Policing within a Professional Framework

Michael E. Cavanagh

PEARSON

Prentice
Hall

Upper Saddle River, NJ 07458

Library of Congress Cataloging-in-Publication Data

Cavanagh, Michael E., 1937-
   Policing within a professional framework / Michael E. Cavanagh.
     p. cm.
   Includes bibliographical references and index.
   ISBN 0-13-039570-6
   1. Law enforcement. 2. Police administration. 3. Law enforcement--Moral and ethical
aspects. I. Title.

HV7921.C38 2004
363.2--dc21   2003045617

Editor-in-Chief: Stephen Helba
Director of Production and Manufacturing: Bruce Johnson
Executive Editor: Frank Mortimer, Jr.
Assistant Editor: Korrine Dorsey
Editorial Assistant: Barbara Rosenberg
Development Editor: Susan Beauchamp
Marketing Manager: Tim Peyton
Managing Editor—Production: Mary Carnis
Manufacturing Buyer: Cathleen Petersen
Production Liaison: Denise Brown
Full-Service Production: Naomi Sysak
Composition Management and Page Makeup: Integra Software Services
Design Director: Cheryl Asherman
Design Coordinator: Miguel Ortiz
Cover Design: Steve Frim
Cover Image: Bill Pogue/Stone/GettyImages
Cover Printer: Phoenix Book Tech
Printer/Binder: Phoenix Book Tech

Pearson Education LTD.
Pearson Education Australia PTY, Limited
Pearson Education Singapore, Pte. Ltd
Pearson Education North Asia Ltd
Pearson Education Canada, Ltd
Pearson Educaçion de Mexico, S.A. de C.V.
Pearson Education–Japan
Pearson Education Malaysia, Pte. Ltd

10 9 8 7 6 5 4 3 2 1
ISBN 0-13-039570-6

*To Michael—A good son
and a good cop*

Contents

10   Responding to Violence and Death   258

11   Understanding Psychological Disorders   289

Preface

A heightened interest in law enforcement exists today primarily for unfortunate reasons. Misconduct and serious mistakes at the federal, state, and municipal levels of law enforcement have generated a level of interest by the public and the courts that has not been seen since the civil rights and Vietnam War eras, when law enforcement was caught between conflicting values and pressures and did not always react in professional ways.

The current scrutiny stems from officer misconduct in the streets, during investigations, and in court, often involving high-profile cases that saturate the media on a daily basis. This scrutiny results in criticism that sometimes is well deserved, but at other times it is not, especially when people who have agendas antithetical to effective law enforcement create it. Whether or not this criticism is well founded, it highlights the concept that the law enforcement community and its officers must make some significant changes if they are to regain and retain the respect of the public and the courts.

The theme of this book revolves around this question: How can law enforcement officers increase their level of professionalism in order to work in maximally ethical and effective ways? This growth is necessary because it is the right thing to do, will better serve society, and will increase respect for law enforcement, which is a requirement for better public cooperation. In this context, "law enforcement" includes federal, state, and municipal agencies, and "officer" denotes all sworn personnel, from city police, county sheriffs, state police, and federal agents of all ranks, from entry level to senior executives.

The concept I have striven to make the hallmark of this book is *balance.* I believe it is important to strike a balance between:

- Theory, research, and practice with each informing the other
- What is ideal (nice) in law enforcement and what is real (necessary)
- Positive and critical attitudes toward law enforcement, the latter being necessary if law enforcement is to advance to more professional levels

- A focus on the organizational dynamics of law enforcement and the dynamics of its individual officers
- The principles of law enforcement and those of psychology, with each informing the other
- A professional and a personal understanding of the issues that form the basis of ethical and professional law enforcement

The content and tenor of this book stem from my over 25 years of experience in law enforcement and psychology, which is reflected in many of the examples used to clarify theoretical points.

The book is aimed at a diverse audience: students simply interested in the law and/or law enforcement or majoring in some aspect of law enforcement, law enforcement recruits, academy instructors, field training officers, and other officers, supervisors, and administrators.

The topics addressed are summarized in the following chapter descriptions.

Chapter 1: Ethics in Law Enforcement. Ethics is the foundation of law enforcement; hence, it is the first chapter. What are "ethics"? Why are they important? What can go wrong? How can ethics become woven into the fabric of law enforcement instead of being relegated to codes and mission statements?

Chapter 2: Professionalism in Law Enforcement. Professionalism is the framework within which law enforcement must function. What professional standards can law enforcement measure itself against? What are the elements of a professional agency? What part do respect and professional education play? How important is a college education in law enforcement?

Chapter 3: Models of Enforcement. There are several methods of law enforcement. What are the strengths and weaknesses of the crime control, problem centered, and community oriented models?

Chapter 4: The Individual Officer. A great deal has been written about law enforcement collectively but very little about individual officers. On a personal basis, what separates effective from ineffective officers? What are the obstacles to becoming an effective officer? Why is the incidence of suicide so high among law enforcement officers? How can officers understand and respond to critical incidents in healthy ways?

Chapter 5: The Selection of Officers. The selection process used in choosing new officers lies at the heart of the strength, effectiveness, and health of an agency. Therefore, it is important to know the answer to questions such as these: What differentiates a valid selection process from an invalid one? What are the elements of a sound employment interview and background investigation? Why are there often difficulties in these areas? What should agencies and candidates know about psychological screening?

Chapter 6: Professional Leadership. Leaders are like ship captains: They can propel their agencies forward, throw them into reverse, or leave them dead in the water. What qualities distinguish effective from ineffective leaders? What do leaders need to know about groups and how they function? What should leaders do and refrain from doing? How can leaders build effective teams?

Chapter 7: Interviewing Witnesses. The prosecution of the vast majority of cases that go to trial rests largely on victim-witness and bystander-witness testimony. How accurate is this testimony, and what can be done to increase its accuracy? What are some traps in interviewing both children and adults? How can the methods and accuracy of suspect identification by witnesses be improved?

Chapter 8: Interviewing Suspects. There are two kinds of suspects: innocent and guilty, and it is critically important to be able to distinguish between the two. What goes into a proper preparation for a suspect interview? How can questioning a suspect make or destroy a case? What motivates people to make false confessions?

Chapter 9: Investigative Techniques. Detecting deception in witnesses and suspects is a critical part of a crime investigation. What are polygraph testing, voice stress analysis, and forensic hypnosis, and how accurate are they in detecting deception? What is criminal profiling, and how is it used? Who qualifies to be an expert witness?

Chapter 10: Responding to Violence and Death. One of the greatest challenges for officers is responding to calls in which violence has just occurred. How officers handle these calls can make a significant difference not only to the victims but also to the officers and their agencies. What distinguishes constructive from destructive responses in cases of child maltreatment, domestic violence, sexual assault, elder abuse, and unexpected deaths?

Chapter 11: Understanding Psychological Disorders. Responding to "mentally disturbed person" calls has become routine for most agencies and presents unique challenges. What is the nature of psychological disturbance, for example, personality disorders, substance abuse, mood disorders, schizophrenia, dementia, and Tourette Disorder? What actions should officers take and avoid when encountering people with these and similar disorders?

These topics were chosen for three reasons. First, they represent a cross section of issues and activities officers frequently face and with which they must grapple. Second, they are topics not typically covered to any meaningful degree in college courses, training academies, or continuing education workshops. Third, they are issues in which many people not directly related to law enforcement are interested because these issues are often involved in high-profile cases and become the subject of media attention.

After reading the book, people will be better educated about what constitutes professional practice in law enforcement, as well as the real challenges officers face in their efforts to protect and serve society.

Michael E. Cavanagh

1

Ethics in Law Enforcement

This chapter deals with ethics because ethics is the foundation upon which all other issues in law enforcement rest. Although ethics is a very complex field, for the purposes of this chapter and text, ethics refers to the study of what constitutes right and wrong behavior and is used as synonymous with morality. Ethics in law enforcement is especially important because there is no entity in society, other than the judiciary, that deals with the constitutional rights of people on a daily basis. The primary goals of professional law enforcement are to protect the rights to life, assembly, free speech, liberty, privacy, and property, as well as due process and equal protection under the law. Society bestows on law enforcement the power to enforce the U.S. Constitution, and at the heart of this power is discretion. Officers must exercise good judgment as to whom to arrest, when to arrest, how to investigate crime, and what charges to bring forth.

These decisions, which directly and indirectly affect the welfare of all citizens, can never be ethically neutral; they will be either ethical or unethical. It is with ethics in mind that an agency's values, code of ethics, and policies are crafted. It should be kept in mind that law enforcement officers are also protected by the U.S. Constitution and should be treated accordingly from both within and outside the agency.

When law enforcement not only fails to protect constitutional rights but also, in fact, violates them, serious problems arise in three areas. First, officer misconduct and the scandals it generates sorely affect the public's image of law enforcement.

A report by the National Institute of Justice and the Office of Community Oriented Policing Services (1997, p. 13) describes the following surveys done in 1980 and 1995 that compare the rankings of the top 12 occupations based on how much moral confidence (trust) the public has in each one.

1980	**1995**
1. pharmacist	1. firefighter
2. clergy	2. pharmacist
3. firefighter	3. teacher
4. teacher	4. dentist
5. police officer	5. clergy
6. doctor	6. stockbroker
7. dentist	7. doctor
8. accountant	8. accountant
9. stockbroker	9. funeral director
10. lawyer	10. police officer
11. funeral director	11. lawyer
12. politician	12. politician

As can be seen, the occupation of police officer dropped five places and ranked tenth by 1995. In light of recent scandals, one wonders what would be the rank of law enforcement today despite the slight increase in ratings that may have occurred after the terrorist attacks of September 11, 2001.

A tarnished public image presents not only a public relations problem but also one of great practical concern. As Palmiotto (2000) states:

> When the police lose the community's respect and trust, the department can't be an effective tool in criminal apprehension and in controlling crime. Without the community's support, victims and witnesses will not come forward. This is crucial because victims and witnesses willing to participate in the legal process contribute to the arrest and prosecution of offenders. (p. 69)

The second problem is that police misconduct can be instrumental in sending innocent people to prison, some being sentenced to death. Scheck, Neufeld, and Dwyer (2000, pp. 246, 265) studied 62 cases in which innocent people had been sent to prison for serious crimes, including murder, but were exonerated by DNA evidence. Police misconduct played a part in 50 percent of the cases and prosecutorial misconduct in 42 percent. In the cases in which police misconduct was shown to have occurred, the following indicates the type and frequency of each.

Evidence fabrication	9 percent
Alleged undue suggestiveness in ID procedures	33 percent
Allegation of coerced witness	9 percent
Coerced confessions/admissions alleged	9 percent
Suppressed exculpatory evidence	36 percent
Other misconduct	4 percent

In addition to law enforcement misconduct, prosecutorial misconduct is also involved in convicting innocent people. Among these types of misconduct, four stand out:

Suppressed exculpatory evidence	43 percent
Knowingly used false testimony	22 percent
Coerced witnesses	13 percent
Gave false statements to jury	8 percent

It is no wonder that law enforcement and the courts are no longer automatically trusted by the public, especially by the people most affected by them—the poor and minority groups.

The third problem is that police misconduct has a serious impact on the morale of ethical officers within the agency. They are also victims of officer misconduct. Ethical officers take pride in their integrity and, despite facing the same temptations and occupational and personal stressors as unethical officers, maintain and even strengthen their sense of integrity. Yet these officers suffer the consequences of the misconduct of others: disrespect, suspiciousness, rejection, hostility, embarrassment, and disparaging remarks, even from family and friends. Officer misconduct can exact a high toll on agency morale, cohesiveness, pride, and effectiveness.

The objective of this chapter is to advance ethical awareness and practice in professional law enforcement. Its theme is this: *Behaving ethically is doing the right thing.* To this end, the chapter will address the following issues:

- What does doing the right thing mean?
- Why are ethics important in professional law enforcement?
- How is an agency's subculture related to ethics?
- How do officers justify unethical conduct?
- What is the slippery slope, and where can it lead?
- What types of officers eventually participate in misconduct?
- What are warning signs of misconduct?
- What are antidotes to misconduct?
- What is leadership's role in creating an ethical environment?

DOING THE RIGHT THING

Doing the right thing means behaving both within and outside of the agency in ways that clearly reflect its values, which are codified in its mission statement, code of ethics, and code of conduct. Additionally, it means obeying and enforcing the U.S. Constitution as well as criminal and civil law. Although it might seem that these documents encompass a large number of values, in fact, there are a manageable number of overlapping values: honesty, justice, respect, accountability, freedom, commitment, courage, obedience, loyalty, duty, and caring.

Characteristics

The admonishment to *do the right thing* is less common in law enforcement than the admonishment *do not do the wrong thing*. Although this may appear to be merely a matter of semantics, it is not. Avoiding evil is only half of an ethical commitment; doing good is the other half. For example, the fact that officers refrain from misconduct does not make them good officers. The report on police integrity by the National Institute of Justice and the Office of Community Oriented Policing Services (1997) states:

> . . . Many police officers view integrity simply as the absence or avoidance of wrong-doing. Most wrongdoing is perceived as a violation of policy, procedure, or law. Within this context, there is little focus on the meaning or need for a higher order integrity—moral responsibility, moral decisionmaking, infusion of values in all tasks, and ethical performance regardless of circumstance or location. (p. 42)

Along the same lines, it is important to understand the difference between "acts of commission" and "acts of omission." For example, it is not all right (ethical) for an officer to plant evidence (act of commission), but it is equally wrong (unethical) not to report another officer for planting evidence or to fail to intervene when an officer is acting illegally (acts of omission).

Doing the right thing requires officers to understand that ethical practice begins at home, that is, within the agency. From the top down, officers treat each other with the same honesty, justice, respect, and care that they are expected to show citizens. Sometimes officers, including supervisors, treat fellow officers in ways that would result in a serious reprimand if civilians were treated in a similar manner.

Multifaceted Concept

While doing the right thing appears simple (just act according to the values mentioned earlier), it becomes complex very quickly in the real world of law enforcement because doing the right thing is multifaceted, as can be seen in the following example: A hungry street person shoplifts a carton of milk, which she intends to share with her equally hungry child. In this situation, doing the right thing can be:

Subjective. One officer believes that arresting the woman is the *just* thing to do, while her partner believes it is *unjust*, considering the circumstances.

Relative. The next day, the same woman is caught stealing milk from the same store. This time the same officers agree that the *just* thing to do is arrest and book her at the jail, even though her crime is the same one for which she was *not* arrested on the previous day.

Graduated. Or, the same officers decide that although it would be *just* to arrest and book the woman, it would be even *more just* to issue a citation and release her because it would be *unjust* to punish the child who would be sent to Child Protective Services.

Hierarchical. Or, the same officers decide that it would be the *just* thing to arrest her, but it would be the *caring* thing to drive her and her child to a place where they can receive food and shelter. In other words, in this case, *caring* trumps *justice*.

Competitive. Leaving the above example, the *ethical* right thing can compete with the *legal* right thing. For example, a supervisor orders an officer to use deceit to trap a murder suspect. The supervisor assures the officer that deceit in this circumstance is legal. But in terms of the officer's ethical standards, lying is wrong (unethical) in any situation. What happens now?

Punished. An officer arrests the mayor for drunk driving because his blood alcohol level is more than twice the legal limit. It is the *ethically right thing to do*, but the *politically wrong thing to do*. Sometimes, the latter overrides the former, so the officer is assigned to a desk job until he can "come to appreciate the meaning of 'discretion.'"

Anticipation of Ethical Situations

Doing the right thing calls for intelligence, critical thinking, psychological security, openness to different perspectives, and courage. All this can take time, which is often a luxury in the split-second decisions necessary in law enforcement. Therefore, it is important to anticipate situations in which ethical issues are likely to arise and develop an ethical framework ahead of time.

All of the ethical dilemmas just mentioned could arise within the same week. Multiply this by 20 or 30 years in law enforcement, and it can be seen that of all occupations, law enforcement arguably has the most opportunities for doing good or doing evil. Therefore, it is helpful to have some core values—for example, honesty, justice, respect, and caring—engraved on the officer's moral compass, which is carried at all times.

Personal Reflections _____

1. What is your image of law enforcement in general and your local agency in particular?
2. Have you, or anyone you know, been the object of officer misconduct, and if so, how did it make you feel about yourself and law enforcement?
3. What would you do if you caught a fellow officer "stretching the truth" in a report?

4. What would you do if you caught your supervisor in a lie that could have serious consequences?

5. What would you do if a prosecutor in a high-profile case strongly suggests to you that you *did* Mirandize the suspect, even though you know you did not?

THE IMPORTANCE OF ETHICS

Officers may ask why acting ethically is so important in law enforcement. The short, utilitarian answer is this: Ethical officers stay out of six places they do not need to be—the boss's office, the internal affairs office, the criminal courts, the civil courts, the unemployment office, and prison. Moving to more profound reasons for ethical conduct, there are at least six reasons why ethics in professional law enforcement is important.

The Right Thing to Do

The first and best reason for behaving ethically is that it is the right thing to do, although organizations seldom state this as their reason for acting ethically. Typically, the reasons given to support ethical behavior are utilitarian: It is good for business; it is good public relations; it will make the organization more efficient; it will help attract good job candidates; it will keep the organization out of court; and so on. However, there still is something to be said for doing the right thing simply because it is the honest, just, respectful, caring thing to do. It also, incidentally, creates an inner sense of goodness and peace that makes officers feel good about their job.

Public Image

An ethical agency has a good public image, which can make an officer's job easier. When people trust officers, they feel free to ask for help, pass on information, and give them the benefit of the doubt when the officers are involved in controversial incidents. Citizens will support an agency that is temporarily losing the fight against crime, but they will never support one that is losing the fight against officer misconduct.

Avoid Litigation

An ethical agency need not concern itself with civil lawsuits that have become a reflexive reaction to law enforcement action in our litigious society. Law enforcement agencies are paying out hundreds of millions of dollars each year in lawsuits, some legitimate and some frivolous. There seem to be two kinds of agencies in this regard: those that frequently get sued and those that seldom, if ever, get sued.

Good Reputation

An ethical agency enjoys a good reputation with other agencies and the courts. This is important because agencies, especially smaller ones, often need the assistance of other agencies in investigations and disasters. Ethical agencies do not want to tarnish their reputation and often will not assist agencies with questionable ones. Moreover, prosecutors and judges often automatically accept the testimony of officers with ethical reputations in contrast to that of less trustworthy officers.

Working Environment

An ethical agency provides a good working environment in which officers can trust each other up and down the chain of command and assist each other without wondering who is trustworthy and who is not. In some agencies, ethical officers are reluctant to call for assistance for fear of getting an officer who may use excessive force or steal something, placing ethical officers' careers, if not their lives, in jeopardy.

Conclusion

An ethical agency uses principles of ethics in making decisions: Is what we are planning to do honest, just, respectful, and caring? This gives the agency a philosophy of decision-making—a professional framework in which to ask the right questions. This is in contrast to making decisions based purely on self-serving and/or political considerations. Often, these decisions fall short of being entirely ethical and effective and eventually are likely to haunt the agency.

To state that ethics in law enforcement is important would appear to be self-evident, yet it is not. Some officers see ethics as an "ivory tower thing" that interferes with good police work. Although a great deal of lip service is paid to the importance of ethics in law enforcement, especially by agency executives, little ethics education and training exist. In this regard, Gilmartin and Harris (1998) state:

> Officers who are mentally prepared to face a lethal encounter are more likely to be successful than officers who are tactically proficient but mentally unprepared. Just like lethal encounters, ethical dilemmas occur at the most inopportune times, frequently without warning and with little time to stop and think about the situation. When inadequately prepared, even the most honest, above reproach officers can make inappropriate split-second ethical decisions ... decisions that can result in life changing consequences. If officers are going to survive ethical dilemmas they need to be as mentally prepared as they would be for tactical encounters.

As law enforcement agencies become more professional, the hope is that an increasing number of officers will realize three things: Ethics is extremely important in law enforcement; how ethical issues are handled can strengthen or destroy an agency; and ethical practices can save an agency a great deal of money that can be used for better things.

Personal Reflections _____

1. What is your reaction to the statement, "If a law enforcement agency is legitimately criticized for wrongdoing, a serious ethical violation is always at the heart of the problem"?

2. Do you think people and/or organizations usually act ethically for self-serving reasons rather than because it is "the right thing to do? ("Do not use excessive force, or you are likely to get sued or lose your job?") Why does this occur?

3. This section of the text lists four core ethical values: honesty, justice, respect, and care. What values would you add to this list if you were an agency executive? Why?

THE AGENCY'S SUBCULTURE

It is important to understand the differences between an agency's mainstream culture and its subculture. The mainstream culture consists of the agency's publicly stated values, which are included in items such as its mission statement, code of ethics, and recruiting brochures, and promulgated at academy graduations.

Most agencies, as is true for most organizations, have one or more subcultures, which have different values than the mainstream culture. This is not necessarily bad, because a subculture's values may complement or even enhance those of the mainstream culture. But, when a subculture's values are antithetical to those of the mainstream, tensions arise and can become fractious. This type of rogue subculture, which has recently brought scandal to law enforcement, will be discussed in this section.

This subculture's values are unstated, unpublicized, never mentioned in recruitment brochures or at academy graduations, but everyone in the agency is well aware of them. Like the mainstream culture, the subculture has rules and understandings that, although unwritten, are clear, binding, and often more stringently enforced than those of the mainstream culture. The following is a sample of a malignant subculture's rules and understandings.

- Always be a stand-up cop; never give up or roll over on a fellow officer, even if you have to take the fall yourself.

- You are either with us or against us. "With us" means either you participate in the same misconduct that we do, or you keep your mouth shut about it.

- You do what you have to do in order to make a case against a suspect you think is guilty. "Creative report writing," "testilying," or tampering with evidence may be necessary to see that justice is done.
- You have to teach these people a lesson so they'll respect you.
- We are not social workers. We control the streets, using street justice and attitude adjustments.
- The only people who really care about you and whom you can trust are other cops. Everyone else, including family, is an outsider.
- Few bosses know what they're doing, so we have to stick together and protect ourselves by ignoring or subverting their orders.
- We are above the law. Our badge provides privileges few people have. Our police immunity entitles us to professional courtesies. (A police badge was originally referred to as a "buzzer" because officers used it to "buzz" their way into free entertainment, meals, clubs, even houses of prostitution.) We can even flaunt policies and laws in front of other cops, and they won't dare do anything about it.
- It is us against them. "Them" is everyone who is not "us": the brass, officers who are different (different race, gender, sexual orientation, lifestyle), and all citizens, whether or not they are criminals.
- *We* are the victims. The public does not understand, appreciate, or trust us. They disparage us, sue us, want to tell us how to do our jobs, and file complaints against us when we are trying to make the streets safe for them. This entitles us to do anything it takes to survive and do our job.

These attitudes create a vicious cycle ending with a self-fulfilling prophecy. In other words, when officers act according to these attitudes, good officers and the public *will* reject them, causing the subgroup to become even more isolated from the mainstream culture. This, in turn, reinforces the subgroup's beliefs, which, in turn, leads to even more rejection and isolation. Consequently, the subgroup becomes even more cohesive, powerful, and, at times, dangerous. These officers do not realize that they bring down on themselves all the things they resent: internal affairs investigations, civil suits, civilian oversight, and citizen complaints.

New officers are gradually introduced to the subculture and forced to make one of three decisions: Join the subculture, join the mainstream culture, or try to remain a free agent. For someone not in law enforcement, this sounds like an easy choice, but, especially in larger agencies, the subculture can be pervasive. It includes officers on every level of command from the highest to the lowest. The rule "You are either with us or against us" prevails. No one is allowed to be a conscientious objector or claim neutrality. This is especially true if a new officer's training officer and other supervisors are part of the subculture because they have the new officer's career in their hands. When new officers are admonished to "forget the academy and learn the streets," they often are faced with choosing between academy values and those of the malignant subculture.

Some people believe that the relatively recent addition of college graduates, minorities, women, and homosexuals to law enforcement will diminish the subculture's strength and pervasiveness. However, the presence of these groups may also cause the subculture to feel more intimidated, become further entrenched, and act out more within the agency. With regard to the subculture, Pollock's (1998, p. 118) admonition should be taken seriously: "The informal police culture is the most obvious threat to the internalization of ethical standards."

Personal Reflections

1. How strong do you believe your moral character is? How much real pressure could it stand before cracks begin to appear?
2. How far would you go to become "one of the guys"? Would you rather join the malignant subgroup and be accepted, or maintain your current ethical values and risk social isolation or harassment?
3. What would you do if your supervisors were part of the subculture and made it clear that you "go along to get along" or else receive poor evaluations and assignments?
4. What would you do, in reality, if you observed one of your supervisors steal a newspaper every morning and get a free breakfast?
5. Do you want to be an officer "more than anything in the world," and, if so, how might this make you vulnerable to corruption?

JUSTIFYING MISCONDUCT

Very few officers say to themselves: "I fully realize that what I am about to do is wrong, but I'm going to do it, and if I get caught I will accept the consequences." They are more likely to say: "What I am about to do may seem wrong to some people, but they don't understand that it's necessary to do these things to be part of the team, make ends meet, and lock up the bad guys."

There are as many justifications for officer misconduct as there are types of misconduct. The following are some examples:

- Everyone is doing it. So, it couldn't be that wrong. If you discipline me, you'll have to discipline half the agency, including the bosses.
- I'm entitled to do what I did. If the agency paid me a decent wage and gave me the promotions I deserve, I wouldn't have to do that stuff.
- I did it to help my family. I have to support my family and my dying mother. I can't let them all end up in the poorhouse.
- I did it for the good of society. If we don't show the criminals out there who owns the streets, they'll take over the whole city.

- No harm; no foul. I wouldn't have done anything if it had hurt people, but absolutely nobody got hurt who didn't deserve it.
- It was a well-deserved payback. They hurt us so we *had* to get even. We just can't let stuff like that go without evening the score
- I just made a stupid mistake; that's all. *Everybody* makes mistakes. No cop is perfect. I'm sorry for it. I'm remorseful. Now let's forget about it and move on.
- I just trusted the wrong people. I trusted my buddies, thinking they were stand-up guys, and the next thing I know, I'm in big trouble.
- I was pressured into it. They boxed me in. I had no choice.
- I was drunk or on drugs at the time. So I need help, and losing my job or going to prison isn't going to help my family or me.
- I was just doing a friend a favor. He's got a sick wife and a pile of debts, and I just wanted to help him out.
- I didn't realize it was wrong. I was just told to pick up a package from some guy and bring it back to the station. How was I supposed to know it had drugs in it?
- I was just obeying orders. The sergeant told me to be more aggressive on the street, so I only did what he told me to do.
- I had personal problems at the time. My alcoholic wife left me and took my kids along with half my salary. I just wasn't thinking straight.
- I was just kidding around. We were just playing, and the next thing I know she's filing a sexual harassment complaint against me.
- You can't be a cop as long as I have and avoid this stuff—sooner or later getting caught up in it is inevitable. After a while, the system just wears you down, and you start giving in just to survive.
- The way things are today, you can't obey the rules and do the job that has to be done. If it weren't for the courts and the civil liberties crowd, I could do the job the way it should be done.
- I couldn't stop myself after a while. It was like being addicted to a drug. I developed a habit that I had to keep feeding.

When these justifications are put on paper, they look pretty stupid, and one wonders how ordinarily intelligent officers can use them to excuse everything from accepting gratuities to murder. In fact, the justifications are not much different than those most people use to excuse and explain their misbehaviors on a daily basis. However, when these rationalizations are used in law enforcement to justify misconduct, they are particularly virulent because they involve officers violating their oath, agency policies, or the law. As a result, important institutions are tarnished, and innocent people get hurt. These justifications also clear the path to slippery slopes that become increasingly steep and treacherous.

Personal Reflections _____

1. Of the justifications listed above, which three would you be most likely to use if you were to participate in some misconduct?
2. Why do you think the average intelligent officer would think anyone would believe these justifications?

THE SLIPPERY SLOPE

A slippery slope is a path that leads down ethical embankments. The first one or two steps down the slope are small ones, carefully taken. But as confidence and pressures build, the officer begins to get careless, to hurry, to underestimate the steepness of the slope, and begins to slide a little. Officers may reach out for someone to help break the slide, but more often they find the slide exciting and believe they can stop anytime they want. This is the slippery slope myth: "I can stop whenever I want—I'm on top of it." Every officer in the history of law enforcement who has participated in serious misconduct bought into this myth. As one officer lamented: "Everything was great; then, all of a sudden, I hit the ground going 100 miles an hour and woke up not knowing how I got there."

The typical slippery slope consists of 14 steps:

1. Observe other officers, including admired cops, participating in misconduct.
2. Feel peer pressure to join in the misconduct, to be one of the guys. Everybody else is doing it; it's no big deal.
3. Agree to go along to get along, some penny ante stuff, usually violating some stupid agency policy. No big deal. One safe step down the slippery slope.
4. Agree to violate more agency policies with more serious potential consequences. Won't get caught, good justifications, no sweat. A second, less firm step down the slippery slope.
5. Graduate to committing misdemeanors. Justifications are growing in number, strength, and believability. No one's getting hurt. It's not as bad as drunk driving, which people, including cops, do all the time.
6. Graduate to committing felonies. Justifications are firmly entrenched, working like a general anesthetic on the conscience. Nothing to it. Should have done this stuff a long time ago.
7. Felonies become so exciting, easy, and lucrative that misconduct is more fun and fulfilling than police work, which is getting less interesting by the day. Slipping down the slippery slope has now become a free fall. No stopping now. But who wants to stop?

8. Felonies become incorporated into the job: half a shift for police work, half a shift for felonies. Pager beeps, officer disappears, not available for calls. So routine, officer talks about it in the locker room, at the cop bar. Invulnerable—the sure sign that the end is near.

9. A good cop or a good citizen, or a bad citizen bent on revenge, drops a dime to the agency. The ground is beginning to come up fast.

10. Internal affairs investigates, taps phones, videotapes meetings, audits books, interviews witnesses, including fellow cops. Builds a case.

11. Get a call from a "white shirt." Have to talk forthwith, and bring a union rep or a lawyer.

12. Lie to the Internal Affairs Bureau about misconduct—a stand-up cop rolls over on no one. Got the wrong guy, sorry.

13. Confronted with slam-dunk evidence. Can't we work something out? Stand-up cop takes a dive, rolls over on good buddies for some future consideration. Justifications fill the room but they don't work. Whoever thought they would?

14. Tell the family—that's the worst part. All the great buddies disappear. Not only a felon now, but worse, a snitch. Terribly alone. No money. Legal bills. Second, third mortgage on house. Hits the media—everyone knows. Lose dignity and maybe even family and own life.

An officer could stop the slide at any one of the fourteen steps. However, as the steps progress, the slide's momentum increases exponentially. One of the saddest parts is that, in all likelihood, at one time many of these officers were decent people: good family people, good friends, good cops who cared about others, were even religious. But somewhere, sometime, someplace, something went terribly wrong.

Personal Reflections

1. How can an individual sense that he or she is on the first step of the slippery slope?

2. Before becoming "dirty cops," all law enforcement officers were "clean cops." What causes this dramatic change?

3. Why do so few police partners and spouses confront officers during the slide down the slippery slope?

MOTIVES FOR MISCONDUCT

Unfortunately, it is not easy to pinpoint where misconduct begins. In some officers, it is caused by a character defect; for example, an antisocial disorder present from childhood.

In other officers, it is psychological weakness. Deep down, despite outward appearances to the contrary, these officers are insecure and need to latch onto others they perceive as stronger in order to feel strong themselves. It does not take much peer pressure to get them to join the strong, powerful officers of the subculture.

In some officers, it is sensation seeking. These officers thrive on excitement, risk, novelty, danger, pushing the envelope. They cannot tolerate boredom, which is often a large part of law enforcement. So, what can officers do that is exciting? If their moral compass is functioning properly, they can be assets in some law enforcement specialties—undercover work, entry teams, rescue teams, and drug enforcement. On the other hand, if their moral compass is not functioning properly, they may seek excitement in using their authority to steal money, drugs, and property; have illicit sexual relations; gamble; shake down or beat up criminals. Sometimes these officers commit crimes more for the "rush" than for any material gain.

In still other officers, it is greed, that is, the need to accumulate money and possessions past the point of necessity and to the point where it controls their lives, causing other important needs and values to pale in comparison. In the greedy person's mind, money and possessions are related to intelligence, power, prestige, and popularity. The more material goods they have, the more they believe they possess these qualities, of which no one can ever have enough.

In certain officers, it is revenge. They enter law enforcement with a child's fantasies and ideals, but then reality gradually sets in. Their enthusiasm is squelched, and their dreams are dashed or become nightmares. They feel unappreciated by the agency and the citizens to whom they are giving their best efforts. They perceive themselves, sometimes accurately, as victims of unfair practices, political machinations, broken promises, and backstabbing. The problem with having unrealistic expectations becomes apparent when the expectations are unmet, and anger and resentment fill the void. Where else are these feelings going to be aimed but at the agency and citizens that broke promises they never made? Hence, these officers, mostly unconsciously, act out in ways meant to eventually harm both the agency and society in general.

Finally, in the case of some officers who "go bad," no one will ever know what went wrong, whether job or family stressors or substance abuse pushed them over the brink, or whether something was wrong at birth and, like a time capsule, did not become activated until early or middle adulthood. Even the people who believe they know them best—parents, spouses, and lifelong friends—are shocked to discover the officers were living a double life for many years.

Personal Reflections

1. Do you think good officers can "go bad," or do you think that unethical officers have a serious character flaw that predates entering law enforcement?

2. What is your theory as to why otherwise good officers participate in misconduct?

3. Why do you think psychological screening and background checks fail to catch moral character defects in some or many officers?

WARNING SIGNS OF UNETHICAL CONDUCT

There are no foolproof warning signs, outside of the obvious ones, that foreshadow unethical behavior. However, some behaviors are worth considering. Whenever two or more people work or live closely together, a rhythm develops, almost like a faint melody in the distance, but people do not notice it until the person sounds "a bit out of tune." At this point, the listener reacts with something like this: "Are you OK? Is everything all right? You have seemed a little different the last few weeks." Some of the out-of-tune behaviors that may be symptomatic of unethical behavior follow.

Disappearing

Officers begin to "disappear." They are not where they usually would be, where they are expected to be at certain times during the shift or even off duty. Other officers ask them: "Where were you? We've been trying to raise you on the radio." When confronted with disappearances by spouses, the officers become defensive: "What do you *mean*, where have I been? I've been working my tail off; that's where I've been!" When this response is deemed unsatisfactory ("You didn't answer my question"), officers lie and usually not very well at first, because they are caught off guard. These lies should be seen as a clear danger sign.

Changing

Officers' moods begin to change: The easygoing officer becomes irritable, the industrious officer lazy, the extroverted officer introverted, the happy-go-lucky officer depressed. Officers pay more or less attention to their physical appearance, eat and drink more, sleep less; tardiness and absenteeism increase; attendance at church decreases; smoking resumes. Their financial status may undergo significant changes. They spend money of dubious origin ("I fell into a little money") or no longer have money for planned family vacations ("My salary's just not keeping up with the economy"). After the misconduct becomes public, fellow officers and family state: "You know, I noticed he began to change about a year ago. I probably should have done something about it then."

Distancing

Distance develops in work and family relationships. Officers who were once close to spouses, children, parents, friends, and fellow officers become increasingly distant, physically and emotionally guarded, and unavailable. Half the time they pull away from people; the remainder of the time they act in ways that cause people to push them away.

Drifting

These officers' thinking drifts, as it becomes affected and infected. The main symptom is being distracted, "being somewhere else." The officers are not concentrating, paying attention, listening to what others are saying. They are off in the distance, missing important communications at work and at home.

Hiding

A secret life begins. Officers who have never conducted personal business on duty now must break away to run a few errands. Officers who once made a point of telling everyone their business are now whispering into phones and locking desk drawers. At home, the following "script of secrecy" is played out with increasing frequency.

> "Where did you go after the shift?"
>
> "Nowhere. I worked overtime."
>
> "How come all this overtime isn't showing up on your paycheck?"
>
> "I took it as comp time."
>
> "Who was on the phone?"
>
> "No one. Just work."
>
> "Who keeps phoning and hanging up when you're not here?"
>
> "Probably the wrong number."
>
> "There's something going on. What is it?"
>
> "What are you, my mother now?"

Typically, the people most likely to hear these discordant notes are the officer's partners, spouse, and parents. But often these people, especially the spouse, are the least likely to confront the officer about the behavior. Those close to the officer do not want to have to admit that someone they care so much about and have trusted for so long would be doing something seriously wrong. Family members and friends also do not want to create tension in the relationship. Consequently, it is not uncommon for family members and partners to sense that something is wrong for a long time but be reluctant to seriously confront the officer. This is one reason for involving officers' families in ethics training, so that there is 360-degree support in this area of extreme professional and personal importance.

Personal Reflections

1. What do you think is the first real warning sign that an officer is beginning to act unethically?
2. When an officer acts heroically, partners and spouses often take some credit for this behavior. When an officer gets caught for ethical violations, should the same people share some of the responsibility?

ANTIDOTES TO OFFICER MISCONDUCT

Just as there are no foolproof warning signs, there are no foolproof antidotes to officer misconduct. But two attempts can be made in that direction. First, officers can go through an ethical self-examination to help them make ethical decisions. Second, officers can use critical thinking to address the classic justifications they use to excuse misconduct.

Ethical Self-Examination

The ethical self-examination includes the following questions:

1. If I'm already conjuring up excuses for some planned action, how could it be ethical? Ethical behavior does not require excuses.
2. What is the cost-benefit ratio of what I plan to do? If the benefit is that I earn a few extra dollars or have a little excitement, but the cost is the risk of losing my job, family, and reputation, is it really worth it?
3. Would I do what I'm planning to do if I knew it was going to be televised on the evening news, because it just might be?
4. If I do what I'm thinking of doing and my family finds out, what would they think of me, and is what they would think of me what I really am?
5. Do I really believe that if I do something unethical, I won't eventually get caught? Don't I realize that every officer who ever got caught had complete confidence on one thing: He would *never* get caught—no way, not in a million years?
6. Do I realize that, even if I don't get caught, I'll "catch" myself? That on some level, I'll pay the price by feeling a deep sense of guilt, shame, or disgust that will never go away and will spoil all the nice things for the rest of my life?

7. What does my planned behavior say about the values and beliefs that my parents, relatives, teachers, and clergy instilled in me? Don't these count anymore? Have I formulated a better value system that will enrich my life and my family's life more than the values of my upbringing?

8. What if my spouse, my children, or my parents did what I'm thinking about doing? What would I think and feel about them? What would I say to them?

9. Have I talked over my plans with my spouse and friends, in and outside of law enforcement? If not, why not? If what I'm going to do is all right, this should not be a problem.

10. If I were a supervisor, would I want somebody for whom I am responsible to do what I plan to do, or would I be furious at the officer for placing the agency, as well both our reputations and careers, in jeopardy?

If reflections such as these are an integral part of an ethics education program and of each officer's personal thinking, ethical decisions will be brought into sharper focus.

Critical Thinking

A second antidote to officer misconduct is to use critical thinking to debunk the basic premises officers use to justify their own and other officers' unethical behavior. The following are some common justifications for unethical conduct.

Loyalty.   Officers should be loyal to each other. Yet, it is important to distinguish between authentic and misplaced loyalty. The dictionary definition of *loyalty* is "to be faithful to the constituted authority of one's country." Translated into law enforcement terms, loyalty is faithfulness to the agency and its values, mission statement, and code of ethics. Authentic loyalty includes being faithful to all those who abide by the constituted authority of the agency. Loyalty to officers who violate this authority and the law is a perversion and is never a justification for unethical behavior.

Stress.   Law enforcement can be stressful for two reasons. One is that officers often face high-risk situations such as armed suspects, hostile mobs, vehicle pursuits, foot chases, and so on. A second cause of stress is the incompetence and injustice sometimes present in law enforcement, as it is in all occupations. Officers will be confronted with supervisors who cannot make decisions or who make deplorable ones, and by fellow officers whose poor judgment and lack of skills make them liabilities. Moreover, it is not rare for politics to trump justice, so officers may not get the appreciation, assignments, promotions, or salary increases they deserve. The stresses that incompetence and injustice create often rival or surpass those created by the physical challenges and risks of the job.

Officers can react to stressors constructively or destructively. They can deal with them positively by developing the skills to pinpoint the nature of the stressors and try to reduce them, changing their attitudes toward them, or by leaving the situation if the stressors are impervious to change and doing significant harm. Officers can deal with stressors destructively by letting off steam through excessive drinking, illicit sex, drug use, or venting aggression in destructive ways. Being under stress is a reason to learn to handle it constructively and is never a justification for unethical behavior.

Lack of Support.   Some officers blame lack of support from the community they serve as an excuse for their unethical conduct: "If the community refuses to help us, we'll have to take over and do things our way." In reality, officers' perceptions that the public does not appreciate them are generally inaccurate. When officers act professionally and ethically, public support will usually result. For example, in a survey (Dautrich, 1998) representative of Connecticut residents, 92 percent of the respondents reported great, or at least some, confidence in both state and local law enforcement. In addition, 85 percent of the Connecticut respondents said they would be willing to work with local police in a community anticrime program. It is unlikely to be a coincidence that 73 percent of the respondents indicated that police met their standards for ethical conduct and 91 percent said they have never felt unfairly treated by police because of their race.

However, even if communities are antipolice, police misconduct is never justified. A lack of community support and appreciation is never a justification to act unethically.

Lack of Compensation.   Many law enforcement officers feel they are not adequately compensated for what they do. Rather than argue the point, which is arguable in many situations and agencies, suffice it to say that before applying for a position in law enforcement, a candidate should gather six pieces of information:

- What are the salary and typical increments?
- What are the benefits: insurance, vacations, sick leave, and retirement?
- What is the schedule of shift rotations?
- What are the chances for regular promotions?
- What are the responsibilities and risks of the job?
- What kind of lifestyle do I expect to live, and do the answers to these questions give me good reason to think I will be able to live it as a law enforcement officer?

People can enter law enforcement to be professional, ethical officers because of, or in spite of, the financial remuneration and other benefits of the job. Discovering at some point in time that they are not making enough money to support their lifestyle is a reason to change the lifestyle or find a more lucrative job; it is never a justification to act unethically.

Making Mistakes.   Law enforcement officers are only human and will make mistakes, just as this is true for those in any occupation. But critical thinking must be introduced into the picture. First, unethical conduct is never "a mistake." Lying, cheating, stealing, being drunk on duty, using excessive force, taking a bribe, tampering with evidence, or getting involved in illicit relationships cannot be considered a mistake. The dictionary defines *making a mistake* as "misunderstanding or misperceiving something." What is there about a code of ethics and the U.S. Constitution that is open to misunderstanding or misperception? Oversteering a vehicle during a pursuit is a mistake; getting the victim's and the witness's names confused in a report is a mistake; kicking in the wrong door is a mistake. Beating someone who is in handcuffs is *not* a mistake. Unethical conduct is the result of an informed, willful, and premeditated decision. And, as some case law states, premeditation can occur "in an eye blink of time"; it does not require minutes, hours, or days.

Both law enforcement agencies and the courts hold that it is appropriate and legal to hold law enforcement officers to higher standards than ordinary citizens. Therefore, while being human includes making mistakes, sometimes serious ones, it never justifies unethical conduct.

Sticking Together.   Cohesiveness among officers is important. There is nothing inherently wrong with wanting to become "one of the guys" (except for the sexist connotation). Yet the question must be asked: Who are "the guys," and what must an officer do to be considered one of them?

If the guys have problems with substance abuse, honesty, corruption, or brutality, then new officers may have to prove their worth by participating in these behaviors. Then, once new officers participate in even one act of misconduct, the guys own them because the act can be held over their heads for the rest of their careers. Consequently, new officers need to join the "good guys" and avoid the "bad guys," or become free agents, which is possible but often quite difficult, depending on the health of the agency's mainstream culture and the strength of the malignant subculture. In any case, wanting to be a part of the team is never a justification for unethical behavior.

Officers are accountable for their behavior and need to cleanse themselves of any subconscious potential justifications before behaving in ways that they and their families may live to regret.

Personal Reflections

1. What would I do if my police partner were sending out warning signals of unethical behavior?
2. What kinds of misconduct could I keep silent about, and what kinds could I not?

3. Is your paycheck your reward, or do you also need understanding, appreciation, and other perks to do your job well?

4. Where do you draw the line between making a mistake and committing an unethical act?

5. Would you have the strength to remain a free agent in law enforcement, or would you have to join some group—the good guys or even the bad guys?

CREATING AN ETHICAL ENVIRONMENT

Administrators and supervisors set the agency's ethical tone. They generally possess the education, knowledge, experience, and authority to affirmatively set ethical standards and see that they are met. When ethical problems arise in an agency, it is not because the agency lacks a code of ethics; it is because the leadership itself does not live by the code and does not actively enforce it on a daily basis, looking the other way when ethical violations occur.

Research and common observation bear this out. A new executive coming into a scandal-ridden agency sets a new ethical tone and immediately promulgates it, from top administrators down to the newest recruits. In a short time, the message gets across: Shape up or ship out. Other than a few administrative transfers, nothing else changes: same officers, same stressors, same assignments, same temptations, and same citizens. Basically, the only thing that has changed is the top executive who creates an ethical tone by example, the force of his or her personality, the enforcement of professional ethics, and a zero tolerance for unethical behavior.

When ethical misconduct comes to light, administrators typically blame the problems on "a few bad apples." However, in the vast majority of cases, the problem is not a few bad apples, but a "bad barrel." In other words, unethical conduct, especially that which has been present for some time and more especially if it is widespread, is known about by supervisors and administrators who actively or passively condone it. This occurs because these leaders are gaining something from the unethical conduct materially (money or goods) or socially (the acceptance and support of the unethical officers).

For better or for worse, leaders directly and indirectly affect an agency's ethical environment. Good leaders in professional law enforcement agencies promote ethical standards by the following actions.

Setting an Example

The personal and professional behavior of good leaders is beyond reproach; they have ethical credibility. They scrupulously abide by the agency's code of ethics and mission statement, avoiding even the perception of wrongdoing. They treat all officers with respect, fairness, and compassion. Their off-duty and on-duty behaviors make a statement: This is how I expect you to conduct yourself because it is the right way to act in order to remain a member in good standing with this agency.

Administrators and supervisors who have morally chaotic personal lives or whose behavior states, "Do as I say, not as I do," or, worse yet, "Let's not let ethics get in the way of good police work," will contribute significantly to ethically bankrupting the agency. As soon as leaders place themselves in an ethically compromised situation, even once, they are likely to lose forever any ethical clout they may have had. ("How can the lieutenant say anything about our appropriating some old stuff from the property room when everyone knows he uses his departmental vehicle to go on vacation?")

Leaders who pad budgets, lie to personnel, drive while intoxicated, have illicit relationships, accept gratuities, treat people unfairly, cover up misdeeds, accept graft, appropriate agency property, sleep or drink on duty, or take agency vehicles for private use send a clear message: "If I can do it, you can do it."

These leaders, from executives to field training officers, are the bad barrel that houses and protects the bad apples. The report by the National Institute of Justice and the Office of Community Oriented Policing Services (1997) sums up the point:

> How do police leaders influence the integrity of police employees? A critical first step in assessing, instilling, and maintaining integrity within the police culture is to ensure that police executives model appropriate behaviors.
>
> If a chief of police or deputy chief fails to convey information in an honest, direct way to employees; if officers are assigned to specialty units or promoted based on a process that is deemed less than fair and equitable; and, if executives allocate resources to cater to the whims and demands of influential people, can officers and civilian employees be expected to maintain a level of integrity that surpasses that of their bosses? Within any police organization, can employees be held to a higher standard of integrity and moral responsibility than that demonstrated by their executive officers and political leaders? (p. 87–88)

Monitoring the Agency's Culture

Most organizations have subcultures in addition to a mainstream culture. One type of subculture states: "Sometimes you have to bend the rules a little to get a job done." This entails occasionally taking some shortcuts and doing some end runs to get a particular job done expeditiously. Because these behaviors do not strictly abide by agency policy, many leaders tend to look the other way ("Don't tell me how you're going to do it—just do it.") For example, detectives "borrow" a surveillance van from the motor pool because to track down the appropriate supervisor and complete the necessary paperwork would result in a loss of precious time in setting up the surveillance.

The second kind of subculture is the "Sometimes you have to do clearly unethical and/or illegal things to get the job done (or to augment your income or to have a little excitement)." Clearly, effective leaders must stop this subculture as soon as it begins. Participating in it in any way, including looking the other way, creates a serious ethical offense for which there is no legitimate justification and for which there should be appropriate sanctions. Silence by leaders communicates consent and is as unethical as actually committing the unethical acts (just as the lookout at a bank robbery is as responsible as the actual robbers).

While "bending the rules" may be justifiable in some limited situations in which the rules thwart what they were meant to accomplish, "breaking the law" is never justified in any circumstances, no matter what perceived good might result. It is the responsibility of leaders to make certain officers understand the differences between the two.

Eliminating the Code of Silence

The code of silence allows unethical behavior to flourish and go unsanctioned. Leaders can eliminate the code of silence, directly participate in it, or passively allow it to exist. Good administrators take four steps to eliminate the code of silence.

First, they are open and honest about the problems that exist in the agency for three reasons: It is the right thing to do; it sends the clear message that openness is valued and secrecy is devalued; and it peremptorily takes the wind out of the sails of those who eventually may discover agency secrets and expose them.

Second, good leaders have a zero tolerance level for all unethical conduct, minor or major, and address and deal with it appropriately. No unethical conduct "slips under the radar"; all unethical acts are documented and appropriately addressed. When there is no unethical conduct, there is no need for a code of silence.

Third, executives in a professional agency make it clear that anyone, including the highest-ranking administrators, will be severely disciplined up to and including termination for ignoring or covering up unethical conduct.

Fourth, the terms snitch, rat, and whistle-blower are expunged from the agency's vocabulary. Leaders promote loyalty to integrity and law enforcement over loyalty to people, especially officers who engage in activities that tarnish the image of law enforcement and place the careers of those closest to them in jeopardy. No heroism is involved in protecting criminals, especially those within law enforcement.

Professional leaders who are able to eliminate the code of silence exhibit the following traits:

- They want, above all else, to do the right thing.
- They have the courage to incur the wrath and rejection of those who indulge in unethical conduct.
- They carry it as a badge of honor that the unsavory people in the agency no longer like or trust them.

- They take responsibility and accept criticism for any unethical conduct that occurs on their watch, but also take credit for unearthing and stopping it as soon as it comes to their attention.
- They realize that the cancers hidden by the code of silence metastasize and cause serious damage to the vital organs of the agency.
- They realize that, ethics aside, the code of silence is a myth because, like family secrets, agency secrets have a short shelf life before they are discovered and publicized, often to the everlasting embarrassment of the agency.

Trautman (2001) summarizes this issue: "If an organization intends to make a genuine effort to prevent the code of silence from placing loyalty to people ahead of loyalty toward principle, its leaders must have and communicate a sincere commitment to integrity."

Recruiting and Training Officers with Ethics in Mind

With respect to recruiting, professional leaders oversee thorough background checks and realize that simply because candidates have not committed a felony does not make them ethical. These leaders not only examine what people have *not* done but, as importantly, what they *have* done to demonstrate that their lives are based on honesty, justice, respect, and caring. Professional leaders direct police psychologists to include integrity tests in the screening of candidates. Becoming more selective in terms of recruits is easier said than done in an era in which retirement is high and recruitment is low, an era in which agencies are seriously debating whether a candidate's drug history should be an impediment to being hired in law enforcement.

The selection process does not stop once the person is hired, but continues through the academy and extended probation periods during which instructors and field training officers teach and model ethical behavior, as well as look for early warning signs of unethical conduct. Ethics education (classroom lectures) and training (group discussions that center on wrestling with relevant ethical dilemmas) are generally either nonexistent or inadequate both in training academies and in continuing education curricula. An extensive survey of ethics training in law enforcement was conducted by the International Association of Chiefs of Police United States (1998), which distributed 4,500 surveys and received 900 returns. One result indicated over 70 percent of respondents reported that their agency provided only four classroom hours or less for ethics training. Only 17 percent reported they had an eight-hour segment reserved for ethics training, still relatively few hours compared to the importance of the topic.

Moreover, existing ethics training often simply consists of "Don't be stupid" admonitions, which have little effect on people who do not believe that they could ever be so stupid to begin with. Finally, ethics education must be attitude centered and not behavior centered or code centered. Behavior flows from attitudes; consequently, ethical attitudes must be fostered if ethical behavior is to follow.

The International Association of Chiefs of Police United States (1998) summarizes the critical role of supervisors in creating and maintaining a pervasive and enduring ethical atmosphere:

> Supervisors can no longer absolve themselves of responsibility for misbehavior or personnel under their command. The prevailing attitude of being a popular supervisor rather than being an ethical supervisor must be reversed. This level of organization, more than any other, must be constantly inundated with ethical situational training and scrutinized for indications of unethical behavior or dilemmas. The consensus of all members of the ad hoc committee identified this level of the police organization as essential in setting the ethical culture in the police profession. (p. 18)[1]

Strengthening the Internal Affairs Bureau

At times internal affairs bureaus have participated in two questionable practices. First, their attitudes and tactics may be as devious and unethical as the behaviors they are investigating. As a result, both ethical and unethical officers will refuse to cooperate with internal affairs investigators whenever possible.

Second, at the other end of the scale, internal affairs investigators have been inclined to investigate citizen complaints superficially and then conclude that the charges were unfounded in order to protect the officers and the agency.

Administrators can strengthen their internal affairs bureaus by the following actions:

- Assigning only the most respected, principled, and professional officers to these units
- Monitoring internal affairs procedures to ensure that all parties, both officers and citizens, receive equal and fair treatment
- Making it crystal clear that the purpose of an investigation is to discover the truth, not to protect the reputation of individual officers or the agency
- Ensuring that internal affairs bureaus are independent entities, which report only to the chief executives of the agency

Executives should realize on a daily basis that they set the ethical tone for the entire agency by behaving ethically themselves and holding their commanders at every level personally and professionally responsible for the conduct of their officers. The message must be clear: "If a few bad apples must go, the sides of the barrel around them must go as well." One must tread lightly in many situations in law enforcement, but ethics is not one of them. The administration's attitude should be this: We have made our ethical standards and sanctions clear to everyone in the agency, so it is assumed that all ethical violations are knowingly and willfully committed; hence, accountability and sanctions will be measured in this light.

When law enforcement was in the early stages of trying to progress from simply being a secure job to a respected profession, signs were posted around station houses: "No more fat cops stealing apples." Today, this sentiment, unfortunately, seems quaint. For law enforcement to consider itself a profession and to be viewed as such by the public, it must keep its house clean and deal with law-breakers within law enforcement with the same dedication it affords to those outside of law enforcement.

Personal Reflections

1. What do you think about leaders whose motto is "Do what I say but not as I do"?
2. What do you think it feels like to work in a situation in which your coworkers are misbehaving, and no one in charge is willing or able to do anything to stop it?
3. With respect to the code of silence, what would you do if you were aware of misconduct but everybody told you to forget about it?
4. Why do you think some leaders in organizations are reluctant to get tough on unethical behavior and practices within the organization?

Summary

It is critically important for officers to understand the necessity of ethical practice in law enforcement. It is not "an ivory tower thing" or an effort to be politically correct or appease the public. Ethical practice is the foundation of law enforcement, which is witnessing daily what happens when the foundation starts crumbling. It is also important to be aware of the personal and organizational influences that can erode ethical practice, placing agencies and careers in danger, to say nothing of the effect of officer misconduct on honest officers and other innocent people.

Finally, it is not only the responsibility of executives and supervisors to root out unethical officers. Ethical officers constitute the vast majority of officers in any agency and have the numbers and the power to expose unethical officers and bring them to the attention of the appropriate people. They need to do this because it is the right thing to do and because they are paying a high price for the actions of the few unethical officers. As Pollock (1998) states:

> To scrutinize and analyze police misconduct and the police role in society is not to disparage the thousands of officers who perform their job in an exemplary manner and epitomize the best of law enforcement. It is important to keep in mind as we discuss issues of law enforcement ethics that the majority of officers are honest and ethical and spend their careers simply trying to do a good job. These men and women usually don't appear on the front page of newspapers or on the evening news, but they pay the price for the few who do through decreased public confidence and even public scorn. (p. 135)

References

Barker, T., & Carter, D.L. (1994). *Police deviance* (3rd ed.). Cincinnati, OH: Anderson Publishing.

Boyer, P.J. (2001, May 21). Bad cops. *The New Yorker*, 58–82.

Crank, J.P., & Caldero, M.A. (2000). *Police ethics: The corruption of a noble cause.* Cincinnati, OH: Anderson Publishing.

Dautrich, K. (1998). *Criminal justice policy foundation survey.* Storrs, CT: University of Connecticut Center for Survey Research and Analysis.

Delattre, E.J. (2001). *Character and cops: Ethics in policing* (4th ed.). Washington, DC: AEI Press.

Gilmartin, K.M. (1998). Ethics-based policing . . . undoing entitlement. Retrieved October 4, 2002, from the World Wide Web: http://www.gilmartinharris.com/entitlement.htm.

Gilmartin, K.M., & Harris, J.J. (1998). Law enforcement ethics . . . the continuum of compromise. Retrieved October 4, 2002, from the World Wide Web: http://www.gilmartinharris.com/law_enforcement_ethics.htm.

Goodman, D.J. (1998). *Enforcing ethics: A scenario-based workbook for police and corrections recruits and officers.* Upper Saddle River, NJ: Prentice Hall.

Harrison, B. (1999). Noble cause corruption and the police ethic. *FBI Law Enforcement Bulletin, 68* (8), 1–8.

Hess, A.K., & Weiner, I.B. (1999). *The handbook of forensic psychology.* New York: John Wiley.

International Association of Chiefs of Police United States (1998). Ethics training in law enforcement. *Police Chief, 65* (1), 14–24.

Jones, J.R. (1998). *Reputable conduct: Ethical issues in policing and corrections.* Scarborough, Ontario, Canada: Prentice Hall Canada.

Kappeler, V.E., Sluder, R.D., & Alpert, G.P. (1998). *Forces of deviance* (2nd ed.). Prospect Heights, IL: Waveland Press.

Klockars, C.B., Ivkovich, S.K., Harver, W.E., & Haberfeld, M.R. (2000). *The measurement of police integrity.* (NCJ181465). Washington DC: U.S. Department of Justice.

Morgan, B., Morgan, F., Foster, V., & Kolbert, J. (2000). Promoting the moral and conceptual development of law enforcement trainees: A deliberate psychological educational approach. *Journal of Moral Education, 29,* 203–219.

National Institute of Justice and the Office of Community Oriented Policing Services (1997). *Police integrity: Public service with honor.* (NCJ 163811). Washington, DC: U.S. Department of Justice.

Palmiotto, M.J. (2000). *Community policing: A policing strategy for the 21st century.* Gaithersburg, MD: Aspen Publishers.

Pollock, J.M. (1998). *Ethics in crime and justice* (3rd ed.). Belmont, CA: West/Wadsworth.

Scheck, B., Neufeld, P., & Dwyer, J. (2000). *Actual innocence.* New York: Doubleday.

Skolnick, J.H., & Fyfe, J.J. (1993). *Above the law: Police and the excessive use of force.* New York: Free Press.

Trautman, N. (2001). Truth about police code of silence revealed. *Law and Order Magazine* (Online version). Retrieved April 11, 2001, from the World Wide Web: http://infobase.thirdcoast.net/clients/lawandorder.

U.S. Department of Justice (2001). *Principles for promoting police integrity.* Washington, DC: U.S. Department of Justice.

U.S. Department of Justice, Office of Justice Programs (1999). *Use of force by police: Overview of national and local data.* Washington, DC: U.S. Department of Justice.

Vicchio, S.J. (1997). Ethics and police integrity. *FBI Law Enforcement Bulletin, 66* (7), 8–13.

Walker, S. (1999). *The police in America: An introduction* (3rd ed.). New York: McGraw-Hill.

Walker, S., Alpert, G.P., & Kenney, D.J. (2001). *Early warning systems: Responding to the problem police officer.* Washington, DC: U.S. Department of Justice.

Weisburd, D., & Greenspan, R. with Hamilton, E.E., Williams, H., & Bryant, K.A. (2000). *Police attitudes toward abuse of authority: Findings from a national study.* (NCJ181312). Washington, DC: U.S. Department of Justice.

2

Professionalism in Law Enforcement

There has been heightened discussion over the past few years as to whether law enforcement is a profession, in contrast to being an occupation or "just a job." Some people argue that it is a profession; others believe it is not currently a profession but should strive to become one; others hold that, by its very nature, it can never be a profession; still others argue law enforcement should not become a profession because doing so would curtail much of its freedom to meet the unique needs of its officers and constituents.

This book's objective is to use professionalism as a framework in which to advance the practice of law enforcement to higher levels. To accomplish this, it is important to acquire a basic understanding of the nature of a profession. To this end, the following topics will be discussed: the standards of a profession, the elements of a professional agency, the importance of respect, professional training and education, and the issue of college education for law enforcement officers.

STANDARDS OF A PROFESSION

Although no agreed-upon set of standards defines a profession, the following qualities are most frequently mentioned when the topic arises.

Code of Ethics

Simply having a code of ethics does not make an organization a professional one. A code of ethics, in addition to high-sounding principles, must have three qualities. First, it must be concrete and specific. If it is abstract and philosophical, it will have little meaning to the members of the organization. For example,

"Officers will live a life of integrity," is virtually meaningless in contrast to "There is zero tolerance for dishonesty and corruption."

A second criterion of a meaningful code of ethics is that it is consistently and evenly enforced. Today, almost every law enforcement agency in the country has a code of ethics, but how many of them actually enforce it *consistently*, not just when there is political pressure to do so, and *evenly* throughout the chain of command? Because the honest answer to this question is "relatively few," it is fair to state that relatively few law enforcement officers take their agency's code of ethics seriously. Although they may have personal ethics, they regard the agency's code as only window dressing rather than as a factor in their everyday activities.

Finally, an authentic code of ethics requires members not only to abide by the code but also to report those who violate it to the appropriate people. Without this requirement, members can personally abide by the code but legitimately stand by while others violate it, thus damaging the entire profession.

When this criterion is applied to law enforcement, it raises two questions: Does law enforcement have a consensually agreed-upon code of ethics? Are the ethical codes in law enforcement continually and evenly enforced?

Mastery of an Established Body of Knowledge

The two parts to this criterion are an "established body of knowledge" and "mastery." The former means that a profession is based on a foundation of literature that includes theories, research, and principles of practice. *Mastery* means that the material is understood, integrated, and effectively applied.

When this criterion is applied to law enforcement, two questions arise. Does law enforcement have an established body of knowledge? Does it, like medicine and law, have a deep reservoir of knowledge that everyone in law enforcement should know even before officers specialize in a particular area of law enforcement? For example, all physicians know a great deal about general medicine before specializing in a particular branch of the field. Can a comparable statement be made by law enforcement?

Appropriate Level of Education and Training

Professions require education and training ordinarily to the baccalaureate level or beyond in order to truly grasp the established body of knowledge. Understanding and integrating theories, principles of practice, and research in any field requires intelligence, commitment, experience, critical thinking, and exposure to related disciplines.

When this standard is applied to law enforcement, two questions arise. First, do the entry-level educational requirements provide officers with the tools to grasp and use the body of knowledge that will hopefully become available to them? Second, are the educational requirements at least relatively consistent across all agencies?

Professional Experience

Experience adds to knowledge and vice versa, which is the reason that supervised experience is necessary in professions before its members can practice autonomously. This experience, often in the form of internships or clerkships, further enhances professional education by providing opportunities to put the theories and research into practice: to sharpen competencies, increase knowledge, develop interpersonal skills, increase confidence in handling a wide range of situations, and grow into a professional identity.

When this standard is applied to law enforcement, the following questions arise. First, how much practical experience does law enforcement typically require before officers are permitted to work without close supervision? Second, are the experience requirements relatively consistent across all agencies?

Best Practice and Maintenance of Competence

Professionals practice in a way that reflects the best and most current knowledge in their field. Conventional wisdom, common sense, pet theories, and tricks of the trade are replaced by practices based on sound theory and research, and consistent with the levels of knowledge and practices of the profession at its best.

Continuing education, especially in perishable skills, is necessary in order to keep current with the profession's best practices. Keeping current with the literature, attending in-house and external education sessions, and discussing practices with peers accomplish this. Typically, professionals spend from 20 to 40 hours per year in continuing education. Assessment of the individual's current competence is regularly done by examination, performance appraisal, and peer evaluations.

When this standard is applied to law enforcement, it raises two questions. First, do law enforcement agencies provide the ongoing opportunities to keep current with constantly changing theories, research, and practice, so that officers will be conversant with them? Second, do officers internalize this knowledge and apply it in their work, or do they ignore it and continue with their "If I don't already know it, it must not be worth knowing" attitude?

Sharing of Knowledge

Professionals do not view knowledge as a privately owned commodity to be kept, or even hidden, from other members in the profession. Because professionals are concerned about the quality of their profession as a whole, sharing knowledge is important. For example, medicine and law each have scores of professional journals and offer hundreds of workshops to update their members so that the profession as a whole will flourish, as well as the people the profession serves.

When this standard is applied to law enforcement, three questions arise. First, is the sharing of knowledge among agencies a common practice? Second, are individual agencies generating new knowledge to share with other agencies? Finally, do agencies seek the knowledge of other agencies?

Accreditation Associations

Professions typically develop associations that oversee credentialing, licensing, setting standards, defining entrance requirements, and disciplining members who violate rules and regulations. This provides quality assurance in terms of both the competency of the members and the services they render. It also ensures uniformity, so that every member, regardless of geographical location, meets the same standards and abides by the same rules.

When this standard is applied to law enforcement, two questions arise. First, do agencies have external professional oversight that sets standards of admission and practice and monitors compliance? Second, is accreditation national, so that law enforcement agencies throughout the country have virtually the same entry requirements, education, and training?

Whereas these criteria of a profession are clear, the topic of professionalism is more complex. The questions that need to be answered as the debate continues include the following:

- Does law enforcement have to meet all these criteria to be considered a profession?
- Why is it important for law enforcement to be considered a profession, as long as it does what it is supposed to do?
- Are there drawbacks as well as benefits attached to being a profession?

Personal Reflections

1. After reading this section, do you view law enforcement as a profession? Explain your answer.

2. Do you think any agency enforces its code of ethics evenly across all ranks, or is it selectively enforced? Why do you think this occurs?

3. Some people in law enforcement do not believe it should become a profession because doing so will hinder its objectives. What do you think of this position?

ELEMENTS OF A PROFESSIONAL AGENCY

Whether or not law enforcement is a profession, or should or should not strive to become one, lies outside the parameters of this book. What lies squarely within its parameters, however, is the fact that law enforcement can always become more *professional*, whether or not it is a *profession*. Being a professional law enforcement agency includes the following elements:

- Generating new knowledge in a continuous way, in contrast to working from information that dates back to the training academy or a book read or a workshop attended a few or many years ago
- Using knowledge based on sound theory and research, in contrast to acting according to pet theories and "tried and true" methods that are more tried than true
- Having a contemporary, enlightened, and highly efficient organizational structure, in contrast to one that is archaic, stale, and gridlocked
- Treating all employees, citizens, and criminals with civility, in contrast to treating anyone in a dismissive, denigrating, or abusive manner
- Understanding that officers' age, years of experience, and rank are not nearly as important as their knowledge and maturity, in contrast to believing that officers who are older, more experienced, or higher ranking are necessarily more reasonable and knowledgeable
- Possessing an accurate and steady moral compass that functions in all climates, in contrast to one swayed by organizational politics, peer or community pressure, or personal insecurities
- Evaluating both the effectiveness of individual officers and the organization as a whole on a regular basis, in contrast to assuming everything is fine until a situation arises that proves it is not
- Respecting bodies of knowledge in addition to police science—for example, psychology, philosophy, business, sociology, political science, and criminal justice—in contrast to believing that anything worth knowing was learned during the first few years on the job
- Possessing a code of ethics, code of conduct, and mission statement that are taken seriously and enforced, in contrast to those whose only function is public relations and the decoration of office walls
- Offering incentive systems that reward education and afford opportunities to increase knowledge, in contrast to an anti-intellectual attitude that demeans education as unnecessary and perhaps even a hindrance
- Having an organizational culture based on honesty, respect, caring, integrity, and conscientiousness, in contrast to one based on backdoor deals and an "all means justify the ends" philosophy
- Offering clear rewards for outstanding work and clear punishments for ineffective or unethical behavior, in contrast to ignoring both of these behaviors or overusing one and underusing the other
- Having a clear understanding that an organization's prestige and respect must be earned through efficient and principled performance, in contrast to being based on public relations gimmicks

Personal Reflections _____

1. Having read the criteria for a profession, do you believe that law enforcement is a profession? If so, why? If not, why not?
2. What difference does it make whether law enforcement is a profession or is regarded as a profession by the public?
3. What do you think the difference is between *being* a professional and *acting* professionally?

THE IMPORTANCE OF RESPECT

When Bernard Kerik was the police commissioner of the New York Police Department, he had officers conduct civility tests. They would randomly contact 50 officers each month and pretend to be citizens asking questions or requesting service. On the average, for every 50 officers contacted, 2 performed exceptionally well, 2 passed, and 46 failed the civility test. In response to the survey results, Kerik (2001) states:

> We're constantly on the lookout for bad cops. Last year Internal Affairs ran one thousand integrity tests, offering bribes and using other tests to weed out dirty cops.
>   . . . But a far more insidious problem, I'm convinced, is this institutional arrogance and rudeness.
>   . . . If I could just convince street cops of this one thing—that they need to be respectful, that they don't need to antagonize people—I'd cut complaints to the Civilian Complaint Review Board in half. (pp. 88–89)

If there is one word that differentiates the professional officer from the unprofessional one it is this: respect. The word *respect* literally means "to look at something twice." Applying this concept to law enforcement, it means officers should look twice at themselves, as well as at the citizens and criminals with whom they interact.

Looking Twice at Themselves

Everyone can remember a parent or teacher admonishing: "Jimmy, just *look at yourself*!" which translated into "You should see what you look like to other people!" Professional officers start the shift looking at themselves in both a real and a psychological mirror: Do I *look* professional? Does my uniform look clean and pressed, with shoes, badges, and name tag shined? Do my posture and physique elicit respect? In this regard, it is useful to compare American law enforcement officers with those in England. The bobbies in England typically appear to be in good physical shape and dressed in a manner that denotes pride in themselves and their work. Although some American officers may scoff at this comparison, officers in England are highly respected, even by criminals, not only because they are in a position of authority but also because their appearance and professional demeanor evoke respect.

Professional officers also look twice at themselves to see how they are viewed by citizens, including criminals. While some officers may be quite pleased with their personal image ("An aggressive crime fighter who takes nothing from nobody"), they are completely blind to how they are perceived by others, including professional fellow officers who are thoroughly embarrassed by the conduct of these officers. Civilians are not always mistaken in their perceptions when they view some officers as pigs, Gestapo, racist, bullies, stupid, or even criminals.

Looking Twice at Citizens

Officers' true motives for entering law enforcement come to light in their interactions with citizens. A common question in preemployment interviews is "Why do you want to go into law enforcement?" and an equally common reply is "To help people—to give back to the community." When this represents the officers' true motives, interacting with the public is typically a positive experience for all concerned. One does not have to wait until recruits hit the streets to discover their true motives for entering law enforcement. A prosocial attitude that engenders positive, helping behavior in social situations will be clearly seen in the recruits' history and academy behavior, whereby they are anxious to help classmates succeed.

On the other hand, some officers enter law enforcement for consciously or unconsciously negative motives. An officer who, deep down, really does not like people is analogous to a physician who actually does not like patients and an attorney who really does not like clients. These officers' attitudes toward ordinary citizens run the gamut from being dismissive to cynical to ridiculing. Once these officers are unleashed on the public, their true motives surface: to have a license to make citizens feel as stupid, powerless, and inept as the officers feel about themselves and to avenge past personal hurts and failures. To these officers "to protect and serve" means to protect their fragile egos and serve their antisocial needs. At a minimum, these attitudes will result in inappropriate behavior and citizen complaints and, at the maximum, will lead to the officer being sued, terminated, or killed.

The first stage of looking twice at citizens is to see their presenting behavior—the behavior that is most noticeable. The most common presenting behaviors stem from anxiety, fear, concern, anger, confusion, depression, and desperation. When people experience these states, they are often "not themselves"—the state they are experiencing takes over their personality. When this occurs, they often make demands of officers ("You *must* arrest my husband." "You *can't* arrest our son."). When officers cannot meet these demands, the citizens often become angry at the officer toward whom they should be the least hostile and the most appreciative.

At this point, officers must look twice at the citizen *and* at themselves. Looking twice at the citizen entails sidestepping the person's demands and frustrations and seeing the very frightened person behind the actively or passively aggressive façade. When people are very upset, which is usually the only time they call the police, they often act uncharacteristically—they do not intend to disrespect officers, demand things, or accuse officers of taking sides or being uncaring, incompetent, or prejudiced. The citizens typically do not mean these things but are simply "crazy with fear." The proof of this is often seen when upset people calm down and become embarrassed and apologetic for their behavior.

Unprofessional officers allow their egos to become central to the interaction and may respond in two ways. They may react with a "contempt of cop" arrest in which the only thing the person violates is the officer's ego. Or, when people get upset with them, officers may proclaim: "Look! Before we go any further: If you're going to talk to me like that, I'm out of here!" Imagine a patient in pain screaming demands and complaints at a physician, and the physician responding the way this officer did. The "Don't talk to me that way!" response does four things: It adds stress to an already stressful situation; it makes the officer's job more complicated; it causes the person to have negative feelings toward the officer and the agency; and it decreases the likelihood of the person calling for help in the future, an effect that could have regrettable results.

Professional officers transcend the drama when the citizen cannot. They are patient, calm, and allow the upset person to vent. The problem can become more clearly defined and the solution more easily attained when officers create a calm, respectful environment.

In addition to recognizing they are becoming aggravated with the complaining citizen, officers need to examine how they would react if they were the citizen in the same set of circumstances. For example, when off-duty officers call police for help or are stopped for a traffic violation, they can be as belligerent as any citizen if they feel the officer is ineffectual or heavy-handed. When officers recognize this human tendency within themselves, it can engender a sense of compassion, a sense of "feeling with" the citizen who is reacting as most other human beings would in similar stressful circumstances.

Looking Twice at Criminals

With respect to interacting with criminals, the same principle just discussed applies: Officers should keep their egos out of their work. Officers have three choices when dealing with criminals: to relate professionally, to relate on the same level as the criminal, or to relate on a level below that of the criminal. Officers who relate on a professional level have only one agenda—to enforce the law and keep the peace in the most effective and expeditious way possible. Analogously, an emergency room physician has only one agenda when treating an intoxicated driver who seriously injured him- or herself and others in a collision he or she caused—to treat the injuries in the most effective and prompt way possible. The agenda does not include yelling insults at the patient, inflicting unnecessary pain, prolonging the agony of the surgical intervention, or ridiculing the patient in front of others. Physicians who were to act in this manner even once would find their jobs in serious jeopardy and would be shunned by their colleagues. No one would think they were cool, tough, humorous, or righteous.

The retort could be made that whereas the physician's life is not in danger when interacting with patients, officer–criminal interactions can be dangerous. This only reinforces the point: If there is anyone on earth who should not disrespect and unnecessarily upset anyone, it is an officer taking a criminal into custody.

Officers who match or surpass the disrespect of criminals must realize that the criminals have just won the contest by reducing the officer to a level that is no better, and sometimes is worse, than the criminal's. Moreover, this is not simply a matter of professionalism; it is also a matter of survival. Therefore, no matter how contemptuous criminals are and how heinous their crimes, there is never a legitimate reason to treat them in ways that officers would not want their family, friends, supervisors, reporters, or a civilian review board to witness.

Personal Reflections _____

1. Think about your direct and indirect experiences with law enforcement officers. Did you see professional or unprofessional behavior? Discuss the differences as you see them.

2. Respond to an officer's statement: "It's all well and good for people outside of law enforcement to talk about treating people on the street with respect, but what they don't understand is that it's a jungle out there, and we are dealing with animals most of the time."

3. Respond to an officer's statement: "I give people the same respect they give me. If they respect me, I respect them. If they don't respect me, I don't respect them. It's that simple."

4. Why do you think it's so hard for people, including law enforcement officers, to see themselves as others *actually* see them and not as they *think* others see them?

5. If you were (or are) an officer, what would you do if you observed another officer ridiculing a suspect in front of others?

TRAINING AND EDUCATION

If professionalism is to develop in law enforcement, it must be introduced at the beginning of the officer's career—at the academy. This section addresses academy education, training, and instructors.

Training versus Education

There is both a semantic and a real difference between training and education. Training answers the student's question: "What should I do when a certain situation arises?" For example, a medical student might ask: "What should I do when arterial bleeding doesn't stop, even after I hold the pressure points?" A law enforcement recruit might ask: "What do I do when my gun jams?" These tend to be mechanical issues that are dealt with by using rote responses acquired through many hours of drilling. There is nothing wrong with this; after all, it is important to know how to stop bleeding or unjam a gun.

Education answers the student's question: How can I acquire knowledge that enables me to relate to myself, people, and events in the most effective, ethical, and helpful ways possible? The question is not which form of learning is better, but how best to combine the education and training into a holistic curriculum, as is done in college lecture-laboratory courses.

In the professions, education always precedes training. For example, an intern would never be allowed to make a surgical incision without first being educated with respect to the anatomy and physiology involved in the situation so that of all the possible incisions that could be made, the intern makes the right one in the right place at the right time.

In contrast to education and training in professions such as law and medicine, training often stands alone in law enforcement, which can cause officers to react to all people and situations as if they are identical. For example, officers may be trained always to separate a feuding couple at domestic dispute calls so that order is maintained and peace restored.

However, in a professional education environment, officers are first educated as to the basic psychological dynamics involved in domestic conflicts, so that their actions will not be automatic but tailored to the situation. Educated officers will know it is sometimes better not to separate the parties but allow them to express their anger in the controlled, safe environment created by the calm and mediating officers. This allows the couple to vent their anger and allows it to dissipate while the officers are present. Separating the couple may bring temporary peace, which may quickly be breached when the officers leave because the couple's anger has incubated and festered during the separation period.

Having a two-dimensional curriculum (education and training) does not add much time to a typical academy program if it is done correctly. For example, a 16-hour segment dedicated to conflict resolution can be designed so that psychologists teach the theoretical aspects on the first day and the academy officers teach the practical segment on the second day. This plan would provide a holistic approach to the situation. Bringing in outside instructors would add to the expense but would be well worth it in terms of avoiding problems when the recruits hit the streets.

The Quality of Academy Instructors

The quality of academy instructors is critical because they introduce recruits to both law enforcement in general and the specific agency in particular. They have a captive audience that is typically impressionable and often uncritically accepts what instructors say and do. For better or for worse, many veteran officers can remember each of their academy instructors by name and personality. What they tend to remember most is not the course content, but the instructors' attitudes and behaviors, some of which the officers consciously or unconsciously adopted as their own.

For this reason, academy instructors should be the best the agency has to offer, which means many things. Good instructors

- Have a great deal of practical experience in the subject taught, in contrast to general experience in law enforcement but little or none in the subject they teach
- Care about the recruits both as students and as individuals, in contrast to using students as a means to an end (a paycheck, adulation, a chance to exercise power)
- Have knowledge based not only on experience but also on a sound academic foundation of theory and research, in contrast to solely relying on what they learned from experience, which may, or may not, have produced valid learnings
- Have a positive attitude toward people and institutions, including the agency, in contrast to being hostile, demeaning, cynical, or paranoid
- Possess compassionate toughness, meaning they can be both compassionate and tough when appropriate, in contrast to specializing in one or the other
- Are obviously enthusiastic about their subject in contrast to being bored by the topic, themselves, their students, and life in general
- Are good role models, meaning that they not only teach respect, conscientiousness, and honesty but also model it daily with their students, in contrast to a "Do as I say, but not as I do" style of teaching
- Impart knowledge but also draw it out of their students so each is educating the other, in contrast to a unilateral relationship in which the instructor crams knowledge down the throats of the students who are expected to simply regurgitate it on exams
- Take their teaching seriously, which includes constructing good examinations that truly test knowledge, in contrast to constructing elementary-level examinations and giving the students the answers before the test, so that they will all pass and make their instructor look good.
- Possess great patience, remembering the stupid things they said and did when they were in the academy, in contrast to demanding perfection from imperfect human beings

- Possess humility and realize they do not know all the answers and that they make mistakes in class, in contrast to having all the answers, never admitting mistakes, and being defensive when students challenge them
- Have good self-monitoring skills, meaning that they are continually aware of their own behavior and its effect on their students, in contrast to lecturing away oblivious that one-third of the class is asleep, another third is frustrated, and the final third has left the classroom
- Communicate clearly, both verbally and nonverbally, giving good examples to explain complicated points, in contrast to lecturing in confusing, disjointed ways, relying on war stories to save the day

As can be seen, good academy instructors are not run-of-the-mill officers. They should be screened with the same rigor as that applied to any officer going into a highly specialized assignment in which the stakes are high. To do anything less does a disservice not only to the students and the agency but also to the citizens who will be on the receiving end of each recruit's actions.

Personal Reflections _____

1. What is the most important trait you believe all academy instructors should possess?
2. What is the worst trait an academy instructor can have?
3. How do you think young people going through a law enforcement academy today view macho, "Don't take anything from anybody" instructors?

COLLEGE EDUCATION

There is continuing and sometimes heated debate as to whether a college degree should be a requirement for entry-level positions and promotion in law enforcement. Six national commissions and the federal courts have recommended that the minimum education level for entry positions in law enforcement be a baccalaureate degree. For example, as far back as 1967, the President's Commission on Law Enforcement recommended that "all police personnel with enforcement powers have baccalaureate degrees." The federal courts (*Davis* v. *City of Dallas*, 1985) echo this sentiment: "The need for police officers who are intelligent, articulate, mature, and knowledgeable about social and political decisions is apparent. . . . College education develops and imparts the requisite level of knowledge."

The American Bar Association in its *Standards for the Urban Police Function* states:

Police need personnel in their ranks who have the characteristics a college education seeks to foster: intellectual curiosity, analytical ability, articulateness, and a capacity to relate the events of the day to the social, political and historical context in which they occur. (Mayo, 2002)

Finally, citizens are weighing in on the issue. An editorial in *The Press of Atlantic City, New Jersey* (2000) states:

Police officers cannot have it both ways.

They cannot talk, at salary-negotiation time, about how much policing has changed in recent years, about the complex issues officers must deal with today, about how they are trained *professionals*—they cannot say all this and simultaneously oppose the growing movement to require today's police officers to have college educations.

Because the officers are right—policing *has* changed. An officer must deal with complex inter-personal issues, myriad legal issues, *technology* issues. They need the kind of broad-based knowledge that comes with a college degree, preferably a full, four-year bachelor's degree. Not that the world isn't full of fools with college degrees. Or that there aren't countless police officers out there who excel at their jobs with no higher education other than what they have learned on the street.

But the exceptions do not disprove the rule: Modern policing is a complicated affair that requires brains as well as brawn. Every town should require its new officers to have bachelor's degrees.

This section will focus on five ways to address the issue. First, law enforcement has been fond of claiming that officers must be "all things to all people": psychologists, attorneys, counselors, ministers, social workers, and judges. The average number of years in college and postgraduate education required to enter these professions is eight. When multiplied by these six professions, the total number of years of college education comes to about a half century. Therefore, it seems reasonable to conclude that at least two to four years of college education should be required for entry-level candidates in law enforcement if they are to wear all these hats.

Second, the demands of law enforcement today are infinitely more complex than they were even a decade ago. Officers do not just issue citations, direct traffic, arrest drunks, check doors, and occasionally break up a fight. Today, officers need to be more knowledgeable and sophisticated in order to confidently approach the "routine tasks" of law enforcement and deal with them effectively and expeditiously. The Occupational Information Network (2000), which was derived by occupational analysts from the *Dictionary of Occupational Titles*, lists 46 skills important for police patrol officers. The 20 most important skills listed in rank order can be seen in Table 2.1

Even a superficial reading of this list indicates these are not skills the average high school graduate possesses to any meaningful degree. Each skill requires a fair amount of education and training to reach a level of acceptable performance in law enforcement.

Third, it must be understood that no skill is an all-or-nothing phenomenon. For example, officers without any college experience may protest they are critical thinkers without ever having set foot on a college campus. Assuming their

TABLE 2.1 *Important Skills for Police Patrol Officers*

Skill	Description
Active listening	Listening to what other people are saying and asking questions as appropriate
Problem identification	Identifying the nature of problems
Critical thinking	Using logic and analysis to identify the strengths and weaknesses of different approaches
Social perceptiveness	Being aware of others' reactions and understanding why they react the way they do
Service orientation	Actively looking for ways to help people
Information gathering	Knowing how to find information and identifying essential information
Speaking	Talking to others to convey information effectively
Information organization	Finding ways to structure or classify multiple pieces of information
Judgment and decision making	Weighing the relative costs and benefits of a potential action
Reading comprehension	Understanding written sentences and paragraphs in work-related documents
Writing	Communicating effectively with others in writing as indicated by the needs of the audience
Active learning	Working with new material or information to grasp its implications
Monitoring	Assessing how well one is doing when learning or doing something
Coordination	Adjusting actions in relation to others' actions
Systems perception	Determining when important changes have occurred in a system or are likely to occur
Identification of key causes	Identifying the things that must be changed to achieve a goal
Negotiation	Bringing others together and trying to reconcile differences
Synthesis/reorganization	Reorganizing information to get a better approach to problems or tasks
Idea generation	Generating a number of different approaches to problems
Idea evaluation	Evaluating the likely success of an idea in relation to the demands of the situation

Source: Occupational Information Network, "Details of Skills for Police Patrol Officers." Retrieved May 13, 2002, from the World Wide Web: http://online.onetcenter.org/cgi-bin/occ_details.

self-assessment is accurate, the question arises: Could they have increased this skill dramatically by developing it over the course of four years of college?

Fourth, the assessment of officers' competencies in the skills mentioned in Table 2.1 might best be reflected in investigating a crime, writing a report, and testifying in court, which is the "final examination" at the end of the process. These are not exotic tasks, but the work of officers from the first day on the job. The general level of competence of officers testifying in court indicates a great deal more education and training are needed to develop the skills described in the table.

Fifth, it is of interest to evaluate the arguments made against requiring a college education for entry-level positions.

- "Some of the best officers on the job have never had a day of college." This argument is flawed for several reasons, one of which is an error in logic, which is going from the particular to the general. A comparable argument highlights the flaw: "The best football player on the team never seriously practices; therefore, I don't think it's important for the other players to practice."
- "We've got some college graduates on the job, and they're some of the stupidest people in the agency." This argument is flawed in the same way as the previous example, which can be seen by using another analogy: "We've got some range instructors who can't shoot worth a darn, so we shouldn't bother sending our instructors to range master school."
- "There's no empirical evidence that college graduates make better officers than do noncollege graduates." This argument is interesting because officers who make it often belittle the importance of empirical evidence for any other issue in law enforcement. For example, no empirical evidence exists that males make better officers than females, yet a large number of male officers firmly believe this to be true. Despite the fact that some studies have attempted to measure the effects of college education on officers' performance, it is virtually impossible to design methodologically sound studies to measure whether one variable causes someone to be a better officer (or a better anything else) because there are too many uncontrollable variables. For example, do college-educated officers perform well because they went to college or simply because they are intelligent, which may have nothing to do with college, except that they were intelligent enough to be accepted into college?
- "Even if a college education were required, agencies could never agree what curriculum would be best suited for a career in law enforcement." This is a nonissue. The intellectual competencies required to complete almost *any* academic major will be directly and indirectly relevant to the knowledge and skills discussed previously in this chapter.
- "Many small and rural agencies do not need college-educated officers because they do not face the same challenges that larger agencies do." One

response to this argument is that wherever human beings gather, there will be human problems, some of which are serious and will be addressed by officers in an enlightened, ineffectual, or damaging way. A second response is that if small and rural agencies, which typically have used a reactive approach to law enforcement, wish to move toward community oriented and problem-solving approaches, they will need officers who possess the same skills as those needed in metropolitan areas.

- "College graduates are difficult to supervise because they think they already have all the answers." In addition to being a gross overstatement, this view raises some interesting points. One is that intellectual maturity is not synonymous with emotional maturity. It may be that, in some cases, officers who are college graduates need to learn diplomacy and humility to develop into truly fine officers. On the other hand, some non-college-educated supervisors may feel threatened by college-educated officers and become unnecessarily contentious. When tensions do arise, they often stem from college-educated officers applying critical-thinking skills to various situations. Non-college-educated supervisors often interpret this behavior as the officer questioning their authority when the officer was merely attempting to analyze and understand issues and events rationally. Law enforcement agencies still entrenched in the paramilitary model do not welcome critical thinking. "Don't ask 'why'—just do it!" is an insecure, regressive attitude that is prevalent in many law enforcement agencies. For this reason, college graduates need to look closely at an agency's culture before deciding to apply for a position within it.

Whether or not agencies require a college degree has some important practical implications. One is that this requirement would shrink the pool of potential candidates because many people interested in law enforcement may not be able to attend college, while those who do attend college may find other careers more interesting and lucrative. On the positive side, the introduction of college graduates into law enforcement might well increase the organizational effectiveness of and respect for law enforcement as it faces new, serious challenges.

It is important to acknowledge that some great law enforcement officers never attended college, just as some great college professors never took a course in education or had a practicum in teaching. Yet both education and law enforcement are changing dramatically, so that young people entering both fields today would better serve themselves and their constituents by becoming educated in the important issues that continue to develop in education and law enforcement. Carter and Radelet (1999) summarize this issue:

> Importantly, then, the role of education in professionalism is to ensure that police officers are informed decision makers who base their actions on a logical interpretation of facts and application of diverse knowledge. Clearly, a consensus that higher education enhances the quality of police performance exists. By inference, we may also conclude that education contributes to professionalism, but does not guarantee it. (p. 148)

The Police Association for College Education (PACE) is a professional organization dedicated to helping agencies meet the standards recommended by several national commissions and the federal courts with respect to the goal of all officers having a bachelor's degree. The organization can be contacted at www.police-association.org.

Personal Reflections

1. Do you believe entry-level officers should have a college degree? Explain your answer.

2. Of the twenty skills important for police officers in Table 2.1, which three do you believe are the more important?

3. In which of the twenty skills would you rank yourself highest? Lowest? What can you do to improve the latter?

4. If a compelling argument exists against requiring entry-level officers to possess a college degree, what would it be?

5. Whatever you think about the college education requirement for entry-level officers, at which rank, if any, would you require a bachelor's degree?

Summary

Whether or not law enforcement is a profession or aspires to become one, officers should conduct themselves in a professional manner. This relates not only to how officers treat the public but also how they treat each other throughout the chain of command.

Officers can ask themselves: How closely does walking through the workplaces of physicians and attorneys resemble walking through a law enforcement facility? Is there little or no difference with respect to the following?

• The physical atmosphere, neatness, cleanliness, and orderliness
• The manner in which the professionals and office staff treat their patients and clients
• The way colleagues and office staff treat each other
• The way they dress, speak, and generally comport themselves

Although at first glance this may appear to be an unfair comparison, in reality it is not. It is true that physicians and attorneys have more financial resources with which to decorate their offices, but it does not require money to keep offices clean and orderly and to treat people with respect.

It is not unheard of for police stations to be as poorly maintained as some of the worst buildings in the city, and for officers and office staff to treat civilians and each other in ways that would not be tolerated in a professional setting.

Certainly, this is not the case in all agencies, but officers know better than anyone that it occurs in too many agencies. The more that officers respect themselves, where they work, the people with whom they work, and the people for whom they work, the more the term *professional* will be applied to them. Until the public perceives officers as professionals, they will not be afforded the respect and advantages professionalism affords. As Conser and Russell (2000, p. 479) reflect: "A major challenge to policing, if it is a profession, is to engage in systematic analysis of all that it does for the purpose of discovering truths about its practices and desired outcomes. It then follows that those practices that are not effective should be changed or discontinued."

*R*eferences

Bayley, D.H., & Shearing, C.D. (2001). *The new structure of policing.* (NCJ187083). Washington, DC: U.S. Department of Justice.

Carter, D.L., & Radelet, L.A. (1999). *The police and the community* (6th ed.). Upper Saddle River, NJ: Prentice Hall.

Carter, D.L., Sapp, A.D., & Stephens, D.W. (1988). Higher education as a bona fide occupational qualification (BFOQ) for police: A blueprint. *American Journal of Police, 7* (2), 1–27.

Conser, J.A., & Russell, G.D. (2000). *Law enforcement in the United States.* Gaithersburg, MD: Aspen Publishers.

Dantzker, M.L. (2000). *Understanding today's police* (2nd ed.). Upper Saddle River, NJ: Prentice Hall.

Davis v. *Dallas.* (1985). *777* F. 2nd 205, 5th Cir.

Kerik, B.B. (2001). *The lost son: A life in pursuit of justice.* New York: HarperCollins.

MacDonald, H. (2000). How to train cops. *City Journal, 10* (4), 46–61.

Mayo, L.A. (2002). Certificate presentation address by executive director Louis Mayo. *Pace Newsletter, 3* (2), pp. 1–3.

Mitchell, I., Juliff, P., & Turner, J. (October 1998). Harmonization of professional standards, Draft. Retrieved May 19, 2002, from the World Wide Web: http://www.ifip.or.at/minutes/C99/C99_harmonization.htm.

Occupational Information Network (2002). Details of skills for police patrol officers. Retrieved May 13, 2002, from the World Wide Web: http://online.onetcenter.org/cgi-bin/occ_details.

O'Connor, T. (2002). Police professionalism and accreditation. MegaLinks in Criminal Justice. Retrieved April 14, 2002, from the World Wide Web: http://faculty/ncwc.edu/toconnor/417-4176lect08.htm.

President's Commission on Law Enforcement and Administration of Justice (1967). *Task force report: The police.* Washington, DC: U.S. Government Printing Office.

Today's police officers—College required. Editorial. (2000, September 6). *The Press of Atlantic City, New Jersey.* Retrieved May 28, 2002 from the World Wide Web: http://www.policeassociation.org/college_required.htm.

Travis, J. (1995, February 10). *Education in law enforcement: Beyond the college degree.* Address at Forum on the Police and Higher Education presented at the Center for Research in Law and Justice, Chicago. Retrieved April 19, 2002, from the World Wide Web: http://www.ojp.usdoj.gov/nij/speeches/police.htm.

3

Models of Enforcement

No one method of law enforcement is effective for all people at all times. What works in one section of a city may be a miserable failure in another; moreover, what works for one agency may tear at the fabric and morale of a neighboring one. Therefore, law enforcement must not only search for better ways of doing things but also do so in a professional manner, using a good deal of critical thinking, in contrast to simply following fads based more on wishful thinking than hard reality. When considering models of enforcement, agencies should be familiar with both the positive and the problematic aspects of each model, so that they can make an informed decision. To this end, the following models of enforcement will be discussed and analyzed: crime control, problem oriented, and community oriented.

HISTORICAL PERSPECTIVES

Citizens have been directly involved in policing from the beginning of time; just as there were "citizen soldiers," there were "citizen constables." In the early 1800s in England, Sir Robert Peel, who was home secretary (secretary of state), faced many of the problems that law enforcement faces today: poverty, homelessness, alcoholism, unemployment, slums, domestic violence, and a meltdown of social values. In response, he formulated what have come to be known as the Peelian Principles. The following are four of these principles:

1. The more that the community gets involved in crime prevention, the less police must make arrests and use physical force.
2. Police should seek the support of the community, not by pandering to public opinion, but by enforcing the law impartially and freely offering service and friendship to all members of the community without regard to their wealth or social standing.

3. There should not be an artificial distinction between "the police" and "the public." The police are also the public, and the public are also the police. This means that it is everyone's responsibility to protect their own and others' civil rights, as well as to prevent crime.

4. The real sign of police efficiency is not visible police action but the absence of crime and disorder. (Reith, 1952, p. 154)

Putting these principles into practice, constables (police officers) ran soup kitchens, founded homeless shelters, and established medical infirmaries as an integral part of their duties.

This community oriented philosophy of law enforcement was brought to the United States by immigrants from the British Isles, many of whom became law enforcement officers. For example, in the eighteenth and nineteenth centuries, it was the duty of officers in the United States to establish playgrounds, lecture in schools, counsel wayward youth, mediate family and business disputes, clean the streets, find shelter for the homeless, and even inspect vegetables in the markets. They responded to *all* calls for assistance, whether it was to fix a leaky faucet or lecture a philandering husband. Yet, they also made their fair share of arrests.

As can be seen, crime prevention and community policing are not "new age" but "old world" concepts. No one, in or out of law enforcement, viewed these officers as "social workers," even though social work was very much in existence at that time. In fact, it was from this era that the concept of a "tough cop" arose, a uniquely American image.

Over time, as crimes and social service agencies increased, law enforcement gradually shifted to a crime control model and increasingly transferred its community outreach to social service agencies. However, in the 1960s and 1970s, two influences came together that caused both law enforcement and the public to question the efficacy of the crime control model. One influence was what many perceived to be the misconduct of law enforcement (excessive force, illegal wiretaps and searches, planting evidence) in its attempts to constrain Vietnam War protestors. The second influence was a spate of research indicating that the crime control model had virtually no effect on the suppression of crime.

These confluences led to a virtual consensus in both the law enforcement and civilian communities that a different method of policing had to be tried. As Cox (1996, p. 230) states: "The message has finally become clear: the police cannot control crime or maintain order by themselves. The involvement of citizens other than police officers in crime prevention, apprehension of offenders, and order maintenance is absolutely essential." Two models of law enforcement evolved that directly involved the community: the problem oriented model and the community policing model. To place these models in proper perspective, the crime control model will be used as a frame of reference.

Personal Reflections _____

1. What do you think of the Peelian Principles? Should they be followed today, or are they too "old-fashioned" to work?

2. Many people today agree that law enforcement needs the cooperation of citizens to do its job efficiently. However, many citizens do not want to "get involved" in helping the police. Why is this so, and what, if anything, can be done about this attitude?

THE CRIME CONTROL MODEL

The crime control (crime fighting) model of law enforcement focuses on patrol, arrest, and retrospective investigation (investigating crimes after they have been committed). This is the image most people have of law enforcement. However, it has become apparent that this model has been more successful in clearing the streets of criminals than it has been in preventing and reducing crime.

For example, in the year 2000, law enforcement agencies nationwide had a 20.4 percent clearance rate, which is quite low. With respect to violent crimes, 47.5 of cases were cleared, in contrast to 16.7 of property crimes. This is due to the fact that investigative resources are dedicated more to personal, in contrast to property, crimes. Breaking down these statistics into subcategories reveals the following clearance rates (Federal Bureau of Investigation, 2002):

Violent Crimes

Murder	63.1
Aggravated assault	56.9
Forcible rape	46.9
Robbery	25.7

Property Crimes

Larceny/theft	18.2
Motor vehicle theft	14.1
Burglary	13.0

These statistics do not include misdemeanors and infractions. Clearance rates are not necessarily arrest rates because some crimes are solved without an arrest, nor are they conviction rates, which indicate the number of arrested people who are actually convicted of a crime. Moreover, when it is recognized that only one of three serious crimes is reported, it is clear that the crime control model is ineffective in reducing crime.

These statistics, along with rising citizen alarm, have generated research into the effectiveness of specific tactics of the crime control method. Several studies (Skolnick & Bayley, 1986, pp. 4–5) found that none of the following tactics reduced crime:

1. Routine foot patrolling
2. Routine motorized patrolling with one officer
3. Routine motorized patrolling with two officers
4. Rapid response times
5. Increasing the number of patrol officers
6. Increasing agency budgets
7. Increasing the number of investigators
8. Saturation patrolling of high-crime areas
9. Imprisoning more criminals
10. Sentencing more people to death

Not only did none of these tactics, singularly or in combination, reduce crime, but when the number of patrol officers was significantly decreased due to budgetary cutbacks or work stoppages ("blue flu"), crime rates remained virtually unaffected. This leads Bayley (1994) to state: "That police are not able to prevent crime should not come as a big surprise to thoughtful people. It is generally understood that social conditions outside the control of police . . . determine crime levels in communities" (p. 10).

Two caveats regarding the research findings on specific patrol tactics should be pointed out: Some of the methodologies used were flawed, and the results do not indicate that crime control policing is useless. No one is suggesting that officers be taken off the streets, only that the crime control method is ineffective as a crime suppressant.

Personal Reflections

1. Why do you think the crime control model does not prevent crime? When people see others arrested and going to prison, does that not make them think twice about committing crime, especially the *same* crime?

2. With respect to the crime control model, why do you think crime clearance rates are generally so low?

3. Of the 10 patrol tactics discussed in this section, which ones would you have thought do reduce crime, even though, in fact, they do not?

THE PROBLEM ORIENTED MODEL

A model that arose out of the social upheaval of the 1960s and 1970s is the problem oriented model proposed by Goldstein (1979). This model was the product of theorizing and extensive research over a number of years. The intent has never been to replace the crime control model, but to significantly lessen the need for it by reducing the commission of crime.

The philosophy underlying problem oriented policing holds that many situations offensive to a community are not separate incidents but form patterns that can be traced to a common root cause. Once the root cause is identified and reduced or eliminated, the offensive situations, including crime, will be reduced or eliminated. However, police cannot do this alone.

Characteristics of the Problem Oriented Model

Problem oriented policing requires the input and cooperation of the community that nominates problems and solutions and works with police to unearth the root causes. Figure 3.1 offers an example of this model. Using this figure, the following discussion shows how the problem oriented model would be implemented.

Observe incidents. In this example, seven offensive incidents are brought to the attention of the police through their direct observations and/or reports from citizens. Not all the incidents are crimes; for example, overdoses are medical incidents, while psychosis and fear are psychological incidents, but all are "offensive" in that the community is offended, that is hurt, by their presence.

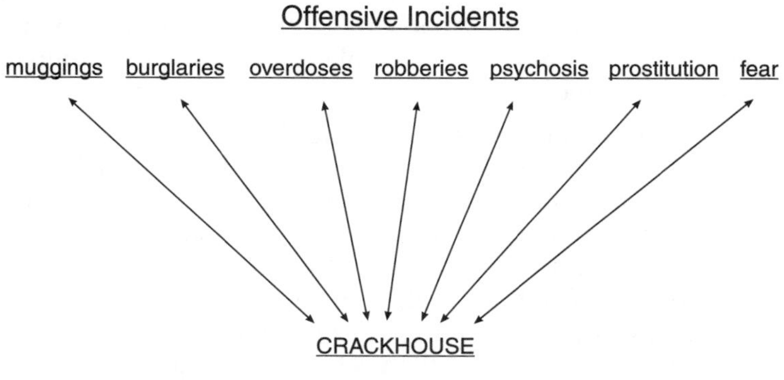

Offensive Incidents

muggings burglaries overdoses robberies psychosis prostitution fear

CRACKHOUSE

FIGURE 3.1 The problem oriented model.

Initiate problem oriented tactics. After observation, officers can initiate problem oriented tactics, the traditional process referred to by the acronym **SARA,** as discussed here (Eck & Spelman, 1987):

> **S**can: Officers and citizens scan the environment in a radar-like fashion to ascertain what incidents are causing problems in the community.
>
> **A**nalyze: Officers and citizens use a checklist to see whether a pattern develops: Who are the perpetrators, victims, and witnesses? What exactly is occurring? Exactly when and where is it occurring? What have officers and citizens attempted to do about these incidents in the past? Why were they not successful? What specific suggestions can be made to discern and solve the problem?
>
> **R**espond: Officers and citizens respond to what hopefully are several ideas gleaned from the analysis stage to discover whether a specific problem is causing these incidents. The problem must have the following characteristics for police to take action:
> - It must cause reoccurring incidents, in contrast to a few, sporadic ones.
> - It must constitute a serious and shared concern within the community, in contrast to being the pet peeve of a handful of officers or residents.
> - It must fall within the general purview of law enforcement, in contrast to being a purely civil problem; for example, squalor in the neighborhood that can be referred to other municipal agencies.
> - It must lie within the means of the officers and citizens to solve it; for example, it will not be cost prohibitive or overly tax the resources of the law enforcement agency or the community. A careful cost-benefit analysis will determine this.
> - The members of the community must largely nominate it, because they are the major stakeholders. However, there will be instances in which police administrators nominate the problem based on their crime analysis, and other instances in which line officers nominate problems based on their observations. In either case, officers must enlist the support of the community because they cannot solve the problem alone. The issue should not be perceived solely as a "police problem" but as a "community problem" that requires a joint effort to solve.
>
> **A**ssess: Officers and citizens evaluate the results: what worked, what did not work, and what was learned that could be used in future endeavors. It is important that this assessment be based on research data: on surveys and statistical analysis and not simply on impressions or feelings. In the end, the problem may be solved, substantially reduced, reduced only to a limited degree, or not solved. The failure to solve the problem can occur when the police and/or the community lack the resources or commitment necessary to solve the problem, or if the problem is larger or more entrenched than anyone imagined.

Conclusion.   Referring again to the example in Figure 3.1, as a result of officers and citizens scanning and analyzing, they concluded that a single crack house, operating 24 hours a day, was the main cause of the seven types of incidents occurring within a six-block radius. The police then responded by surveilling the crack house, arresting dealers and customers, and calling building inspectors who condemned and boarded up the house. As a result, these seven types of incidents were significantly reduced, making 36 blocks, 3,000 residents, 2 schools, and 3 playgrounds safer.

Comparison with Crime Control Model

The problem oriented model differs from the crime control one in a number of important ways, as can be seen in Table 3.1

It is important to note that while the models are different, they are not mutually exclusive. For example, crime control officers can seek community assistance in problem solving, and problem oriented officers can investigate crimes and make arrests. It is incorrect and counterproductive to claim that one model is superior to the other. These models complement each other, and until crime disappears from the face of the earth, both will be necessary.

Technology and the Problem Oriented Model

The creative use of technology has made a significant contribution to the problem oriented model of law enforcement. The most effective and popular tool is COMPSTAT, which stands for "computer generated statistics." The concept of COMPSTAT originated in the New York Police Department in the mid-1990s and is currently used by many agencies throughout the United States.

TABLE 3.1   *Differences between Crime Control and Problem Oriented Models*

Crime Control Model	Problem Oriented Model
• Reactive: reacts to crime after it occurs	• Proactive: prevents crime before it occurs
• Perceives incidents as *independent* events	• Perceives incidents as often *related*, part of a pattern or cluster
• Focuses only on *crime*	• Focuses on criminal *and* noncriminal incidents, for example, fear
• Officers *alone* address crime	• Officers *and* community address not only crime but also social disorder
• Success largely measured in number of arrests	• Success largely measured by reduction of crime, social disorder, and fear

The philosophy of COMPSTAT is that crime prevention and solution can be effectively addressed only when law enforcement agencies have a clear and current picture of where crime is occurring so that proactive and reactive approaches can be combined in a systematic fashion.

This philosophy is based on four principles:

1. Accurate and current intelligence must be disseminated to the entire agency—from the top executives to the officers walking a beat. This information is gathered from crime and incident reports as well as patrol and 911 logs, and it is mapped according to the type of event, the time it occurred, the location where it occurred, the response time of officers, and the disposition of the event. Information on the perpetrators and victims, as well as on the quality-of-life complaints that fall short of constituting a crime, are also noted. COMPSTAT is a technologically advanced version of the old pin maps, in which colored pins are placed on a map designating the locations where various types of crimes and collisions occurred during the previous month. Often these pin maps were months and even years outdated and gave no detailed information other than the fact that a specific incident had occurred.

2. COMPSTAT maps are then presented each week to the command structure, the media, and interested citizens. Each district commander is called upon to assess the information relevant to his or her district; explain why crime decreased, remained the same, or increased; and describe what will be done to address these issues during the next week. In large jurisdictions, the discussion often includes outside agencies: the FBI, ATF, DEA, highway patrol, county sheriff, probation and parole officers, the prosecutor's office, and so on. The proposed tactics that follow from this review must be clearly articulated, practical, and have a high probability of success. The results are then reported at the next week's meeting.

3. The tactical plan must be immediately and effectively initiated. Specific officers are selected to match the crime or incident that has been targeted. These officers meet and work as a team and are deployed immediately to the areas of concern. They have six days to accomplish their tasks and make their commander look good at the next week's meeting. As one officer said: "When we make the commander look good, we all look good. When the commander looks bad, well—we're all in deep trouble." This creates a pressure to solve problems in an expeditious and lasting manner because *everyone* in the process is held accountable.

4. Addressing the target concerns is only half the battle. Relentless follow-up is necessary: Were the fires extinguished for good, or did they just go underground and resurface a few weeks later? It is never assumed that a problem is solved forever.

The results of COMPSTAT appear to be quite promising (Dussault, 2000). For example, New York reported 1,946 murders in 1993. After several years of COMPSTAT, the number was reduced to 629. Even though crime had a 23 percent decline nationally during those years for the most serious crimes, New York's decrease was three times the national average. In Philadelphia, murder and auto theft rates declined 15 percent in the first year of COMPSTAT. In New Orleans, a 24 percent drop in violent crime was achieved after COMPSTAT was used for one year.

Although it seems that COMPSTAT has been remarkably successful, even when compared to national declines in crime, a few concerns exist:

- While accountability is appropriately a key element in COMPSTAT, it should be exercised in a professional way and not in one that humiliates commanders and officers. Other enterprises, such as business and the professions, have strict accountability without "motivating by humiliation," a tactic that has been used in some agencies.

- Demographically describing crime areas by geographic location, sex, race, and ethnicity has raised concerns that stereotyping and reduced property values will increase, as well as make public the names of offenders who have already served their sentences, people who are only suspects in crimes, and the victims of violent crimes, including rape. The demographic issue is one of the countless catch-22 dilemmas that law enforcement faces. If it does not plot demographics, crimes will not be reduced in the highest-crime areas. On the other hand, plotting demographics can be viewed as racist and a violation of civil rights. Making the names of offenders, suspects, and victims public does not have to be an inherent part of the process.

- The pressure placed on commanders and officers is intense and can lead to overzealous practices that threaten the civil rights of both criminals and innocent citizens, including the use of excessive force, illegal searches, and mass arrests that may include innocent people. The command structure must help officers draw as bright a line as possible between quality arrests that will stand up to legal scrutiny and arrests for the sake of statistics and public relations. A part of the weekly assessment meetings must include the number of citizen complaints and lawsuits that were threatened or filed in order to keep the situation in proper balance.

Challenges of the Problem Oriented Model

As is true with any plan of action in law enforcement or any other organization, challenges exist in the effective practice of the problem oriented model. Knowing the challenges of any operation beforehand is critical in spotlighting situations in which maximum thought, ability, and energy need to be focused. The following are some basic challenges involved in the problem oriented model.

Education and training.   Both administrators and line officers are often insufficiently educated and trained in the problem oriented model, which results in confused and ill-conceived efforts on the part of officers, followed by discouraging results. These results are interpreted by some people as proof that the model does not work, yet the actual problem is not the model but its implementation. Problem oriented policing is neither a quick fix nor a quick study. It is a subspecialty of law enforcement, similar to special operations or narcotics enforcement, that requires intensive education and training, far more than the few days of academy or in-house training typically offered. Education should consist of teaching the theory, philosophy, psychology, sociology, criminology, and organizational dimensions of problem oriented policing, a concept that defies simplistic "anybody can do it" thinking.

Although it is impossible to indicate the exact amount of time that should be allotted to education and training in the problem oriented model, some frames of reference are available. For example, if some states require an 80-hour course to obtain an advanced baton instructor certification, it is reasonable to believe that at least a comparable amount of time should be dedicated to learning the theory and practice of the problem oriented method of policing.

Budget.   Agencies often struggle to maintain at least minimum staffing levels and budgetary funds, and problem oriented policing requires time away from traditional policing, money for education and training, and overtime pay to attend community meetings. Administrators need to understand that, in the long run, the problem oriented model may be more cost effective than the crime control model in terms of money and time. Moreover, problem oriented policing significantly raises officer morale by removing the feeling that officers are merely "shoveling the same garbage day after day" and increasing the feeling that they are making a tangible difference.

Organizational change.   Problem oriented policing requires organizational change, which can pose a threat to some administrators. In contrast to the traditional chain of command, line officers are the "experts" because they are the ones immersed in the communities and therefore have more information than administrators with respect to assessing and solving community problems. Consequently, the input of line officers is critically important to the success of the operation. This does not mean that administrators lose power or control. Power is not a fixed entity but an expandable one; for example, the fact that salespeople know their territory far better than their supervisors do and therefore are often more expert in this respect, does not diminish the supervisor's power and control; in fact, it could expand it as the territory expands.

Officers in the problem oriented model need to be given more freedom, autonomy, discretion, and trust than is generally afforded traditional patrol officers. Information gathering and consulting in the community is a dynamic process often not amenable to the micromanaging that occurs in traditional policing. Constant monitoring of an officer's activities and whereabouts is often not possible, and this is where trust enters the picture.

The performance appraisal of problem oriented officers cannot be identical to that of officers in the traditional model: number of calls, citations issued, arrests, investigations, court appearances, commendations, and so on. These activities are quantifiable; that is, they can be counted and assigned numerical totals; for example, a patrol officer made seven felony arrests last month. Problem oriented policing does not lend itself easily to quantification; it is much more qualitative. How is the reduction of fear and an increase in the health, respect, and safety of the community accurately measured? Therefore, a method of assessment should be created to adequately reflect and measure the officer's performance. These same considerations must apply when addressing the criteria for promotion and other rewards for outstanding performance.

Finally, problem oriented policing requires a reasonable degree of continuity in the relationship between the officers and the community. It takes time, sometimes a good deal of time, for officers to acquire a real sense of what is going on in the community and to build a sense of mutual trust. Often, just as officers are beginning to get a handle on things, they are transferred to another assignment. This causes everything to revert to ground zero, which, among other negative side effects, is a major source of discouragement to the community.

Cooperation with other agencies.   The problem oriented model often requires the close and willing cooperation of several municipal and state agencies: public health, social services, public works, parks and recreation, building inspection, fire inspection, tax assessor's office, housing development, and so on. In addition to these agencies, private businesses, churches, and synagogues can be helpful in certain situations. It may also include municipal, county, state, and federal law enforcement agencies, as well as the prosecutor's office and judiciary. This cooperation is often difficult because it is not rare for each group to have its own bureaucracies, political agendas, and turfs to protect, as well as attitudes toward the police.

To build good working relationships with all these entities requires knowledge and diplomacy, best accomplished with a two-pronged approach: police administrators meeting with their counterparts in these organizations, and line officers making frequent contact with individual employees and supervisors in the same organizations. Ideally, each city should sponsor workshops that include police, members of other municipal agencies, and business and church leaders to orient everyone to the problem oriented model of policing and how it needs community support if it is to succeed.

Patience.   As was stated earlier, the problem oriented model does not constitute a quick fix. It takes time, measured in years, not weeks or months, to gather momentum and take effect. Patience is often required because massive resistance to problem solving can exist within a community. What is one person's problem is another person's income (drug dealers and pimps), tax deductions (a landlord's vacant buildings), or claim to fame ("community leaders" who use community problems as a power base). These individuals can sabotage efforts at problem solving by spreading misinformation and impugning the motives of the police.

Even when problems are solved, they seldom remain solved forever. Many problems are like a rash—as soon as the treatment stops, the rash reappears or a new one appears someplace else ("Just as we close down the crack houses, a string of massage parlors opens up."). Problem oriented policing is not for the impatient or faint of heart. Like parenting, it takes endless patience and effort, but if it is done correctly, it also can be very satisfying and rewarding.

Protect constitutional rights.   As is true with all models of policing, the problem oriented model must often straddle the thin line between protecting the constitutional rights of one group of citizens and trampling the rights of another. Much more than the crime control model, the problem oriented model is fraught with a myriad of competing interests. For example, the distinction must be made on a daily basis between disordered behaviors and illegal ones. People have a right to be unclean, unsavory, scary looking, crazy, homeless, prejudiced, antipolice, hostile, stupid, abrasive, neo-Nazis, Ku Klux Klanners, anarchists, and "a blight on the community." They also can generally congregate where they want, talk to whom they wish, assemble in groups, maintain privacy over their person and possessions, make a fair amount of noise, use a certain amount of profanity, stay out as late as they want, possess an assortment of instruments that *could* be used as weapons or burglary tools, have rowdy kids, be in illicit relationships, and disturb the peace of police officers.

Although officers and the majority of the community may consider these behaviors unpleasant, unsightly, or aggravating, they generally are protected by the Constitution and, therefore, are not illegal. In their efforts to solve problems on the one hand, officers must be careful not to create more serious ones on the other by violating the civil rights of some members of the community.

Premature diagnosis.   Perhaps the biggest temptation and mistake in problem oriented policing is to diagnose a problem prematurely, which results in frustration, wasted time, and even harm. Problem analysis is the critical element in problem-solving calculations. "Everybody" might agree as to what the problem is, but frequently everybody is wrong, because everybody does not always consist of people who are objective, sophisticated, perceptive, rational, and farsighted. Analogously, although everybody, including nurses and physicians, knows that the problem causing a child's headaches is that he is malnourished (all you have to do is *look* at him, for goodness sake), these people could be seriously mistaken. A proper assessment of the child may reveal that high levels of lead from the ancient water pipes in his building are eating away his brain.

So, while the child is being fed more nutritious food every day, his brain is starving to death, as are those of all the other tenants in the building in which he lives.

Research, logic, patience, perspicacity, and consultation are necessary to ferret out the problem from the complicated web of symptoms it can produce. Diagnosing the problem requires the ability to take an overview of situations, not getting lost in the trees. It takes the ability to "connect the dots," to take disparate incidents, place them in a latticework, and trace them to their least common denominator without getting sidetracked by enticing detours and shortcuts along the way.

Personal Reflections

1. What are your thoughts about the problem oriented model? Would it work to reduce crime significantly, or do you think it is too idealistic?
2. Of the seven challenges of the problem oriented model, which two do you think are the biggest ones, and why?
3. In comparing the crime control and problem oriented models, which one do you think the people in your community would prefer?

THE COMMUNITY ORIENTED MODEL

The philosophy underlying the community policing model holds that social disorder in the community spawns crime; therefore, the community has the major role and responsibility in diagnosing and preventing both social disorder and crime. The community has the information and latent resources to do the job; law enforcement's role is to gather information from the community to help create a healthy and safe environment. From this philosophy evolve strategies (for example, increased community vigilance) and tactics (for example, civilian patrols).

Definition of the Model

Although several definitions of community oriented policing exist, the following attempts to craft a clear and concise one: Community policing consists of assigned officers forming a partnership with the members of a community, the purpose of which is to empower the community to take the actions necessary to increase its health and safety. There are four elements to this definition:

Assigned officers. The community oriented agency has dedicated specifically trained officers to the community, for a reasonable amount of time, and their primary function is to work with the community to increase its health and safety.

A partnership. A relationship develops between the officers and the community, which is marked by *mutual* cooperation, trust, respect, and support.

Empower the community. Officers help create an environment in which community members develop the direction, motivation, competencies, and confidence to act in unified and constructive ways to accomplish their goals.

Health and safety. The police and community work together to transform social disorder, which is associated with medical, economic, social, and psychological problems, as well as with crime, into social order.

A major force in the recent history of models of community policing is the broken windows theory espoused by James Q. Wilson in 1982. This theory has three major premises (Wilson & Kelling, 1989):

1. Neighborhood disorder, left to fester, communicates the message that no one cares about the neighborhood, which sends an invitation to predators that they can take over the neighborhood.
2. This creates a paralyzing fear in residents of the neighborhood, so that they cannot take steps to rectify the situation.
3. It is the role of police to embolden the citizens and, with their help, gradually restore order and peace to the neighborhood.

Distinguishing Characteristics

Two basic differences exist between the problem oriented and the community policing models. First, the problem oriented model employs a top-down, vertical approach. It traces a cluster of already occurring specific offensive incidents to their root causes (primarily reactive), whereas the community oriented model employs a horizontal approach, attempting to reduce social disorder across the board *before* it causes significant offensive incidents (primarily proactive).

Second, officers who address specific problems and spend most of their time doing crime control policing largely orchestrate the problem oriented model. On the other hand, the community oriented model is largely orchestrated by the community, addresses community-wide problems, and is sponsored by officers whose full-time deployment is in community policing. Although community policing officers can use the problem oriented model as one of their tools, problem oriented officers are not involved in the broader full-time work of community policing.

In defining community policing, it is equally important to distinguish what this law enforcement model does *not* include. Contrary to what many descriptions state:

- Community policing does not require that the entire agency be immersed and totally dedicated to the concept of community policing in order to work. Although such commitment might be ideal, it is not essential. If it were, very few agencies, if any, would be doing effective community policing.

- Community policing does not require the command structure of agencies to be organizationally and geographically decentralized, and research confirms this point (Wycoff & Skogan, 1994, p. 89). Even social service agencies, including the Salvation Army, do not have "decentralized" organizational structures. Law enforcement agencies that do effective community policing have not dismantled their traditional organizational structure but have modified it to accommodate community policing, especially on the levels of midmanagement and first-line supervision.

- Community policing does not need to create false and divisive dichotomies between the crime control model and the community policing one. It does not imply that officers who feel more comfortable working in the crime control model are "macho cops" who only want to arrest people and kick in doors, nor does it imply that those who are more comfortable working in the community policing model are "social workers" and not "real cops." There is plenty of room in law enforcement for both kinds of officers.

- Community policing does not necessarily draw sharp distinctions between "reactive" and "proactive" policing. These concepts need not be mutually exclusive. Officers in the crime control model who spend only 20 percent of their time dealing with crimes often do proactive policing between calls, while officers who do community policing make arrests, especially because they are more likely to "on view" crime than are crime control officers patrolling in their vehicles.

- Community policing does not imply that simply attaching the word *community* to any police activity makes it "community policing." For example, foot patrol, bike patrol, crime prevention programs, community relations, and community programs, such as DARE, may be important but are not, in themselves, community policing as it is generally understood. In other words, "policing the community" is not the same as community policing.

Challenges in Community Policing

Because community policing is broader, more intense, and more complicated than either the crime control or the problem oriented model, it presents some specific challenges, including the following.

History of the community.   Officers should not assume that their first day in the community marks the first day of the community's existence. Often communities have a remembered and anecdotal history that predates the officer's birth. These memories of police contacts may be positive or negative, which means that new officers may be met with appreciation and relief or with suspicion and hostility. Therefore, officers need to tread lightly and take time to learn how the community has defined them long before it ever met them. Knowing the history of the community is also important in order to understand what worked and failed to work in the past, so that officers do not continue to reinvent the same useless wheel.

Political entanglements. Officers should avoid political entanglements, which is often easier said than done. Typically, communities are labyrinths of competing and conflicting claims (needs, values, visions). Each group, in its efforts to enlist the officer's allegiance, will offer compelling reasons why truth and justice is on its side, and why rival groups are greedy and selfish, if not outright criminal. For example, in a conflict between "the people" and "the landlords," officers may become swept up in the righteousness of "the people's" cause against the greed and lack of concern of "the bloodsucking landlords." However, officers would do well to remember that the land-lords are also the people and have the same rights and protections as the rest of the community. Therefore, rather than take sides, officers would be better advised to assume the role of mediator in helping different factions resolve their problems.

Diversity issues.   Officers need to be seismographically sensitive to the diversity issues in the community. This sensitivity has three dimensions. First, officers need to be aware of their own prejudices regarding race, gender, religion, age, disability, socioeconomic status, sexual orientation, and so on. It is a rare individual in any society who does not harbor some conscious or unconscious bias against at least one group of people. Even the unconscious prejudices of officers manifest themselves and can be easily spotted, especially by those sensitive to such issues.

Second, officers need to be careful as to how they "reach out" to people who are different than they are. Attempting to adopt the language, mannerisms, and attitudes of other races and cultures—for example, a Caucasian officer referring to a black man as "bro" or a Latino man as "amigo"—is not likely to melt much ice. Officers are more likely to earn respect by being themselves and not by pretending to be someone they are not. Good-natured bantering about racial issues with people racially different than the officer, despite its good intentions, is more likely to be perceived as offensive than helpful.

Third, officers must be aware that whatever their race, it can be an issue in the community, and no officer is exempt, even when he or she is the same race as many people in the community. For example, both white and black officers working in a largely black community are likely to experience some racial tension, as will Hispanic officers working in either white or black communities. Officers should be prepared to be racially stereotyped, understand that it is not personal, and transcend it to do their job professionally.

The "blame game."   Officers should refrain from playing "the blame game," which is common in any group of people experiencing problems. The first stage of most conversations will consist of some variation of "We're the victims, and they're the perpetrators." Officers are expected to take the side of the victims against the perpetrators. But, three points should be kept in mind. First, there is a saying in law enforcement that is often true: Today's victim is tomorrow's perpetrator. In other words, there is often sufficient blame for problems in the community that most people must assume part of it due to their acts of commission or omission. Second, as long as everyone is blaming everybody else, no one is left to take responsibility for a problem, which guarantees that it will never be solved. Third, as mutual blaming escalates, so do hostility and the threat of violence. Officers would be well advised to sidestep the blame game and focus on asking each involved group: What can *you* do to bring about some resolution to the problem?

Involve the community.   Officers should not lose sight of the word *community* in *community policing*. Due to their training and experience, officers tend to be take-charge people, which is appropriate in most of their roles. It becomes natural for them to carry these attitudes and behaviors into community policing, whereby the community merely becomes an instrument for officers to accomplish their goals for the community. Sooner or later, this personal and social engineering will result in community disaffection and withdrawal.

Officers need to realize their leadership is part of a two-phased process. In the first phase they are more active, orienting people to the nature of community policing and helping organize its foundations. As the community begins to coalesce and come alive, the second stage evolves in which officers hand the reins over to the community and act more as facilitators and consultants than leaders.

Moreover, it is important for the community policing program to be that of the *agency* and not of individual *officers*. When individual officers get transferred to another assignment, the program should have sufficient momentum and continue to thrive. Programs built entirely around a few popular, dedicated officers will fold when these officers leave. Ideally, if both the officers and the community do their jobs, the time will come when the community does its own policing, and the officers can move on to other assignments.

Importance of law enforcement.   Above all else, officers are involved in law enforcement, which is impossible to forget in the crime control model but can be forgotten in community policing. Officers should be aware of three cautions. First, the temptation exists not to take enforcement action when it would be appropriate to do so—not to want to upset the very members of the community with whom the officer is trying to establish rapport. This is a delicate issue in which discretion must be exercised, but discretion means making prudent decisions; it does not necessarily mean looking the other way.

Second, officers should be careful not to "go native"; that is, forsake their law enforcement role and become fully immersed in the culture of the community they are supposed to be policing. This can happen in several ways.

- Becoming involved in business deals in the community in an effort to augment income
- Becoming romantically/sexually involved with members of the community
- Carousing with community members outside of work
- Becoming involved in the community's illegal enterprises: buying/selling drugs, gambling, visiting prostitutes, and so on

In fact, the original reason for taking officers out of communities and placing them in patrol vehicles was to remove them from the temptations involved in becoming too close to a community.

Third, officers are often more public as community police officers than they were in their previous assignments. Whatever they do or say will have ripple effects that, for better or worse, reach the farthest ends of the community. The word gets around about officers: He stopped traffic and walked a little girl across the street; she visits the elderly shut-ins; after he eats, he throws his trash in the street; she spends half her time flirting with the men; he went to bat for us at the city council meeting; she drove my aunt to the clinic. Officers should realize that both friendly and critical eyes are on them every second of the day, which is likely to have positive or negative repercussions at some future time.

Realistic expectations.   It is easy for new community policing officers to harbor unrealistic expectations with respect to their role and how they will be received by the community. When unrealistic expectations are unmet, which is frequently the case, officers become frustrated and may reduce their involvement in the community ("If they don't care; I don't care"). Officers sometimes feel that they were sent to save the community and the community should respond with appreciation. In most cases, the community did not *invite* the officers into the community; they were *assigned* by their agency. These officers are "outsiders" by virtue of living outside the community and being police officers (even if they live in the community, they are still cops).

Moreover, the presence of these officers reflects the inadequacy of the community, that it is unable to help itself. A point of empathy here may be to reflect on how officers feel about civilian oversight. Officers generally do not welcome or appreciate it because it implies that they are incapable of taking care of themselves. This is similar to how some community members feel about community policing. Finally, as discussed in the section on problem oriented policing, some factions in the community may resent the officers' presence because it interferes with their own questionable operations and disrupts their power base.

Officers should be sensitive to these challenges and not be surprised or hurt when their hard work is unappreciated or even ridiculed. Just as counselors experience negative transference (resentment) from their clients, community policing officers will experience negative transference from some segments of the community. Officers need to understand these dynamics and remain focused on the reasons they are in the community in the first place: to increase the health and safety of *the community* and not to get their personal needs met.

Unique Challenges

Just as the crime control and problem oriented models require officers to possess certain competencies to function effectively in those models, the community policing model also has its own unique set of competencies that officers should possess. The following challenges are largely unique to community policing.

Develop abilities. The community policing model requires many special abilities that, while ideal in all officers, are not essential in the other models. The most important traits include the abilities to do the following:

- Communicate well with groups and facilitate group discussions, which includes good speaking skills, a facilitative demeanor, and a willingness to truly listen to all segments of the audience.
- Relate well and in a continuous fashion with diverse groups—people of all ages, races, cultures, religions, educational and socioeconomic levels, as well as those with different personalities and politics. The concept "in a continuous fashion" is important. Most officers can relate well with *anybody* for the length of a 10-minute call for service, but to *live* with a very diverse community for a year or two or more is quite different.
- React well to the "maximum effort—minimum results" syndrome. Especially in the early stages, officers "go all out" in their efforts to deal with an issue and often see a minimum yield on their investment. Maturity, frustration tolerance, and perseverance are required to stay the course.
- Relinquish appropriate amounts of control, delegate authority, and trust in the abilities and goodness of the majority of the people.
- Be humble—admit mistakes and ignorance and ask for help from everyone willing to offer it.
- Maintain one's bearings in the eye of storms, not getting swept up in the undertow of other people's expectations, demands, pressures, and emotions.
- Respond well to hostility from people who believe, correctly or incorrectly, that they have been abused by police, and avoid the natural reaction: "If that's the way you feel toward us, we don't need to be here." Sometimes

the most hostile people can become the most cooperative when their anger is listened to and respected.

- Get personal needs to be liked, loved, respected, needed, esteemed, important, successful, popular, and in control met *outside* of the community. Officers are in the community to nourish the people, not to be nourished *by* them.
- Understand the rudimentary principles of psychology, sociology, and criminology as they relate to community policing, so that dynamics that do not seem to make sense can be understood and dealt with accordingly.
- Be creative—think outside the box; try things that no one else has tried; contact people and institutions that no one else has contacted, seeking support and counsel.
- Be farsighted—see beyond the immediate situation and understand that even simple decisions can have positive and negative ripple effects that extend in all directions.
- Think critically—go beyond appearances and understand, without being cynical or paranoid, that things are seldom what they seem; understand that the more important the issue, the greater the number of layers that must be considered before final actions are taken.
- Respond to the people in the community with respect, regardless of their circumstances, in contrast to being paternalistic or cynical.

These abilities should be present, at least to a reasonable degree, if officers are to be effective in community policing.

Understand social disorder.   It is important for community policing officers to truly understand and appreciate the nature of social disorder. This sounds simple enough until one looks at what "social disorder" entails. Depending on the community, it may include, but not be limited to, squalor, poverty, unemployment, addiction, untreated physically and mentally ill and retarded people, neglected children and elderly, ignorance, injustice, hunger, homelessness, roving packs of dogs, gutted buildings, vermin-infested streets and housing, family dysfunction, overcrowding, prejudice, racial tensions, graffiti, rubbish, broken streets, nonfunctioning water mains and hydrants, inadequate street lighting, broken fire escapes, rowdy teenagers, constant noise, putrid smells, a meltdown of social values, unreliable transportation, long waiting lists at clinics and rehabilitation centers, abandoned vehicles, rundown schools, empty churches, and so on. Note that, although crime is part of social disorder, none of these conditions is a crime in the usual meaning of the word.

All these conditions dovetail into a syndrome of similar feelings: depression, anxiety, confusion, alienation, isolation, hostility, cynicism, suspiciousness, helplessness, and hopelessness. The theory underlying community policing is that some people living in these conditions participate in antisocial behavior to anesthetize their pain (through alcohol and drugs); to vent their hostility (through muggings and stabbings); to experience some pleasure (through illicit sex); to feel some excitement (through burglary and robbery); or to feel a sense of power (by joining a gang). This syndrome often comprises the beat of the community policing officer.

Select and train officers.   The process of preparing to do community policing requires careful selection of officers, lengthy education and training, a supervised practicum, and strong agency support if it is to be even reasonably successful. In addition to the abilities described previously, officers involved in community policing need to demonstrate that they possess the qualities of intelligence, maturity, sociability, and a commitment to the principles of community policing.

With regard to education, although it is probably true that recruiting for community policing should focus on college graduates, this is not a panacea for at least two reasons. First, most of the abilities required to be a good community policing officer have more to do with personality than with academic intelligence and knowledge. Second, at this point in the economy many college graduates are choosing to enter more lucrative careers.

Education should include at least the following topics, which are an integral part of the community policing model. Although they are important to varying degrees in all models of policing, they are particularly important for success in community policing because of the unique broad range of challenges it presents.

- Ethical issues in community policing
- Philosophy of community policing
- Decision making
- Conflict resolution
- Time and stress management
- Problem solving
- Diversity issues
- Mediation and arbitration
- Public speaking
- Principles of organizations
- Crisis intervention
- Cost-benefit analysis
- Leadership and "followership"
- Consultation, counseling, and referring skills
- Advocacy theory and practice
- Needs assessment
- Principles of psychology, sociology, criminology, and management
- Public relations
- Victimology

With regard to training for community policing, each block of classroom lectures should be followed by a "lab"; that is, officers are presented with real-life scenarios that will sharpen and test the theories learned in the lectures. Instructors can monitor and grade the officers' performance.

The final part of education and training is on-the-job training, which means the officers accompany an experienced community policing officer for a minimum of three months, or until the trainer believes the officers are ready to launch out on their own or as a member of a team.

Community policing, as it is formally understood, is a daunting but possible endeavor. It requires a good deal of money, time, energy, personnel, supervision, and commitment, if the job is to be done correctly and professionally. To do less dooms the effort to failure, and a failed community policing program is not a neutral, private event. Because community policing usually begins with a great deal of fanfare, any failure has to be explained to many important people, including the community that will perceive itself as being "once again abandoned by the police."

Critique of the Model

The following can be considered when evaluating the community policing model.

Validity of premise.   The basic premise that social disorder causes crime is arguable. The fact that social disorder *correlates* with crime does not necessarily mean that it *causes* it. For example, a meltdown of social values (respect, responsibility, honesty, justice, industriousness, compassion) may cause *both* social disorder *and* crime. In other words, if social disorder were to disappear overnight, would crime disappear or even be significantly reduced, or would crime simply become more orderly? Moreover, what can law enforcement officers realistically do to address a meltdown of social values?

Problems with research.   The effectiveness of community policing is very difficult, if not impossible, to assess using traditional scientific methods. The following questions address this concern:

- How are key concepts defined: community, policing, health, safety, social disorder?
- What are the criteria for success and failure? In other words, is the program considered a success because the community *perceives* that crime has decreased even though, in reality, it has not? Is it good that people *feel* more free to walk the streets if, in fact, the streets are just as dangerous?
- How will extraneous variables be controlled? For example, has social disorder decreased because of community policing, because the city began a renovation project in the area, or because a new factory opened up employing several hundred of the area's residents?

- Is the research methodology scientifically sound? Is it valid, reliable, and overseen by objective experts outside of the agency?
- Will the results of the research be taken at face value, or will critical thinking be applied to them?
- Will the study be replicated to ensure reliability of the results?

Research on the effectiveness of community policing has been generally flawed and has yielded inconsistent results. Bayley (1994) addresses this concern:

> The honest answer to the question of whether community policing works is we do not know. . . . From these studies [on community policing] it is difficult to determine whether the effects of community policing are long lasting, displace problems elsewhere, are due mainly to the community policing initiative, or are as substantial as the police and citizens involved with them perceive them to be. . . . In other words, the promise of community policing cannot be fairly determined because of flawed implementation and flawed research. (pp. 117, 118)

Even though the federal government distributed $9 billion in grants to law enforcement agencies between 1994 and 2000 for Community Oriented Policing Services (COPS), the evaluation of the first four years of COPS did not address whether or not the COPS program had had an effect on crime (Roth & Ryan, 2000). This represents the type of thinking often reflected in community policing: Let's put a great deal of time, effort, and money into it, but let's not evaluate whether it really works.

These questions arise: Is it realistic to expect that officers can help effect a significant reduction in a community's social disorder when it has existed for a quarter of a century or more? If the professionals who have worked in the community for years (physicians, nurses, social workers, counselors, ministers, community organizers) have not been able to reduce social disorder substantially, can a handful of officers with a few hours of training and other law enforcement responsibilities be expected to do so?

Misplaced responsibility.   Even if law enforcement officers could be successful in reducing social disorder, basically it may not be their responsibility. The responsibility perhaps should be placed with the city's social service agencies. It may be more efficient professionally and financially to increase the number of already educated and trained social service and community workers rather than to require law enforcement agencies to rearrange their philosophy, organizational structure, training, recruiting, and budgeting to do community policing.

Potential for harm.   Community policing is not necessarily a benign endeavor. As is true for most challenging projects, every opportunity to do good is also an opportunity to do harm. Almost by definition, communities targeted for community policing have serious problems, and some are tinderboxes ready to explode at the first spark of tension. Moreover, in areas of serious conflict, good intentions do not count. Sometimes all it takes is an ill-chosen word, a misunderstanding, or an ill-conceived decision by officers to light the spark of a new set of tensions.

Equivocal results.   Because law enforcement agencies have been under great pressure to find a solution to crime, they tend to trumpet their community policing endeavors as "the answer." In fact, community policing is not a quick fix, a silver bullet, or a panacea. Moreover, the results are not always promising. In a thorough study of the effects of community policing in two cities, the only consistent declines in crime in both cities were in car thefts and burglaries. Moreover, there was an increase in the number of assaults on officers in both cities (Schobel, Evans, & Daly, 1997).

Oliver (2001) summarizes the research:

> The findings through program evaluation in regards to a variety of programs implemented under community-oriented policing have shown very mixed results. In some cases the level of fear was reduced, but satisfaction with police did not go up. In other cases, crime rates, local problems, and calls for service dropped, but citizen fear increased. (pp. 349–350)

Spurious fear reduction.   As Oliver indicates in this quotation, perhaps the most consistent finding from the studies on community policing is that it reduces fear in the community. However, the finding must be viewed in the context of the "crime-fear paradox," which means that people under the most imminent threat of crime are less fearful of becoming victims than are those slightly removed from the center of crime.

One explanation of this phenomenon is that people in high-crime areas build up a tolerance for it as well as the defense mechanism of denial to remove the threat from consciousness. In contrast, those in the "rear areas" hear the sounds of battle but have not developed defenses to ward off fear because the danger is not imminent. If this theory is valid, then it could be that the more that people find themselves in the center of battle zones, the less fear they will report, giving a spuriously positive picture of the situation.

Personal Reflections

1. What is your general feeling about community policing as it is defined in this chapter?
2. Which two cautions involved in community policing should officers be most aware of, and why?
3. Which challenge of community policing do you think would take the greatest effort to overcome, and why?
4. Which two controversies regarding community policing do you think are closest to making a good argument against community policing, and why?
5. Despite the problems involved in community policing, do you think it is still worth a try? Why? Why not?

Summary

In the final analysis, scientifically answering the question "Does community policing work?" is analogous to scientifically answering the question "Does capital punishment work?" Both issues are so heavily laden with a virtually endless number of confounding variables — factors that can never be adequately controlled — that the justification for their continuance must lie mostly, though not entirely, outside of pure scientific analysis.

Perhaps the DARE (Drug Abuse Resistance Education) program is a prototypal example of this. In general, there is little or no evidence that DARE significantly reduces illegal drug use (Truth, DARE, and Consequences, 2001). Yet, DARE continues to be a popular program within law enforcement. DARE may be justified for reasons other than its effectiveness in reducing illegal drug use; for example, it can foster a close working relationship between students who are at a vulnerable age, their parents, teachers, administrators, and police. So, even if DARE does not seem to deter illegal drug use, it may have significant dividends for all concerned. However, this justification must be arrived at by a serious, objective cost-benefit analysis and not simply by good feelings and high hopes to be valid and supportable.

In summary, the worth of community policing is vigorously debated. For example, Doerner (1999) argues:

> The police belong in the crime-suppression business. They already have too many unfinished law enforcement tasks awaiting their attention without saddling them with the extra burden of a social agenda. Community policing is very labor intensive. In an effort to raise the quality of life, advocates would redeploy already scarce police resources and reallocate them to perform activities for which the police are not adequately trained.
>
> The bottom line is very simple. If the goal is to mend the social fabric and make more social services available to less fortunate people, then hire social workers. If the priority is law enforcement, then equip police officers with the proper tools and let them do their jobs. (p. 193)

On the other hand, Stephens (1999) states:

> Traditional policing, with its emphasis on a war on crime, has not succeeded and has no chance to succeed. It is based on myths and false premises.
>
> Community-oriented policing, with its emphasis on community peace, is extremely difficult to initiate and sustain in practice. It takes visionary leadership, creative employees, partnerships, networks, and a constant proactive, preventive focus. But it can succeed spectacularly. Major successes have already been documented. (p. 202)

References

Alpert, G.P., & Piquero, A.R. (2000). *Community policing: Contemporary readings* (2nd ed.). Prospect Heights, IL: Waveland Press.

Bayley, D.H. (1994). *Police for the future.* New York: Oxford University Press.

Bureau of Justice Assistance, Office of Justice Programs (1994). *Understanding community policing: A framework for action.* (NCJ148457). Washington, DC: U.S. Department of Justice.

Carter, D.L., & Radelet, L.A. (1999). *The police and the community* (6th ed.). Upper Saddle River, NJ: Prentice Hall.

Cox, S.M. (1996). *Police: Practices, perspectives, problems.* Boston: Allyn and Bacon.

Doerner, W.G. (1999). War on crime. In J.D. Sewell (Ed.), *Controversial issues in policing.* (pp. 190–194). Boston: Allyn and Bacon.

Dussault, R. (April 2000). Maps and management: Comstat evolves. *Crime and the Tech Effect,* a supplement to *Government Technology.* Retrieved November 12, 2002, from the World Wide Web: http://www.govtech.net/magazine/crimetech/Apr00/CTEtoc.phtml.

Eck, J.E., & Spelman, W. (1987). *Problem solving: problem-oriented policing in Newport News.* Washington, DC: U.S. Department of Justice, Office of Justice Programs, National Institute of Justice; and Police Executive Research Forum.

Federal Bureau of Investigation (2002). *Crime in the United States 2000: Uniform crime reports.* Washington, DC: U.S. Department of Justice.

Glensor, R.W., Peak, K.J., & Gaines, L.K. (1999). *Police supervision.* New York: McGraw-Hill.

Goldstein, H. (1979). Improving policing: A problem-oriented approach. *Crime and Delinquency, 25* (2), 236–258.

Kaufman, M. (1999, August 3). Study fails to find value in DARE program. *Washington Post.* Retrieved July 2, 2002, from the World Wide Web: http://www.mapinc.org/drugnews/v99.n797.a09.html.

Kelling, G.L. (1999). "Broken windows" and police discretion. National Institute of Justice Research Report. (NCJ178259). Washington, DC: U.S. Department of Justice.

Oliver, W.M. (2001). *Community-oriented policing: A systemic approach to policing* (2nd ed.). Upper Saddle River, NJ: Prentice Hall.

Palmiotto, M.J. (2000). *Community policing: A policing strategy for the 21st century.* Gaithersburg, MD: Aspen Publishers.

Reith, C. (1952). *The blind eye of history.* London: Faber and Faber, Ltd.

Roth, J.A., & Ryan, J.F. (2000). *The COPS program after 4 years—National Evaluation. A National Institute of Justice Research in Brief.* (NCJ183644). Washington, DC: U.S. Department of Justice.

Schobel, G.B., Evans, T.A., & Daly, J.L. (August 1997). Community policing: Does it reduce crime, or just displace it? *The Police Chief,* 64–71.

Sewell, J.D. (Ed.). (1999). *Controversial issues in policing.* Boston: Allyn and Bacon.

Skolnick, J., & Bayley, D. (1986). *The new blue line.* New York: Free Press.

Stephens, G. (1999). Peace in the 'hood. In J.D. Sewell (Ed.), *Controversial issues in policing* (pp. 196–203). Boston: Allyn and Bacon.

Truth, DARE, and Consequences (2001). *Law Enforcement News,* February 28, pp. 1–10.

Wilson, J.Q., & Kelling, G.L. (February 1989). Broken windows: Making neighborhoods safe. *Atlantic Monthly,* 46–52.

Wycoff, M.A., & Skogan, W.G. (1994). Community policing in Madison. In D. P. Rosenbaum (Ed.), *The challenge of community policing: Testing the promises* (pp. 75–91). Thousand Oaks, CA: Sage Publications.

4

The Individual Officer

Much is written about law enforcement officers collectively, but very little about officers as individual human beings. This is unfortunate. The welfare of each officer should be of paramount importance to agencies because an agency is only as strong as its weakest officer. This is seen time and time again—a small handful of officers who are "nobodies" diminish the public's respect for an entire agency. When this occurs, the agency typically dismisses the problem as simply a case of a "few bad apples," failing to mention that apples do not go bad overnight but only after a period of time when many people stand by and watch the apples gradually rot. When officers manifest psychological disturbances, from addictions to depression to schizophrenia, agencies typically camouflage the problems or, when forced to deal with them, define them as personal problems rather than ones that may have existed for some time with the agency ignoring or only superficially addressing them.

It is increasingly important for agencies and individual officers to become more aware that officers are human beings first and officers second (or spouses/parents second and officers third). To this end, this chapter will address the following topics: the officer as a human being, obstacles to becoming an effective officer, critical incidents, and officer suicide.

THE OFFICER AS A HUMAN BEING

Historically, law enforcement has portrayed its officers as superhuman, and the media have conveyed this image to the public. Although this is less the case today, there still remains a culture in law enforcement that perceives officers as superior to mere mortals, also known as "citizens."

This attitude causes three problems. First, according to "the bigger they are, the harder the fall" principle, when officers make honest mistakes or behave unethically, they immediately go from being "gods" to being "pigs." At this point defenders respond: "But cops are only human and cannot be expected to act otherwise," which would not need to be said if everyone believed it to be true in the first place. (When a bank teller makes a mistake, no one ever says, "But bank tellers are only human," because no one has ever believed otherwise.)

Second, society has thrust many roles on officers, and law enforcement has accepted these roles, so officers are expected to be superhuman. The mantra of law enforcement has become that officers not only enforce the law but also must be psychologists, sociologists, criminologists, counselors, ministers, mentors, negotiators, lawyers, role models, teachers, community organizers; as well as experts in driving, firearms, and defensive tactics; and paragons of virtue. An officer who falls short in even one of these areas must be prepared for repercussions, not only from citizens, but from the agency as well. This attests to the fact that the myth of the superhuman officer endures despite overwhelming evidence that it defies reality.

Third, the most serious problem is that many officers believe they are, or should be, superhuman, acting as if they do not have the same mundane needs, feelings, strengths, and weaknesses as everyone else. This attitude is seen most dramatically in the massive resistance so many officers have to reaching out for help from other officers, family, friends, clergy, or counselors.

The combination of these three problems often creates an intense pressure on officers to deny and squelch their humanity, and not share in the human condition. As a result, human conflicts can metastasize not only into personal problems but also problems on the job and at home.

This section addresses the humanity of law enforcement officers and how accepting and dealing with it daily is at the heart of being a good officer, as well as a good spouse, parent, and friend.

Human Needs and Competencies

Psychological needs and the competencies required to get them met satisfactorily are the core of psychological health. Psychological needs are analogous to food: The more nutritious and plentiful the food, the more healthy a person will be. Problems arise when not enough nutritious food is available, or the food is toxic, or sufficient food is available but the individual is unwilling to eat it, as in anorexia nervosa. In these cases, starvation and sickness occur and can eventually result in death. People with good psychological diets are psychologically healthy, those with average diets are psychologically normal, and those with poor diets are psychologically abnormal (disturbed, dysfunctional).

Just as food does not magically appear on the table, psychological needs do not get met automatically. Just as people must have the ability to obtain food, they need certain competencies to have their psychological needs met satisfactorily. The following eight needs are basic to becoming a fully developed, psychologically healthy human being.

The need to feel secure. The need to feel secure includes the needs to feel free from physical and psychological threat or harm, to let down one's guard and feel safe, relaxed, and peaceful in situations and relationships.

The opposite of feeling secure is feeling insecure, always having one's guard up, expecting and sensing harm in situations and relationships. Insecure individuals view life as a battlefield on which, at any time, something or someone can psychologically injure or destroy them.

The basic competency required to feel secure is trust in oneself and others. Secure people have a good sense of who they are. As a result, they are able to handle most threats that arise, either by neutralizing them or by leaving the situation. Secure individuals realize that, for the most part, people are not out to hurt them. When the threat of harm appears, they trust it can be worked out in constructive ways. Secure people also make others feel secure, whereas insecure people tend to make others feel insecure, which puts them off balance and makes them less of a threat to the insecure person.

At work, secure officers can concentrate on the issues at hand and not worry about protecting their flank. Their ego is intact, allowing them to admit ignorance and mistakes, to rise above the taunts and disrespect of citizens, and honestly to consider the ideas of people who disagree with them. Insecure officers' main objective is to protect their egos from assaults. They typically overcompensate for their fears and weaknesses by acting smarter and tougher than they are, operating on the principle that the best defense is a good offense. They tend to put down others in order to feel superior and intimidate people in order to keep them at a safe distance. Insecure officers are generally difficult to educate because they have all the answers and to supervise because they are so defensive. It is likely that insecure officers do not have many friends in the agency, which makes them even more insecure, and they tend to receive an inordinate number of citizen complaints because of their overbearing attitudes and preemptive strikes.

The need to feel accepted. The need to feel accepted encompasses the desires to feel liked, included, acknowledged, affirmed, and/or loved. The opposite of feeling accepted is feeling different, ridiculed, isolated, lonely, and always on the fringe of friendships, groups, and social activities.

The basic competency required to feel accepted is to first accept oneself, one's strengths and weaknesses. People who accept themselves tend to enable others to feel the same way, whereas those who do not feel accepted tend to make others feel unaccepted so as not to feel alone in their isolation.

Officers who sense that they are accepted and liked tend to relate comfortably with others. Like secure officers, they can concentrate on the issue at hand because they are not worried about whether people like or dislike them, whether their decisions will make them popular or unpopular, and whether they will be accepted or rejected. In other words, they do their job in a healthy way and let the chips fall where they may.

Officers who do not feel accepted spend a good deal of energy trying to be accepted and liked by everyone. This causes them to be ingratiating and easily manipulated by people who pretend to befriend them to get something in return. These officers are particularly vulnerable to prostituting their values for acceptance, a dynamic that makes them easy prey to a rogue subculture. This neediness creates tension in that their constant efforts at trying to win acceptance have a suffocating effect on others.

The need to feel worthwhile.   The need to feel worthwhile includes the needs to feel appreciated, respected, admired, effective, important, and successful. The opposite of feeling worthwhile is feeling stupid, ineffectual, ignored, ridiculed, unimportant, and worthless.

The basic competency required to feel valuable is the ability to fulfill one's roles effectively, to be a good officer, spouse, parent, and friend—in other words, to be a person who is worth knowing. People who feel worthwhile tend to help others feel the same way, and those who do not tend to make others feel worthless in order to even the playing field.

Officers who feel worthwhile take their roles seriously at work and home, spending a good deal of time, effort, energy, and preparation on them. They work hard at becoming the best officer, spouse, parent, and friend. At work, officers who feel worthwhile can concentrate on the issues at hand because they do not continually have to prove their worth to themselves and others. They are realistically confident in their abilities and goodness and are willing to contribute their ideas and talents to improve situations in which they are involved. They are willing to help others succeed and can easily compliment others on a job well done.

Officers who do not feel worthwhile often overcompensate by showing off, trying to convince others and themselves that they are highly competent, effective, and successful. They let it be known at every opportunity how they outwitted somebody, won some battle, and saved victory from the jaws of defeat. This creates tension in that these officers tend to take credit for the good work of others and are blind to the fact that they are not as competent as they think they are.

The need to be intimate.   The need to be intimate includes the needs to be close, open, and honest with selected others, including coworkers, family members, and friends. The opposite of the need to be intimate is the need to avoid intimacy—to be private, keep all thoughts and feelings to oneself, and perceive needing anyone for anything as a sign of weakness.

The basic competency for an intimate relationship is the ability to become close to another individual without losing one's own sense of self, suffocating the other person, or becoming addicted to the other person so that little else in life matters. People capable of intimate relationships enjoy a richness that breeds security, openness, and trust. Those who are comfortable in intimate relationships allow others to get close to them, while those who are uncomfortable keep a safe distance, viewing anything deeper than a superficial relationship as a minefield in which they are likely to get seriously injured.

Officers whose intimacy needs are met in a healthy way can have a few, close friendships in which they are honest and trusting about personal and professional issues. They realize that these relationships take time to develop and cannot be rushed because the foundation of such relationships is deep trust. These friendships can be a real source of support, get officers through the toughest times, make the job worthwhile, and last a lifetime. The only danger is that these friendships with either sex may meet so many intimacy needs that an officer's spouse or partner becomes a substitute player when it comes to sharing on an intimate level. This is especially true when the officers' friends are also their partners with whom they are working 8 to 12 hours each day.

Officers who do not have intimacy needs or get them met primarily outside the job will not feel the need to get close to people at work, which is fine. But officers who bring strong intimacy needs to the job may attempt to force intimacy onto other officers or may enter into illicit intimate relationships with other law enforcement personnel, citizens, or even suspects in criminal cases.

The need to experience stimulation. The need to experience stimulation includes the needs to experience change, novelty, risk, excitement, and challenge. The opposite of feeling stimulated is being bored, apathetic, stale, stuck, suffocated, or depressed.

The competency required to get this need met is the ability to leave the security of the familiar and launch out into the unfamiliar, seeking new experiences that can invigorate life.

Officers with a healthy need for stimulation transmit this enthusiasm to other officers. They are always looking for new challenges and developing schemes to increase their effectiveness. They are rarely bored and do not allow those around them to be bored. They resuscitate dead briefings and meetings with comments, challenges, and ideas, the energy from which can be contagious.

Officers who have no need for stimulation but do their job well will not be a problem. Officers with strong needs for stimulation but without the maturity to modulate it are likely to get into trouble. These are sensation seekers ("adrenaline junkies") whose need to experience thrills, to take it to the edge, can lead them into hazardous, if not illegal, enforcement practices that place their lives and careers, as well as those of fellow officers, in jeopardy. They may also be attracted to the excitement of the underworld—the drugs, sex, and corruption that will destroy them and tarnish the image of law enforcement.

The need to be free. The need to be free includes the need to choose friends, relationships, careers, social activities, values, commitments, and a philosophy of life. The opposite of being free is feeling forced by people or circumstances to stifle personal needs and values in order to gain the acceptance of others, which can be suffocating and life threatening.

The basic competence required to be free is the ability to take the reins of one's life, take the risks and accept the responsibilities of being free, disengage from people who wish to unduly curtail one's freedom, and avoid entering relationships or situations in which life-sustaining freedom will be unduly restricted. People who are truly free tend to free others because they have experienced the importance of freedom, whereas those who are not free tend to enslave others, just as they are enslaved.

Officers who are free, while understanding the limits of freedom, allow themselves to communicate their honest thoughts and feelings in constructive ways. They are healthily independent in their behavior, taking the initiative, seeking new opportunities for growth, and approaching others, including superiors, with suggestions and concerns. They think outside the box and are willing to try innovative approaches to solving problems.

Officers who lack freedom live within self-constraints for which they often blame others or the agency. They remain silent when they should speak up; they remain static when they should be advancing; they are risk aversive when risk is called for; they remain shackled to old solutions to problems; and they resent free people who are advancing while they are regressing.

The need to have fun.   The need to have fun includes the need to experience joy, laughter, play, leisure, pleasure, and beauty. The opposite of having fun is being overly serious, overburdened, irritable, morose, and burnt out. The basic competency required to have fun is the ability to relax, let down defenses, put stressors aside, and possess a sense of vibrancy about life. People who enjoy life make life enjoyable for others, whereas those who are dour tend to make others miserable, based on the principle that misery loves company.

Officers with a keen sense of fun bring liveliness and good humor to the job, which can reduce tension and place things into proper perspective. Their humor is uplifting and never at anyone's expense. They are often at the center of the camaraderie of the agency, which is an important part of job satisfaction, especially when tangible results are few and far between. But these officers' sense of fun is tempered with maturity, which operates on the axiom: There is a time and place for fun, and a time and place for seriousness.

Officers who simply lack a sense of fun will not bring levity to the job, but they also will not cause any damage. However, officers whose sense of fun is not tempered by maturity can cause tension by trying to be funny at the wrong time with the wrong people, by playing practical jokes that are not funny, and by acting the part of the court jester to the annoyance and embarrassment of all.

The need to have an existential purpose in life.   The need for an existential purpose in life means that, in addition to a material purpose (reaching a certain rank or buying a nice home), there is a need to enrich the existence of oneself and others. This is accomplished by increasing the amount of justice, honesty, compassion, hope, respect, love, peace, freedom, and beauty in the world, so that it is a better place in which to live.

The opposite of having an existential purpose in life is having no purpose in life, simply drifting from day to day, or having a purely material, self-centered purpose in life, seeking money, possessions, popularity, power, prestige, and pleasure with no thought of creating a better material, psychological, moral, or spiritual life for others.

The competencies required for an existential purpose in life include a keen sense of perspective, social responsibility, and morality; perspective to realize that there are more important things in life than personal gratification; social responsibility to know that fortunate people have an obligation to help those less fortunate; and morality to sense that an existential legacy of love, justice, freedom, and compassion are more important and enduring than power, possessions, and prestige. People whose existential needs are fulfilled can meet them in others, whereas those who do not can only meet other people's material needs.

Officers whose existential needs are met take home more from the job than a paycheck. Their goal is not only to get evil off the streets but also to put good back on the streets. They do this by taking a little extra effort and, at times, a lot of extra effort, to increase justice, empowerment, trust, honesty, respect, care, and compassion in the community. Generally, this is not done on a large scale or in a flamboyant way, but in individual and small group interactions with children, adolescents, young adults, middle-aged people, and the elderly. These officers view half their job as locking up criminals and the other half as freeing the good people in the community to live a more peaceful existence.

Officers who have not reached the level of existential needs can still be, all other things being equal, fine officers. However, they may not give as much as they could to the communities they serve or bring home the soul-enriching feelings that are possible.

Need Fulfillment

In looking back on this discussion, seven points can be kept in mind.

- Getting needs met is not an inherently selfish pursuit. It resembles foraging for food; until people feed themselves, they are not in a position to feed others. Selfishness enters the picture only when there is a bounty of food, but it is not shared.
- It is the responsibility of adults to get their own needs met. In most cases, people who are psychologically malnourished or even starving have no one to blame but themselves, because either their behavior is counterproductive or they choose to remain in relationships with people who are unable or unwilling to participate in mutually need-fulfilling interactions.

- Some people are psychologically anorexic, meaning that they refuse to accept psychological nourishment from others, even when it is offered, because of fear ("I don't want to get dependent on you"), anger ("I don't need you for anything"), or guilt ("I don't deserve to be happy").
- Each need just discussed can be defined differently by different people. One officer's idea of "fun" is to socialize with other officers after work, but his wife's idea of fun is a family picnic with her parents. When conflicting definitions of a need arise, negotiations and compromises are necessary so that all those involved get their fair share of "psychological groceries."
- People tend to gravitate toward people and situations that meet their needs. For example, an officer gets many of her needs met from her coworkers, so she meets the needs of other officers in return. She gets far fewer needs met at home, where she perceives her husband as whiny and her children as demanding. She is, at the same time, an "esteemed colleague" and "a resented wife." This creates a dangerous vicious cycle in which the more needs she gets met at work, the more boring and frustrating she finds her home life to be, which causes her to want to spend even more time at work and less time at home.
- When one or more important psychological needs are not met over a period of time, psychological hunger pangs occur. For example, an individual may desire to be in an intimate relationship, but this does not happen, causing a deep, gnawing ache. Instead of using the pain as a motivator to address the problem and do something constructive about it, the individual chooses to deaden the pain with psychological analgesics, such as excessive drinking and eating, using drugs, or entering into illicit relationships, all of which are fruitless attempts to fill a void with the wrong ingredients.
- Need fulfillment is closely related to job and marital satisfaction. For example, an officer's priority needs are to work hard and play hard, meaning that between working a great deal of overtime and socializing with fellow officers after work, he is rarely home, especially when his children are still awake. His wife's priority needs are to be a good wife and mother and to spend as much time as possible with her family. The more the officer is "forced" by his wife to discontinue his overtime work and socializing with friends, the less satisfied he will be with both his work and his marriage. These marital dissatisfactions create chronic tensions that can seriously infect both work and family until some compromises can be reached that are at least partially satisfactory to both parties.

Before individuals become law enforcement officers, they are human beings with the same needs, feelings, strengths, and weaknesses as the rest of humanity. They have personal needs that must get met, and they have people at work and at home who have similar needs. Sometimes these needs mesh, sometimes they clash, and sometimes they simply go unmet for lengthy periods of time. It is critically important for both officers and their loved ones to understand the nature of human needs and that the vast majority of problems at work and in relationships can be understood best by viewing them in the context of need fulfillment.

Personal Reflections

1. Of the eight needs discussed in this section, which three are you getting met most? Which three are you getting met least?
2. Psychologically healthy people spend half their time meeting their own needs and half their time meeting other people's needs. How would you grade yourself in this regard, and why?
3. Do you actively try to meet your needs, or do you sit back and wait for others to meet them?
4. When you are feeling badly about yourself or life in general, what need or needs are not getting met that cause you to have these "hunger pangs"?
5. Do you feel that organizations care about meeting the psychological needs of their members? Explain your answer.

OBSTACLES TO BECOMING AN EFFECTIVE OFFICER

One of the saddest things to see in the workplace is employees with great potential and a great future failing to meet their potential or lapsing into self-destructive behavior. Veteran training academy instructors have endless stories about recruits who showed high promise but whose bright star flickered out and crashed to earth somewhere along the way. The following obstacles to becoming an effective officer involve personal, family, and organizational issues.

Personal: The John Wayne Syndrome

The John Wayne syndrome has consciously or unconsciously influenced many law enforcement officers in the past. John Wayne typically played characters who were tough, abusive, prejudiced, hard drinking, hot tempered, humorless, authoritarian, unattached, bullheaded, fearless, chauvinistic, adventuresome, and emotionless (except for an abiding anger, occasional romantic feelings, and a fondness for their horse, which were unconditionally loving and never talked back).

In other words, if John Wayne characters were in law enforcement today, they would be spending their entire life patrolling the streets, meeting with internal affairs, negotiating with divorce attorneys, responding to civil suits, and attending rehabilitation meetings. Still, they would be better than the Dirty Harry character, who would have ended his short career in law enforcement by spending half his life in prison.

So, what do many officers find so attractive and appealing about these caricatures of humanity? It is fair to speculate that a psychological profile on the John Wayne characters would result in at least four common traits and resultant messages:

- I am tough. (I don't have time for mushy feelings.)
- I am brave. (I am fearless in all situations.)
- I am proud. (I am superior and never wrong.)
- I am self-sufficient. (I don't need *anybody*, especially women.)

Because these traits were, and still are, perceived in some circles as the stuff of "real men," and many officers view law enforcement as "man's work" and need to feel like "real men," they have adopted these traits. Some female officers have also adopted these traits to prove to themselves and others that they are just as macho as male officers—a dubious distinction.

However, three major problems result from emulating John Wayne characters. One is that these officers portray a caricature of a human being, one that is stuck at an early adolescent stage of male development, in which intelligence, sensitivity, affection, and compassion are stupid, and fighting, drinking, fearlessness, prejudice, toughness, and chauvinism are smart. This attitude, especially today, causes nothing but trouble within the agency, on the street, in the courts, and in the family.

The second problem is that the John Wayne persona (which means "mask" in Latin) is just that, a mask. Masks are meant to hide things the wearer does not want to see, much less want others to see. In other words, psychological subtitles exist for each message:

- "I am tough" has the subtitle "I am actually very vulnerable."
- "I am brave" has the subtitle "I am actually scared."
- "I am proud" has the subtitle "I actually feel worthless."
- "I am self-sufficient" has the subtitle "I am actually very needy."

Officers who wear John Wayne masks cannot know who they really are (nor can their family or friends) because the masks hide their real strengths and weaknesses. This precludes personality growth because nothing that needs to change ever will.

A third problem is that, when masks get ripped off, it is traumatic for the person, as well as those closest to him or her. It is not a pretty sight to see the tough John Wayne officer unmasked in an internal affairs investigation and end up crying like the terrified child he has always been, or the self-reliant John Wayne officer pleading like the needy child he has always been for his girlfriend or wife not to leave him. In some cases, the unmasking can be so traumatic that the officer commits suicide.

For these reasons, it is past time for law enforcement to lay the John Wayne character to rest. Training academy instructors need to tell the John Wayne recruits on the first day of class that they have the length of the academy to grow up or find a more suitable type of employment. These recruits need to know that there is

- A time to be tough and a time to be gentle
- A time to be heroic and a time to be cautious
- A time to be proud and a time to be humble
- A time to be independent and a time to rely on others

Law enforcement officers do not need to be "real men" or "real women," but real human beings who can relate to themselves, other officers, citizens, and their families in comfortable and authentic ways.

Family: The Spillover Effect

What happens at home can spill over and significantly affect what happens at work and vice versa. Some people think that they can separate the two parts of their lives, and while some do it better than others, it is impossible to do well. It also is not possible to clearly separate job stress from family stress because they are so intricately related. For example, if two officers experience the same traumatic situation at work, it is likely that the officer with a great family life will be far less negatively affected by the trauma than will the officer with a terrible family life. Therefore, it is important for officers to understand how work and family life feed, starve, or poison each other. ("Family," as used here, refers to the unit comprised of officers and anyone they live with, including partners, spouses, children, parents, and siblings.)

A common source of spillover deals with control within the family with regard to family finances, children's behavior, social life, family rules, purchasing activities, assignment of chores, and sanctions for members who violate rules. As long as everyone in the family agrees to the jurisdictional boundaries and who oversees them, no tension will exist. But if jurisdictions are fought over, major tensions can arise that affect the entire family. For example, an officer may feel he has the right to spend his overtime money as he chooses, whereas his wife may feel that she has the right to use that money to pay mounting bills. Collisions often occur at this intersection, creating stress for both spouses and the entire family.

In some families, jurisdictional conflicts are minimal and virtually nonexistent. In some cases this occurs because nobody really cares who does what as long as everyone leaves everyone else alone. In other instances, it happens because everyone is secure and truly loves and respects each other so jurisdictions and rights are evenly distributed, often with little discussion.

However, when tensions exist, either in many areas or in one or two highly charged ones, and they are not dealt with constructively, they invariably spill over into the job. Officers in these situations begin their shift "locked and loaded," hoping that someone will cross their sights so that they can blow them away, thus venting some of their anger, if not rage. God help the first dispatcher who makes a mistake or the first violator the officer stops.

One can only guess how many officers overreact to situations at work, sometimes with lethal results, not because of the nature of the situation, but because they were ticking time bombs with clocks that were set at home. Furthermore, with the invention of the cell phone, these conflicts can be waged throughout the shift, reigniting the fires every few hours. A vicious cycle results: Bringing stress from home causes problems on the job; problems on the job create stress at home, and so on. If both spouses or partners work, the effects of spillover increase exponentially.

The spillover effect is especially problematic for law enforcement officers because of the high-risk nature of the job. If an accountant brings her anger to work, she may angrily snap at a coworker. If an officer brings her anger to work, she may end up using excessive force on a suspect as an outlet for her anger.

For these reasons, agencies can no longer pretend a firewall exists between work and home. Officers and their families need to be educated as to how their work and personal lives are not separate but intricately entwined. Agencies also need to understand that individual counseling for officers may not be as successful as it could be because the officer's problems often are not solely work related or personal but also relational, meaning that relevant family members should be included in the counseling program.

Organizational: Bureaucracy and Injustice

Many officers report that the greatest source of stress is not the high-risk situations they confront in the line of duty, but the stressors within the agency itself. In one survey Violanti and Aron (1993) found that 7 of the top 20 stressors for officers were organizational/administrative. Shift work was ranked as the highest organizational stressor, followed by inadequate support, incompatible patrol partner, insufficient personnel, excessive discipline, and inadequate support from supervisors. In another study, Violanti and Aron (1995) found that the two basic stressors for law enforcement officers were organizational practices and the inherent nature of police work. The organizational stresses included issues such as authoritarian structure, lack of participation in decision making, and unfair discipline. Included in the inherent stressors of police work were situations that threatened to harm the officer either physiologically or psychologically.

For the most part, truly high-risk situations occur only occasionally, relative to daily, unrelenting agency stressors. Moreover, officers can do something about the high-risk situations—they can take control of them, resolve them, and move on to periods of relative peace. This is ordinarily not the case with agency stress.

For the most part, officers must endure it, keep their mouths shut, and ventilate about it privately with other trusted officers. Two examples of agency stressors that are largely unnecessary are bureaucracy and injustice.

Bureaucracy.   A large difference exists between management and bureaucracy. Management simply means directing operations, a necessity in every organization. Bureaucracy, on the other hand, means managing in inflexible, mechanical, unimaginative ways, insisting on petty rules and procedures. Whatever the strengths of military and paramilitary organizations, their suffocating bureaucracy is not one of them. An interesting paradox of bureaucracy in the military is the rationale given to support its existence—when war does break out, all personnel will be prepared to do everything "by the book." Yet, in reality, war is the precise time when "the book" is thrown out and the ingenuity of leaders takes over, wins battles, and is rewarded.

Business organizations with the bureaucracy present in law enforcement could not successfully compete in a free market economy. Law enforcement agencies can get away with their bureaucracies because they are monopolies, but they pay a price in terms of organizational stagnation, poor morale, and a lack of productivity.

Agency executives, managers, and supervisors need to ask themselves the following questions:

- Is every bit of paperwork I require absolutely necessary? Could *some* of it be eliminated without dire consequences?
- Do I absolutely have to hold as many meetings and briefings as I do? Could some of the material discussed at meetings be communicated by e-mail, memo, or posted on bulletin boards?
- Do officers have to check with me or report to me as often as I require? Could I give them a little more freedom to use their own initiative and judgment?
- Do officers absolutely have to log every move they make? Can they limit their logging to significant incidents and let the radio log do the rest?
- Do I respond to officers' requests and questions in a timely manner? Can I work on a "within 24 hours" principle of returning messages so that officers do not have to make repeated requests?
- Do I encourage officers to come up with creative ideas and solutions? Am I secure enough to let my officers think outside the box, especially if the box is wrapped with hundreds of yards of red tape?
- Do I believe the agency needs to be as compartmentalized as it is? Can some walls be removed to expedite the free flow of ideas and information?

It is typical of bureaucrats to insist that every inch of red tape is absolutely necessary to hold the agency together. Yet, if a new chief executive takes over who is as allergic to red tape as the officers, half of the "absolutely necessary" red tape can "absolutely" disappear overnight.

Injustice.   High on the list of officers' stressors and complaints is being treated unjustly by their agency. This does not mean that, in fact, they are. For some officers, the simple fact that they are not receiving what they feel entitled to is perceived as an injustice. Because feelings of entitlement seem to be assuming epidemic proportions in society, increasing numbers of officers are likely to perceive they are being treated unfairly, whether or not they are.

But it is undeniable that unavoidable and avoidable injustice exists in law enforcement, as it does in any organization. Unavoidable injustice is part of living in an imperfect world. As one ethics professor is fond of saying: "There is 'justice,' and there is 'just is.'" For example, one officer may use reasonable force while arresting a well-placed citizen, but be unjustly accused of using excessive force. As a result, he must endure a prolonged internal affairs investigation. On the same day, his partner may have used clearly excessive force arresting a gang member and never hear about it again. This is unfair in the world of distributive justice, but not uncommon in the world of law enforcement, and there is not much anyone can do about it, except complain and move on. However, probably half of the injustice officers endure is avoidable. Because of this, supervisors must ask themselves: Without fail do I

- Treat others they way I would expect to be treated in a similar situation, or does that thought never enter my mind?
- Accept uncritically the negative things I hear about an officer, or do I tell the officer what I heard and offer her the opportunity to give her side of the story?
- Perceive constructive criticism by my officers as important and helpful, or do I secretly resent it and get revenge later?
- Receive information in confidence from officers and keep those confidences, or do I concoct some rationalization that allows me to violate that confidence?
- Give my officers ongoing corrective feedback about their performance, or do I save it and dump it on them at their yearly evaluation?
- Divide desirable and undesirable assignments equally among officers, or do I favor my friends with the desirable ones and give the less desirable ones to officers I dislike?
- Recommend officers for promotion based solely on their merits, or do I allow personal feelings and political considerations to contaminate my recommendations?

Honest answers to these questions will offer some idea as to how justly officers in a particular command are being treated. It is important to understand that the most pernicious organizational virus is avoidable injustice. It scorches the agency's infrastructure and can spread like wildfire, meaning that injustice breeds injustice up and down the organizational ladder and payback becomes the rallying cry. Therefore, it is of the utmost importance for *all* officers, no matter their rank, to consciously place the highest priority on treating each other in ways they would expect to be treated in the same situation.

Personal Reflections

1. Why do you think some people, both males and females, must act tough all the time? What are they trying to prove to themselves and others?

2. Everyone knows people who suffer from the John Wayne syndrome. Despite what they think about how impressive they are, how do they really come across to others?

3. How have you experienced the spillover effect in your life? What can you do to reduce it in the future?

4. If you were in a position of authority, what three things would you do to prevent management from regressing into bureaucracy?

CRITICAL INCIDENTS

A critical incident is an event that could generate so much stress for officers that they lose their psychological equilibrium, causing symptoms that disrupt their normal functioning. This definition has two parts. First, it is an event that *could* create disequilibrium, but does not necessarily do so, depending on the nature of the incident, the officer's pre-incident personality, the officer's perception of the incident, and the psychological supports available to the officer. The symptoms that the incident generates, for example, insomnia, may be mild, moderate, or severe; be short term (a few hours to a few days) or long term (a few weeks, months, or years); be immediate (experienced at the time of the incident) or delayed (not experienced until several days or even weeks after the incident).

Second, critical incidents often generate a crisis, meaning that the resultant stress overwhelms the officer's psychological defenses and causes symptoms that significantly impair the officer's functioning. For example, the officer may not only experience insomnia but also panic attacks, intrusive images of the incident, prolonged periods of crying, loss of appetite, increased alcohol consumption, and temper outbursts. It is important to reiterate, however, that not all critical incidents result in a crisis.

Crisis intervention is different from traditional counseling in that it is immediate, incident focused, short term (one to three contacts), simple (direct and practical), and often takes place in the field. Its goals are modest: Stabilize the symptoms so they do not continue to escalate, reduce the distress, restore the officer to pre-incident functioning, and facilitate access to further counseling when appropriate.

In law enforcement, the following events can take on crisis proportions:

- Being involved with mass casualties, such as occur in natural disasters, terrorist attacks, bus accidents, airplane crashes, large structure fires
- Being involved in a shooting: shooting a suspect, being shot or shot at, or being a witness to a shooting
- Being involved in a life-threatening assault, as the victim or as the officer attempting to subdue a suspect
- Being severely injured in an accident, such as being in an automobile accident, being struck by an automobile, falling from a roof
- Investigating an extraordinarily heinous crime, especially one involving multiple victims, children, or elderly people
- Being sued, especially for punitive damages, as a result of taking, or failing to take, some action
- Being accused of a serious crime or violation of agency guidelines—an accusation that could result in termination or prison
- Having committed a serious mistake, for example, accidentally shooting a firearm and injuring or killing someone, crashing a patrol vehicle into innocent people and seriously injuring or killing them
- Having a partner or other officer commit suicide
- Making an error in judgment that causes other officers or innocent citizens to be seriously hurt or killed
- Being required to testify against one's partner or other officers, a situation with serious consequences for all concerned

The proliferation of guns and illegal drugs on the street, a generation of criminals who feel they have nothing to lose by being sent to prison or killed, the high rate of litigiousness, and the anti-law enforcement attitudes present in today's society all add up to the real possibility that officers and their families will experience one or more of these incidents over the course of a career. And, if officers do not personally experience a critical incident, they may have to live through one vicariously with a partner or other officers and their families.

Reactions to Critical Incidents

It is important for officers and their families to become at least mentally prepared for such events, so that they will know what to expect, how to react, and how to help each other.

The psychological reactions to critical incidents are personal in nature, meaning that some officers will have little reaction, others will seem to have no immediate reaction but will react at a later time, others will have an acute reaction lasting a relatively short time, and still others will feel devastated and never fully recover.

Some officers may not require any intervention, others require short-term crisis intervention, and still others need long-term counseling. Some families do not miss a beat, others go through a difficult period for a short time, and still others never fully recover. In fact, sometimes the family may experience a more difficult time dealing with the incident than the officer does. For example, some officers who are shot soon return to duty relatively unscathed, while members of their families dread every day their spouse or parent goes to work for the remainder of their lives.

Officers in a crisis state can experience a wide variety of repercussions, caused by stress surging through them and causing psychological short circuiting and power outages. Therefore, it is important to know the kinds of symptoms to expect. A danger always exists in listing symptoms that officers can experience because this could create a self-fulfilling prophecy, meaning that it could bring about symptoms in a suggestible person who might otherwise not experience them. Keeping this in mind, the following are some symptoms that may follow a critical incident.

Cognitive symptoms. These may be recurring and intrusive thoughts regarding the critical incident, as well as negative thoughts about oneself ("It's all my fault"), about coworkers ("They're going to blame me"), about one's family ("They don't really care or understand"), about one's career ("I'll never be a cop again"), and about life in general ("Maybe I should just pack it in").

In the worst case, officers become obsessive about the incident, ruminate about it and perhaps experience flashbacks, or slip into a psychotic state, which is rare.

Affective symptoms. These are deep feelings of fear ("What's going to happen to me and my family?"), anger ("Why was I placed in that situation?"), guilt ("I should have done something differently"), depression ("Everything seems hopeless"), loneliness ("No one else can ever understand what I'm feeling"), and confusion ("I don't know whether I'm coming or going").

In the worst case, officers become angry and lash out at others, especially family members and close friends, or become depressed and unable to function, possibly considering or even committing suicide, which is rare.

Psychophysiological symptoms. These are headaches, dizziness, distorted vision, impaired hearing, stomach cramps, diarrhea, nausea, vomiting, loss of sexual desire, sexual dysfunction, menstrual problems, heart palpitations, profuse sweating, loss of hair, numbness in the extremities, rashes, hyperventilation, panic attacks, loss of appetite, insomnia, tremors, fatigue, agitation.

In the worst case, officers become so physically debilitated that they simply fall apart and are unable to care for themselves or concentrate on anything beyond their physical state, which is rare.

Placing Stress in Perspective

Law enforcement can be very stressful, yet many other occupations are also stressful. Emergency room physicians have their unique stressors—even one mistake in the midst of the chaos in an emergency room can cost lives. Pilots, especially military pilots, have their unique stressors—law enforcement officers do not know what multitasking under maximum stress is until they fly an F16 jet, especially in war games or combat. Attorneys prosecuting or defending a dangerous felon, or suing or defending a large corporation have their unique stressors—losing a case can have life-altering effects for everyone involved, including the attorneys.

Nevertheless, law enforcement officers have a unique stressor that no civilian occupation faces. People are willing to kill them, and officers must be willing to kill others in life-threatening situations. This represents an ever-present stress, more so in some jurisdictions and assignments than in others. However, a mythology surrounds law enforcement that it is *the* most dangerous and stressful occupation. In reality, some occupations are two to ten times more dangerous. Table 4.1 (Bureau of Labor Statistics, 2002a) presents a sample of occupations that have higher fatality rates than law enforcement (police and detectives) for the year 2000.

With respect to nonfatal occupational injuries and illnesses, the Bureau of Labor Statistics (2002b) lists only the top 10 occupations, and law enforcement is not included in that number. The occupations listed are truck drivers, laborers (nonconstruction), nursing aides and attendants, construction laborers, janitors and cleaners, assemblers, carpenters, cooks, cashiers, and registered nurses.

Law enforcement publications that list occupational stressors often overstate the intensity and number of stressors, as if they are more frequent and intense than those in other occupations. These stressors include enduring bureaucratic red tape, political infighting, catch-22 situations, shift and holiday work, 50- to 70-hour work weeks, inept leadership, injustice regarding salaries and promotions, exposure to lawsuits, poor working conditions and environment, job burnout, feelings of hopelessness, unfair judgment by the public, "burst stress"—long periods of calm followed by high-intensity action—and so on.

Viewing these items objectively, it can be seen that they are present in many occupations. This is clearly seen when officers leave law enforcement for higher-paying jobs and often long for the days when they only had to cope with the stressors of "the job."

The amount of stress in law enforcement should be perceived objectively, so that realistic attitudes and remedies can follow. Two significant problems result from ignoring the fact that many other occupations are as stressful as, if not more stressful than, law enforcement.

TABLE 4.1 *2000 Fatality Rates by Occupation*

Occupation	Fatalities per 100,000 Employed
Timber cutting and logging	144
Moving equipment operators	121
Sailors and deckhands	121
Fishers, hunters, trappers	104
Airplane pilots and navigators	100
Water transportation	100
Railroad operators	100
Mining operators	79
Structural metal workers	59
Taxicab drivers	52
Coal miners	50
Garbage collectors	43
Farm managers	39
Excavating machine operators	30
Roofers	30
Construction laborers	28
Truck drivers	28
Electrical workers	21
News vendors	21
Firefighters	15
Police and detectives	12

Source: Bureau of Labor Statistics, *2000 Census of Fatal Occupational Injuries* (Washington, DC: U.S. Department of Labor, 2002), p. 4.

Cowboy mentality.   After a long, hot day of driving cattle across arid plains and fighting off the elements, predatory animals, and cattle rustlers, cowboys would feel entitled to go out on the town and get drunk, pick fights, and shoot off their guns and mouths. Officers who believe they have the toughest job in the world sometimes develop a cowboy mentality that entitles them to let off steam in inappropriate ways that are personally and professionally risky. Yet the fact is that law enforcement officers are not cowboys but people claiming to be members of a profession. The time has come for cowboy behavior to be seen for what it is—a sign of not being able to handle stress in a healthy manner. After all, even cowboys do not act like cowboys anymore.

Self-fulfilling prophecy.   Officers who believe they have "the most dangerous and stressful job in America" may begin to feel overwhelmed by stress and become symptomatic because this is "what is supposed to happen to cops."

A typical, though not universal, pattern occurs when officers react to a critical incident with agitation, depression, or a combination of both. Instead of allowing themselves to feel the full brunt of these feelings and making some healthy life changes—including career changes, in order to reduce them—they mask the symptoms through self-medicating behavior. The most common forms of self-medication are smoking, excessive drinking and eating, gambling, and sex. In some cases, the use of illegal drugs is added to the mix. These behaviors have the effect of throwing fuel on a fire because not only do they fail to address the original problem, they also place the officer and others at risk, the fallout from which simply increases the symptoms.

Cautions Regarding Advice

It is important for officers experiencing stress to be cautious about accepting "one size fits all" advice, even from officers who "have been there" and mental health professionals. Examples of advice that may be appropriate in some situations but not in others include the following:

- "The more you express your emotions, the better you'll feel." Expressing emotions after a critical incident can be good. However, some officers, at least for a time, need to hold on to their feelings until they can get them under control and feel safe sharing them with others.
- "Try not to think about it; keep yourself distracted with other things." Although this may be a good strategy for some officers, others need to revisit the incident many times to desensitize themselves to it gradually. In other words, they "wear out" the memory by thinking about it often.
- "Keep a diary of what you're thinking and feeling, then read it to understand your experiences better, objectify them, and move on." This is not always helpful because it may cause some officers to delve into themselves in ways that bring up feelings they are not ready to face. It may also focus the officers more on introspection than on dealing with the more pressing parts of the reality facing them.
- "Take some medication to help you feel better and cope with the situation until you're ready to do it on your own." Some officers may need medication to help them deal with the critical incident. However, most officers will not need medication, which, though helpful in certain limited circumstances, can also be misprescribed and abused, leading to addiction. This only compounds the problem.
- "Join a group of officers who 'have been there'; they know what you're going through and can help you better than anyone else." Officers who have recovered from a critical incident sometimes can be helpful. Yet they also can possess a dogmatic belief that their way of recovering is the only one and will work for everyone, when, in fact, it may only cause frustration when others try it.

- "You can't withdraw from people. You must let others in to help you, especially your family." Some officers need time to accept their situation before allowing others to become involved. Moreover, this advice assumes that all families are equally empathic and accepting.
- "You must get some professional counseling." This may be good advice, but some officers have such negative feelings toward "shrinks" that their resistance to counseling would scuttle the entire process and create more stress. Moreover, some officers have the ability to cope with the situation on their own without professional help.
- "You can't hang on to your fear (anger, guilt, depression, loneliness, confusion) because it will eat you alive and eventually kill you. You must let go and move on with your life." This advice is unlikely to help any officer because people cannot simply order their deeply entrenched feelings to disappear. When officers try to do this and fail, they feel even more frustrated than they did prior to receiving the advice.

Advice of any sort can be good, unhelpful, or harmful; therefore, giving advice, no matter how well intentioned, is not necessarily a benign endeavor. For example, suggesting that an officer take medication could be particularly pernicious if the officer has a history of addiction (to alcohol, gambling, food, sex, exercise, work), which the advice giver may not be aware of or recognize as a danger sign. Although a physician should check out an officer's history before prescribing medication, this does not always occur.

Officers experiencing the effects of a critical incident should consider the worth of all advice. However, they should accept only the advice they feel is best suited to them at any particular point in the recovery process. No advice, no matter how good, fits all officers at all times during their recovery. Every officer is unique and thus will have a different way of recovering from a critical incident.

Intervention Considerations

Some issues in crisis intervention may be especially important for both officers and counselors to consider.

Turning point.   A crisis is not necessarily a negative event. The word *crisis* means a turning point, a turn that can be made in a positive or a negative direction. The direction of the turn depends less on the nature of the incident itself and more on the officer's perceptions of the incident and support systems. Whether the critical incident is getting shot, witnessing gruesome carnage, or getting fired, it can move officers to reevaluate themselves, their lives, and their values in ways that lead them in a better direction.

Triage and counseling.   Crisis intervention is not the same as traditional counseling. It is what first aid is to surgery. Keeping with the analogy, four situations can occur:

- An officer may not feel well, but not require first aid.
- An officer may require first aid, but not surgery.
- An officer may require first aid and surgery.
- An officer must be rushed directly into surgery.

The triage decision needs to be made by both the officer and the crisis counselor.

Modalities.   Crisis intervention has several modalities. It can be done in a group; for example, rescuers at the site of mass casualties often meet in groups of 5, 10, or 15 with one or a team of crisis counselors. Individual officers can meet with one or more counselors. It also can be done with the family of the officer. In this situation, the entire family, including children, meets to better understand how they can support each other during the period of crisis.

Crisis intervention can focus on helping the officer in one or all of the following dimensions: the physical dimension of the incident, dealing with physical injuries or symptoms; the psychological dimension, dealing with the cognitive and emotional symptoms created by the incident; or the spiritual dimension, dealing with religious and spiritual issues that often arise during a crisis reaction.

Crisis intervention can be done in the field, as close to the incident site as possible; in the officer's agency; in the counselor's agency; or in the family home.

Which modalities are used depends upon the nature of the incident, the physical and psychological states of the officer, the wishes of the officer and the officer's family, and the policies of the officer's and counselor's respective agencies.

Cautions Regarding Crisis Intervention

Crisis intervention is not necessarily a benign procedure. All good intentions aside, crisis intervention, like any other endeavor, can be helpful or harmful. Officers and agencies should consider the following points.

Counselor qualifications.   In some states people can refer to themselves as "counselors" regardless of their qualifications. Unqualified people can be hired by schools, clinics, and hospitals, as well as become private consultants. Some law enforcement agencies use their officers as crisis counselors because they have earned the proper professional credentials, have "therapeutic personalities," apply for the position, or have experienced a critical incident themselves.

People lacking the academic and professional qualifications to do crisis intervention can do a good deal of harm, as can qualified people whose personal theories of law enforcement and psychology nullify what they should have learned in their courses and internships. The following are some mistakes counselors can make.

- *Stereotyping officers.* Counselors' personal attitudes toward officers can militate against their being able to truly respect, understand, and empathize with the officer they are counseling. For example, if counselors believe that all officers are "control freaks," they will focus the counseling on the officer "letting go," a strategy that may be countertherapeutic in a specific case.

- *Intervening prematurely.* Not every officer who has experienced a critical incident needs crisis intervention. As stated earlier, a crisis is not an event, but a reaction to an event that may or may not reach crisis proportions. When counselors intervene in a case that has not reached a crisis point, they may well cause officers more discomfort than if they were left alone. The role of counselors is not to force-feed officers crisis intervention. If it is clear after a brief discussion that the officer is asymptomatic and expresses no need for intervention, the contact should end.

- *Being too directive.* Crisis intervention tends to be more directive than traditional counseling because time constraints do not allow for lengthy excursions into what officers think would be best for them. On the other hand, officers must have some input in deciding what would best help them at a particular point in time. Counselors who take over the decision making ("Take a week off from work; don't answer the phone; get a lot of exercise; don't smoke or drink alcohol; spend as much time with your family as possible") may be steering an officer in the wrong direction.

Resistance to counseling.   Resistance in counseling is a two-way street. When officers resist counseling, the reasons are generally fourfold: They believe seeking help is a sign of weakness; they do not think highly of the psychological community; they do not think civilians can understand them; and they do not trust that what they say will be held in confidence, especially if the counselors are employed by the agency. It is too late to attempt to deal with these issues after a critical incident has occurred and officers are in a crisis state. These issues must be addressed in a thorough and honest manner *before* critical incidents occur as part of the education and training offered in academy and continuing education classes and workshops.

Counselors can also resist attaining the intended outcomes of crisis intervention when their attitudes are countertherapeutic. For example, if a female counselor does not particularly like men or believes they enter law enforcement to extend their "power trip," her reaction to a male officer may be more of a hindrance than a help. If a male counselor does not particularly like women or believes they enter law enforcement only to prove they are just as good as men, his reaction to a female officer may be more of a hindrance than a help. This raises the point that not only should counselor education and training address these issues, but so should law enforcement agencies who refer their officers to counselors.

Confidentiality.   It is important to understand the difference between confidentiality and privileged communication. Confidentiality is a *professional concept* that holds that communications between a client and counselor must ordinarily be kept private. For example, an officer tells a critical incident counselor (or any counselor) that he really did not see a weapon in a suspect's hand as he claimed in his report. This would likely be considered a confidential communication, meaning that the counselor could not divulge it to anyone, including the agency. A privileged communication, on the other hand, is a *legal concept* that holds that communications between a client and a counselor are ordinarily protected from being divulged *in a legal proceeding*. This distinction raises two key issues.

First, counselors, whether professionally credentialed or not, may be bound by the principle of confidentiality but may not have "the privilege," meaning they must divulge client communications in a legal proceeding. The Supreme Court has ruled that only state-licensed counselors "have the privilege," meaning that unlicensed counselors, despite college degrees and professional certifications, must divulge their client communications when subpoenaed by a court (*Jaffee* v. *Redmond*, 1996). Therefore, in the previous example, if the counselor were unlicensed, she would be required to divulge the officer's statement concerning filing a false report if subpoenaed to testify in a criminal or civil proceeding.

Second, the word *ordinarily* in the description of confidentiality and privileged communication is important. Numerous exceptions to the principle of confidentiality exist depending on state laws. For example, if officers admit to certain behaviors such as child abuse or being a danger to themselves or others, confidentiality may not apply. If a third party, such as the officer's spouse, partner, or supervisor, is present at the counseling session, confidentiality also may not apply, even in the absence of a subpoena.

With respect to privileged communication, the principle never holds in cases in which the counselor is unlicensed and may not even hold with licensed counselors in certain cases. For example, an officer who has seen a counselor is sued because of some action he took. He voluntarily testifies in court about some statements he made to his counselor, but wants to invoke "the privilege" with respect to others. The problem is that once he waives the privilege for some communications, he waives it for all communications with his counselor. Therefore, the counselor would have to supply the court with all of the officer's statements. Because federal and state laws may differ in some ways, and state laws often differ from each other, officers and their agencies must be clear about federal laws as well as their state laws governing privileged communication.

Although officers could decide never to talk with counselors because of these issues, this information must be placed in a proper perspective. The vast majority of critical incidents do not involve situations in which criminal or civil liability is an issue, or in which officers would be admitting to a counselor that they were a danger to themselves or others, or in which a third party would be present and hear incriminating material. In the world of counseling, these issues rarely arise. However, because of the professional and legal stakes involved, officers and their agencies should approach counseling and the hiring of counselors in an enlightened manner.

Unfortunately, during the course of their careers, officers will encounter critical incidents. Consequently, they need to be psychologically prepared to deal with them and help fellow officers do the same. Perhaps as much as half the stress officers experience in the wake of critical incidents stems from not being psychologically prepared for them. Understanding the causes and effects of critical incidents can go a long way toward softening their impact when they occur.

Personal Reflections

1. What do you think is the worst thing that could happen to officers, not including being killed?
2. Why do you think two people can witness the same critical incident and one is devastated by it while the other, although distressed, does not miss a day of work?
3. Of the typical advice given to people who have experienced a trauma, which would you have been likely to give before you read this chapter?
4. Why are some people so resistant to counseling? How would you encourage them to get counseling if you thought it was the best course of action?

OFFICER SUICIDE

Suicide among law enforcement officers is a matter of great concern for good reason. Unfortunately, very few studies deal with the topic, so it is difficult to accurately determine the actual suicide rate for law enforcement officers. One large agency estimates that as much as 67 percent of officer suicides were purposely misclassified as accidental, natural, or "cause undetermined" (Violanti, 1995).

This problem exists for two reasons. First, agencies are reluctant to disclose their suicide rates for fear of harming their reputation. Second, suicide in law enforcement is likely to be underreported to protect the officer's family and allow them to collect several benefits. Families of officers killed in the line of duty are entitled to a $100,000 federal payment, maximum pension benefits, and access to programs that pay for the funeral and other expenses (Armstrong, 1998a). This does not include benefits from the officer's agency. When officers commit suicide, the families are likely to lose these and other benefits.

Despite the fact that accurate statistics are difficult to ascertain, the following information seems to be reasonably accurate:

- Approximately 300 law enforcement officers commit suicide each year.
- Approximately twice as many officers commit suicide as are killed in the line of duty.
- The law enforcement officer suicide rate is approximately three times that of the general population.
- Officers are one and one-half times more likely to commit suicide than they were a decade ago.
- Officers have the third highest suicide rate among 130 occupations.
- Retired officers kill themselves at a rate of five to ten times that of the general population (Armstrong, 1998a, 1998b, 1998c; Seligmann & Holt, 1994).

Several hypotheses have been offered to explain the high suicide rate of officers. These include access to guns, high job stress, alcohol abuse, domestic problems, psychological disturbance, financial problems, the cynical police culture, and involvement in corruption and scandal. Although any or all of these factors can contribute to officer suicide, they do not represent a sufficient cause, because many officers can experience all eight of these factors and never even think of, much less commit, suicide.

Decision Points

Along the same lines, it is important to point out that external stressors in themselves do not drive officers to suicide ("The job killed him"). In fact, the causes of suicide are varied and complex, ranging from biological to psychological to sociological to spiritual. However, in many cases people who commit suicide go through two lengthy decision periods during which they can alter their course toward self-destruction.

The first decision period occurs when officers are manufacturing the stressors that will eventually weigh heavily on them. They decide to abuse alcohol or drugs; they choose to behave in ways that cause domestic turbulence; they decide that their work is more important than their family; they make a decision to spend more money than they have; they decide to take shortcuts at work; they choose to get involved in ethically questionable conduct; they decide to hang around with other officers who have serious problems; they choose to live life on the edge; they decide to live a double life; and so on.

The second decision period occurs after the stressors come into existence, when officers can decide to respond to them constructively or destructively. For example, officers can seek or refuse professional help for their addictions, family problems, or stress overload. They can decide to address their financial problems by altering their lifestyle, or they can maintain or even augment it in the face of mounting bills. They can choose to address job-related stress by requesting a transfer to a less demanding assignment, or they can "gut it out" until the stress overwhelms them. They can commit to mend some fences with their family or simply withdraw into isolation. They can decide to socialize with a healthier group of officers or to "hang where the fun and excitement are," and so on.

The point is not to blame anyone for officer suicide—not the officers, their agencies, their coworkers, or their family and friends—but to understand that suicide does not occur in a vacuum. It is not the solitary act that it is often portrayed to be, but occurs in a social context that includes everyone who, after the officer's suicide, finds himself or herself saying: "Maybe I should have seen something and didn't"; or "I knew there was something going on with him, but never got around to talking to him about it"; or "I mentioned my concerns once to her, but she assured me she was fine, so I let it go." The purpose of this section is to help prevent people from ever having to second-guess themselves after a loved one, friend, or fellow officer commits suicide.

Warning Signs

Everyone in law enforcement from chief executives to recruits, as well as the family and friends of an officer, should be aware of the early warning signs of suicide. These signals are often present for months and even years prior to the actual suicide. The sooner these signals are detected, the sooner officers can be offered the help they need. No foolproof warning signs of suicide exist, but the following often appear in the psychological autopsies of people who eventually commit suicide.

Verbal cues.   Verbal cues are comments made casually or pointedly that infer the officer is consciously or unconsciously thinking about suicide.

- "Well, you won't have to put up with me much longer."
- "I have a way of getting back at everybody."
- "I think the only time I'll finally get some peace is when I'm dead."
- "I've come up with a solution to all my problems."
- "Life isn't worth the effort any more."
- "For the first time, I can understand how somebody could commit suicide."

Fellow officers, family, and friends typically react to these statements by ignoring them or saying things such as: "Oh, come on, what are you talking about? You're going to get through this and be better than ever." Instead, as uncomfortable as it might be, people should directly respond to these comments, try to learn what is behind them, and get the officer help as soon as possible.

Nonverbal cues. When officers begin to behave in clearly uncharacteristic ways, the people who care about them should be concerned. The following are some behavioral cues:

- *Depression:* sadness, apathy, fatigue; disturbance in concentration, sleep, appetite, sexuality; loss of a sense of fun, enthusiasm, joy, purpose; feelings of helplessness and hopelessness, alienation, loneliness, worthlessness and guilt; recurrent morbid thoughts, including suicidal ideas.
- *Explosive behavior:* loss of temper, yelling, assaulting, throwing objects, making threats, getting in fights, using excessive force.
- *Withdrawal:* wanting to be alone, ignoring friends, staying in their room or glued to TV, disappearing for periods of time.
- *Accidents:* being accident prone—getting involved in vehicle collisions, accidental gun discharges, injuries from physical confrontations, falling down stairs, getting burned in fires, getting cut from glass.
- *Disinterest:* losing interest in people, family, sports, hobbies, local and world events, religion, sex.
- *Overindulgence:* eating, drinking, smoking too much.
- *Recklessness:* driving and handling weapons carelessly, taking senseless risks on the job, "tombstone courage," swimming, skiing, diving in high-risk situations, having unprotected casual sex.
- *Exit decisions:* deciding to leave what may be nourishing situations—filing for divorce, quitting a good job, breaking off a friendship, disowning children, quitting social organizations, discontinuing church attendance.

The common theme underlying all these behaviors is self-destructiveness. The officer is likely to end up worse off after any of these behaviors than before them. These behaviors should not be ignored or rationalized away. People need to confront the officer with the behavior, try to ascertain the reasons for it, and steer the officer in the direction of help.

Situational cues. Suicide often, though not always, follows a specific event or chain of events, some of which include an unwanted divorce, discovering a spouse's or partner's infidelity, losing custody of children, sudden financial reversal, the breakup of a romantic relationship, the death or impending death of a loved one or oneself, being named in a scandal, being arrested, being fired, facing retirement. None of these events, or even a combination of them, is a sufficient cause of suicide because, if it were, everyone experiencing them would commit suicide. These events can be contributing causes, that is, they can be "the last straw" in the life of a very depressed or otherwise dysfunctional officer.

External precipitating situations do not have to be present to trigger a suicide. Many suicides are triggered by internal dynamics—thoughts, feelings, and experiences that no one else has the slightest inkling exist. These suicides "come out of nowhere" and are particularly traumatic to fellow officers and other survivors.

The worst equation with respect to suicidal potential is verbal comments directly or indirectly hinting at suicide, plus nonverbal behaviors that are self-destructive, plus significant situational stressors, plus alcohol, plus a gun.

Understanding Suicide

Many people are often involved when an officer commits suicide. The officers themselves must bear the major responsibility for their act. It is ironic and sad that officers, along with many others in the helping professions, are more capable of helping others than they are of helping themselves and asking for help from others. Almost without exception, an officer's suicide comes at the end of a long string of destructive decisions, which involve three areas: the officer's personal, family, and work life.

Officers can ask themselves three questions:

- Is what I am currently doing in my life good for my physical, psychological and spiritual health? If not, why am I doing it?
- Am I in a relationship or situation that is detrimental to my physical, psychological, or spiritual health? What can I do to make the relationship better? If the relationship or situation is unalterable, why am I choosing to remain in it?
- When loved ones and friends tell me they're concerned about me, how do I react? Do I listen to them, openly and seriously discuss their concerns and take them to heart, or do I become indignant, brush them off with a joke or superficial assurances?

With respect to the officer's family life, parents, spouses, adult children, and other relatives can ask three questions regarding the officer.

- Am I comfortable with the way he's been acting lately, or do I sense that things are not right? If I sense things are not right, what am I going to do about it? Am I going to express my concerns immediately, keep my mouth shut, or wait for the "right time," which I know will never come?
- If I share my concerns and am brushed off, what do I do? Do I give up, assuring myself that I did my best, or do I keep after him in a loving way?
- If his behavior is damaging our family or me, and my efforts to discuss these concerns are to no avail, what do I do then? Do I let the damage continue and increase, or do I offer a serious ultimatum: Either we get professional help or we break up, because I can't let you destroy all of us?

The officer's agency can ask three questions:

- Are we becoming concerned about him and, if so, what are we doing about it? Are we communicating our concerns in no uncertain terms, or do we figure, "He's a big boy and can take care of himself," and decide not to intervene?
- Have we instituted education programs about officer suicide at every level of command down to the training academy? Or, do we believe that such a move would only highlight the problem and cause unnecessary concern and publicity?
- Have we taken steps to create confidential professional counseling for officers in locations away from the agency so that no embarrassment or punishment accrues to the officers seeking it, or do we feel getting help is the officer's business?

Conclusion

As can be seen, suicide prevention in law enforcement agencies requires a three-dimensional approach, involving a good many people, the expenditure of money, and a good deal of education and dedication. In preliminary studies of agencies that have such plans, the number of suicides has dramatically decreased. Violanti (1996) sums up the situation:

> Suicide leaves survivors shaken and in search of answers that may never be found. Police suicide can devastate the morale of entire agencies and leave individual officers with intense feelings of guilt, remorse, and disillusionment.
>
> By its very nature, suicide is an act of desperation, carried out when less drastic avenues of relief seem unavailable or inadequate. Police agencies should ensure that these other avenues are available.
>
> Because most studies suggest that law enforcement officers are at a heightened risk for taking their own lives, police agencies also should be at the forefront of developing and implementing suicide intervention programs. As is true with addressing any problem, the first and most important step is to recognize that the problem exists. With regard to police suicide, this fact can no longer be ignored. (p. 23)

Personal Reflections _____

1. Why do you think law enforcement officers have such a high suicide rate?
2. What do you think is the main cause of suicide in anyone's life?
3. Of all the signs that may indicate an individual may be headed for suicide, which do you think are the three most significant ones?
4. It is easy to say that people should confront loved ones or coworkers who seem depressed and possibly headed for trouble, but what makes this easier said than done?

Summary

Before anything, law enforcement officers must get their personal needs met, both at home and at work. It is as important to be psychologically fit as it is to be physically fit. When officers get into trouble, it is rarely because they are in poor physical shape, but more often because they are in poor psychological condition.

One factor that interferes with officers becoming effective is adopting a "tough guy" personality that, in today's society, not only is an outmoded caricature but also can get officers and their agencies into a lot of trouble. It is rare for mature, balanced, intelligent officers to find themselves facing citizen complaints and internal affairs and grand jury investigations.

Despite what officers may claim, it is virtually impossible to leave the job at the door when they arrive home. They may think they do, but their spouses and children know full well that they do not. Officers also may claim they do not bring family stressors to the job, but their fellow officers know full well that they do. It is important to realize that each aspect of life infuses the others with nutrients or toxins that can significantly influence officers' overall welfare.

The agency's organizational dynamics can directly interfere with officers being as effective and satisfied with their job as they could be. Unnecessarily intrusive and time-consuming policies and politics can demoralize officers to the point where their main objective at work is to hide from bosses and get lost in the hinterlands of their beat.

Because law enforcement officers must face situations such as officer suicide and critical incidents on the job, it is important for agencies to provide their members with opportunities to get into psychological shape and help them deal with stressors when they arise. An agency is only as strong as its individual officers, so every agency has a vested interest in developing and maintaining both the physical and psychological health of its members.

References

Armstrong, D. (1998a, August 23). Suicide epidemic spreads through police ranks. *Boston Globe*, A1.

Armstrong, D. (1998b, August 24). Police suicides rely on tools of guns, alcohol. *Boston Globe*, A1.

Armstrong, D. (1998c, August 24). Law enforcement agencies keep quiet on police suicides. *Boston Globe*, A8.

Barker, J.C. (1999). *Danger, duty, and disillusion*. Prospect Heights, IL: Waveland Press.

Bureau of Labor Statistics (2002a). *2000 Census of fatal occupational injuries*. Washington, DC: U.S. Department of Labor.

Bureau of Labor Statistics (2002b). *Summary of nonfatal occupational injuries for 2000*. Washington, DC: U.S. Department of Labor.

Cavanagh, M.E. (1988). What you don't know about stress. *Personnel Journal, 67* (7), 52–59.

Cavanagh, M.E., & Levitov, J.E. (2002). *The counseling experience: A theoretical and practical approach.* Prospect Heights, IL: Waveland Press.

Finn, P., & Tomz, J.E. (1996). *Developing a law enforcement stress program for officers and their families.* Washington, DC: U.S. Department of Justice.

Ford, W. (1998). *Managing police stress.* Walnut Creek, CA: The Management Advantage.

Goleman, D. (1995). *Emotional intelligence.* New York: Bantam Books.

Hart, P.M., & Wearing, A.J. (1995). Police stress and well-being: Integrating personality, coping and daily work experiences. *Journal of Occupational and Organizational Psychology, 68* (2), 133–156.

Jaffee v. *Redmond* (1996). 116 S.Ct. 1923, 1996 WL 315841 (U.S. III)

Kappeler, V.E., Sluder, R.D., & Alpert, G.P. (1998). *Forces of deviance: Understanding the dark side of policing* (2nd ed.). Prospect Heights, IL: Waveland Press.

Kates, Allen R. (1999). *Copshock: Surviving posttraumatic stress disorder (PTSD).* Tucson, AZ: Holbrook Street Press.

Klein, J. (2002, March 18). The supercop scenario. *The New Yorker,* 72–78.

Quinnett, P. (1998). QPR. *FBI Law Enforcement Bulletin, 67* (7). 19–25.

Rogers, L.K. (2000). *Post traumatic stress disorder: A police officer's report.* Ypsilanti, MI: Proctor Publications.

Seligmann, J., & Holt, D. (1994, September 26). Cops who kill—themselves. *Newsweek, 124* (13), 58.

Sheehan, D.C., & Warren, J.I. (Eds.). (2001). *Suicide and law enforcement.* Washington, DC: U.S. Department of Justice.

Snipes, D., & Snipes, C. (2000). The issues of privilege v. confidentiality in counseling with law enforcement officers. Retrieved October 28, 2000, from the World Wide Web: http://www.geocities.com/HotSprings/Spa/7762/confidentiality.html.

Violanti, J. (1995). The mystery within: Understanding police suicide. *FBI Law Enforcement Bulletin, 64* (2), 19–24.

Violanti, J. (1996). *Police suicide: Epidemic in blue.* Springfield, IL: Charles C Thomas.

Violanti, J.M., & Aron, F. (1993). Sources of police stressors, job attitudes, and psychological stress. *Psychological Reports, 72,* 892–904.

Violanti, J.M., & Aron, F. (1995). Police stressors: Variations in perception among police personnel. *Journal of Criminal Justice, 23* (3), 287–294.

5

The Selection of Officers

The selection of officers is critical to the success of any professional law enforcement agency. The axiom "The best way to prevent personnel problems is not to hire personnel problems in the first place," is never truer than when it is applied to law enforcement. Most officers who consistently create problems probably should not have been hired in the first place. Once hired, it is often difficult to get rid of them because of the job protections available in public service agencies. Amendola, Weber, and Mercer (1998) set the tone of this chapter:

> Is it always possible to accurately predict the future behavior of an employee? The short answer is no, but there are certainly ways to increase your odds. The stinging consequences of police misconduct are provoking many law enforcement agencies to re-evaluate their personnel selection, training, and employment standards. (p. 2)

Consequently, a screening process based on professional principles is important if agencies are going to hire the people most likely to become ethical, productive, and physically and psychologically healthy officers. There are four reasons for agencies to be enlightened in this regard:

- Contemporary law enforcement is faced with infinitely more challenges than it was even 10 years ago.
- Problematic officers divert attention and resources from the daily demands of the job, which are sufficiently challenging in themselves.
- The expense incurred in recruiting, training, and supervising officers through their probationary period can be many thousands of dollars, money that is lost every time an officer leaves the agency.
- Because officers within the agency usually fill promotional openings, the selection process not only determines the agency's recruits but often its future leaders.

The effective selection of candidates, however, is easier said than done. In good economic times people who would be excellent law enforcement candidates often take their talents into careers whose pay and benefits clearly surpass those offered by many, if not most, law enforcement agencies, whereas in bad economic times many people who normally would never consider going into law enforcement apply for jobs simply for the sake of financial security. Unfortunately, the question often becomes not how high to set the bar but how low to set it and still get acceptable candidates.

Historically, a dramatic improvement has occurred in law enforcement hiring procedures. In the early days, people could get a job in law enforcement by being politically connected and making a donation to local politicians' coffers. This "selection process" often, though by no means always, attracted men who were primarily interested in job security, not a few of whom increased their income by behaving in ethically and legally corrupt ways.

Fifty years ago, the selection of officers, even in large agencies, sometimes consisted of a 10-minute interview with the chief during which he made the hiring decision based on the most subjective criteria imaginable, such as a firm handshake. After passing this interview, the candidate was sworn in and given a uniform and gun, even in cases in which the candidate had never held a gun, much less fired one. Although this kind of selection process can still be found in some sections of the country, for the most part the situation has improved dramatically. It seems fair to state that the process is 50 percent better than it was in "the good old days," but often 50 percent short of where it should be in a professional organization. More and Wegener (1992) describe one of the primary challenges in selecting law enforcement officers in today's world:

> Police administrators must come to grips with one simple fact of life. They are dealing with a new breed of employee. Modern police personnel are more sophisticated than their predecessors. They are better educated, more participative, and much less resistant to change. They demand respect and expect to be treated as professionals. While money is still a magical word in the police subculture, it has a much different meaning than it did a generation ago. Salaries and fringe benefits have been improved to the point where more money, in and of itself, no longer serves as the primary motivator. Police officers demand more. Most of them want to do meaningful work that meets their conscious and subconscious higher order needs for growth, self-esteem, and a sense of fulfillment. (pp. 173–174)

Therefore, the overall objective of this chapter is to focus on professionalizing these procedures so that the quality of present and future law enforcement officers can improve significantly. To this end, the following topics will be discussed: the selection process, employment interview, background investigation, and psychological screening.

THE SELECTION PROCESS: AN OVERVIEW

Before deciding on the criteria to be used for selecting candidates, law enforcement agencies should consider the following topics that are basic to the hiring process.

Legal Aspects of Employee Selection

The legal factors involved in the hiring process are varied and complex and should be fully understood by those involved in the hiring of law enforcement candidates. The following are a few basic legal considerations pertaining to federal law.

The Civil Rights Act, Title VII (1964, amended 1972) prohibits unfair discrimination based on race, religion, color, sex, and national origin. People in these categories are referred to as "protected groups."

The Age Discrimination in Employment Act (1967) prohibits discrimination against applicants or employees age 40 or older. This means that an agency cannot legally reject candidates who are 40 years of age or older simply because of their age unless it can be proven that these people cannot perform the essential functions of the job for reasons not related to age.

The Uniform Guidelines on Employee Selection Procedures (1978) prohibits the use of a selection procedure that creates an adverse (disparate) impact on a protected class, unless justified by demonstrated job relatedness or business necessity. Adverse impact is legally determined by the four-fifths rule, which requires that the percentage of candidates selected from a protected class must be at least four-fifths (80 percent) of hires from any other group. For example, if 50 percent of the white applicants for a position are hired, 40 percent of the applicants from the protected class must be hired.

The Americans with Disabilities Act (1990) prohibits employers from discriminating against qualified individuals with disabilities; that is, those who can perform the essential functions of the job with, or without, reasonable accommodation. This act also prohibits asking about medical and psychological conditions in tests or interviews before a conditional job offer. Even if the candidate volunteers this information, interviewers are not permitted to pursue the topic and must move the interview in another direction.

Although inquiries about race, ethnicity, or age generally are not expressly prohibited under law, asking such questions may well raise red flags in the candidate as well as any oversight agency that reviews the hiring process. The reason is that it brings up this issue: Why is the agency asking these questions if its conscious or unconscious intent is not to discriminate against people in these protected classes? It is also important to understand that, in addition to federal laws, state and municipal laws may apply to employment selection. For example, some states include homosexuals as a protected class.

The conditional job offer.   A conditional job offer is made when the candidate has successfully cleared all the hurdles up to the point at which the agency must elicit information regarding the candidate's physical and mental health. At this point, the Americans with Disabilities Act requires an organization to make a conditional job offer to the candidate. In other words, a job offer is made on the condition that the candidate can pass physical and psychological examinations that assess abilities and attributes necessary to perform the essential functions of the job. It is only at this point that candidates can be asked questions relating to possible physical and psychological disabilities that may or may not disqualify the candidate from being given a final job offer.

Before a conditional job offer is made, agency personnel may inquire about a candidate's ability to perform specific job tasks but not about the possibility of the presence of a physical or psychological disability that could disqualify the candidate. For example, a legitimate question might be: "If this room were on fire, could you drag me out of it to safety?" whereas an illegitimate question might be: "Do you have any physical condition that would make it difficult or impossible to drag me out of this room?" Although these differences may seem subtle, they are nevertheless important to understand if a selection process is to be legally defensible.

Essential job functions.   The only purpose of an employment selection process is to predict future performance. In other words, it asks this question: Will this candidate be able to perform the essential functions of the job? If any segment of the selection process does not address this question, it does not belong in the process and may well be illegal.

Various methods can determine the essential functions of a job. One way is to perform a task analysis that involves having employees already in the job compile a list of tasks critical to its successful performance and have them rate each task on a scale as to its frequency and importance for job success. In addition to a task analysis, supervisors and their employees can complete inventories, such as the Position Analysis Questionnaire, the Job Elements Inventory, the Fleishman Job Analysis Survey, and the Personality-Related Position Requirements Form. These inventories can provide the agency with a list of essential job functions.

Approach to Selection

Selection in law enforcement today typically operates according to a multiple hurdles approach, which means that candidates must clear a number of hurdles before being hired. There are two reasons for the large number of hurdles, certainly far more than would be present in the selection process for most jobs. First, agencies want to hire the top people for the job, those with the highest qualifications who will best fit the needs of the particular agency.

The second reason is that agencies want to avoid negligent hiring lawsuits, meaning that if an organization hires someone it should have known had problems, and those problems surface after the officer is hired, the organization can be sued for any subsequent damage the officer causes, often for large amounts of money.

Failing to clear any one of the hurdles disqualifies the candidate from further participation in the process, regardless of how many hurdles were previously cleared or how well they were cleared.

The number and sequence of hurdles may differ slightly from one agency to another, but the following is a typical sequence:

1. Assessment of application forms and résumés
2. Physical agility test
3. Agency oral and/or written examination
4. Background investigation and polygraph test
5. Conditional offer of employment
6. Psychological examination
7. Medical examination

The rationale underlying the sequence of hurdles is that they rank from the least to the most costly to administer. Additionally, the Americans with Disabilities Act requires a conditional offer of employment before prospective employees take psychological and medical examinations.

Typically, law enforcement agencies use a "weeding out" and "screening in" process in which only poor candidates are weeded out and all other candidates are screened in. This creates significant problems because borderline candidates are accepted and often become problematic officers. A more professional approach aims at screening in only good candidates and weeding out both borderline and poor candidates. This process may reduce the number of candidates, but those selected will be more qualified and more likely to become effective officers. The larger the candidate pool, the more freedom the agency has to disqualify borderline candidates.

The selection process has also become more complicated in the last decade because of the increased interest in the screening process due to egregious misconduct by officers in high-profile cases. This has caused the focus to be on screening out candidates likely to participate in unethical and illegal conduct. However, the focus must also be extended to candidates whose abilities to think clearly, feel compassionately, and act responsibly are suspect. It is not only unethical officers that create serious problems; it is also officers who, while ethical, make unbelievably poor decisions in their professional and personal lives.

In summary, there are at least two basic reasons to take only the best candidates. One is moral—it is the right thing to do. The second is utilitarian—agencies are increasingly being held liable for the behaviors of the officers they hire and retain (see *Bonsignore* v. *The City of New York*, 1981).

Agency Self-examination

Before launching out on recruitment drives, law enforcement agencies need to do some serious soul-searching as to not only what candidates can offer the agency but also what the agency can offer the candidates. A good match between a candidate and an agency is a two-way proposition. If all an agency can offer a candidate is a badge, a gun, and some power and excitement, it may well discourage the right people from applying and encourage the wrong ones.

Administrators and recruiting officers can ask themselves some questions as part of the self-examination process.

- Why would the kind of person we want to recruit (bright, enthusiastic, open-minded, educated, innovative, assertive, motivated) want to join our agency?
- Would I encourage my son or daughter, husband or wife, to join our agency?
- Would the kind of person the agency wants to recruit enjoy working:
  - In the physical environment of our facilities?
  - In our organizational culture?
  - Under our command structure?
  - In an agency with our turnover and promotion rates?
  - For an agency that offers our salary and benefits?
  - For an agency that treats its rank-and-file officers the way we do?
  - For an agency with our respect for education, including continuing education?
  - For an agency that has our reputation?
- Would the agency feel comfortable having candidates meet privately with a representative sample of its rank-and-file officers to learn more about the agency than is included in recruiting brochures?

The basic point is one that is commonly ignored in the recruitment of candidates: Is the exchange ratio between what successful candidates will give to, and receive from, the agency equal, or is the agency getting a much better deal?

Realistic Job Preview

One method of looking out for the interests of candidates as well as those of the agency is to give candidates a realistic job preview. Many businesses have discovered that these previews help weed out candidates who will not be satisfied working for the organization and screen in those with realistic expectations of what working for the organization will entail.

A realistic job preview can be provided in an interview, or through brochures or videotapes that offer an honest, objective, and realistic picture of what awaits candidates who are accepted into the agency. In addition to the attractive aspects of law enforcement, this procedure reviews the less attractive ones, such as the real possibility of working shifts that disrupt family life, being assigned duties that candidates may not only lack interest in but also actively dislike, being assigned to partners with whom the candidate has nothing in common, working in high-risk situations, witnessing a good deal of pain and suffering, having to work on legal and family holidays, working hard on a daily basis to get a promotion that may take many years to receive, having to spend significant portions of each shift writing reports.

Administrators and recruiting officers may respond to the idea of a realistic job preview by stating: "If we were to do this, we'd lose most of our candidate pool." If this statement is true, the agency needs to be overhauled from top to bottom if it realistically expects to attract and retain good candidates. If the statement is false, there is no reason not to give prospective candidates all the information they need to make an informed decision. The agency may lose some good prospects, but it also will gain candidates with a realistic view of the agency who are more likely to be satisfied with the job and remain with the agency for a longer period of time.

As Schultz and Schultz (2001, p. 66) indicate, an analysis of 40 studies on realistic job previews found them to have a significant positive correlation with subsequent job performance. Those who participated in realistic job previews tended to have lower initial expectations of the job and lower turnover rates. One study indicates employees given brochures that provided realistic job previews were only half as likely to quit their jobs as those who were not given the brochures.

Personal Reflections

1. What are your thoughts about the legal aspects of candidate selection? Do you agree with the laws and guidelines discussed in the chapter and, if not, why not?

2. Does the multiple hurdles approach seem valid to you, or would you like to see a different method used?

3. Why would you, or anyone, want to go into law enforcement today?

4. What do you think about the realistic job preview? Can you think of a legitimate reason why it should not be done?

5. What are some reasons that a candidate with good intelligence and physical and mental health might not become a good law enforcement officer?

THE EMPLOYMENT INTERVIEW

Interviewing candidates is one of the most important parts of the selection process because it gives the agency an opportunity to see firsthand how candidates relate on several levels in a moderately stressful situation. Unfortunately, too often law enforcement interviews are not guided by professional interviewing principles and techniques. Typically, most employment interviews are notoriously lacking in validity and reliability. In fact, Aamodt (1999) states:

> Because the interview is the most commonly used method to select employees, it might logically follow that it must be the most effective. Unfortunately, most evidence suggests otherwise. The typical unstructured interview is a poor predictor of future employee performance. . . . Does this mean that the interview is useless as a predictor of employee performance? Not at all; it just means that care must be taken to ensure that interview questions and decisions are job related. (pp. 171, 173)

For this reason, this section will deal extensively with interviewing in a professional manner in order to make the process more effective and productive, and also to give people considering law enforcement as a career some idea of what to expect in the interview process so they can prepare well for it.

Interview Validity

Interview validity refers to how well an interview actually measures what it claims to measure. For example, law enforcement interviews generally are aimed at measuring qualities such as intelligence, motivation, judgment, communication, assertiveness, trainability, and integrity. The challenge is to create a process that will *actually measure* these characteristics, not simply look as though it does.

The only way to ensure interview validity, or at least to take major strides in that direction, is to keep two clear images in mind. One image is that of the essential functions of the specific job in the particular agency for which the candidate is interviewing; the other image is that of the particular candidate. If there is a good match between the two, the person is likely to be a good candidate for the position; if there is not a good match, the person is likely to be a poor candidate. What appears to be a simple proposition is, in fact, quite complex. For example, when there are three interviewers on a panel, each may have a different image of what the job entails, and all three may have very different images of the candidate by the end of the interview. This means that three different pictures of the job must be matched to three different pictures of the candidate, an exercise bound to lead to an interview with very low validity.

This process can be improved through research, critical thinking, and open discussion before the interviews to arrive at a consensus regarding the essential job functions in the particular agency. A consensus as to the specific competencies and attributes that the job-related tasks require should also be established. This is easier said than done and is a theme to be addressed throughout this section.

Interview Reliability

There are two kinds of interview reliability: intra-interviewer reliability and inter-interviewer reliability.

Intra-interviewer reliability refers to each interviewer being internally consistent. For example, if interviewers use problem-solving ability as a measure of intelligence, they must use it for all the candidates. An interviewer cannot use problem solving with the first candidate, logical thinking with the second, and articulateness with the third candidate and have a reliable interview process.

Inter-interviewer reliability refers to how consistent a panel of interviewers is among its members. For example, one interviewer always uses problem-solving ability as a measure of intelligence, a second interviewer always uses logical thinking, and a third always uses articulateness. While the interviewers may have intra-interviewer reliability because each one judges every candidate by the same criterion, the panel of interviewers lacks inter-interviewer reliability because they are each holding candidates to a different standard of intelligence.

Figure 5.1 is a good example of what happens when interviewers lack both intra-interviewer and inter-interviewer reliability across a wide range of unstructured interviews. In this classic study (Hollingworth, 1929), 12 experienced sales managers interviewed 57 applicants in unstructured interviews as to their potential to become successful salespeople. As can be seen, the interviewer ratings *of the same candidate* ranged from a low of 1 to a high of 55. These results clearly demonstrate that experienced interviewers are not necessarily competent ones and contribute to the low reliability as well as low validity of unstructured interviews.

Interviewer-training workshops are the most effective method of learning professional interview techniques, and some of the issues they cover will be addressed and evaluated in this section. Students who have a long future of job interviews ahead of them, either in law enforcement or other careers, also can consider this material as an aid in preparing for and succeeding in interviews.

Any interview technique should be measured against the following criteria.

- How much information is likely to be gained?
- What specific kinds of information are likely to be gained?
- How much stress will the candidate generally experience?
- How valid and reliable is the technique likely to be?
- Who controls the interview, the candidate or the interviewers?
- How much "truth" is likely to be elicited from the candidate?
- What is the likelihood of legal challenges arising?
- How complicated is the technique?
- How much time, effort, and money does it require?

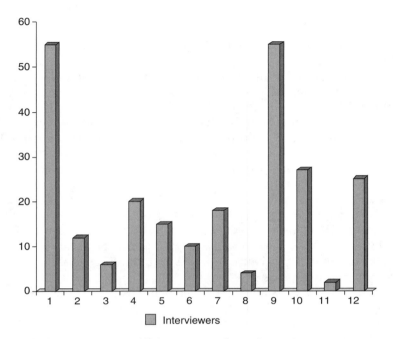

FIGURE 5.1 Ratings of the same applicant by 12 interviewers.
Source: From H. L. Hollingworth, *Vocational Psychology and Character Analysis* (New York: Appleton, 1929), p. 132.

The Unstructured Interview

The unstructured interview, as the name implies, lacks standardization both in content and sequence. Interviewers on the same panel ask whatever questions occur to them at any point in time and in no particular sequence; some questions may be followed up and others may not. It is conceivable that six different candidates could be interviewed by the same panel on the same day for 45 minutes each and never be asked the same question.

The time frame also is not standardized, meaning that some interviews by the same panel last 30 minutes, others 40 minutes, and still others 50 minutes. Nor is the scoring standardized. Some interviewers give the heaviest weight to integrity, others to intelligence, and still others to assertiveness. Typically, candidates are rated according to gut feelings or intuition, which is based on vaguely defined criteria, such as attractiveness, intelligence, character, or personality.

Although unstructured interviews are by far the most common because they require no preparation and little thought, they have low validity and reliability and are a fertile ground for lawsuits.

The Structured Interview

In the structured interview, the questions are job related, precisely phrased, and asked in the same sequence to every candidate, whether there are two candidates or two thousand. The time frame is exactly the same for each candidate, because each is asked the same questions and allotted the same amount of time to answer them. The scoring is standardized in that there are specific behaviors being evaluated—for example, the ability to communicate clearly—and each behavior is allotted the same range of points—for example, 1 point for a poor response, 3 points for an average response, and 5 points for a good response. In other words, every candidate for the job goes through the same interview, even if there are several different teams of interviewers, which is not ideal but sometimes necessary. Although no two interviews, regardless of how well standardized, will be exactly the same, these procedures generally double the validity and reliability of structured interviews over unstructured interviews (Huffutt & Hunter, 1994).

There are three types of structured interviews.

The broad-focused interview.   This is aimed at obtaining a general picture of the candidate. The questions follow this theme: Tell us who you are so we can match the picture you give us with the picture we have of the job for which you are applying. It is important to keep in mind that these questions follow all the standardized procedures mentioned above. In other words, they are job related, phrased precisely, asked in the same sequence within the same time frame, and scored according to a set of established criteria. They are not simply commonsense questions, asked randomly by different interviewers over varying periods of time.

Here are examples of some typical questions:

- How did you come to be interested in law enforcement?
- What do you know about law enforcement?
- Why do you want to become a law enforcement officer?
- How long have you been interested in law enforcement?
- Why do you think you would be a good law enforcement officer?
- Assuming you would not be a perfect officer at the time of hire, what are a few things you would have to work on to become a good officer?
- What prior experiences in your life do you believe would help you be a good officer?
- What would be your favorite assignment in law enforcement?
- What do you think you would like best and least about law enforcement?

Although these are not very sophisticated or penetrating questions, they can yield some significant information regarding intelligence, articulateness, self-confidence, affability, seriousness of purpose, and the ability to remain focused on a task.

Note that all the questions are *job related.* There are no questions such as these: What are your hobbies? What kind of books do you read? What kind of friends do you have? What does your father do? If you had to be a vegetable, what kind would you be?

The advantage of the broad-focused interview method is that the format is simple to use once a consensus is reached regarding the questions and scoring procedures. The disadvantage is that these questions hand over control to the candidate in a relatively stress-free encounter, which means there will not be an opportunity to assess the candidate's behavior under stress. The broad-focused interviewers should not be the same as those used in the following types of interviews because the information elicited could be prejudicial and positively or negatively affect the objectivity of the interviewers using other methods.

The past-focused interview. This focuses on real past events in the candidate's life, the purpose of which is to ascertain how the candidate handled them. Typically, the interviewers arrive at a consensus regarding a list of job-related competencies on which to evaluate the candidate. A sample list might include integrity, assertiveness, judgment, intelligence, and stress tolerance.

The interviewers then go down the list and ask the candidates to describe real-life situations in which they have been involved, in which one of the competencies on the list was at issue. A typical scenario would be this: "We are going to ask you about some real-life situations you've faced as an adult and ask you to describe one incident you handled well and another you handled poorly. For example, tell us about a situation in which you were honest when you didn't have to be and one in which you were dishonest." A standard follow-up question after the admission of not handling a situation well is this: "Why did you handle it that way and what, if anything, would you do if you were faced with the same situation today?"

The main object of this type of interview is to discover how the candidate reacted to real-life situations in terms of a number of job-related competencies. The expected result is that, after four to six scenarios, the candidate will reveal some strengths and weaknesses that can be matched with some critical law enforcement functions.

The advantage of this method is that it taps into actual behaviors and demonstrates how the candidates think and feel about job-related situations. The disadvantage is that the candidates may take inordinate amounts of time racking their brains for relevant situations, which could use up valuable interview time. Other possible disadvantages are that the candidate may censor past situations in order to look good, and that invasions of privacy could inadvertently occur, depending on the nature of the situations candidates dredge up.

The future-focused (situational) interview. This involves asking hypothetical questions dealing with the future. The theme is this: What would you do if you found yourself in a situation in which. . . ? There are several steps in the development of this method.

First, supervisors in a representative sample of departments within the agency are asked to list the essential job functions that officers are required to perform. For example, a patrol supervisor may list "using discretion" as one of the functions.

The essential job function is then translated into a question: "What would you do if you went to a domestic disturbance call where a husband and wife had been arguing? Both have scratches and bruises on their arms where they grabbed each other. Both cool down when you arrive, and neither wishes any action to be taken. They have three small children and no relatives or friends in the area. You have three choices: arrest both of them, arrest one but not the other, or arrest neither. What do you do?"

Next, the supervisors brainstorm to arrive at benchmark answers; that is, those that would be given by good, average, and poor officers. For example, they may decide that a good officer would arrest neither party, ensure the peace, and refer the couple to social services. The average officer would arrest the party who inflicted the most damage and leave the other to care for the children. The poor officer would arrest both parties and call protective services to take the children.

After arriving at benchmark answers, the supervisors can brainstorm for sample follow-up (probe) questions: "Why did you take the action you took? OK, you would not arrest anyone. But the law says if a party inflicts observable physical damage to another, arrest is mandatory. *Now* what would you do?"

Scores can then be assigned to the scenario and follow-up questions. For example, a good answer would merit 5 points, an average one 3 points, and a poor one 1 point. A score of 4 can be given for answers that fall between 3 and 5, and a 2 is given for answers that fall between 1 and 3.

Finally, the benchmark answers are validated by interviewing a representative group of officers who have been ranked as good, average, or poor by their supervisors or by some other criteria to see whether their answers match the hypothesized good, average, or poor officer responses. In cases in which the statistical correlations are high, the benchmark answer is validated and kept. If matches are low, the answer is discarded and a new one tried until all the benchmark answers have been highly validated. Once the validation process is completed, the scenarios and follow-up questions can be used in actual employment interviews.

The advantages of future-focused interviews are that they present situations that officers face daily and hence are job related. This method places a healthy degree of stress on the candidates and tests their ability to think, act, and communicate under pressure. Moreover, it is legally defensible because the questions are derived from research on people who are sworn officers. Finally, as long as the job remains the same, the scenarios can be used year after year.

One disadvantage of situational interviews is that they take a long time to develop and validate, a task best left to professional researchers. Also, depending on the time allotted for the interview, often only two to four scenarios can be presented. While a good deal of information can be gleaned that cannot be obtained from other methods, the information is more narrowly focused than it is, for example, in the broad-focused interview.

Leaderless Groups

Interviewing by the use of leaderless groups consists of randomly assigning five to eight candidates to a group with no leader. Two to four interviewers present the group with two to four problems to solve, depending on the amount of time allotted for the interview. The candidates must all work together within a specific time frame to form a consensus as to how to solve the problem.

An example of a problem might be this: "You are members of a street gangs task force, and your sergeant is a great guy. He's smart, tough, courageous, but also genuinely cares about each of you, both professionally and personally, and has bailed you out of trouble on more than one occasion. One night, after a violent struggle with a gang member who resisted arrest, the gang member who had been handcuffed spit on the sergeant. In response, your sergeant flung the gang member to the ground, where his head hit the curb, placing him in a life-threatening coma. No one other than your unit witnessed this incident. You have 15 minutes to decide how your team will present what happened at the scene to a group of internal affairs investigators who will question you separately. It is your responsibility to keep the discussion on track and end the discussion on time."

Before the session, the interviewers have reached a consensus as to what scenarios to use, what job-related behaviors to look for, and how the scoring will be done. Each candidate is scored, for example, on a scale of 1 to 5 on each of five, six, or seven job-related behaviors, such as articulateness, assertiveness, integrity, sociability, leadership, stress tolerance, ability to listen, mediation, and problem solving.

The advantages of this interview method are that it creates a real-life situation in which candidates must both cooperate and compete with each other under pressure. It also is economical in terms of time in that as many as eight candidates can be interviewed in the same period it takes to have one individual interview.

One disadvantage of this procedure is that although the scenarios and scoring can be standardized across groups, the group members cannot be standardized. In other words, one group may be a "dead group," in which one member emerges as a star, whereas in a "live group" the same member would come across as only average or even poor. Another disadvantage is that some candidates may not do well in a group setting but would flourish working alone or with one or two partners. When this is the case, these candidates would be at a marked disadvantage.

Assessment Centers

Assessment centers were originally used only in promotion examinations but recently have been used in the entry-level selection process because of their relatively high validity. An assessment center creates an environment that mimics functioning in the real world of work. Scenarios based on a wide range of job-related tasks and played out by actors are presented to the candidates. Over the course of a day, candidates participate in six to eight exercises in which, for example, they may have to counsel a juvenile, mediate a dispute between people of different races, present a talk to high school students, write a police report on an incident the candidate observed, confront a partner about an unethical act, interview a rape victim, and so on.

Like standardized interviews, all the candidates get the same scenarios, in the same sequence, are scored according to the same criteria and, ideally, by the same assessors.

Examples of job-related scoring criteria could be the abilities to

- Plan, organize, prioritize
- Make good decisions in a timely manner
- Function well under stress
- Relate well with others, including authority
- Be tough minded, yet compassionate
- Communicate well
- Be observant
- Facilitate difficult situations

The assessors should be carefully selected and formally trained. Often a panel of assessors comprises agency personnel, personnel from an outside agency, mental health professionals, and local citizens who have an understanding of the type of officers their community needs.

The advantages of assessment centers are that they simulate real-life situations that candidates will confront in law enforcement and also place candidates under stress in order to see how they respond. The scenarios sample a wide range of behavior, which gives candidates the feeling that they have been tested in a legitimate way. The disadvantages are that assessment centers require a great deal of thoughtful preparation, time, energy, and several assessors and actors to be available on a continuing basis.

The following table represents the validity coefficients of various selection techniques. These coefficients represent the effectiveness of these techniques in predicting future job performance (Aamodt, 1999, p. 131).

Selection Technique	Validity
Structured interviews	.51
Cognitive ability tests	.51
Assessment centers	.37
Personality tests (conscientiousness)	.31
Unstructured interviews	.23
Reference checks	.16
Application blank	.10
Handwriting analysis	.00
Projective personality tests	.00

Problems in Interviewing

Professionally trained interviewers are aware of errors that can significantly diminish the validity and reliability of interviews. The following are some of the more common ones.

Prior knowledge bias. When interviewers gain information about the candidate from sources outside of the actual interview, it can consciously or unconsciously interfere with their objectivity. For this reason, interviewers should not be privy to the candidate's résumé, application forms, autobiography, and so on. Questions about these issues should be dealt with in a different forum, for example, the human resources department.

Contrast error. This error can occur when a candidate is contrasted with the previous candidate. For example, candidates who immediately follow excellent candidates may receive a lower grade than they would if they had followed average or poor candidates and vice versa.

Interviewer prejudice. Interviewers can have the same racial, gender, religious, and political prejudices as anyone else. For example, interviewers who do not believe women or homosexuals should be in law enforcement will likely reflect these attitudes in their evaluations even though these characteristics are not job related.

Negative information bias. Interviewers tend to weigh negative information revealed by candidates more heavily than positive information. For example, a drunk driving arrest five years prior to the interview may be more heavily weighted than a commendation for saving a life during the same period.

Primacy error. The impression the candidate makes in the first minutes of the interview often colors the remainder of the interview. A good first impression can overshadow negative information later in the interview, and a poor first impression can overshadow later positive information.

Intuition error. Many interviewers, perhaps especially those in law enforcement, believe they have a sixth sense for sizing up people based on many years of dealing with the public. As will be discussed in Chapter 8, Interviewing Suspects, law enforcement officers are no more successful than anyone else at "seeing through" people.

Similarity error. Candidates who are similar to the interviewer are likely to be ranked more highly than those who are dissimilar. For example, white male college-educated interviewers are likely to rate candidates who share these characteristics higher than candidates who, for example, are black females without a college education.

Overemphasizing nonverbal behavior. Interviewers may tend to read too much into the candidate's nonverbal behavior, such as poor eye contact necessarily meaning the candidate is lying, or crossed arms necessarily indicating the candidate is being defensive. Interpretations of nonverbal behavior are as likely to be incorrect as correct.

Halo error. A positive halo error occurs when interviewers form a strong positive impression based on one piece of information and allow it to overshadow negative information. For example, the fact that a candidate was an all-state athlete in high school may overshadow the fact that he flunked out of college.

A negative halo error occurs when interviewers form a strong negative impression based on one piece of information and allow it to overshadow positive information. For example, the fact that a candidate flunked out of college two years prior overshadows the fact that she has become serious about her life and worked productively since then.

Inter-interviewer conflict. Sometimes interviewers on the same panel simply do not like each other and so, at least unconsciously, give lower ratings to candidates that the disliked interviewer seems to like. For example, a feminist interviewer may rate poorly a male candidate that a macho male officer obviously likes.

One of the problems with interviewer errors is that they are often unconscious and, therefore, not self-correctable. However, evidence indicates that workshops in error avoidance can reduce some errors as much as 90 percent (Wexley, Yukl, Kovacs, & Sanders, 1972).

Conclusion

The following points can help interviewers increase their professionalism.

1. Personal opinions of the ideal candidate for a career in law enforcement should be ignored and replaced by this question: Does the candidate meet the essential job functions of the position? Whoever else the candidate is or is not cannot be considered when evaluating the candidate.

2. Standardization is a critical element that applies to *all* valid and reliable interview methods. Every candidate must have virtually the same interview experience, so that the interviews are reliable and provide a level playing field for all candidates.

3. Interviewers should realize that their verbal and nonverbal behavior can significantly influence the candidate, for better or for worse. For this

reason, interviewers should assume a consistently professional demeanor with all candidates, friendly but businesslike, much the same as a physician who has a pleasant manner but also has a serious job to do. Candidates should leave the interview not having the slightest idea of how well they did based on the reactions of the interviewers.

4. Interviewers are responsible for providing all candidates with a professional interview environment that is comfortable, quiet, neat, smoke-free, and devoid of interruptions and distractions.

5. Interviewers should score each answer immediately after it is given rather than at the end of the interview to avoid forgetting pertinent information and being influenced by the opinions of other interviewers before the final scoring is done. Discussion of the candidate's performance should only be held *after* all the scoring is finished, so that one interviewer does not unduly influence the others.

6. Interviewers should not try to reach a consensus in scoring candidates. Instead, each interviewer's scores should be averaged with those of the other interviewers.

7. Interviewers should never ask unscripted questions, not even "Just out of curiosity. . ." questions, or make unscripted comments to a candidate, no matter how neutral sounding or well intentioned. Even departing remarks should be the same for all candidates. As a proper conclusion, interviewers can thank candidates for coming to the interview and having an interest in the agency. Telling candidates they did a good job or otherwise indicating that they passed the interview is ill advised, especially if they did not pass the interview.

8. Interviewers must decide how to record the interview. Two schools of thought exist regarding this. One holds that the more that is recorded, the better, which means videotaping the interview in a way that the faces of both the candidate and interviewers appear on tape. The other school holds that record keeping should be minimal, which means it is restricted to the scoring forms and attached comments, if any. This decision should be made only after consulting legal counsel and agency executives.

Employment interviewing is serious business, especially in law enforcement, because the stakes are high. Hiring the wrong person or not hiring the right person can be costly to the agency in terms of reputation and lawsuits. Therefore, job interviewing is not for amateurs, nor for agencies that lack the commitment or resources to do them professionally. The agency's responsibility is to select interviewers based on professional training and interviewing experience rather than on years of service or demonstrated interest in interviewing. Hopefully, the time will come when interviewers will be required to have at least the same amount of formal training and certificates as field training officers and background investigators often do.

Personal Reflections

1. Think back on your previous job interviews. What type were they, and how valid and reliable do you think they were?

2. What do you think your strong and weak points would be as a person being interviewed? How can you work on the weak points?

3. Consider the types of interviews discussed. (a) Which do you think would be the most effective at distinguishing good from poor candidates? (b) Which would you prefer to go through?

4. What kinds of people do you think should not be chosen as interviewers?

5. Of the ten problems in interviewing, which three do you think probably occur the most frequently? Why do you think they do?

THE BACKGROUND INVESTIGATION

The background investigation of candidates is a critical part of the selection process according to this principle: The best predictor of future performance is past performance. The traditional objectives of a background check can be framed in two questions:

- Can the candidate function on a level of performance required in law enforcement?

- Does the candidate have the integrity necessary for a career in law enforcement?

The answers to these questions are sought from the significant people in the candidate's life, such as relatives, teachers, employers, or neighbors. Obviously, the answers to these questions are important, but they also fail to present as full a picture of the candidate as could be developed in a background investigation.

The main problems with typical background investigations are fourfold. First, they are often done in a cursory way, either because of the large number of candidates and the few investigators available to do them, or because the investigators are untrained or lazy. Second, background investigations often take so long that the agency is forced to hire candidates before the background checks are completed.

A third problem is that background investigations are often perceived as a tool to exclude candidates, rather than as an instrument for screening in only the best candidates. Many candidates pass their background checks because they are "not bad" rather than because they are "very good."

Finally, confusion often exists about what can be legally asked during a background investigation, especially since the Americans with Disabilities Act was enacted. In one sense, the questions allowed depend on whether the background check is done before or after a conditional offer of employment. In either case, however, a general principle can be helpful: Do not ask direct questions of the candidate or respondents (those contacted for references with respect to the candidate) regarding the candidate's physical or mental health. Those questions should be left to physicians and mental health professionals. However, if necessary, the investigator can pose job-related scenarios that can elicit pertinent information: for example, a respondent may be asked: "If Joe had to climb over a typical backyard fence to catch a suspect, how easily do you think he could do it?"

Background investigations can be enhanced with relative ease by standardizing the ratings of investigators and respondents. This would avoid the haphazard approach to background checks that has often been the case, as well as put a great deal of information about the candidate into a meaningful whole.

The following example of how this could be done applies only to rating the candidate's personality and behavior as it relates to law enforcement, and does not include other important areas that should be covered in background checks, such as family; employment, medical, legal, and credit history; driving record; and military background. Respondents can be given or sent the following form (see Box 5.1).

Box 5.1

Background Investigation: Respondent's Rating of Candidate

Candidate:_____ Respondent:_____ Date:_____

Thank you for taking the time to answer a few questions that will help us get to know the candidate better. Please be completely honest in your responses, so our picture will be as accurate as possible. Your responses will be added to those of many other people before we make a final decision with respect to the candidate.

1. In what capacity have you known the candidate (relative, teacher, employer, friend, etc.)?_____
2. How long have you known the candidate (answer in terms of months or years)?_____
3. How well do you know the candidate? Choose *only* from very well, moderately well, not well._____
4. When was your last meaningful contact with the candidate?_____

Please rank the candidate on the following behaviors on the following scale:

Low	Below Average	Average	Above Average	High
1	2	3	4	5

Write the appropriate ranking number in the box that follows the behavior being rated. For example, if you rank the candidate high in integrity, write a 5 in the box following integrity. Each of the 20 behaviors to be ranked is followed by words or phrases that clarify the meaning of that behavior. If you feel you are not in a position to judge the candidate on a specific behavior, place an "X" in the box.

1. Adaptability ❑
   - flexible
   - not rigid
2. Alertness ❑
   - observes details
   - responds rapidly to situations
   - anticipates situations
3. Appearance ❑
   - neat and clean
   - appropriate demeanor
   - appears confident
4. Assertiveness ❑
   - confronts difficult people and situations
   - takes charge when appropriate
5. Independence ❑
   - self-directing
   - has own ideas and values
   - resists social pressures
6. Industriousness ❑
   - hardworking
   - committed
   - enthusiastic
7. Integrity ❑
   - honest
   - fair
   - ethical
8. Intelligence ❑
   - learns quickly
   - problem solves
   - remembers well
9. Judgment ❑
   - makes thoughtful decisions
   - uses discretion
   - considers consequences of acts

10. Leadership   ❏
    - seeks leadership positions
    - sought out for leadership positions
    - accepted by others as a leader

11. Mental Health   ❏
    - rational thinking
    - accurate perception of reality
    - emotional stability

12. Open-mindedness   ❏
    - open to new ideas
    - open to changing behavior
    - open to different lifestyles

13. Responsibility   ❏
    - dependable
    - meets deadlines
    - accepts accountability for actions

14. Sensitivity   ❏
    - aware of people's feelings
    - compassion for less fortunate

15. Sociability   ❏
    - relates well to others
    - interested in people
    - accepted by others

16. Stress Tolerance   ❏
    - reacts to stress well
    - does not become flustered
    - energized by stressors

17. Trainability   ❏
    - wants to learn
    - admits mistakes
    - learns from mistakes

18. Trustworthiness   ❏
    - keeps promises
    - keeps confidences
    - does not backstab

19. Verbal Skills   ❏
    - uses correct grammar
    - can be clearly understood
    - speaks confidently

20. Writing Skills
   - spells correctly
   - uses proper grammar
   - writes clearly and understandably

If you would like to clarify any of your responses or add comments, please feel free to do so.

After background investigators receive these rating scales from the respondents, they can average them, using the following format in Box 5.2.

Box 5.2

Computation of Respondents' Ratings by the Investigator

Candidate:_____ Investigator:_____ Date:_____

Following are the *averages* of the ratings that respondents gave to the above candidate. Each item reflects the average score from the respondents who gave a numerical score for the item. No items given an "X" (no knowledge) are used in computing the average. These ratings are divided into three groups of respondents:

- Knows the candidate well
- Knows the candidate moderately well
- Does not know the candidate well

	Well	*Moderately*	*Not Very Well*
Adaptability	❑	❑	❑
Alertness	❑	❑	❑
Appearance	❑	❑	❑
Assertiveness	❑	❑	❑
Independence	❑	❑	❑
Industriousness	❑	❑	❑
Integrity	❑	❑	❑
Intelligence	❑	❑	❑
Judgment	❑	❑	❑
Leadership	❑	❑	❑
Mental Health	❑	❑	❑
Open-mindedness	❑	❑	❑
Responsibility	❑	❑	❑

	Well	*Moderately*	*Not Very Well*
Sensitivity	❑	❑	❑
Sociability	❑	❑	❑
Stress Tolerance	❑	❑	❑
Trainability	❑	❑	❑
Trustworthiness	❑	❑	❑
Verbal Skills	❑	❑	❑
Written Skills	❑	❑	❑

After background investigators completely document their interviews with the candidate, as well as all the respondents' ratings, they prepare a final summary using the following form (see Box 5.3).

Box 5.3

Summary Rating of Candidate's Personality by the Investigator

Candidate:_____ Investigator:_____ Date:_____

After interviewing the candidate and performing a thorough background check, I would rate the candidate in the following ways, using the same rating scale that was given to respondents.

Adaptability	❑	Mental Health	❑
Alertness	❑	Open-mindedness	❑
Appearance	❑	Responsibility	❑
Assertiveness	❑	Sensitivity	❑
Independence	❑	Sociability	❑
Industriousness	❑	Stress Tolerance	❑
Integrity	❑	Trainability	❑
Intelligence	❑	Trustworthiness	❑
Judgment	❑	Verbal Skills	❑
Leadership	❑	Written Skills	❑

Impressions and Comments

These rating forms have four qualities: They cover a broad range of job-related behaviors; are standardized for each candidate; are quantified, rendering numerical scores for comparison; and leave room for comments on issues not covered by the scales. This represents a vast improvement over many background investigation practices that are often done in a haphazard, superficial, and unstandardized manner.

Personal Reflections _____

1. Knowing what you now know about background checks, what makes you feel comfortable and uncomfortable about the prospect of undergoing one?
2. What issue do you personally fear the most about a background check?
3. Of the twenty behaviors listed on the checklist, on which three would you score the highest and which three the lowest? What can you do to raise the lowest-rated behaviors?

PSYCHOLOGICAL SCREENING

Perhaps the most controversial screening instruments are those involved in psychological assessment. The main reason for the controversy is that false positives can result; that is, candidates who pass the psychological screening may be discovered to have psychological problems of one type or another. There are three thoughts, however, to keep in mind regarding this criticism.

First, assessing such abstract phenomena as the workings of the brain and psyche are infinitely more challenging than assessing concrete things such as physical agility and heart rate. One cannot realistically expect the same accuracy in assessment in the former as in the latter.

Second, the polygraph test is routinely used without question in screening law enforcement candidates, yet there is no reason to believe its accuracy is any higher than that of psychological screening. (See Chapter 9 for a discussion of polygraph testing.)

Finally, this question must be addressed: What is the alternative to psychological screening of candidates? Although it is true that such screening is better at weeding out the more psychologically dysfunctional candidates than those with more insidious dysfunctions, it seems reasonable to hold that some screening out is better than none, both professionally and legally.

Law enforcement agencies have long held that psychological screening (psychological interviews and testing) should be left solely to mental health professionals because they are the experts in that field. Typically, the only interaction between the agency and mental health professionals is that the agency refers the candidate for evaluation, and the mental health professionals send the agency a report and a bill. This does not constitute a professional relationship between the agency and the mental health professional. Analogously, even though contractors are experts at remodeling houses, the homeowners who employ them must keep close contact with them, so that the remodeling meets the homeowners' needs. A homeowner would never tell a contractor: "You're the expert. Do what you want and let us know when you've finished."

This section discusses how agencies can become active partners with mental health professionals in order to develop and maintain a psychological screening program that meets the unique needs of the agency in an effective and legally defensible way.

Psychological screening is likely to be one of the more legally vulnerable parts of the overall selection process, so who the mental health professionals are and what they do should be monitored by the agency at least as carefully as the agency oversees its other operations. Failure to do so can incur vicarious liability if litigation occurs, because the mental health professionals are hired by the agency.

Choosing Mental Health Professionals

Choosing the right mental health professional is the first step in developing a scientifically and legally valid screening process. Agencies should never choose mental health professionals solely on reputation or the fact that they submitted the lowest bid. The agency should interview mental health professionals by asking questions such as these:

- What interests you in working for law enforcement?
- What do you think motivates people to go into law enforcement?
- What agencies have you worked with? What agencies are you no longer working with? Why not?
- Have you followed up on officers whom you passed on the psychological exam to see how accurate your predictions were over time?
- What do you look for in a good officer, and what are your automatic disqualifiers?
- What is your overall pass–fail ratio?
- May we see a copy of the questions you ask candidates and your reasons for asking them?
- What psychological tests do you administer? Why did you choose them, and can you send us their descriptions and their validity and reliability coefficients?
- Can you describe the topics you would cover in a typical report? Do you pass or fail candidates, or do you make graduated recommendations (highly recommend, recommend with reservations, do not recommend)?
- Are your reports technical? Will we, as laypeople, be able to understand them?
- Can you send us sample reports you have written for law enforcement agencies with identifying information redacted?
- How do you perceive the agency's role in the screening process?

- What difficulties, if any, have you experienced in working with law enforcement candidates or their agencies?
- What psychological theory do you subscribe to, and how does it influence your work?
- What differences, if any, are present in evaluating a law enforcement candidate in contrast to a candidate for any other job?

There is no reason to feel uncomfortable interviewing people who can do a great deal to help or harm the agency. In fact, secure mental health professionals will welcome the opportunity to explain who they are and what they do and will respect the agency for its enlightened approach to the process. If the agency perceives the mental health professional as a viable candidate for the job, a check of résumés and references is necessary to complete the process.

Psychological Interview

It is important for agencies to have some knowledge of the psychological interview done by mental health professionals. In the same spirit as homeowners not telling contractors how to do their job but, at the same time, having a vested interest in how they perform, the agency can keep tabs on what occurs in the psychological interviews of its candidates. The following considerations will help the agency do this.

All mental health professionals have their own image of what constitutes a good law enforcement officer. It is important for this image to match the agency's image because, if it does not, the mental health professional will be recommending candidates who may not fit the agency's needs and not recommending those who do. For this reason, the professional's and the agency's images must be kept continuously in view in order to avoid confusion and conflict.

Some mental health professionals purposely place candidates under pressure to evaluate how they handle it. It is important to realize that there are two kinds of pressure: constructive and destructive. Mental health professionals may apply constructive pressure to get candidates to stretch their psychological muscles. ("Six months from now you stop me for drunk driving. You recognize me and know that the local paper publishes the names of people arrested in the county, which will ruin my reputation. Look me in the eye and tell me what you're going to do.")

Destructive pressure can be damaging to the candidate and the agency. ("What are you, only about 5 feet 2 inches tall? I've seen people like you before—you want to be cops so you can bully people the way you've been bullied your whole life. Don't you think there could be just a little bit of truth in this?") In addition to denigrating candidates, this attitude creates a no-win situation for them. If they react with anger, they are insecure; if they react timidly, they are too weak to be a cop. Agencies need to monitor what happens in psychological interviews by randomly debriefing candidates after they have been examined but before they know the results.

Psychological interviews for personnel selection purposes have different legal parameters than those done for clinical purposes. Mental health professionals must be careful in three areas. One deals with invasion of privacy. All questions in a psychological employment interview should be directly job related. Therefore, questions about candidates' private lives (race, marriage, divorce, religion, sex, including sexual orientation, and so on) run the risk of being legally contested, which is clearly not the case in typical clinical interviews.

A second area deals with not recommending candidates for psychological reasons. This brings the Americans with Disabilities Act into the picture: Can candidates be denied a job, any job, because at one time they had a psychological disorder or currently have one that is under control or will not interfere with job performance?

The third area for caution involves the situation in which candidates typically are required to sign a waiver stating they will not request to see the psychological report that is sent to the agency. When candidates who were not hired because they failed the psychological examination insist on seeing the report, the waiver may have dubious legal standing and have legal ramifications for the mental health professional and the agency. The mental health professional's position on this issue should be solicited as well.

These issues should be openly and perhaps frequently discussed to make the psychological interview process as professional and liability proof as possible. The psychological interview often includes administering intelligence and personality tests. Agencies should acquire some basic knowledge as to the nature of these tests and their statistical validity and reliability. This information can be obtained from the mental health professional who administers the tests.

Screening in Perspective

It is important to place psychological screening (interviewing and testing) in a proper perspective. In one sense, the mental health profession is like law enforcement—people tend to grossly overestimate or underestimate what each can do. Perhaps the best way to describe the parameters of psychological screening is to compare it to medical screening, because they are similar in a number of areas.

First, both render a general picture of the candidate's health, but are not geared to pick up the countless subclinical (not readily observable) symptoms. A medical examination may determine that a candidate has a heart murmur, but not that he is in the beginning stages of prostate cancer, which may be even more problematic. A psychological examination may determine a candidate is prone to depression but may not discover she also has a borderline personality, which may become more troublesome.

Second, both medical and psychological screenings render a picture of a candidate that is only valid at the time of the examination. People change and younger people are more inclined to change than older people. Some people who are examined at 22 years of age are in better physical and psychological shape at age 30. Unfortunately, the opposite also can be true. Some people who are poster candidates for law enforcement at 22 years of age are physically and/or psychologically in very bad shape by the age of 30. These progressions and regressions are virtually impossible to predict.

Third, no examination is absolutely foolproof. Candidates can lie about their physical history, lose 30 pounds for the physical examination, and appear to be in good physical health, only to gain the weight back 6 months later. People can lie about their psychological history and be clever enough to give all the right answers during the psychological interview and testing, thus giving a false picture as to who they really are.

Finally, any examination is only as valid as the examiner. Some medical and psychological examiners are excellent practitioners, some are incompetent, and most fall someplace in the middle. For this reason, it is as important to screen the medical and psychological examiners of candidates as it is the candidates themselves.

These four points often provide the answer to this question: Why didn't the so-called experts see these problems in this officer a few years ago when they examined him?

A realistic view of psychological (and medical) screening is that it is far better than no screening but perfect screening does not exist. Ideally, it would be helpful if officers were required to be medically and psychologically examined every few years, a policy that would be in their interests as well as those of the agency. This would preclude, in many cases, fitness-for-duty evaluations that enter the picture only when officers are in serious trouble.

Personal Reflections

1. What do you think about the psychological screening of candidates for law enforcement or any job?
2. Would you feel confident about going through a psychological screening procedure? If so, why? If not, why not?
3. Would you feel more confident taking cognitive (intelligence, aptitude, ability, and achievement) tests or personality tests? Why do you feel that way?
4. Do you believe that, in reality, the playing field is level for all candidates, or do you think it is level for some and uphill for others? Why do you think this?

*S*ummary

In summarizing this chapter, five points can be kept in mind. First, because no single selection instrument has overwhelming validity and reliability, it is important to use several before rendering a final assessment of the candidate. Second, a professionally and legally acceptable screening includes valid and reliable interviews and tests, only job-related questions, and no adverse impact. In other words, every candidate competes on the same level playing field. The only variable being measured asks this question: Who can perform the essential functions of the job and who cannot?

A third point to keep in mind is that who does the screening is as import-ant as, if not more important than, what is done in the process. In other words, the assessment tools cannot be better than the people administering them. For this reason, great care must be taken to choose properly trained interviewers, background investigators, and mental health professionals. Agency interview-ers and background investigators who learned on the job and mental health professionals with little or no experience in personnel assessment in general or law enforcement in particular may experience difficulty in the face of legal challenge.

Fourth, by the end of the entire selection process, a picture of the whole candidate should emerge, which includes the physical, intellectual, emotional, social, and moral dimensions of behavior. Finally, the agency must take extra-ordinary steps to secure the confidentiality of all screening results. Interview and test results and all reports are strictly confidential and should not be avail-able to, or shared with, anyone (including secretaries and janitorial staff) who does not have an official need to know.

The importance of selection is important to each individual officer, the agency, and the community. As Gaines and Kappeler (1992) state:

> The personnel selection process is one of the most important administrative functions in a police department. It is the process through which the agency is rejuvenated by importing vital new human resources. Since officers often have complete careers with one agency, if the initial selection decision is poorly made, the department is faced with retaining an inferior officer for 20 years or more. Thus, selection decisions have long term, momentous implications for a department. No matter how well a department is organized or administered, if the police officers who must perform daily police responsibilities are not of the highest caliber, the department will not reach its full potential in terms of maintaining order, reducing crime, and providing important services to the community. (p. 107)

*R*eferences

Aamodt, M.G. (1999). *Applied industrial/organizational psychology* (3rd ed.). Pacific Grove, CA: Brooks/Cole.

Amendola, K.L., Weber, R.W., & Mercer, B.S. (March–April 1998). Minimizing the risks: Personnel selection strategies. *Community Policing Exchange, V* (19).

American Educational Research Association, American Psychological Association, and National Council on Measurement in Education (1999). *Standards for educational and psychological testing.* Washington, DC: American Educational Research Association.

Bayley, D.H. (1994). *Police for the future.* New York: Oxford University Press.

Bonsignore v. *The City of New York* (1981). 521 F. Supp. 394.

Community Policing Consortium (1994). *Recruitment and selection for community policing.* Monograph. Washington, DC: Community Policing Consortium. Retrieved April 8, 2002, from the World Wide Web: http://www.communitypolicing.org.

Doerner, W.G. (1998). *Introduction to law enforcement: An insider's view.* Woburn, MA: Butterworth-Heinemann.

Domash, S.F. (2002). Who wants this job? *Police, 26* (5), 34–39.

Gaines, L.K., & Kappeler (1992). Selection and testing. In G.W. Cordner & D.C. Hale (Eds.), *What works in policing? Operations and administration examined* (pp. 107–123). Cincinnati, OH: Anderson Publishing.

Hollingworth, H.L. (1929). *Vocational psychology and character analysis.* New York: Appleton.

Huffutt, A.I., & Hunter, A.W. (1994). Hunter and Hunter (1984) revisited: Interview validity for entry-level jobs. *Journal of Applied Psychology, 79* (2), 184–190.

Kass, J. (2000). Fight over hiring cops who once used drugs. *Christian Science Monitor, 92* (35), 1.

McKeever, J., & Kranda, A. (2000). Recruitment and retention of qualified police personnel. *Big Ideas for Smaller Police Departments, 1* (2), 3–14.

More, H.W., & Wegener, W.F. (1992). *Behavioral police management.* New York: Macmillan.

Occupational Information Network (2000). *Testing and assessment: An employer's guide to good practices.* Washington, DC: U.S. Department of Labor Employment and Training Administration.

Schultz, D.P., & Schultz, S.E. (2001). *Psychology and work today* (8th ed.). Upper Saddle River, NJ: Prentice Hall.

Wexley, K.N., Yukl, G.A., Kovacs, S.Z., & Sanders, R.E. (1972). Importance of contrast effects in employment interviews. *Journal of Applied Psychology, 56,* 45–48.

6

Professional Leadership

As is true for any organization, leadership is a key to success, mediocrity, or failure in professional law enforcement agencies. It is extremely rare for employees, or an organization as a whole, to thrive in the absence of good leadership. As More and Wegener (1992) state:

> Empirical evidence and common sense suggest that an organization's performance is closely related to the quality of leadership. While leadership may not be the only important variable in the success or failure of a collective effort, it is an essential one. There is absolutely no doubt that inept leaders lower employee morale and hamper police operations. (p. 364)

Unfortunately, law enforcement has a long history of promoting officers to leadership positions on the basis of several variables, but true leadership ability has not always been one of them. In order to increase the professionalism of law enforcement, agencies need to place officers in leadership positions based purely on their tested competence to lead and not on in-house or external political rewards or pressures.

Many definitions of leadership exist, but a clear and concise one is this: Leadership is the ability to persuade people to commit themselves to the goals of an organization and work together to achieve them. This definition clearly indicates that not everyone in a leadership position is a leader, and leaders can emerge naturally from nonleadership positions. Conflict often arises when a group follows the natural leader who has emerged from the group rather than the designated leader who has been appointed by the administration.

The majority of the literature on leadership in organizations is aimed primarily at business and industry rather than paramilitary organizations, such as law enforcement. Therefore, the realities of law enforcement organizations must blend with modern leadership theory and practice to generate meaningful thought and discussion.

Unfortunately, because of their nature, law enforcement agencies do not have a broad range of opportunities to practice and experiment with leadership styles. These encumbrances are real and stem from a number of causes. Law enforcement organizations generally suffer from being paramilitary in structure, which allows little room to "think outside the box," to be democratic, creative, unique, or laissez-faire.

A number of good reasons exist for this encumbrance. Law enforcement officers carry nonlethal and lethal weapons, which can cause bodily injury and death. They participate in raids, hostage situations, vehicle pursuits, foot chases, physical encounters, and sniper incidents, and respond to demonstrations, riots, domestic violence calls, crimes in progress, and people who are crazed due to drugs or mental illness. They also have the right to deprive people of their freedom and property. All of these acts call for a different kind of leadership and organizational structure than do insurance companies, computer firms, universities, or social service agencies, all of which have very different purposes, mandates, and liabilities.

Moreover, law enforcement has an infinitely larger pool of stakeholders than do other organizations. For example, on the level of municipal policing, stakeholders include the mayor, city council, citizen oversight committee, citizenry within the agency's jurisdiction, community activists, media, prosecutor's office, judiciary, civil service commission, and police officers' association and union.

The potential to do great good and great harm, coupled with constant scrutiny by the stakeholders, necessarily creates leadership styles and organizational structures that constantly tighten and loosen the reins across an infinite number of situations 24 hours each day. No other organization works within these constraints. Consequently, although healthy modernization needs to occur in law enforcement leadership in order to keep up with increasing knowledge, responsibilities, and the new breed of officers, leadership styles that work well in insurance companies and universities cannot be automatically transplanted into law enforcement.

While about half the status quo in traditional law enforcement leadership models must change to be effective in today's world, the other half may have to remain as it is. The challenge is to know which half must go and which half must remain. This chapter attempts to shed some light on the development of professional leadership in law enforcement through discussing the following topics: leadership and personality, leadership and behavior, leadership and the situation, leadership failure, and the functions of leadership.

LEADERSHIP AND PERSONALITY

The personality of a leader—*who* the leader *is*—is an important factor in leadership success or failure. Although no one set of personality traits defines effective leaders, both research and common observation indicate that individuals who are, or are perceived to be, effective leaders possess similar personal qualities. It should be noted that personal qualities do not necessarily translate into actual behavior. For example, an officer may be very sensitive as a parent, but not as a supervisor or street cop. As will be seen, personal qualities are potentials that may or may not be actualized, depending on other factors.

The following section describes some of the key personal qualities that have been identified in effective and ineffective leaders.

Qualities of Effective Leaders

Ethical.   Professional leadership requires the supervisor to be ethical—to be principled, just, honest, respectful, caring, and trustworthy. Some people are always ethical, whereas others are selective. For example, some leaders never lie or only lie when telling the truth would upset the bosses or cause a guilty person to go free. A few leaders routinely lie, no matter the circumstances.

Ethical leaders avoid this officer reaction: "Basically, we don't trust him. He lies like a rug, and wheels and deals in ways that are going to get us all in a jam one of these days."

Intelligent.   People want their leaders to be intelligent, but it is important to realize that intelligence is not a monolithic trait but has several dimensions. For example, some people have good theoretical intelligence but lack practical intelligence and vice versa. Some people have both types and others have neither. Some people who have both may lack a third type of intelligence—social intelligence. For example, community policing leaders may have good theoretical intelligence (understand the philosophy and principles of community policing) and good practical intelligence (organize and synthesize well), but they may have poor social intelligence (relate to people in abrasive ways). Therefore, despite their good theoretical and practical intelligence, they would be disastrous community policing leaders. This would also be true of officers who have good social intelligence but are lacking in one or both of the other kinds of intelligence.

The professional leader uses his intelligence to avoid this officer reaction: "How can such a smart person do so many stupid things?"

Assertive.   People want their leaders to be assertive: to communicate their thoughts, feelings, expectations, and values in a forthright manner; to face difficult people and situations squarely; and to be an advocate for them in the face of injustice.

Assertiveness can be a general trait. For example, leaders can be assertive across situations; they can be selective—assertive with civilians but not with superiors; and some leaders are generally unassertive. Being assertive is not the same as being aggressive—intimidating, arrogant, demanding—which is antithetical to effective leadership.

Healthy assertiveness avoids this officer reaction: "She lets people get away with murder because she lacks the courage to confront them, and she never goes to bat for us with the citizens or the bosses."

Responsible.   People want their leaders to be responsible—to respond to problems immediately and effectively, to cope with turmoil calmly, to handle criticism constructively, to admit failure honestly, and to treat people as individuals.

Responsibility can be a general trait. For example, leaders can be responsible in all situations, or the trait can be used selectively—leaders are responsible in their dealings with superiors but not with their officers, and less so with citizens. Still other leaders are irresponsible across the board.

Being a responsible leader avoids this officer reaction: "He doesn't have a clue as to what's going on around here. He's always a day late and a dollar short and blames us for the consequences."

Self-monitoring.   Leaders should be self-monitoring, that is, aware of how they come across to people and how their behavior is subtly influenced by people's reactions. Good leaders sense immediately when people are registering interest or disinterest, hope or despair, understanding or confusion, respect or ridicule, and make the appropriate behavioral adjustments.

Leaders are also sensitive to how others make them feel: secure or insecure, competent or incompetent, strong or weak, accepted or rejected, and deal constructively with these dynamics. Some leaders are generally self-monitoring, while others are selective, being self-monitoring with supervisors but not with officers or citizens. Certain leaders are never self-monitoring.

Leaders who are self-monitoring avoid having officers state: "She babbles away all day and is blind to the fact that she is either boring us to death or really infuriating us at any given point in time."

Motivated.   People want their leaders to be motivated to lead—to enjoy the challenges, responsibility, action, power, and opportunity to make positive changes. Wanting to lead can be a general or selective trait. Leaders may enjoy supervising a SWAT unit but dread overseeing a secretarial staff. Some leaders do not feel comfortable in any kind of leadership role.

Motivated leaders act in ways that avoid this officer reaction: "He's just not a leader. He got the position by being an excellent *follower* during his career, and someone thought this was good preparation for being a *leader*. Big mistake."

Sociable.   People want leaders with good interpersonal skills—who like, respect, trust, and enjoy being around people. These leaders not only are easy to talk to but also approach others on a regular basis to see how things are going and to elicit feedback that will make everyone's job easier.

Some leaders are generally sociable, while others are selective; that is, they are sociable with superiors but not with their officers, or sociable with citizens but not their superiors. Some leaders are unsociable, preferring to work alone and remain distant.

Sociability allows leaders to avoid this officer reaction: "She knows the job, but her people skills leave a lot to be desired, which makes it difficult to really know her or go to her with problems."

Psychologically balanced. People want their leaders to be psychologically balanced—to have an intellect that governs emotions, and emotions that humanize their intellect. They are not so intellectualized that feelings are squelched, nor so emotional that little room remains for reason. Some leaders are generally balanced psychologically, while others are selective. Leaders may be balanced when things are going well, but thrown off balance under stress, becoming unreasonable or overly emotional. Some leaders are always out of kilter psychologically.

By acting in a psychologically balanced manner, leaders avoid this officer reaction: "One day he's great; the next day he's the epitome of reason but cold as a fish. On still another day his emotions drive out all reason. We only approach him every third day."

Persuasive.   Persuasive leaders present their ideas so that people *want* to follow them because everyone will benefit by doing so. Unpersuasive leaders may have good ideas but lack the ability to sell them. On the other hand, domineering leaders foist their ideas onto others without fully engaging their cooperation.

By acting in a persuasive way, leaders avoid this officer reaction: "She's got some good ideas, but she just rams them down our throats whether we agree with them or not. We don't feel that we're really part of this operation."

It is important to note that these personal qualities are not all-or-nothing traits, but are present in degrees. For example, a leader could be very sociable, quite sociable, somewhat sociable, unsociable, or antisocial. In most situations, only leaders who fall into the first two categories would be potentially good leaders, all other factors remaining the same. Because personal qualities are basically set by adulthood, they are not easily modified. For example, it is highly unlikely that an unsociable officer will become sociable as a result of leadership training.

In addition, it seems fair to say that all eight qualities just described need to be present, at least to an average degree, for a leader to be effective. To put it another way, which one, two, or three of these traits could a leader lack and still be effective?

Qualities of Ineffective Leaders

The following is a sample of the qualities that research (Hogan, Curphy, & Hogan, 1994) and common observation indicate are often found in ineffective leaders.

Untrustworthy.   Untrustworthiness is a major cause of leadership failure. It refers primarily to the one unforgivable organizational sin—the betrayal of a trust by breaking promises and confidences—but also refers to being dishonest, unfair, and unpredictable.

This violation follows the "one strike and you're out" rule. It takes only one violation to eliminate the leader as a person to respect, trust, or follow in the eyes of the victims of the violation. Law enforcement leaders must choose between never *breaking* a promise or confidence and never *making* promises or *giving* assurances that any confidences will be honored. The latter may often be the more realistic and prudent option.

Overcontrolling.   Authoritarian leaders who exert too much oversight, domination, and control and who micromanage as a management style and not simply as a short-term necessity are likely to fail. This style of management denotes distrust, implying the officers are too stupid or lazy to be left alone. This attitude breeds resentment among the officers and results in passive–aggressive obstruction, such as foot dragging, or outright rebellion, such as refusing to follow directives. Second, overcontrolling leaders breed secrecy among the officers who do not want their supervisor to know what they are doing, especially if they are making mistakes. These secrets invariably come to the supervisor's attention, causing the officers to increase their resentment and go further underground.

Weak.   Weak leaders cannot make decisions, confront problematic officers, answer questions directly, or broker the needs and concerns of the group to their supervisors. Their behavior is controlled by fear—the fear of upsetting people, of making mistakes, of failing. This generates resentment and ridicule ("Our fearless leader was nowhere to be found"), and a rudderless group, which simply drifts or is taken over by an emergent leader, for better or for worse.

Insensitive.   These leaders are "bulls in a china shop." They tease people in cruel ways ("Just kidding"), make jokes at others' expense, fail to grasp the delicate nuances of situations, berate people in front of others, make politically incorrect comments, and, as a matter of principle, say the wrong things, to the wrong people, at the wrong time, in the wrong place, and under the wrong circumstances. Insensitive leaders are perceived by their officers as walking time bombs ready to explode at exactly the wrong time. This causes officers to seek cover whenever their leader enters the scene.

Rigid.   Rigid supervisors are set in their ways, whether they are 25 or 55 years of age. They are unwilling or unable to adapt to new, changing situations and tend to perceive reality in terms of black or white, right or wrong, all or nothing. No middle ground, no gray, no ambiguity, no uncertainty, and no two sides to an issue or room for compromise are allowed. These leaders are the captains of their ships, ordering their own speeds, consulting their own navigational charts, unilaterally deciding on ports of destination, all of which may have little or nothing to do with the group's capabilities, needs, or goals. This behavior typically results in the crew stopping the ship dead in the water, or declaring a mutiny and sailing for their own ports, causing organizational dissention and chaos.

Leadership qualities comprise only one-third of the equation for effective leadership. These qualities must be translated into leadership behavior, and the success of this combination depends on the leadership situation, that is, the people who are to be led and the factors that make up their situation.

Personal Reflections

1. Of the eight personal qualities discussed above, which three do you believe are more important and why?
2. Do you agree with the axiom "Leaders are born, not made? Explain your answer.
3. Think of some of the leaders in your life. Who was the best leader, and who was the worst leader? Explain your answer.
4. Looking at yourself objectively, which personal quality could help you become a good leader, and which quality do you need to work on in order to become a good leader?

LEADERSHIP AND BEHAVIOR

In addition to knowing *who* effective leaders are, it is important to know what they *do*. The National Institute of Justice and the Office of Community Oriented Police Services (1997) emphasize the importance of this issue:

> In modern police service, leaders must do more than articulate right behavior; they must exhibit right behavior. The leader must ensure that the agency's values and principles are articulated, and he or she should include input from the department's stakeholders. The leader then must provide followthrough and ensure that the values and principles are expressed, communicated, and reinforced throughout all aspects of the department's operations, administration, and service. (p. 47)

The following behaviors are associated with effective leadership.

Communicating Clearly

Good leaders are constantly communicating with their officers, genuinely demonstrating interest in the individuals and their work and asking for honest feedback. They operate according to the MBWA principle (management by walking around). They prove that their interest is genuine by remembering previous conversations and following up on the questions, concerns, and suggestions of their officers. The opposite of the MBWA principle is the MBBS principle (management by being scarce). By communicating, a leader can avoid this officer reaction: "He talks but never says anything; he hears but never listens."

Defining Their Role

Good leaders define their role as leaders and the role of their officers by continually communicating "This is what I do and don't do. And this is what you do and don't do." Role and jurisdictional ambiguities and misunderstandings are eliminated because everyone knows exactly what is expected at any given time. Role defining prevents the sentiment "Everyone is in charge, and no one is in charge, so we have chaos."

Anticipating Problems

Leaders anticipate problems before they occur, or at least before they reach crisis proportions. Their elevated, 360° view of the terrain enables them to see trouble approaching and head it off. They anticipate what will happen when a new member joins the group or when the promotions list is posted, and do what they can to help people deal positively with these situations. Their officers are never in a position to complain: "Why are we always getting blindsided by things?"

Adapting to Situations

Good leaders have a fluid style of management that adapts to each new situation. They know when to micromanage and when to macromanage, when to "drop the hammer" or give a little slack, and when to call for a "full court press" or for a "time out." They do not have a one-size-fits-all style of management that in actuality only fits about one-third of the situations that arise. Their officers are never left complaining: "She's like a mechanic with only one tool who tries to fix *everything* with it, and it simply doesn't work."

Using Power Properly

Good leaders possess power that they earned by being knowledgeable about the job and being liked and respected. They do not have to gain power by pulling rank or threatening punishment. They use their power for the good of the group—to increase group cohesiveness, productivity, morale, resources, and prestige, and to decrease distractions caused by ineptitude, malcontents, political pressures, and red tape. Officers are never left in the position of lamenting: "He's a good guy, and he tries hard, but he lacks the clout to be taken seriously."

Conveying Their Vision

Good leaders have a vision and convey it to the group. They have one eye on where they are and one on where they want the group to be in the future. They perceive the status quo simply as a launching pad for something better—an opportunity to develop new programs, new ways to get financial and technical support, new training opportunities, new methods of career advancement, and new ways to enlist the support of their superiors and the community. These leaders present their visions in a way that transforms the group and allows it to adopt the leader's vision as its own. As a result, the group never complains: "We're tired of doing and hearing the same old things. We're stuck and can't seem to move forward in any direction."

Making Good Decisions

Good leaders make good decisions, which include the following steps:

- Define the situation clearly.
- Gather as much pertinent information as possible.
- Consult with others involved in the decision.
- Assess the long- and short-term consequences.
- Search for hidden factors and agendas.
- Calculate the cost-benefit ratio.
- Make the decision in a timely manner.
- Convey the decision, as well as the reasons for it, to all the stakeholders.

Officers are never placed in the position of saying "I don't know which is worse—when she tries to make decisions and screws them up, or when she just refuses to make a decision."

Setting Attainable Goals

Good leaders set goals that are

- Specific and clear
- Sensible and realistic
- Inherently motivating
- Measurable in one way or another
- Periodically evaluated
- Time limited
- Rewarded when met

When these goals are set, the group can never legitimately complain: "Half the time he sets goals that are entirely unrealistic or are meant to impress his superiors, and other times we have *no* goals—we just respond to one crisis after another and accomplish nothing."

As is true for leadership qualities, these behaviors are not all-or-nothing phenomena, but each must be present to some degree for good leadership to occur. Again, which one, two, or three of these behaviors could a person not exhibit and yet still be considered an effective leader?

Personal Reflections

1. Of the eight leadership behaviors just discussed, which three do you think are the more important and why?
2. What is the difference between leadership qualities and leadership behavior? If people have good leadership qualities, won't they automatically have good leadership behavior?
3. Thinking of the leaders who have had authority over you, what behaviors did the best ones manifest the most and which ones did the worst leaders manifest the least?
4. Imagining yourself as a leader, what behaviors do you exhibit that would help you be a good leader? What leadership behaviors do you feel you need to improve to become a truly effective leader?

LEADERSHIP AND THE SITUATION

The nature of the group to which leaders are assigned is the third determining factor of effective leadership. Professional leaders should be aware that they must respect certain realities in the groups they supervise. The following qualities can be taken into consideration.

Respect for Individual Differences

Each individual is unique with different genes, life experiences, perceptions, feelings, needs, beliefs, attitudes, values and hopes. Unfortunately, one of the biggest mistakes leaders make is to forget this fact and treat officers like a "matched set," assuming that what is helpful to one officer is helpful to all.

It is important for leaders to interact often with their officers personally and collectively in order to learn what each needs in order to be satisfied and productive. The importance of personal interaction has been accepted for some time in business, but it generally has been resisted by law enforcement as too "touchy feely" for a paramilitary organization. However, even the military has come to accept the necessity of relating to people in ways that actualize their personal potential as well their potential to help the group.

Respect for the Group's Maturity Level

Some groups are more mature than others; that is, they are more developed intellectually, emotionally, socially, and morally. Although maturity is often related to age and experience, this is not always the case. For example, it is possible for a group with an average age of 40 to be less mature than one with an average age of 25. Therefore, leaders should calibrate their approach to each group's level of maturity. In general, the more mature the group, the more leaders would be well advised to macromanage, to allow the group the freedom, autonomy, and authority to do their work as they see fit. Serious problems are likely to arise if the leader micromanages the group, telling them how to do their work, insisting on daily progress reports, and regimenting the workday. On the other hand, leaders of immature groups would be well advised to micromanage, to keep close tabs on the group, and to offer individuals an appropriate amount of direction, in contrast to being democratic or laissez-faire.

Respect for the History of the Group

With the exception of newly formed groups, most groups have a history that directly and indirectly affects their current behavior, sometimes significantly. This history includes the group's

- Successes and failures and what caused them
- Experience with authority; how justly or unjustly they feel they have been treated in the past
- Experience with previous leaders; what worked and what did not work
- Morale as measured by spirit, absenteeism, transfers, turnover rate
- Perception of itself as high or low functioning

To ignore a group's history, to adopt a "forget the past and focus on the present and future" approach, is counterproductive for two reasons. First, for better or for worse, a group cannot forget its past, and second, it should not forget the past because it gives clues as to what will work or not work in the future. This is priceless information for a group and a leader to possess.

Respect for the Group's Potential

Every group has a maximum level of performance, just as individuals do, and the leader's role is to help the group maximize its potential to reach that level. However, not all groups are created equal. Some have great natural resources—a vast array of talent, excellent secretarial and technical support, and a user-friendly, ergonomic work environment. Their potential is virtually limitless. At the other end of the scale are groups with modest talent, negligible support services, and a deplorable working environment. Their potential is limited.

To ignore these realities can have deleterious effects. For a high-achievement, success-oriented leader to take over a group with modest ability and limited resources and expect the group to accomplish great things will likely lead to mutual frustration and resentment. Although a good leader can help a lagging group with good potential to accomplish good things eventually, by definition, a group with modest potential can at best accomplish only modest things, and everyone involved, including the leader's supervisors, should recognize this reality.

All three factors—personal qualities, behavior, and the situation—must be positive for effective leadership. Two out of three will not suffice. Administrators must take this information seriously when assigning officers to leadership positions. Simply to declare that an officer has leadership potential and to be confident things will work out well does not justify assigning an officer to a leadership position, especially an important one.

Whatever one thinks about it, the days are gone when strictly authoritarian leadership will work. ("Your job as a leader is to *make* the group come around to *you*. You don't *ask* them—you just *tell* them!") This does not mean that leaders must kowtow to the needs or whims of a group, but it does require an interactive relationship between leaders and group members so that the work-related needs of both are sufficiently met.

In any endeavor, the best predictor of the future is the past. Ideally, officers who have been successful as leaders in a particular situation are likely to be successful in similar situations in the future. Officers who have leadership qualities and demonstrated leadership behaviors should receive training that correlates with the particular leadership situations for which they are being considered.

Personal Reflections

1. Respect for individual differences is an important leadership trait. Why do you think such an obvious concept is so often ignored in practice?

2. When a group you belong to gets a new leader, what is the first thing you look for that will reduce or increase your anxiety about him or her?

3. A new leader tells a group: "The sky's the limit if we work like a team." What do you think about the wisdom of this pep talk?

LEADERSHIP AND FAILURE

Leadership in many organizations is often ineffective, and law enforcement is no exception. Schultz and Schultz (2001) address this by referring to summaries of research on leadership effectiveness:

Some 60 to 75% of American workers believe that the worst thing about their job, and the greatest single cause of stress, is their boss. The most common complaints from workers are that supervisors are unwilling to exercise authority, tyrannize subordinates, and treat employees as if they were stupid. (p. 193)

A study of law enforcement officers (Brown & Campbell, 1990) found that bureaucratic policies, poor leadership, weak administrative support, role ambiguity, and the incompetence of fellow officers create more stress for officers than do the physical risks of the job, witnessing the effects of violence, and public criticism.

In a study that asked 113 police chiefs to rate their predecessor's performance on a scale ranging from 1 (poor performance) to 7 (outstanding performance), the current chiefs responded that their predecessors would have been given a score of 3.3 by the rank-and-file officers, a score of 3.6 by the community, and a score of 3.1 by the local government (Cordner & Kenney, 1996, p. 11). If officers were to receive these scores in evaluations, their performance would be described as "does not meet agency standards."

Causes

How does such a sad state of affairs exist in law enforcement? The following reasons for promoting officers often lead to ineffective leadership.

- Officers can be promoted to a leadership position because they did an outstanding job in their last position, but lack the competencies required to be an effective leader in the new position. This is the Peter Principle—being promoted to one's level of incompetence (Peter & Hull, 1996).
- Officers can be assigned to a leadership position because they score well on tests and perform well in assessment centers. These evaluations seem better at screening out potentially poor leaders than screening in potentially good ones. The reason may be that such evaluations focus far more on specific professional skills and far less on personality traits and situational factors.
- Officers can be assigned to a leadership position for political reasons: to meet the requirements of consent decrees, as a reward for past favors, for being ingratiating or remaining silent about irregularities, or because they know where the bodies are buried.
- Officers can be assigned to a leadership position precisely because they are ineffectual, weak, docile, lazy, or otherwise dysfunctional by bosses who are insecure and do not want assistants who will threaten them by being more intelligent, energetic, professional, popular, or mentally healthy than they are.
- Officers can be promoted to leadership positions because they were "kicked upstairs" where they supposedly will do less damage than they did in their previous position.
- Officers can be assigned to leadership positions because no one else wants them.

In appointing leaders, the principle of unintended consequences should be kept in mind. This means the motivation for promoting an officer to a leadership position may meet a short-term organizational or political need, but the ultimate effects of the decision may be disastrous.

Situational Problems

Unfortunately, some situations endemic to law enforcement actually foster ineffective leadership. The following are some of them.

- An authoritarian, military attitude holds that might makes right, that those in authority rarely do wrong, and, when they do, others cover up for them, so that nothing ever comes of it, except possibly a transfer or promotion.
- An inbred, incestuous atmosphere places virtually everyone in the same law enforcement family. All officers go through basically the same training academy, progress through the ranks together, and often socialize with each other. These close ties militate against a willingness to promote only the deserving, to demote the undeserving, and to sanction leaders who have behaved unprofessionally, unethically, or illegally ("We protect our own").
- The presence of police officer associations, police unions, and civil service boards often make it virtually impossible to get rid of ineffective leaders, unless they are convicted of major ethical or legal violations. Simply being ineffective is neither unethical nor illegal. Therefore, ineffective leaders can have lifetime tenure to damage both the people they oversee and the agency as a whole.
- Law enforcement is a monopoly. It has no free market competition to force it to be on the cutting edge, put out the best possible product, recruit the best leadership available, get rid of the dead wood, and bring in people with fresh ideas. The CEO of a major corporation, who is also familiar with law enforcement, perhaps put it best: "If I ran my company like most law enforcement agencies are run, I'd be out of business in six months."

Although these situations are generally but not universally true, it does not mean that law enforcement cannot change or do a better job of fostering effective leadership within its current parameters. Beliefs and attitudes concerning leadership in law enforcement need to change significantly. Ideas based on tradition and myth ("Give him the promotion; he'll grow into the job") must be replaced by the knowledge that comes from research, experts, and the experience of leaders in highly functioning organizations.

Whatever one thinks of it, the days are past in most organizations when, if a group is having significant problems with their leader, the group members are fired and the leader is assigned to a new group. Today, unless the groups are clearly dysfunctional on their own, their leaders are more likely to be removed, and the group remains. If only out of concern for their careers, leaders need to understand that leadership is interactive, a two-way street with each side teaching and learning from the other.

Ineffective Leaders as Symptoms

While it is easy to point the finger at ineffective leaders as the problem, in fact they are only symptoms of larger problems that will be framed by the following questions.

- Who appointed the leader? What were the motives of the person (or persons) who appointed the leader? Were the motives purely professional (the candidate showed every indication of being an effective leader in the assigned position)? Or, were the motives political (the candidate was "connected," was owed a favor, or was loyal)?
- What was the candidate's track record with regard to leadership qualities and behaviors in previous similar positions? Did the candidate have a good track record, no track record, or a problematic one?
- Was the candidate given formal leadership training for a period of time commensurate with the importance of the specific position? Or, was the candidate simply thrust into the position on the basis of high hopes?

There is no foolproof method for choosing leaders. Sometimes the best candidates turn out to be the worst leaders, and the worst candidates may develop into the best leaders. The more a professional, formal selection process measures the variables discussed in this chapter, the greater the chances that effective leaders will emerge. This selection process takes a good deal of time and money, but ineffective leadership can eventually cost the agency infinitely more time and money and, perhaps more importantly, the loss of the respect of officers and the community. The effects of poor leadership in law enforcement are frequently seen in the daily media, so this is not merely a theoretical concern.

Personal Reflections _____

1. Of the six poor reasons for promoting officers, which two do you think are the more common ones?
2. Thinking back on poor leaders in your life, how did these people end up in leadership positions?
3. Of the five qualities of ineffective leaders, which three do you think are more common, and why?
4. Of the situations endemic to law enforcement that interfere with choosing truly effective leaders, which two do you think are most frequently present and why?

LEADERSHIP AND ITS FUNCTIONS

Effective leadership has many functions that require skill and experience. Outstanding leaders perform all these functions well; dysfunctional leaders perform them poorly; and most leaders fall somewhere in the middle. This section discusses some of the critical functions of leadership—those that will have a significant impact on the agency and the leader's career. These functions are motivating employees, evaluating employees, creating a healthy culture, and modulating stressors.

Motivating Employees

All theories of motivation related to employee performance seek to answer the same question: What can I do to create an environment in which employees are highly productive and satisfied in their work? Because it is no longer possible for leaders to simply tell their employees, "Here's your job for the day. Don't come back until it's finished," it is important for leaders to have at least some understanding of the nature of motivation. To this end, three theories of motivation will be discussed: expectancy theory, equity theory, and learning theory.

Expectancy theory.   Expectancy theory holds that employees will be motivated to work well when two expectations are met – that their work will result in a well-defined outcome, and the outcome is one that they value. If either or both of these elements is lacking, employees will not be motivated to put their minds, hearts, and souls into the job. For example, DARE officers may be told that, as a result of their efforts, the students and teachers at a school will develop good relationships with police officers, turn to them for counsel, give them crime-related information, and, most importantly, that drug use will significantly diminish. Because the officers value these outcomes, they will begin the year highly motivated. If their expectations are met, their motivation increases; if they are not met, motivation decreases. It is the leader's role to offer realistic and valued outcomes and to see to it that the outcomes are met.

Equity theory.   Equity theory, also called exchange theory, holds that employee motivation is associated with input–output ratios. Input is measured by how much the employee puts into the job (education, experience, time, effort, sacrifice). Output is measured by how much the employee gets out of the job (salary, benefits, promotions, prestige, appreciation). If the ratio is balanced, or at least fairly balanced, the employee will be motivated to work well ("I'm getting a good deal—or at least a fair deal—at work").

If the ratio becomes quite unbalanced, for example, input far surpasses output, or output far surpasses input, motivation will diminish. The reason in the former situation is obvious – "I'm really getting ripped off at work"—but the latter is less obvious. The problem with the latter situation can be seen in an employee's response "If I'm getting all kinds of perks for doing minimal work, I'm going to slack off even more and still get more perks than I deserve." Leaders have the responsibility to see that input–output ratios remain relatively balanced.

Learning theory.   Learning theory holds that leaders motivate employees by a system of rewards and punishments and by setting a good example. When employees work well, they are rewarded; when they do not, they are punished. Rewards can vary from a pat on the back to a promotion. Punishments can run the gamut from a stern look, to a reprimand, suspension, or termination. This theory requires a leader to

- Have a good understanding of what employees are doing in order to reward or punish effectively
- Reward and punish evenly and equally and act in fair, unbiased ways
- Reward and punish as close to the act as possible. Delayed rewards and punishments lose their effect.
- Recognize individual differences. One person's reward (a plaque at a public ceremony) could be another person's punishment (being embarrassed by public acclaim). Some people are motivated only by rewards and are demotivated by punishments, and vice versa.

In addition to motivating by a system of rewards and punishments, leaders motivate by acting as role models. Leaders who work well in all facets of their role will provide a picture and set a standard for disciplined, enthusiastic, and effective performance.

These theories complement each other and are likely to be operative in all situations in which motivation is an issue.

Evaluating Employees

Assessing employees' job performance is an important part of leadership because a good deal depends on these evaluations. Evaluations can be used to change assignments, promote or demote, commend or reprimand, assign to advanced or remedial training, give feedback to employees, and recommend a fitness for duty examination or termination. Moreover, a large number of agencies rate supervisors on the quantity and quality of *their* evaluations of officers. Last but not least, evaluations can end up in grievance procedures or in criminal and civil courts where each word will be scrutinized.

The underlying principle of every performance evaluation is this: *The only objective of a performance appraisal is to evaluate performance.* The critical question to be asked regarding a supervisor's evaluation of an employee is this: *Is it a fair and accurate representation of the employee's performance*? With this principle and question in mind, leaders can be acutely aware of the following cautions.

Limit comments. The evaluator's comments should be limited to the employee's actual performance, to concrete behaviors that have been seen, heard, read, or reported with corroborated evidence. Evaluators should refrain from describing personality traits (friendly, cooperative, dedicated, or stubborn, moody, lazy). *Who* the employee *is* does not matter. *What* the employee *does*, or does not do, is *all* that matters. So, instead of stating, "Officer Smith is irresponsible," the evaluator should write, "Officer Smith's reports are consistently late and incomplete."

Avoid personal biases. Evaluators should not allow their personal feelings, whether or not they are favorable, to influence their assessments. It is irrelevant that an officer attends the same church as the evaluator or that an officer is living with a homosexual partner. These issues are unrelated to performance and should not influence a performance appraisal.

Do not rely on unsubstantiated hearsay. Relying on hearsay regarding an employee is especially likely to occur when leaders do not know the employee well or lack the time or courage to question the employee about the hearsay. Hearsay is often partially or completely inaccurate, so it is precipitous to include it in a performance appraisal.

Refrain from impugning motives. Supervisors should not include in evaluations *why* they believe officers act the way they do. For example, a supervisor writes: "At times, Officer Jones is overly aggressive on the street, probably because she's new and wants to impress the other officers." Officer Jones's aggression can be explained without divining her motives.

Avoid recency errors. This means an employee's performance should be evaluated over the entire evaluation period (six months or one year) and not on the most recent positive or negative behaviors.

Avoid halo effects. Evaluators should not give employees a positive evaluation because of a high-profile positive action they took, ignoring all the negative behaviors (positive halo effect), or give a poor evaluation based on the employee's high-profile negative action, ignoring all the positive behaviors (negative halo effect).

Avoid distribution errors. There are three types of distribution errors: (1) leniency error—giving everyone high evaluations, whether or not they deserve them; (2) strictness error—giving everyone low evaluations, whether or not they deserve them; (3) central tendency error—giving everyone average evaluations, whether or not they deserve them.

Avoid cognitive errors.   There are two kinds of cognitive errors: (1) misinterpretation of an employee's behavior, for example, interpreting an employee's critical thinking as disrespectful; (2) selective memory, that is, remembering an employee's behavior that fits the supervisor's preconceived notion of the officer ("He's lazy") and forgetting behaviors that contradict the preconception.

Avoid surprises.   In most cases, employees should not learn anything new during their evaluation interview. Effective leaders keep employees current by giving them positive and corrective feedback throughout the evaluation period. The purpose of the interview is simply to review and document the information, not to dump a year's worth of negative feedback on the employee.

Many supervisors dislike doing performance evaluations because they take time, entail assertion of authority, require them to confront negative behaviors, may be used against them in a grievance procedure, and may be ignored despite all the work that went into them. Nevertheless, performance evaluations are a critically important part of a leader's role. The more that supervisors learn to compose professional evaluations, the more enjoyable they become because they often effect needed changes in employee behavior, which benefits both the employee, the supervisor, and the agency.

Creating a Healthy Subculture

Leaders always create a subculture within the group they supervise, whether or not they realize it. Leaders communicate this message, directly or indirectly, consciously or unconsciously: "This is how we do things around here." Every subculture has unwritten and unspoken rules that sometimes make it difficult for newcomers to know the difference between acceptable and unacceptable behavior. Often veteran members of the group will pull newcomers aside and inform them about how they are expected to act.

Subcultures run the gamut from being carbon copies of the mainline culture to being antagonistic toward it. Effective leaders are aware of what a subculture is and verbally and nonverbally make it clear to the group what kind of subculture they want to create. The following messages directly or indirectly illustrate the elements and sentiments that constitute a healthy subculture and are offered more for their spirit than their literalness.

Ethics.   "We do the right thing—the honest, just, and respectful thing. We treat people the way we want to be treated or want a loved one to be treated, no matter who they are or what they've done. There's no room in this group for people who treat people, including each other, in dishonest, unfair, or disrespectful ways. We would rather lose a case in court than lose our pride and integrity; therefore, we employ zero tolerance for violations of our code."

Authority.   "I'm the boss, which involves four things. First, I am ultimately responsible for everything we do; therefore, I have to know everything that goes on in this group. A cardinal sin is not to inform me immediately when there's a problem, which precludes me from helping you solve it. Second, I can't be a good boss if you're not completely honest with me about my leadership. If you agree with how things are going, let me know; if you don't, let me know. I take constructive feedback as a sign of respect, not as disrespect. Third, it means I'm here for you; you're not here for me. I'll help you in any way I can and back you to the hilt, as long as you're right. Finally, I'm smart enough to know that I don't have all the answers. I know stuff you don't know, and you know stuff I don't know. We need to share information on a daily basis, so we're all equally smart."

Cohesiveness.   "We are a team, which has two aspects. First, we work together. We share information, the workload, and responsibility for doing a good job. We help each other out and don't want situations in which the right hand doesn't know what the left hand is doing or people hide information from or snipe at each other. We won't tolerate prima donnas or sluggards. We don't have to give up our individuality to be a member of the group, but we have to give up our selfishness and insecurities.

"A second aspect of cohesiveness is that we watch out for each other. If people are going through a tough time, we help them out. We don't ignore or hide behavioral problems that affect our work—drinking, using drugs, depression, shoddy work, excessive force, questionable behavior and friends, and so on. These are not personal problems that are nobody's business but group problems that are everybody's business. We need to get these people help before they lose their careers or their lives. We cover for people, but we don't cover up for them, the latter being a favor to no one. It is up to the group to monitor itself; it is not just my responsibility. We put our fires out before someone else has to do it and before they burn us up. This is just being smart. Anything else, while it may be well intentioned, is stupid."

Service.   "We exist to serve the public; the public does not exist to serve us. We often forget this, especially in the heat of battle. We view the public as a nuisance, as the enemy. Certainly, some of them are, but the vast majority of people support us and, even if they don't, we're still here to serve them. To serve people, we need to know what they need and don't need; otherwise, we're serving ourselves and not the public. I take citizen complaints seriously and will investigate each one in a manner that is fair both to the citizen and to you. If you don't feel comfortable with this, there's a simple solution—don't act in a way that will place you in that situation. Most of us come into the job to help people—sometimes we have to remind ourselves of that."

Fun.   "Law enforcement is not a game, but it should be fun. Fun is the oil that keeps our engines from burning out. Show me a burnt-out cop, and I'll show you someone who stopped having fun a long time ago. There's humor in almost everything, and we need to take time to see it. Forming friendships and socializing after work are important parts of this job—part of the benefits that other people who don't work as closely as we do don't enjoy. If the day comes when this job is no longer fun, when you start dreading work, if you're 30 years old and planning your retirement, come to me for a closed-door meeting. We'll work together to resuscitate you and bring you back to life for the sake of your health, career, and family. If we're unable to do this, I'll ask for your resignation from this group because I don't want to put my life and those of other group members in the hands of someone who really doesn't want to be here anymore.

"In summary, I'm here to serve you, to make your job easier and your career more fulfilling. If you've got suggestions, concerns, problems, or questions, pull me aside, and I'll do what I can to help. At any rate, this is the way things are done around here, because it's the best way I know to keep the public and this group healthy and safe."

Modulating Stressors

Leaders have the responsibility for modulating stress in their officers, that is, keeping it within reasonable bounds as much as possible. Stress is like the temperature in a room—it does not have to climb to the level of an inferno if someone is present to operate the thermostat. The following characteristics mark supervisors who do well at keeping group stress within tolerable limits.

Allow venting.   Good leaders continually encourage officers to vent their feelings of frustration and pressure in appropriate ways. They also realize that unexpressed feelings build up and can cause the individual to burn out, blow up, or self-medicate (use alcohol, drugs, food, or sex to kill the pain or self-destruct). Ventilating feelings can be a therapeutic act in itself and may allow supervisors to actively reduce or eliminate the causes of stress.

Promote communication.   Good leaders create a communication network aimed at preventing and reducing stress by making it clear that *everyone*

- "Has their ear," not just the favored or the loudest
- Can ask for, and should be secure enough to accept, corrective feedback
- Knows what is expected, eliminating confusion and double messages
- Is in charge of rumor control, checking out rumors and squelching false ones
- Says what one thinks so no one has to be a mindreader

- Asks for help when things become overwhelming
- Gets confidential counseling if the need arises

Monitor dynamics. Good leaders closely monitor the group's interpersonal dynamics, taking immediate action in cases of unhealthy competition, rumor mongering, bullying, backstabbing, inappropriate banter, sexual or racial remarks (even "just kidding" ones), practical "jokes" that are not funny, ethically questionable behavior, tardiness and absenteeism, and palming off work onto others. They recognize that these behaviors can create more cumulative stress in a group than even critical incidents do.

Clarify policies.   Good leaders present formal and informal agency policies reasonably and clearly. They realize that stress occurs when officers get confusing, and even contradictory, directives that flow from agency policies. For example, officers ask: "Do we have a pursuit policy or not? Sometimes we do, and other times we don't. What exactly constitutes a pursuit? When do we break off a pursuit? What happens if we decide not to pursue and a serial rapist escapes when we could have stopped him? Which of the three supervisors yelling at us on the radio during a pursuit do we listen to? It seems if we catch the bad guy and no one gets hurt, that's a good pursuit. If we catch the bad guy but somebody gets hurt, that's a bad pursuit. If we don't catch the bad guy and someone gets hurt, that's a very bad pursuit and 30 days on the beach. Can someone please clarify our pursuit policy before someone gets hurt or in trouble?"

Ecologically and ergonomically aware.   Good leaders recognize that some situations in the working environment cause chronic stress, often on a low-grade level, which can be the most pernicious because it accumulates and is least likely to generate action to eliminate it. The following situations are well known to be stressors:

- *Overcrowding.* No place to move or have privacy
- *Noise.* Phones ringing, people shouting, radios blaring, air conditioners and heaters clanking
- *Temperature.* Rooms that are freezing or sweltering, often within the same hour
- *Lighting.* Lights that are too bright, too dim, continually flickering
- *Odors.* Putrid smells emanating from all kinds of unpleasant sources
- *Décor.* Naked radiators, peeling paint, decrepit furniture, filthy floors, leaking plumbing, missing tiles, chronically overflowing wastebaskets
- *Health hazards.* Cigarette smoke, closed ventilation systems where germs incubate and spread, electromagnetic radiation from older computer monitors, unhygienic restrooms and eating areas

- *Equipment.* Inadequate weapons, safety equipment, and first-aid supplies, poor vehicle maintenance, poor work systems that cause physical injuries such as carpal tunnel syndrome and repetitive motion injury

Overseeing Groups and Teams

By definition, leaders lead groups, not single individuals. Therefore, it is important for leaders to have at least a basic understanding of the nature of groups and how they operate. A group is not just a congregation of individuals; it is more than the sum of its parts. Each group has a personality of its own, a fact to which instructors can attest as they have some classes that are great, others that are lifeless, and still others that they wish were lifeless. Almost every endeavor in law enforcement requires group participation and teamwork. Effective leaders lead groups well; ineffective leaders are led by groups. This section deals with a number of issues that relate to leading groups and teams.

Build teams.   It is important to build groups into teams. The concepts of group and team are not synonymous. A group could be in existence for years and never be a team. A group is simply a bunch of people. A team is a group of people dedicated to working closely together to achieve mutually agreed-upon goals.

In attempting to transform a group into a team, leaders can start by asking the group some basic questions. In these questions, the word *group* is used instead of *you* to accentuate the fact that it is up to *the group* to answer these questions and make the decisions, not only the leader or one or two of the more vocal or senior members.

- What does the group want to accomplish? What are its long-term and short-term goals? What are the group's task goals, the projects the members want to accomplish? What are their interpersonal goals, the ways they want the group to relate to each other to accomplish these goals?
- How will the group prioritize each of its goals, from the highest to the lowest?
- What specific resources will the group need to accomplish each goal?
- What obstacles, if any, does the group foresee within or outside the group that could interfere with goal attainment, and how does it plan on dealing with the obstacles?
- What will the rules of the group be with respect to sharing information, workload, responsibility, and dealing with people outside the group? What are some basic "dos" and "don'ts" that must be agreed upon to ensure group cohesion and productivity?
- How often does the group want to meet for the specific purpose of assessing progress toward its goals?
- How does the group perceive the supervisor's role in the group process?

Avoid groupthink.   Team cohesiveness is good, but only up to a point. It is possible for a team to become so cohesive that the members act and think as one, which is often seen as a virtue but, in fact, is not. This commonly results in groupthink, which means everyone sees everything in the same way and makes decisions accordingly. There is little open, thoughtful, vigorous debate during which all sides of an issue are critically examined and several different perspectives are advanced. Groupthink causes tunnel vision that excludes information that could well have brought about a better decision.

Use committees judiciously.   Forming groups and committees to work on projects and solve problems is good, but only up to a point. It seems that whenever leaders are too busy, tired, or disinterested to take time to address an issue, they assign it to a committee, which takes countless hours to address the issue and arrive at a few suggestions. When considering committees, leaders can ask the following questions:

- Could the issue in question be better addressed by one or two highly motivated people rather than by a committee of only marginally motivated people? In other words, is this committee really necessary?

- How many members should a committee have? Five members are generally considered ideal because there are enough people to bring different ideas to the table, but not so many as to be redundant.

- What typically bogs down committees? Two things interfere with progress in groups and in committees: (1) *Social loafing*, meaning that group members exert significantly less effort in a group than if they were doing the job alone. This has three manifestations: the "free rider" effect, which means that, because the group is progressing so nicely, one or two members do little work, just going along for the ride; the "sucker effect," which means that members who were working hard significantly reduce their efforts because they feel like a "sucker" when they realize they are doing most of the work; and the "getting lost in the group" effect, which means that members who do not want to work hide in the midst of busy members, happy to go unnoticed. The antidote to social loafing is for leaders to hold each member accountable for an equal share of the work. (2) Members who talk too much and listen too little can have a chilling effect on group performance because they usurp an inordinate amount of time talking or repeating things that were already said but that they failed to hear because they were not listening. It is the leader's responsibility to encourage the *group* to address this problem, because it is a *group* problem.

Timing.   How long a committee should last is an important consideration. Unless it is a standing committee, the active life of most committees is between four and six meetings. After that, members tend to lose interest and miss meetings. *Ad hoc* committees, formed to address specific issues, should be time limited; that is, members know from the outset they have only two, four, or six sessions to address the issue. This helps motivate action and gives the committee a light at the end of the tunnel.

Resolving Group Conflict

Most groups experience conflict at one time or another; therefore, it is important for leaders to understand the nature of group conflict. The first point to understand is that not all conflict is bad and to be avoided. In fact, the absence of conflict can be a problem when it indicates the group has become stagnant, fearful, uncaring, depressed, or is so satisfied that it is languishing in the warmth of complacency. In these cases, leaders need to jump-start the group so it becomes operational. Healthy conflict can be generated in several ways.

- By directly challenging the group's stagnation or complacency in constructive ways ("We're hitting on about four out of six cylinders, and we really need to find out why, so we can increase our efficiency")
- By playing the devil's advocate at meetings, challenging the members to critically assess themselves and what they are doing or not doing
- By encouraging the group to set new work standards and debate about what the standards will be and how they will be met

One caution to keep in mind is that generating conflict in a group must be done in a positive manner, emphasizing the overall welfare of the group rather than in a way that destructively pits group members against each other or the leader. Conflict is like fire—it can keep the group warm and vibrant, or it can incinerate the group. The leader's responsibility is to maintain a controlled burn in the group, that is, a fire that will keep things warm but not rage out of control.

Generally, it is not what a group does that distinguishes between constructive and destructive conflict, but how the group does it. The following situations will generate conflict; how the conflict is handled will determine the constructiveness or destructiveness of the result. Group members can generate conflict by the following actions:

- Being completely honest with each other
- Disagreeing with each other
- Dealing with frustration and pressure
- Confronting each other about problematic behavior
- Competing with each other for success
- Challenging established policies or practices
- Introducing new ideas
- Placing responsibility for failures
- Dealing with a violation of group rules

All of these actions are likely to generate conflict, and both the group and the leader are responsible for dealing with these issues in a positive, group-strengthening way. The following framework is not meant to be a recipe or script, but merely a theoretical construct of how this can be accomplished.

"We've got some issues to discuss. We can go about this in one of three ways. We can pretend they don't exist and hope they'll go away on their own. The problem with this is they won't go away; they'll only fester and spread and take us down, sooner or later. We can deal with them by putting each other down, which just brings the whole group down. We can deal with them as a group issue—we've got an issue that affects all of us, and we need to pull together to resolve it. Each one of us, including me, has blind spots, weaknesses, and makes mistakes once in a while. If we can be secure enough to accept this, we'll probably resolve these issues a lot more comfortably and quickly."

If leaders take this type of approach, they must set an example by not denigrating group members and by admitting their own mistakes. This will clear a path for the rest of the group ("If Sarge can admit he messed up, maybe I can admit it when I do").

Personal Reflections

1. If you could only use one of the three theories of motivation just discussed, which one would you choose, and why?

2. What do you think is the biggest mistake leaders make in evaluating officers, and why do you think leaders make this mistake?

3. What is your understanding of an agency or company culture? How important is the culture in the overall picture of agency functioning or morale?

4. Discuss this statement: "Team cohesiveness is good, but only up to a point."

5. Discuss this statement: "Forming committees to work on a project is sometimes, but not always, a good idea."

Summary

Leadership is a two-edged sword in practically every conceivable way. It presents an opportunity to do great good or harm, experience significant success or failure, receive vast praise or blame, earn deep respect or disrespect, and progress in or derail one's career.

Leadership in general, but especially in law enforcement, is a critically important role and should be taken seriously. In this era of civil unrest, rampant litigation, media attention, police scandals, and officers leaving law enforcement for safer and more lucrative careers, the professional law enforcement agency must carefully select and train people for leadership positions. Officers can no

longer be promoted to these positions because it is their turn; because it is politically correct; or because they are well connected, have paid their dues, have a
college degree, or have command presence. The stakes are now too high for law
enforcement to view leadership as a reward rather than as a serious responsibility that calls for "the right stuff"—the right personal qualities, behaviors, situation, training, and support from the agency.

*R*eferences

Aamodt, M.G. (1999). *Applied industrial/organizational psychology* (3rd ed.). Pacific Grove,
   CA: Brooks/Cole.

Brown, J.M., & Campbell, E.A. (1990). Sources of occupational stress in police. *Work
   and Stress, 4,* 305–318.

Cavanagh, M.E. (1985). Personalities at work. *Personnel Journal, 64* (3), 54–64.

Cavanagh, M.E. (1987). Employee problems: Prevention and intervention. *Personnel Journal, 66* (9), 39–47.

Cordner, G.W., & Kenney, D.J. (Eds.) (1995). *Managing police organizations.* Cincinnati,
   OH: Anderson Publishing.

Glensor, R.W., Peak, K.J., & Gaines, L.K. (1999). *Police supervision.* New York: McGraw-Hill.

Hogan, R., Curphy, G.J., & Hogan, J. (1994). What we know about leadership: Effectiveness
   and personality. *American Psychologist, 49,* 493–504.

International Association of Chiefs of Police (1999). *Police leadership in the 21st century:
   Achieving and sustaining executive success.* Recommendations for the President's First
   Leadership Conference. Washington, DC: International Association of Chiefs of Police.

International Association of Chiefs of Police (2000). *Police accountability and citizen review:
   A leadership opportunity for police chiefs.* Washington, DC: A Project Response Publication, International Association of Chiefs of Police.

Jones, T.L. (1998). Autocratic vs. people-minded managers. *Law and Order Magazine, 5*
   (Online version). Retrieved from the World Wide Web: http://infobase.thirdcoast.net
   /clients/lawandorder/archiveissues.

Jurkanin, T.J., Hoover, L.T., Dowling, J.L., & Ahmad, J. (2001). *Enduring, surviving, and
   thriving as a law enforcement executive.* Springfield, IL: Charles C Thomas.

More, H.W., & Wegener, W.F. (1992). *Behavioral police management.* New York: Macmillan.

National Institute of Justice and the Office of Community Oriented Policing Services
   (1997). *Police integrity: Public service with honor.* (NIJ163811). Washington, DC: U.S.
   Department of Justice.

Peter, L.J., & Hull, R. (1996). *The Peter principle.* New York: William Morrow.

Schultz, D., & Schultz, S.E. (2001). *Psychology and work today* (8th ed.). Upper Saddle
   River, NJ: Prentice Hall.

7

Interviewing Witnesses

The eyewitness testimony of both victim witnesses and bystander witnesses is a crucial determinant of whether a case will be brought against a suspect and whether a jury will find the suspect guilty or innocent. As Vrij (1998, p. 105) states: "Evidence in criminal trials is often based upon eyewitness testimonies: It has been estimated that around 77,000 people a year in the USA are charged with crimes solely on the basis of eyewitness evidence." Loftus (1979, p. 9) notes: "Jurors have been known to accept testimony pointing to guilt even when it is *far* outweighed by evidence of innocence."

This information should serve as a stark reminder to law enforcement and citizens alike that eyewitness testimony is an area fraught with potential problems, and that all law enforcement officers, not only investigators, need to interview witnesses in a professional and effective manner. As Walker (1998) notes, the Rand Corporation's 1979 study on criminal investigations states:

> The single most important determinant of whether or not a case will be solved is the information the victim supplies to the immediately responding patrol officer. If information that uniquely identifies the perpetrator is not presented at the time the crime is reported, the perpetrator, by and large, will not be subsequently identified. (p. 78)

The behavioral sciences have learned a good deal about eyewitness testimony in the past quarter century, and this knowledge has been acquired by many in the judicial system, including defense attorneys. The days of officers asking witnesses a series of commonsense questions and marching into court with the answers and their witnesses in tow are quickly coming to an end. Unfortunately, at the present time, law enforcement education and training with respect to interviewing are often inadequate. The need for a professional approach to interviewing is seen in Fisher's (1995) comments:

Despite the importance of eyewitness information in criminal investigation, police receive inadequate training to interview cooperative witnesses. They make avoidable mistakes that minimize the amount of eyewitness information elicited and contribute to inaccurate recollections.

. . . Because formal training is often lacking or of such meager quality, many police are either guided by intuition or they learn on the job, by trial-and-error or by observing more senior partners conduct interviews. As a result of this laissez-faire attitude, police often maintain a less-than-rigorous attitude toward interviewing. As one police investigator said, "Basically, you just ask them who, what, when, where, why, and how." (pp. 732, 734)

This chapter first addresses the nature of eyewitness testimony followed by a discussion of the psychological aspects of interviewing witnesses, leaving the legal aspects to other sources. To prepare for being in a position to interview witnesses effectively, officers need to have a clear understanding of the dynamics of eyewitness accounts. They can then focus on the goal of eliciting accurate and complete testimony from both adult and child witnesses. When officers have a firm understanding of the psychological dimensions of interviewing, they can be more confident in the strength of their witnesses, the soundness of their cases, and the effectiveness of their court presentations in the face of increasingly sophisticated cross-examination. To this end the following topics will be discussed: eyewitness testimony, officer self-evaluation, memory theory, the retrieval environment, the state of witnesses, the cognitive interview, avoiding traps, interviewing children, and methods of identifying suspects.

EYEWITNESS TESTIMONY

The accuracy or inaccuracy of eyewitness testimony has enormously important repercussions. As Goodman and colleagues (1999) state:

How accurate is eyewitness testimony? Part of our fascination with this question derives from the fact that people's fate may hang on human memory, which is known to be fallible. Innocent people accused of serious crimes through eyewitness reports face false imprisonment, financial ruin, and loss of reputation. And not only can the fate of the accused rest on witness accuracy, but so may the fate of the victim; for instance, if an accurate victim is not believed, the victim may endure further assaults by the perpetrator and disillusionment with the legal system. (p. 218)

Inaccurate Eyewitness Testimony

A classic example of inaccurate eyewitness testimony causing great damage to an innocent person is the case of Father Bernard T. Pagano, a Catholic priest. An individual called "The Gentleman Bandit," because he was so nice and apologized to his victims, committed a series of armed robberies near Wilmington, Delaware. State police distributed composite drawings of the suspect based on several victim descriptions. Anonymous calls led officers to Father Pagano, who resembled the composite drawing. At trial, *seven victims* identified the priest as the robber. When conviction looked imminent, the true robber, 15 years younger and in jail for other crimes, stepped forward and admitted his guilt. One can only imagine the upheaval this caused the priest as well as his parishioners, family, and friends during the long period between arrest and trial.

Unfortunately, the accuracy of eyewitness testimony is not nearly as high as most people, including law enforcement officers and jurors, believe. The memory process includes many opportunities for memories to be lost or distorted, even in the most intelligent and well-intentioned people. As Wrightsman (2001) states: "Studies in the psychological laboratory or controlled field studies that simulate a crime and then determine the degree of accuracy of eyewitnesses confirm the fear that false identifications by bystanders occur with frightful frequency" (pp. 121–22).

Recently, due to the use of DNA testing and heightened interest in the death penalty, the accuracy of victim-witness and bystander-witness testimony is being questioned on several fronts. For example, a study by Wells and colleagues (1998) examined 40 cases in the United States in which innocent people were convicted of serious crimes and served time in prison, five of them on death row. After DNA analysis exonerated these individuals, they were declared innocent and released from prison. In these 40 cases, 36 (90 percent) involved erroneous eyewitness (including victim-witness) evidence. When combining *all* the witnesses involved in the 40 cases, 31 were victim witnesses (2 cases had 2 victim witnesses) and 10 were bystander witnesses (1 case had 5 bystander witnesses), all of whom were wrong and helped send 40 innocent men to prison. These cases were chosen for analysis solely because DNA exonerated innocent men, not because of the rate of erroneous witness identification. This analysis points out, among other things, that the testimony of victim witnesses, who in most cases clearly saw and heard the perpetrator, is not necessarily more accurate than that of bystander witnesses.

Another study of falsely convicted defendants by Scheck, Neufeld, and Dwyer (2000) examined the wrongful convictions of 62 defendants later found to be innocent based on DNA evidence. There were 15 (9.3 percent) instances of false witness testimony and 52 (84 percent) of mistaken identification. There was 1 mistaken bystander witness in 34 cases, 2 in 14 cases, 3 in 2 cases, 4 in 1 case, and 5 in 1 case (pp. 263–264).

This question then arises: How can so many people be so wrong about such serious matters? These and many other studies lead to the inescapable conclusion that far too many mistakes are being made in preparing cases in the area of eyewitness testimony. However, a great deal can be done to increase the accuracy of eyewitness accounts. As is stated in *Eyewitness Evidence: A Guide for Law Enforcement* (1998) published by the U.S. Department of Justice: "During the past 20 years, research psychologists have produced a substantial body of findings regarding eyewitness evidence. These findings offer the legal system a valuable body of empirical knowledge in the area of eyewitness evidence" (p. 1).

OFFICER SELF-EVALUATION

The officer's first step in conducting a witness interview is to prepare psychologically for it whenever possible. This is easier to do when officers have made an appointment to meet with witnesses and more difficult at a fresh crime scene. In either case, however, officers can develop a pre-interview attitude that they can carry, even unconsciously, into every witness interview. This attitude flows from two sets of self-reflection questions:

1. "How much pressure, if any, am I under to solve this case and carry it through to a successful prosecution?"

    Moderate pressure can be facilitative because it can fuel highly productive and successful behavior. However, insufficient pressure may cause officers to be lackadaisical, which leads to such witness reactions as hostility: "If this cop doesn't care, I sure don't care." On the other hand, too much pressure can lead officers and, subsequently, witnesses to make mistakes, thus sabotaging the case ("This cop is trying to put words in my mouth").

    The pressure on the officer can be internal and external. Internal pressure is self-generated and occurs when officers try too hard to make the case, pressuring themselves, victims, and witnesses to the extent that mistakes are made that can have serious consequences for all concerned.

    External pressure stems from without—from victims, their families and neighbors, the officer's coworkers and immediate supervisors, the neighborhood where the crime was committed, the officer's family, the media, city officials, and the executives of the agency.

    The worst case for the officer is to have great internal pressure pushing out and great external pressure pushing in, creating the ingredients for spontaneous combustion. Officers continually need to check the gauge on these pressures in order to relate to witnesses in ways that help rather than hinder the process.

2. "What are my attitudes toward witnesses in general and this witness in particular? Do I see that this witness genuinely wants to help, cooperates despite the stressors involved, will make mistakes despite his or her best efforts, is sometimes frightened and therefore sometimes reluctant, and is someone who needs my continuing patience and support? Or, do I view this witness as stupid, a source of frustration, a waste of time, or somebody who is going to really mess up my case?"

    Officers' attitudes are clear to the witness from the very first contact and set the tone for the remainder of the relationship. Generally, positive attitudes evoke positive attitudes, or at least neutral attitudes in hostile witnesses, whereas negative attitudes evoke negative attitudes, even in the most positively disposed witnesses. Having a positive, or at least a neutral, attitude toward a witness is not just a public relations tactic. It is a necessity if eyewitness testimony is to be accurate and complete.

If good rapport exists between officers and witnesses, both are likely to go to great lengths to help each other. When rapport is poor, both are likely, at least unconsciously, to make each other's job as difficult as possible, even if it hurts the case. Leaving humanitarian motives aside, if officers want to get the most cooperation from witnesses, even hostile ones, they need to treat them as they would want to be treated, or have a loved one treated, in the same situation.

Personal Reflections

1. Have you ever wanted to share something of importance with people who seemed so distracted that they hardly paid attention to what you said? How did it make you feel about that person and the whole situation?

2. How well do you typically pay attention to people when they want to tell you something that is important to them? Do you pay complete attention, ignoring all distractions, or do you let your mind wander to what you want to say next?

MEMORY THEORY

One of the basic problems in interviewing eyewitnesses is the failure to use a proper theory of memory on which to base interview questions. The following describes a theory of memory that provides a framework for officers with respect to interviewing witnesses, writing reports, and testifying in court.

The *reconstructive theory of memory* (Nairne, 2002) is the one most accepted by psychologists. The term *reconstructive* comes from the idea that memories are never exact representations of a perceived event but rather a "reconstruction." Memory is added to, subtracted from, or changed in other ways, so that at any given point in time, it may resemble the actual event closely or not at all. This theory holds that memory has three parts: acquisition, retention, and retrieval.

Acquisition (Encoding)

As witnesses observe a crime, they acquire information. Even at this early stage, several conscious and unconscious psychological events can occur in a split second that interfere with the memory being accurate and complete. Among these events are the following.

Stereotyped expectations.   A white man hears gunshots coming from a liquor store and sees a black man with a gun running out of the store. He is certain that the man is the robber and shooter when, in fact, the man is an off-duty police officer chasing the white perpetrator. This misperception stems from the witness's stereotypical idea that if a crime has been committed and it is not clear whether a black or white man committed it, it is more likely the black man did.

Selective perception.   In the stress of the situation just described, the witness experiences tunnel vision ("gun focus"), and so can describe the gun but not the man with the gun except that he was a black male. The witness failed to see the white perpetrator who was only a few feet away from the pursuing off-duty officer. He also experienced auditory exclusion: He did not hear the man with the gun yell: "Freeze—police officer!" on two occasions.

Maximizing/minimizing.   The same witness *maximizes* the size of the man with a gun. He perceives him as 6 feet 2 inches and 230 pounds, when, in fact, he is 5 feet 11 inches and 200 pounds. He also *minimizes* the number of gunshots; he perceives two when, in fact, there were three.

Experiencing illusions.   The witness perceives the event, but in a distorted, misleading way. He "swears" he saw the owner of the store, whom he knows, also chase the man with the gun out of the store when, in fact, the owner was not working that day.

As can be seen from even these few examples, people do not remember *reality*, only their *perceptions of reality*. Memory can be very malleable. Moreover, little or no correlation exists between witnesses' confidence and the accuracy and completeness of their recollections. The practical problems that can arise from misperceptions can be enormous, from convicting an innocent person to freeing a guilty one.

Retention (Storage)

The perceptions of the crime are encoded in the brain, which then stores them for future reference. As in the case of acquisition, several conscious and unconscious events can occur over time to interfere with the accuracy and completeness of an individual's memory and recall. The following is a sample of these intervening variables.

Time delay.   Memories left unattended in storage—that is, not periodically refreshed—can decay, disappear, or become vague and distorted. For this reason, especially in important cases, officers should speak frequently with witnesses between the event and the trial to refresh their memory and make it tamper proof.

Postevent suggestion.   After the crime, witnesses may learn things about the event and believe they actually witnessed them at the time of the crime; for example, a witness learns some time after the crime that the perpetrator was wearing a black watch cap. Although she did not see a hat on the perpetrator, after a while her account not only includes that the perpetrator wore a *hat* but a *black watch cap*.

Forgetting/repressing.   In addition to the natural forgetting that occurs over time, victims of and witnesses to a traumatic crime can push the memory into the deepest recesses of their storage area. The effect is that witnesses have no recollection (psychological amnesia) or only partial recollection of the crime. This memory may be lost forever or recovered accurately or inaccurately at a later date.

Mistaken transference.   Witnesses can mistakenly transfer the identity of someone else to the suspect. For example, after a great deal of thought, a witness suddenly thinks he remembers the identity of the suspect, confusing the suspect with someone he had seen at some other time, possibly in the area where the crime was committed, but who had no connection with the crime.

Own race bias.   Witnesses are better at accurately identifying people of their own race, probably because they spend more time with them. A study by Malpass and Kravitz (1969) indicated that when asked to examine slides of black and white faces, white observers were more accurate with white faces than with black faces. Black observers gave equally correct responses for both white and black faces. In their study of wrongfully convicted people who were later freed due to DNA evidence, Scheck, Neufeld, and Dwyer (2000) found that 35 percent of Caucasians misidentified an African American defendant. However, this must be viewed against the backdrop of other related statistics: Twenty-eight percent of Caucasians misidentified a Caucasian defendant, and 24 percent of African Americans misidentified African American defendants. Only 1 percent of Caucasians misidentified a Latino defendant, and no Latinos misidentified an African American defendant. There were no statistics on the percentage of African Americans who misidentified Caucasian defendants.

Even in this brief, oversimplified presentation, it can be seen how at least nine psychological events can significantly and negatively affect accurate and complete recall of a crime.

Retrieval

After memories have been acquired and retained, they have the potential to return to consciousness. These memories can be totally or partially accurate, inaccurate, or forgotten. Below is a diagram of the possible domino effects that can occur in memory processing.

	Acquisition	Retention	Retrieval
Line 1:	accurate	accurate	accurate
Line 2:	accurate	inaccurate	inaccurate
Line 3:	inaccurate	inaccurate	inaccurate
Line 4:	accurate	forgotten	forgotten

It is the task of officers to try to keep Line 1 intact between the crime and testifying in court. In Line 2, officers can attempt to rehabilitate the inaccurate retention and return it to its original accurate state. In Line 3, officers can do little, because the retrieval inaccuracy began at the moment of acquisition. In Line 4, officers can attempt to refresh and retrieve the witness's recollection of her originally accurate acquisition.

The greatest danger for officers at this point is postevent suggestion. In their zeal to confirm their theory of the crime, officers can consciously or unconsciously give the witness new information that can become incorporated into the witness's storage area and later be retrieved as fact rather than as an artifact of postevent suggestion. Even when the officer's suggestion is unconscious and inadvertent, it can cause serious problems for the prosecution when defense attorneys cross-examine on this pseudo-memory.

Sometimes when people experience an event so traumatic that they are unable to process it, they psychologically repress it as though it never occurred. At a later time, often many years later, an event may thrust the repressed memory into consciousness. For example, a woman may have been sexually molested when she was 3 years of age, repressed the memory for 20 years, and, in the course of counseling, this memory surfaces.

Although heated debate surrounds the legitimacy of "recovered memories," few deny that victims can have psychological amnesia about a traumatic event under certain circumstances. When the recovered memories concern possible criminal actions, officers will often have to become involved in interviewing these victims and witnesses. Therefore, officers can be mindful of the following points.

- The fact that a person "remembers" a past trauma does not mean that it occurred in reality. On the other hand, the fact that a person cannot remember a trauma, even with the help of counseling, hypnosis, or sodium amytal, does not mean it did not occur in reality.
- Memories of trauma are not necessarily either accurate or inaccurate; they can be both.
- There may be no relationship between the vividness of a memory and whether or not the event actually occurred.
- The fact that a person recants a memory of a trauma does not necessarily mean that the trauma did not, in fact, occur.
- The fact that a person is currently psychologically disturbed does not necessarily indicate that her memory of the trauma is false; maybe she is disturbed *because* she has repressed the memory of the trauma.

- The fact that a person sincerely and vehemently denies the existence of a trauma does not necessarily mean that it did not occur.
- It is virtually impossible to distinguish between true and false memories without corroboration.
- Because of repression, people do not report trauma when it occurs. This renders invalid the claim: "If it really happened when she said it did, she certainly would have told *somebody* at that time."
- Simply because a person recovers memories of a trauma that are found to be accurate does not necessarily mean that *all* the person's memories of the event are also accurate.

Officers should not formally take a position in the recovered memory debate based on their own opinions. Scores of experts who have thoroughly researched this area for many years are divided on the topic because of the profound complexity of the issues involved. Officers can, however, become informed on the key issues, so that they can discuss them intelligently.

Officers also should be familiar with their state laws pertaining to the admission of "recovered memory" evidence in criminal cases because laws differ from state to state. Brown, Scheflin, and Hammond (1998) offer an extensive review of repressed memory and the law and conclude:

> Criminal cases that turn exclusively on repressed memory will be hard for prosecutors to win, unless the repressed memory provides details not previously reported or known, thereby authenticating the veracity of the memory. The presence of additional evidence supporting the repressed memory will always be helpful and, in most states, will likely be necessary. (p. 518)

Personal Reflections

1. How many times in your life in normal situations were you *convinced* that you saw somebody you recognized on the street and later discovered that person was miles away when you thought you saw her?
2. How many times in your life was someone *convinced* that she saw *you* someplace, but it clearly was not you?
3. How many times in your life have you been immersed in a highly stressful situation, were *convinced* you saw or heard something that did not, in fact, happen, or *did not* see or hear something that *did*, in fact, happen?

THE RETRIEVAL ENVIRONMENT

The retrieval segment of the memory process is the most important for two reasons: It yields information about a crime, and it is the only aspect of the process over which officers have some control. Retrieving memories is far more complex than simply asking a witness: "So, what happened at the liquor store?" Officers can create a facilitative retrieval environment, which maximizes rather than minimizes the potential for helping witnesses retrieve memories that are both accurate and complete.

There are two kinds of retrieval environments: physical and psychological. Ideally, the physical environment should be comfortable, quiet, private, and devoid of distractions and interruptions, including phone calls. For this reason, the typical police station is probably the worst place to hold a serious interview. Officers can identify with the plight of witnesses if they picture themselves trying to have a critically important conversation in a place that is loud and distracting with someone who is attending to other business half the time. Often officers need to be creative in finding at least a tolerable location for the interview.

Creating a psychological environment begins at the instant of first contact, even if it is simply a short phone conversation to set up an appointment. The officer's choice of words, tone of voice, facial expression, demeanor, body language, and manner of dress communicate a clear message. Basically, officers communicate one of two messages: "I'm very busy, so you're going to have to meet with me as soon as possible so I can get this out of the way and get to my other cases," or "I'm looking forward to working with you because, between the two of us, we might be able put these suspects away for a long time." First impressions of the officer typically set the tone for the rest of the relationship and are usually difficult, though not impossible, to change.

After positive first impressions are formed, maintaining rapport must be a continuing process, not something to get out of the way so the real work can get done. Officers who have the attitude "I don't care if witnesses like me or not; I'm not in a popularity contest. I've got a job to do, and I'm going to do it," are unlikely to succeed because witnesses often are unable to relate to them in a positive manner. The following are some basic rapport-building messages and their polar opposites:

- "I respect you," in contrast to "You look like a pretty shaky witness to me."

- "I appreciate your coming forward," in contrast to "As if I don't have enough grief in my life, I have to deal with you."

- "I understand this is very difficult for you," in contrast to "This is my twentieth rape case this year, so it's no big deal."

- "You can trust that I know what I'm doing," in contrast to "I'm drowning in work—who are you, and what case are you here about?"

- "What I need from you is an accurate and complete picture of what you saw on the night in question," in contrast to "Here's a pencil and some paper. Let me tell you what you saw that evening."

- "Sometimes being a witness isn't easy—it's understandable if you are confused, upset, unsure, and even want to correct your account as we progress," in contrast to "You'd better get yourself together because this is important stuff, and we can't mess it up."

Establishing and maintaining good rapport is not only the *right* thing but also the *smart* thing to do. On a purely practical level, officers will obtain far more information from relaxed, confident, trusting witnesses than from scared, hostile, and suspicious ones.

In the same vein, it can be very helpful and efficient to give witnesses an information sheet to help them understand the process and put them at ease. An example of such a document is presented in Box 7.1.

When the case goes to court, officers can present this victim/witness orientation form as part of their professional and good faith efforts to obtain honest, accurate, and complete information from the witness. In cases in which the victims/witnesses are unable to read or understand the form, officers can go over it with them.

Box 7.1

What You Should Know as a Victim or Witness

As the victim of a crime or a witness to a crime, it is very important that you remember, as accurately and completely as possible, exactly what you observed so that justice can be done. Please read the following and sign it, and if you have any questions, feel free to ask them.

It is perfectly all right to:

- Admit you can't remember something. Do not guess, infer, fill in gaps with what "probably happened," and *never lie*, even for a "good cause."
- Tell the officer if you are feeling pressured to say things you do not feel comfortable about.
- Make mistakes and admit them immediately, so that wrong decisions will not be made on the basis of misinformation.
- Say *anything* that comes to your mind as it relates to the crime, even if you feel it is silly, stupid, crazy, or doesn't make sense. Sometimes things that sound stupid can actually have a bearing on the case.
- Identify the portions of your account that you feel more confident about and that you feel less confident about.
- Correct your story if necessary—sometimes our memories can play tricks on us, and the officer understands this.
- Make contradictory statements; between you and the officers these will be cleared up.

- Admit how you feel as the process continues. You may experience a wide range of emotions (fear, anger, guilt, depression, confusion), which are important to share with officers.
- Admit whether you have heard things about the crime afterward and whether others have spoken to you about it, so that officers will know what you actually observed at the crime and what you heard afterward from others, including the media.
- Ask officers any questions you have. There are no stupid questions, just good questions that officers may or may not be able to answer.

Signed _____   Date _____

Officer _____   Date _____

THE STATE OF WITNESSES

Once rapport is established, officers need to know not only what witnesses are going to say but also what kinds of people they are, because this could be more important than what they have to say, especially in court. Officers will want to know the answers to the following questions.

1. What was the *physical* state of the victims/witnesses when they observed the crime? Do they have good vision and hearing? If they wear glasses, did they have them on when they witnessed the crime? Are they sufficiently mobile to have moved around at the crime scene as quickly as they say they did?

2. What is their current physical state? Have they had medical problems since the time of the crime that could affect their testifying; for example, have they had a stroke, developed visual or hearing problems, or do they currently need to take medications?

3. What was the *psychological* state of the victims/witnesses at the time of the crime? Psychological disturbances, strong emotions such as fear or rage, and drugs and alcohol can impair perception and distort observations. It is better to know and work with this possibility than to have it revealed in court.

4. What is their current psychological state? Are the witnesses currently confused, drunk, high on drugs, emotionally unstable? These issues must be addressed before a formal statement is taken and before the witness enters the courtroom. Simply admonishing "Don't shoot up before you go to court" is not a sufficient safeguard.

5. Do the witnesses have a personal stake in the case? Sometimes witnesses have a vested interest in the case. A witness against a suspect

may be a jilted lover, a disgruntled employee, or a jealous friend who is seeking revenge rather than justice. On the other hand, the witness may be emotionally involved with the suspects and may tilt testimony in favor of them. When this is revealed in court, it could be a serious blow to the witness's credibility.

6. How do victims/witnesses feel about being involved in the case? Do they feel comfortable, confident, righteous—or distressed, ashamed, guilty, or tentative due to something they did or failed to do at the time of the crime? For example, if witnesses feel that they should have done more to protect the victim, they may omit observations that bring that fact to light. Are they afraid to testify in court, to be embarrassed or make fools of themselves? Are they afraid of possible reprisals against them or their families as a result of their testimony? If these issues are not dealt with openly as soon as possible, they can haunt the witness's testimony all the way to court, making it too zealous, tentative, confused, porous, or incredible.

Answers to these questions should be obtained as soon as possible; otherwise, witnesses could be like time bombs set to explode at the worst time, right before going to court or while on the witness stand.

Personal Reflections

1. Can you think of a situation in your life when the first impression a person left with you took a long to change or may never have changed?

2. If you witnessed a violent crime, would you freely come forward as a witness, or would you be reluctant in light of the "hassle" it would cause you and possible retribution from the perpetrators?

3. Most witnesses believe they are great witnesses, even when they are mediocre or even horrible witnesses. Why do you think this is so?

4. What reluctance, if any, would officers have in giving victims/witnesses the What You Should Know as a Victim or Witness form to read and sign?

5. Do you think officers ever intentionally overlook the fact that important witnesses are weak and allow them to testify, hoping that the defense attorney will not see the weaknesses?

THE COGNITIVE INTERVIEW

Historically, witness interviews have largely been based on the intuitions and needs of the interviewing officers and not on sound psychological theory and research. This has often created situations in which witness accounts are shaped by the officers' well-intentioned attempts to solve the crime quickly rather than simply elicit an accurate and complete account of what actually happened at the scene. Throughout the remainder of this chapter, the term *witness* will include both victim witnesses and bystander witnesses, unless the context clearly refers to only one or the other. Moreover, when interviews are not standardized, the same witness may give what appear to be conflicting accounts of the event to different officers when, in fact, it is the interview techniques that are in conflict and thus elicit seemingly different versions of the same event.

Professional interviewers recognize the importance of using techniques that are based on what is known about how people perceive and recall events. One technique that has been effective in this regard is the cognitive interview (Milne & Bull, 1999), which has been researched with children as well as adults and generally has been found to be equally effective, increasing witness recall up to 50 percent and more with no more errors or confabulation than typical interview methods.

This method is based on cognitive psychology and combines what is known about memory and recall with psychologically sound interviewing techniques. Because of its solid theoretical foundation, it is more cross-examination-proof than are other methods, and it affords a rationale, logic, and structure to interviews that are lacking in the "flying by the seat of the pants" interviews often conducted by even experienced investigators. The following brief description of the seven phases of the cognitive interviewing method makes it appear simple but, in fact, formal training is required to use it properly.

Phase I: Building Rapport

In this initial phase, officers build a relationship with the witness. While the relationship is an ongoing process, its foundations can be set in the first five minutes of the interview. Through their verbal and nonverbal behavior, officers communicate three basic messages:

> *Empathy message.* "What you've witnessed/experienced must be very upsetting to you, and I certainly can understand that. Would you like to tell us how you're feeling now?"

> *Relaxing message.* "We'll help you through this process all the way. All you have to do is paint a picture of what you observed; there are no right or wrong answers, and we'll do the rest."

> *Humanizing message.* "Let us tell you something about us so you'll know who we are, and we'd like to know something about you so we can both feel comfortable with each other."

Several behaviors can interfere with rapport building, including the following:

- *Being abrupt, businesslike, and impersonal.* "Just the facts, ma'am."
- *Placing pressure on the witness.* "This is very important so there's no room for mistakes here."

- *Interrupting.* "Excuse me, I don't mean to interrupt again, but. . . ."
- *Being critical.* "Wait a minute. You say you were standing *here* and could see all the way *over there?*"

Phase II: Setting the Stage

The four goals of this stage are to

- Advise the witness that intense, focused concentration is necessary. All distractions must be blocked out and, for this reason, the interview should take place in a distraction-free environment.
- Interview at the appropriate time. Whenever possible, witnesses should be interviewed twice shortly after the crime. The first interview occurs immediately after the event, so that memories are fresh. But, ideally a second interview should take place a few hours later. When witnesses have calmed down, their recall is often more accurate and complete. Witnesses often intuitively know this: "I need some time to pull myself together and gather my thoughts."
- Advise witnesses to share everything, even things that seem stupid, irrelevant, or crazy.
- Reassure the witnesses that *they* are the experts as to what happened and therefore will be doing the bulk of the talking and explaining. The officers are merely facilitators and listeners.

Phase III: Establishing Free Recall

Once officers have a general idea of what the witness observed, they initiate the free recall process. Free recall means that witnesses are invited to tell their story in their own words, at their own pace, and without interruption. Officers can simply say to the witness: "Tell me what happened. . ." and sit back and listen. Video- or audiotaping the interview is preferable to taking notes, which is distracting to both officers and witnesses and inadvertently sends messages to witnesses as to what is important and what is unimportant. Notes can be made from the tape at a later time, if necessary.

The principle is that if witnesses are allowed to give full reign to their memories, they will offer a more accurate and complete picture than if officers guide them to places the officers want to go. Witnesses can let their minds wander, like a roving camera, taking in both narrow and wide expanses of the physical and psychological terrain that surrounded the crime, telling what they saw, heard, smelled, felt, or tasted; what they did not observe; and how they felt at different times. Analogously, they are making a documentary film of the crime scene as they perceived it. In free recall, they tell their story devoid of distractions, guidance, interruptions, or judgments as to its accuracy or completeness. The more the officer disappears into the background, the better it is, so that the officer's unconscious facial expressions, body movements, and sighs do not contaminate the free flow of ideas and feelings.

The free recall will likely address the following questions: What happened? Where did it happen? When did it happen? Who was there? Who did what? Where were the other witnesses? Where was the witness? As a result of the free recall, officers should have a fairly clear, general picture of what the witnesses observed. The officers can then focus on specific frames of the picture.

Phase IV: Questioning

In this phase, officers question the witnesses about the content of their free recall.

Preparing the witness for questioning.   Before beginning to question witnesses, officers should prepare the witnesses so they will be receptive to the various types of questions to follow. The following considerations will help officers in this regard:

- Officers encourage the witnesses to form a mental picture that corresponds to each question before answering: "You did a great job telling us what you observed. Now, we'd like to ask you some questions but, instead of going to your brain for the answers, go to your eyes and ears. Let our questions flash a picture on a screen and answer the questions looking directly at the images you see."
- Officers should exhaust all the questions they have immediately after each specific image that the witness describes. Analogously, once they are finished with one picture, they should file it away until the next phase. Continually switching back and forth to different pictures in the same phase can create confusion.
- Officers should ask *only* the questions that stem from the witness's account and in the *order* of the witness's account. In other words, officers should not ask questions about events that the witness did not mention in free recall, nor should officers ask questions outside of the witness's sequence, even if the sequence of the witness's account did not correspond to the actual sequence of events.
- Officers should always begin with open-ended questions before asking specific questions.
- Officers should assure the witness that it is perfectly all right to say "I don't know," or "I don't understand the question."

Types of questions.   Only after the free recall is completed do the officers begin asking questions. Questions should rarely, if ever, be asked during free recall because they can taint or distract from the witness's account. After free recall has been thoroughly exhausted, it is appropriate to ask two types of questions: open-ended and specific questions.

Open-ended questions invite witnesses to recall in their own words and at their own pace what they observed within certain parameters. These questions are meant to flesh out specific parts of the picture that was developed during free recall. Examples of open-ended questions are "What did people do when they saw the knife?" "What did the victim say to the paramedics?" "What did you talk about with other witnesses before you left the scene?"

Open-ended questions are in contrast to *close-ended ones,* which ordinarily can be answered with a simple "yes" or "no," for example: "Were the streetlights on yet?" or "Did you ever lose sight of the suspect?" Open-ended questions are also in contrast to *multiple-choice questions*, for example: "Who saw the knife first—the victim, the victim's sister, a witness, or none of the above?"

Both close-ended and multiple-choice questions not only yield the least information, but their insinuating nature can taint accounts and be misleading. For example, the question "Did you see the knife?" may pressure witnesses to say they saw a knife, when, in fact, they did not.

For some reason, open-ended questions seem to be difficult for officers to ask, possibly because they unconsciously try to angle witnesses into saying what officers want to hear or to simply "cut to the chase." Even officers who insist that they ask mostly open-ended questions discover that, in fact, they do not, when tapes of their interviews are played back to them.

Specific questions are "sweeping up" questions, which should begin only after what can be gained from open-ended questions is exhausted. These questions gather bits and pieces of information that remain after free recall and open-ended questions have been asked. Examples of specific questions are "At what point did you pick up the knife and place it on the sink?" "Exactly where were you standing when the guy with the knife begin slashing?"

Open-ended and specific questions tend to yield the most information with the least potential for contaminating witness accounts because they are based on what witnesses have already said and not on inferences that may lie within the officer's questions.

Phase V: Returning to the Original Retrieval

Once the witness has gone through the free recall phase, followed by officers asking questions about the event, officers begin a second, third, or fourth search of the original retrieval field. The more that witnesses return to the scene of the original retrieval with "fresh eyes," the more new information they are likely to retrieve. This process, however, should not imply that the original retrieval was inadequate: "OK, you're doing great. Now, to wrap up, we need to go back over your story because, if you're like the rest of us, some things may have inadvertently slipped your mind."

Just as officers would not search the same field for evidence in exactly the same way time after time, they should develop new strategies for searching the retrieval field. Some common strategies follow:

- To have the witness begin the account from the finish and work backward to the beginning, or from the middle and work forward or backward.
- To have the witness change perspectives. If the witness was a bystander, the officer states: "Now put yourself in the place of the victim. What do you think *she* saw, heard, felt?"
- To have the witness sketch what was observed, or to stage the scene, using anything available: paper clips for people, erasers for vehicles, pencils for streets, staplers for buildings.

Phase VI: Summarizing

Officers summarize what they heard the witness say. In addition to clarifying the officer's perceptions, this can act as another retrieval search for the witness ("Oh, come to think of it, maybe it was more like 11:30, not 11:00, when I heard the screams"). Once both the officers and the witness are "on the same page," a written statement can be taken, which also acts like a retrieval search.

Phase VII: Closing

Officers thank the witness, adding again that they know this was a difficult experience. They tell the witness how beneficial the interview was and what a great job the witness did under difficult circumstances. They give the witness their business card, inviting the witness to contact them if more information or questions come to mind. Allowing the witness to leave feeling good is important because, in addition to being the right thing to do, it paves the way for further cooperation if the witness needs to testify in court at a later date.

Because the cognitive interview can, at times, be time-consuming, many officers reserve its use for more serious crimes that are likely to be adjudicated in court. However, a brief form of the cognitive interview can also be used in exigent situations in which Phases I, V, VI, and VII can be shortened or eliminated. However, as is true with all shortcuts, the effects are not likely to be as promising nor is the method as likely to withstand the onslaught of cross-examination if the case reaches the courtroom.

Personal Reflections _____

1. Why would some officers resist doing cognitive interviews and why?
2. What do you see as the strengths and weaknesses of the cognitive interview?

3. If you were a witness, how would you feel about going through a cognitive interview? Would you feel it would help you pull together your memories, or do you feel some other interview method would be more helpful to you?

AVOIDING TRAPS

The more important the case and the greater the number of witnesses, the more likely pitfalls will arise in the interview process. This section discusses several problems officers need to avoid, so that their relationships with witnesses can be productive and professional.

Talking Too Much

Officers often talk too much and ask too many rapid-fire questions during interviews. This behavior has a twofold effect: It smothers the witnesses, which prevents proper reflection, and it takes control away from the witnesses and places it squarely in the hands of the officer. This makes it the *officer's* interview, and the witness is reduced to being a passive, reactive recipient of the officer's questions and directives. Part of talking too much is asking witnesses the same question over and over again, the clear inference being that the officer will continue to ask the question until the witness stumbles on "the right answer," which can taint their accounts.

Shaping Witness Accounts

Shaping means sculpting witness accounts to fit the officers' preconceived theory of the crime, whether or not it is accurate. Shaping testimony can occur consciously or unconsciously when officers react to witness accounts with facial expressions, sounds, and body language that denote approval or disapproval; give witnesses information they did not know; ask leading questions; and implant memories.

An example of officers giving witnesses information they did not know is "Are you absolutely certain her boyfriend only stabbed her *once*? A physician at the scene said he stabbed her three times. Could it be possible that you turned away after you saw the first stabbing?" A typical leading question is "You say the shooter was wearing a green shirt. Could it possibly have been a yellow shirt?"

An example of implanting a memory in a child sexual abuse case is "You say the man touched your tummy. I'll bet if he touched your tummy he touched you down there, too, didn't he?" This situation exemplifies the magic formula for implanting memories: a suggestible child, a high-status questioner (a person who is not only an all-knowing adult but also a police officer), and a clearly leading question. It is also the magic formula for getting testimony thrown out of court.

Shaping testimony is a perilous venture, analogous to ice sculpting. A sculpted ice figure can look quite solid, as long as it remains in the atmosphere in which it was shaped. However, as soon as it is moved to a warm environment, it melts. Shaped testimony always looks solid in the police station, but once it enters the warm environment of the courtroom, it melts. This is not a pretty sight to see, especially for the officer who did the shaping.

Ignoring Individual Differences

Individuals can have very different ways of responding to situations and expressing themselves. In other words, there is no one "appropriate" way in which people react to the same stimulus. Although this is obvious, officers often act as though it is not. For example, an officer asks five different witnesses the same question: "Are you *sure* you didn't see more than you're willing to tell me?" She notices that all of the witnesses respond differently.

> Witness A's face blanches, and he suddenly looks intently at the ceiling and finally whispers, "Yeah."
>
> Witness B steadily looks the officer in the eye and immediately responds with an edge in her voice: "I'm sure."
>
> Witness C's hands begin to shake; he looks confused and nervously asks: "Could you repeat the question?"
>
> Witness D takes a deep breath, fixes his eyes at some distant point and finally answers in an exasperated tone, "Of course, I'm sure."
>
> Witness E's face reddens; she leans forward in her chair, and blurts out: "*Of course I'm sure*. What do you *think*, I'm going to come in here and *lie* to you?"

Which witnesses are clearly telling the truth, which ones are hedging, and which ones are clearly lying? Many officers might judge that Witness B is clearly telling the truth, Witness A is clearly lying, Witness C is clearly hedging, Witness D is probably lying, and Witness E could be telling the truth, but her defensive reaction could also indicate she is lying.

The only correct answer is that it is impossible to tell from any of these reactions who is telling the truth, lying, or hedging because *different people can react very differently to the same stimulus.*

The officer's semi-accusatory question may be perceived as a stressor to some of the witnesses but not to others, which will create different reactions. After that, each individual processes the question and its implications differently and responds accordingly. Witness A *always* has that reaction when he's placed on the spot, but he's telling the truth. Witness B has learned the best way to lie is to look people squarely in the eye and affect a rather indignant tone. Witness C flashed back to being asked similar questions by his abusive father, became temporarily distracted, but told the truth. Witness D is insulted by the question, fights back an angry response, takes a deep breath, and tells the truth. Witness E *always* responds to perceived threats this way. She's a fighter and a truth-teller.

Participating in Confirmation Bias

Confirmation bias occurs when officers prematurely arrive at a theory of a crime and the identities of the perpetrators. Instead of weighing accounts of witnesses evenly, they register, at least unconsciously, only those portions that confirm their theory and ignore those that cast doubt on it.

Veteran officers particularly may be vulnerable to this error because, according to their estimation, they have a heightened "sixth sense" for sniffing out what really happened during a crime. Additionally, officers who are under a great deal of internal and external pressure to solve a crime may be especially prone to this error. Perhaps more than any other interviewing error, this attitude is likely to result in the officer arresting the wrong suspect and allowing the right one to remain free.

Confusing Hearing and Listening

It is important for officers to recognize the difference between *hearing* what witnesses say and *listening* to what they communicate. Hearing is a physiological process in which words are registered in the brain, whereas listening is a psychophysiological process by which ideas, feelings, attitudes, and values, as well as words, are registered. Officers can hear every word a witness says but miss the most important aspects of the communication. For example, a witness says: "I sure hope I'm doing the right thing coming forth like this." The officer responds: "You're absolutely doing the right thing—no question about it!" as he pages through his notes. Had the officer *listened* to all of the witness's verbal and nonverbal cues and "read between the lines," he would have dropped what he was doing and responded: "It sounds as though you may have some concerns about this. Why don't you tell me what they are, so I can understand and maybe help you with them?" This response will help the witness feel the officer cares about him as a person as well as a witness and may lead the witness to open up and divulge information that otherwise might not be forthcoming.

Making the Interview Officer Centered
Rather than Witness Centered

Law enforcement officers are used to taking control of situations, which, for the most part, is an appropriate and necessary part of their work. One of the few exceptions to this strategy, however, is in interviewing witnesses. Although it is obvious that witnesses cannot be permitted to take over an interview, they should be given a wide berth to express themselves in ways they feel the most comfortable. They are there to tell their story, not to have someone in the audience (the officers) continually jump on stage and direct each line.

Officers can exert too much control over the witness in the following ways:

- They can pin down the witness with so many rapid questions that the witness cannot breathe.
- They can routinely interrupt the witness; this is rude, distracting, and sends the message that the officer is displeased with the witness's efforts.
- They can routinely direct the witness to focus on areas that are of interest to the officer and away from areas that the witness needs to discuss.

Officer-controlled interviews present two problems. First, they establish the officer as the high-status person—the person who is in charge of and responsible for the success or failure of the interview. In fact, the witness is responsible for the productivity of each interview and therefore must be allowed to actively assume that responsibility.

Second, as the high-status person, the officer will, often unconsciously, establish a set of *demand characteristics*. This means that witnesses, even at less than conscious levels, can sense the officer's "demands" for the witness to respond in certain ways that may not match the witness's memories of the crime.

Failing to Have a Sense of Empathy for Witnesses

Understandably, it is often difficult for officers to maintain high levels of empathy for everyone with whom they deal. Empathy is not infinite and can be depleted by constant demands for it. Moreover, some witnesses, because of their personality, simply do not evoke much empathy. However, this does not change the fact that witnesses need at least some empathy to feel understood and respected in the situation.

Being a witness is often a novel and intimidating experience and, added to this, it may well be the first time the witness has ever spoken to a police officer or entered a law enforcement facility. On the other hand, this case may be the officer's eightieth major felony case of the year, so the current one is just another case and witness to get out of the way. Someplace between having deep empathy and no empathy for witnesses, officers need to find a place for at least some empathy so that mutual trust, respect, and cooperation can occur.

Empathy should remain after the trial, if there is one. Too often, after officers "win" in court, but especially after they "lose," they pay little attention to their witnesses. However, after the trial, many witnesses need closure with officers. If the prosecution was successful, witnesses need to share their relief and perhaps receive a little appreciation from officers. If the defendant was found not guilty, witnesses need even more support because they often feel as if they failed in some way.

Failing to Recognize Common Mistakes

Research (Milne & Bull, 1999, pp. 3–7) has found that officers often repeat the same mistakes in their interviews. An analysis of interview tapes indicates that the following are common, even among experienced officers.

- Officers appropriately begin interviews with free narrative ("Tell me what happened") but, after only seconds, interrupt and ask questions or try to focus the interview. Witnesses soon come to expect such interruptions, causing them to relate their story in brief bursts, thus shaping their story to the officers' prompting and not to the crime being described.
- Officers frequently ask rapid-fire, short-answer questions, often allowing only one second to pass between them, preventing any possibility of elaboration or clarification.
- Officers take complete charge of structuring the interview, casting the witness in the role of a passive participant.
- Officers frequently interrupt witness accounts to ask follow-up questions that were previously asked in the interview, thus thoroughly distracting the witness.
- Officers ask a great many leading questions, often apparently without realizing it ("Did you see the knife a few feet away from the body?"), placing witnesses in the position that, if they are to be a good witness, they *must* have seen a knife.
- Officers frequently use language and jargon far beyond witnesses' ability to grasp, making them feel inadequate.
- Officers have judgmental attitudes ("If you were standing next to the body, how could you *not* have seen the knife only a few feet away?"), which cause witnesses to feel bad about themselves and their efforts.
- Officers concentrate on only one sense ("Then what did you *see*?"), instead of all senses, which include hearing, feeling, smelling, even tasting. A better question is "Then what did you experience?"
- Officers often stop the witness's digressions when, in fact, they may be important sidelights to the story.
- Officers seem allergic to pauses, quickly filling in the slightest bit of silence with a question or comment, rather than understanding that silences are often productive periods during which witnesses are reflecting on important information.

When officers become aware of these common mistakes, they are in a better position to avoid them and make their interviews more effective.

Personal Reflections _____

1. Why do officers feel the need to "shape" witness accounts, and is there ever a good reason for this practice?
2. Why do you think the principle of individual differences is so obvious ("Everyone is different"), but can be completely ignored in some law enforcement practices?
3. Do you recognize confirmation bias as prevalent in our society? When is the last time you perceived only good things in a friend until the friendship broke up, and then you saw only bad things?
4. Do you understand the differences between "hearing" and "listening"? Can you recognize the differences in yourself and others when conversing?
5. Do you understand the concept of "demand characteristics"? Do you know people who, even though they invite you to be completely honest with them, have a way of letting you know exactly what they want to hear?

INTERVIEWING CHILDREN

Over the past few years, increasing numbers of children are coming forth as witnesses to crimes, mostly in child maltreatment and domestic violence cases. Frequently, their testimony is critical because they are the sole witnesses to the crimes. Interviewing children who are witnesses can be especially challenging because they are less developed cognitively, emotionally, and socially than adolescents and adults.

Some people believe that the accuracy of children's memories cannot be trusted due to their lack of overall development. Others believe such generalizations are incorrect—that, given the right circumstances, including a competent interviewer and adequate social supports, children can give quite accurate testimony.

Preliminary and accumulating research tends to support the latter view. For example, as Marxsen, Yuille, and Nisbet (1995) state:

> That young children are more suggestible than adults is well established. This does not mean that the investigative interviewing of children is impossible, only that it requires skill and care. However, the literature's overemphasis on suggestibility can give the police, the judiciary, the media, and the general public the mistaken impression that children are inherently unreliable. (p. 458)

Basic Considerations

The following points, derived from research, clinical observation, and the experience of law enforcement officers (Bull, 1998; Milne & Bull, 1999; Ceci & Bruck, 1993) can offer a framework in which to view interviewing children.

1. The younger children are, the less likely they will remember details of a crime, especially peripheral details. In other words, they are likely to commit more errors of omission than are older children and adults. However, depending on the circumstances, even preschool children can accurately recall some events.

2. Beginning at about age four, children have learned to lie and may lie in their testimony if pressured to do so by adults. However, children rarely concoct events that are beyond their experience. Only about 8 percent of children's allegations of sexual abuse are fictitious, 6 percent due to adults feeding them misinformation. Consequently, only 2 percent of children *initiate* lying in their testimony.

3. Children tend to be more suggestible than adults, and preschoolers seem to be the most suggestible. However, the greater the cognitive and emotional maturity of the children, the more vivid the memory; and the more skilled the interviewer, the less suggestibility will be an issue.

4. Age should not be the sole or even overriding criterion by which to judge competency to give accurate testimony. Good intelligence, emotional and social maturity, and a supportive environment can make a child of four years of age a more competent witness than a seven-year-old who lacks one or more of these elements.

5. Children who are subjected to intimidating interviews are more likely to provide inaccurate information than are those in supportive interviews, possibly because they will agree to anything to terminate the intimidating interview.

6. Children, especially those under six years of age, tend to change their answers to questions that are asked a second time, possibly because they assume their first answer was incorrect. Asking open-ended rather than close-ended questions can help reduce this problem.

7. Children who believe that the interviewer expects them to know the answer to a question, even though they do not, are likely to give *any* answer, but especially a suggested answer, rather than admit they do not know the answer to the question.

8. Good rapport between a child and an interviewer can be a two-edged sword. It can cut for the good because the child may feel secure in the situation and be more forthcoming with information; however, it can also

be a problem because the child wants to please the interviewer, which could include incorporating inaccurate information into the testimony.

9. Children can experience more problems with source monitoring than adults. This means that children can become more confused as to the source of their memory: whether they actually witnessed an event or imagined it, or if they only heard about it from a third party. This is especially true of very young children.

10. Children's memory can be fairly accurate and detailed for a new event that occurred only once, but the memory fades and becomes less accurate with events that are similar to each other, for example, repeated sexual abuse.

11. When children experience a stressful event, it does not necessarily interfere with the accuracy of their memory for that event.

12. Children who receive social support after a stressful event tend to have more accurate memories of the event than those who do not.

Suggestibility

Because the question of suggestibility is prominent in any discussion of interviewing children, officers should be particularly aware of how children's suggestibility can shape their testimony. A review of the literature (Warren & Marsil, 2002) shows that six points should be kept in mind:

1. Suggestibility is not limited to preschool children. Although suggestibility generally decreases with age, elementary school children, as well as college students, still can be very suggestible when being interviewed about an event they witnessed.

2. Suggestiveness is not limited to leading questions. The following interviewing techniques can increase suggestibility:

    Social influence. "All the really smart kids in your class said your teacher touched their private parts. Did he touch you there, too?"

    Reinforcement. "See, you must be really smart too because you noticed what the other really smart kids noticed."

    Invitations to speculate. "When the teacher took Tommy in the bathroom ahead of you, did you think the teacher touched Tommy's private parts?"

3. Suggestibility is not confined to formal interviews. Children can give false accounts of an event during a proper interview because they have been told false accounts by others, because they have been given negative stereotypes of the people involved in the event ("Be careful of men

because they do bad things"), and because of autosuggestibility in which children and adults may distort information to make it fit their preconceived beliefs.

4. Identifying particular children and adults who would be most susceptible to suggestion is often difficult. Although conventional wisdom indicates that older, more intelligent, and mature children and adults would be less suggestible than younger, less intelligent, and immature children and adults, in fact this is not necessarily true. A wide range of factors seem to affect suggestibility, and, at this point in time, there is no valid way to assess what kinds of children and adults will be more or less susceptible.

5. It is difficult to train children to resist potentially suggestive questions. Although some children could be inoculated to a limited degree to resist preinterview and interview attempts to shape their accounts, the number of personal, social, and situational variables involved allow for no foolproof way to make children's accounts tamper proof.

6. Even though neutral, well-intentioned interviewers are taught to avoid directly or indirectly suggestive techniques, they still continue to do so in rather large numbers. These numbers increase even more in law enforcement interviews in which the interviewers have a vested interest in the outcome.

The Interview Itself

As is true for officers interviewing adult witnesses, there is no recipe for interviewing child witnesses. Yet several ideas can be considered and incorporated into the framework of the interview process.

Establishing rapport with the child is important, although laborious attempts to establish it may have the opposite effect. Asking children a few friendly questions about themselves and showing them around the office may suffice.

Officers should try to get a sense of who the children are and how accurate their testimony is likely to be. Although judges usually make the final decision regarding the child's capacity to testify, officers should develop their own assessment first. Some things officers (and later judges) may want to know follow:

- How observant is this child?
- How clearly does the child think?
- How well does the child understand the situation?
- How intelligent and psychologically stable is the child?
- Can the child recognize the difference between telling the truth and lying, between a fantasy and an actual event?

- Is the child's memory of the crime relatively pure, or has it been contaminated with input from interested parties?
- Has the child's account of the crime been consistent so far?
- Does the child appear confident in her account?
- How much of the crime did the child actually witness?
- Who has the child spoken with about the crime?
- How does the child feel about being in the situation?

In many ways, a child witness is only as good as the interviewer who obtains and compiles the testimony and prepares the child to testify. The following points can help interviewers prepare children to become confident, solid witnesses.

Write down questions. As much as possible, officers should write down *all* questions before asking them for two reasons:

- To purge them of any hint of being suggestive or leading. The younger the child, the more tempting it is to ask leading questions, not out of malice but due to an authentic need to be helpful to the child.
- To rewrite any questions in which the language is too advanced for the child's age or too vague or convoluted to evoke a sensible answer.

Avoid disapproval. Most children are very attuned and sensitive to disapproval and tend to perceive people as either "liking" or "disliking" them. Even a sigh of frustration can place an interviewer in the "dislike" category and fracture rapport.

Avoid discounting statements. It is important to avoid the inclination automatically to discount statements by children who are intellectually, emotionally, or physically challenged. Some healthy children can be mistaken in their accounts, while some disadvantaged children can be correct.

Weigh necessity of testimony. Officers should weigh the necessity of exposing a child to the judicial process, especially if the child will be questioned repeatedly and explicitly about sexual abuse or family violence, and may be required to testify against a family member. Even though it is unlikely that officers will have the final say as to the competence of a child witness, they can offer input for others to consider.

Officers can recognize that children are not merely small adults. They often have almost qualitatively different ways of perceiving, remembering, and communicating. As a result, interview techniques that work well with adults may be counterproductive with children. Therefore, officers need to have interviewing strategies and techniques that are especially tailored to children's capabilities and dynamics.

Personal Reflections _____

1. Do you believe that children, in general, make reasonably accurate witnesses? If you do, would you feel comfortable having a child as a witness in a case in which you were innocently named as a suspect? If you do not, why do you believe that children, in general, have less credibility as witnesses than adults?

2. Do you believe all officers have the skills to interview children, or do you believe that, whenever possible, only officers who are specially educated and trained should do the interview? What are the reasons for your answer?

3. What would be the most difficult part of interviewing children for you?

4. What do you think are the two most common mistakes officers make in interviewing children?

METHODS OF IDENTIFYING SUSPECTS

An important part of the interview process is to ask witnesses to identify the person they observed commit a crime. Various media may be used: mug books, composite images, show ups, photo arrays, and lineups. The purpose of these procedures is to identify the guilty people and clear the innocent, both equally important endeavors. These procedures, however, are vulnerable to the same potential errors inherent in interviewing witnesses: for example, memory distortion, susceptible witnesses wanting to please the officer, and overzealous officers unconsciously steering witnesses in the direction of identifying "the correct suspect." For these reasons, officers can be aware of some basic considerations pertaining to suspect identification as well as the different identification techniques.

Basic Cautions

Ten basic cautions are applicable to all identification procedures.

Document procedures. Officers must document each identification procedure in exact and complete detail. The documentation must include the location of the procedure, who was present, the time lines at each segment, the medium that was used (a photo array or a lineup), and the exact words used in the instructions and by the witness identifying the suspect. As is true with all documentation, videotaping is the best medium, audiotaping is second best, and taking detailed notes is better than nothing. It should be kept in mind that defense attorneys will search for any technical flaw in the procedure to render the evidence inadmissible. Officers can expect to be cross-examined on their identification procedures more intensely than on the rest of the witness interview because these procedures are at the heart of eyewitness testimony and offer the most concrete and exacting evidence.

Provide instructions.   The instructions to the witnesses before embarking on any identification procedure must be standardized, especially if there are multiple witnesses. The same instructions, cautions, and encouragement must be presented to all witnesses, and uniform guidelines for answering questions must be established. It can be helpful for officers to have a set of standardized instructions and read them as they would a *Miranda* warnings card, so that they can testify in court that they gave the same instructions to all witnesses.

Develop witness picture.   Before beginning any procedure, officers should help the witness develop a clear mental picture of the suspect and write it down with as much detail as possible. Officers can use this picture as a benchmark against which to measure the witness's later identification of the suspects. It is not unusual, for example, for a witness to insist that the perpetrator had a high forehead but later confidently identify someone with a low forehead in a photo array or lineup.

Isolate witnesses.   If there are multiple witnesses to the same crime, they should be isolated from each other and, whatever the identification procedures, never be allowed to identify the suspects together, as this would legitimately raise the specter that they influenced each other's decision.

Avoid highlighting suspect.   Officers must not create a situation whereby the known or possible perpetrator is highlighted in any way. There cannot be imaginary (or real) arrows pointing to the person officers believe is the perpetrator. For example, if the witness saw tattoos on the perpetrator's arm and only one subject in a lineup has tattoos, that constitutes "drawing arrows" directly at the suspect. An officer's verbal and nonverbal behavior during the procedures can also act as "arrows."

Use objective officer.   It is highly recommended that an officer not familiar with the case and who does not know the identity of the perpetrator administer the identification procedures. This avoids any question about the conscious or unconscious biases of the officer influencing the witnesses or the procedures in any way. Witnesses should be told that the officer does not know the identity of the perpetrator, so they will not read into the officer's reactions.

Avoid relative judgments.   Officers must be aware of the relative judgment error, which means that when witnesses look at a photo array or lineup, they tend to compare the people in the lineup with each other to see which one most resembles their mental picture of the suspect, rather than directly comparing each lineup member to their mental picture of the suspect. Officers must help witnesses avoid this common error, which can cause them to pick out the wrong person.

Elicit certainty statement.   After a witness identifies a person as the perpetrator, officers should not indicate *in any way* that the choice was the right or wrong one. Immediately after their selection, witnesses must make a "statement of certainty" indicating exactly how certain they are that they have identified the correct person. In other words, is the witness absolutely certain, very certain, pretty certain, or kind of certain? This statement of certainty must also be made for people they cleared. Officers can respond to a witness's question—"How did I do; did I pick out the right one?"—with a statement such as "I can't comment on this now. We'll let you know after the investigation is complete."

Avoid tampering.   Because witness confidence is malleable, that is, it can be manipulated after the identifications are made, officers should be careful not to tamper with it. In other words, if witnesses are told they identified the perpetrator or that other witnesses identified the same person, they will be likely to become more confident in their identification, which may, or may not, have been accurate. The more confident they are, the more the case can be seriously compromised if they are wrong. If they are only "kind of certain," and the identification is incorrect, it will have less impact on the case as a whole.

Question accuracy.   As has been noted previously, a high correlation does not necessarily exist between the confidence witnesses have in their perceptions and their accuracy. Officers should not assume that simply because witnesses exhibit a high degree of confidence in their suspect identification that their selection is accurate. Prudent officers can role-play with the witness, taking the part of the defense attorney in a cross-examination to test the strength of the witness's perception and memory. For instance, the officer may challenge: "You said the guy that did the shooting was over six feet tall, but the guy you picked out is five ten. Isn't it true that you're not certain if the guy who shot the clerk is five eight, five ten, six feet, six two, or six four?" The witness's reaction will afford the officer an example of what will happen in court, unless the witness is helped to make more discrete judgments.

Instructions to Witnesses

Before proceeding with any identification procedures, officers should properly instruct witnesses regarding the identification procedure and their role in it. Although these instructions will differ slightly depending on the particular identification process, they follow some general themes. Officers can also present the instruction sheet in court to demonstrate the fairness of the process. A sample set of instructions can be seen in Box 7.2.

If witnesses are unable to read or understand the form, officers can go over it with them.

Media Used in the Identification Process

The following media can be used in the identification process.

Mug books.   Mug books are collections of booking photographs of people arrested for crimes. They are used when the identity of the suspect is unknown; for example, a rape victim can describe the perpetrator but does not know his identity.

Box 7.2

Identification Procedures—Victim/Witness Instructions

Before you begin the identification procedures, it is important to keep the following in mind.

1. The purpose of these procedures is to identify the guilty *and* clear the innocent. Both are equally important. If you *don't* see the suspect, this can be as helpful as if you *do* see the suspect. Do not feel pressure to identify someone just to feel better or to please the officers.

2. The person who committed the crime you witnessed *may* or *may not* be in the presentation of pictures or people. Don't *assume* that the suspect is present, because he or she may not be.

3. If the suspect *is* present, he or she will appear only once in each presentation.

4. Whether or not you identify the suspect, the investigation will continue in order to gather more evidence to clear or convict suspects.

5. If the suspect is present, he or she may not look exactly the same as at the time of the crime. Some suspects alter their appearance after committing a crime.

6. Except for giving you clear instructions as to how to approach the identification procedures, the officers cannot help you identify the suspect or indicate *in any way* whether or not you are zeroing in on the suspect, or if you have identified the correct or incorrect suspect. After giving you instructions, the proper role of officers is to remain silent and listen to you. Officers are not allowed to tell you whether a suspect is actually in the presentation, whether the suspect has changed his or her appearance since the crime, or whether the case rests on your ability to identify the suspect. If you feel any pressure to say or not to say anything during the process, please tell the officer immediately.

7. Don't compare the people in the pictures or lineups with *each other* to see which one most resembles your mental picture of the suspect. Compare each person *directly* to your mental picture of the perpetrator.

8. After each identification, the officers will ask you to make a "certainty statement" that answers this question: "How *certain* are you that the person being examined is guilty or innocent? Are you (a) absolutely certain; (b) very certain; (c) pretty certain; (d) kind of certain? It is okay not to be absolutely certain, but it is important to state your degree of certainty clearly."

Thank you for participating in this procedure. We appreciate your taking time to come in and help us.

Witness Signature _____   Date _____

Officer Signature _____   Date _____

When preparing and presenting mug books, the following points should be kept in mind.

• To reduce witness fatigue and save time, pictures of suspects who have committed the same kind of crime that was witnessed should be shown first, although the witness should not be told this. To simply thrust a series of mug books at a witness, each with hundreds of photos, can cause unnecessary confusion, frustration, and fatigue ("All these faces are beginning to blur into one face and look alike").

• The selected pictures should be reasonably current and at least generally resemble the witness's description of the subject. For example, if the witness confidently describes the perpetrator as white, it is a waste of time to include hundreds of photos of nonwhite people.

• After the witness identifies a suspect, the process need not stop. It can be good practice to ask the witness to look at a "few more pictures just to make sure." Sometimes witnesses see an even better match later in the process.

Composite images.   Composite images are sketches drawn by hand, computer, or using an Identikit that are based on the witness's description of the perpetrator. In using this procedure, the following considerations can be kept in mind.

• If the witness is not reasonably clear and confident with regard to the perpetrator's description, this technique should not be used, because there is too much room for error. It could create a situation in which innocent people are suspect, and guilty people are cleared.

- Officers should avoid showing the witness any photos prior to creating the composite.
- After the composite is completed, the witness should be given ample time to examine it carefully and make final changes in the sketch when appropriate.
- The witness should be advised as to how the composite will be used, disseminated to other agencies, the media, and so on.

Show ups. A "show up" or "cold show" is ordinarily an in-field identification process used when the possible perpetrator is apprehended shortly after the crime. Because the officers may lack probable cause to make an arrest, they can only detain the suspect, hoping that the witness's identification will give them the probable cause needed to make the arrest.

A typical procedure involves the following.

- The witness is told by officers that it is possible, though not certain, that one or more of the perpetrators has been apprehended.
- The witness is then transported in a police vehicle to where the suspects are detained, usually only a short distance away.
- Multiple witnesses should be transported separately. The witnesses are slowly driven past the suspect, who is usually standing next to a patrol vehicle.
- The witness examines the suspect closely to see whether a positive identification can be made.
- The least suggestive scenario is when innocent people are added to the show up, such as undercover officers or bystanders.
- The most suggestive scenario is when the suspect is presented alone, in handcuffs, with the "fruits of the crime" at his feet, for example, the stolen purse, watch, and necklace. Clearly, this technique is the most suggestive and is likely to be vehemently challenged by defense attorneys.

Photo arrays. A photo array, unlike mug shots, consists of a series of photographs that generally include the known or possible suspect and five photos of nonsuspects (a "six pack"). When preparing and presenting a photo array, officers can keep the following points in mind:

- Fillers should resemble the witness's description of the suspect as much as possible to avoid highlighting the known suspect in any way. For example, if the witness describes the suspect as "balding," and the only photo of a balding male is that of the known suspect, this photo array will be legitimately challenged by defense attorneys.
- To "nail down" a witness identification, the procedure should be repeated several times, using different fillers each time, as well as positioning the suspect differently.

- If there are multiple suspects, only one should appear in each photo array, and different fillers must be used with each suspect.

A photo array can be presented in two ways: simultaneously or sequentially; that is, the six or more photos (suspect and fillers) can be shown all at the same time (simultaneously) or each picture shown one at a time (sequentially). In the sequential photo array, the witness must make a decision and statement of certainty after each picture before progressing to the next. Even after a positive identification is made, witnesses should continue to look at the remaining pictures to see whether there is an even closer match and to ensure standardization of the procedure.

The sequential method has several advantages over the simultaneous one, not the least of which is the elimination of the "relative judgment error." Witnesses should not be told how many pictures are in the sequential lineup because this could increase pressure to identify somebody before the pictures run out.

Lineups.   Lineups are composed of a number of people, one of whom may be the known or possible suspect, whereas the others are fillers (nonsuspects). In preparing and presenting lineups, officers can recall the five points relevant to photo arrays because they pertain to lineups as well. In addition, the following points specifically refer to lineups:

- Witnesses can be told that a person's position in the lineup does not indicate one way or another the person's guilt or innocence.
- Fillers should not know who the suspect is because they can unintentionally, through nonverbal behavior, send cues that indicate the identity of the suspect.
- The officer's instructions to the people in the lineup must be standardized; for example, everyone must be told to make the same kind and number of turns, say the same things, and so on.
- In the case of multiple suspects, only one suspect should appear in each lineup.
- If more than one witness is to view the same lineup at different times, the position of the people in the lineup must remain the same.
- When presenting a new suspect to a witness, different fillers must be used.

As is true with photo arrays, lineups can be simultaneous or sequential. In a sequential lineup, witnesses should not be told how many people they will be looking at. It also can be very helpful to videotape all identification procedures to demonstrate that they were done professionally and nonprejudicially. Videotaping lineups can have added advantages in that witnesses can view the tape as many times as necessary in order to make a confident identification and the same tape can be used at different times for different witnesses.

Personal Reflections _____

1. Which of the identification procedures do you believe would be the most likely to yield the correct suspect, and why do you believe this?

2. Why do you think it is often the case that the more confident witnesses are, the less likely they will be accurate?

3. Why do you think that some officers would be reluctant to give witnesses a printed set of instructions, even though it seems a logical and helpful thing to do?

4. If you were an innocent suspect in a crime, which of the five identification procedures would you prefer to be picked out of, and why?

5. Why do you think some officers are reluctant to videotape their identification procedures?

*S*ummary _____

Because of the possibility for erroneous conviction due to mistaken identification by witnesses to a crime, officers need to be carefully trained in eliciting accurate witness testimony. Cutler and Penrod (1995) state:

> Estimates of erroneous conviction rates in the United States generally fall within the 1–5 percent range. However, reducing the hypothesized error rate to .5 percent and relating it to the average number of convictions each year in the United States for serious offenses, which is approximately 1.5 million, this yields 7,500 erroneous convictions each year. The number of convictions does not include less serious (misdemeanor) convictions. (p. 7)

So, although the percentage of erroneous convictions is relatively small, the cost in human tragedy (innocent people languishing in prison, guilty people walking the streets) is very high and intolerable.

On the other hand, few things can be more dispiriting than for officers to have a "smoking gun" case, yet see it evaporate in court because of lazy, inept, or overconfident witness preparation. To lose a witness, especially a key witness, is often more the fault of the officers (or prosecutors) than the witness. Therefore, the anxiety this specter poses can be used to encourage officers to prepare nothing less than a perfect case, a case that cannot be lost in court.

*R*eferences _____

Bartol, C.R., & Bartol, A.M. (1994). *Psychology and law: Research and application* (2nd ed.). Pacific Grove, CA: Brooks/Cole.

Brown, D., Scheflin, A.W., & Hammond, D.C. (1998). *Memory, trauma, treatment, and the law.* New York: W.W. Norton.

Bull, R. (1998). Obtaining information from child witnesses. In A. Memon, A. Vrij, & R. Bull (Eds.), *Psychology and law: Truthfulness, accuracy and credibility* (pp. 188–209). New York: McGraw-Hill.

Ceci, S.J., & Bruck, M. (1993). Suggestibility of the child witness: A historical review and synthesis. *Psychological Bulletin, 113* (3), 403–439.

Cutler, B.L., & Penrod, S.D. (1995). *Mistaken identification: The eyewitness, psychology, and the law.* New York: Cambridge University Press.

Eck, J.E. (1992). Criminal investigation. In G.W. Cordner & D.C. Hale (Eds.), *What works in policing: Operations and administration examined* (pp. 19–34). Cincinnati, OH: Anderson Publishing.

Fisher, R.P. (1995). Interviewing victims and witnesses of crime. *Psychology, Public Policy, and Law, 1,* 732–764.

Goodman, G.S., Redlich, A.D., Qin, J., Ghetti, S., Tyda, K.S., Schaaf, J.M., & Hahn, A. (1999). Evaluating eyewitness testimony in adults and children. In A.K. Hess & I.B. Weiner (Eds.), *The handbook of forensic psychology* (2nd ed.) (pp. 218–272). New York: John Wiley.

Loftus, E.F. (1979). *Eyewitness testimony.* Cambridge, MA: Harvard University Press.

Malpass, R.S., & Kravitz, J. (1969). Recognition for faces of our own and other races. *Journal of Personality and Social Psychology, 13,* 330–334.

Marxsen, D., Yuille, J., & Nisbet, M. (1995). The complexities of eliciting and assessing children's statements. *Psychology, Public Policy, and Law, 1,* 450–460.

Milne, R., & Bull, R. (1999). *Investigative interviewing: Psychology and practice.* New York: John Wiley.

Nairne, J.S. (2002). *Psychology: The adaptive mind* (3rd ed.). Belmont, CA: Thomson/Wadsworth.

Rand Corporation (1975). *The criminal investigation process* (Vols. 1–3). Rand Corporation Technical Report R-1111-DOJ. Santa Monica, CA: Rand Corporation.

Scheck, B., Neufeld, P., & Dwyer, J. (2000). *Actual innocence.* New York: Doubleday.

U.S. Department of Justice, Office of Justice Programs (1998). *Eyewitness evidence: A guide for law enforcement.* (NCJ178240). Washington, DC: U.S. Department of Justice.

Vrij, A. (1998). Psychological factors in eyewitness testimony. In A. Memon, A. Vrij, & R. Bull (Eds.), *Psychology and law: Truthfulness, accuracy and credibility* (pp. 105–123). New York: McGraw-Hill.

Walker, S. (1998). *Sense and nonsense about crime and drugs: A policy guide* (4th ed.). Belmont, CA: West/Wadsworth.

Warren, A.R., & Marsil, D.F. (2002). Why children's suggestibility remains a serious concern. *Law and Contemporary Problems, 65* (1), 127–147.

Wells, G.L., Small, M., Penrod, S., Malpass, R.S., Fulero, S.M., & Brimacombe, C.A. (1998). Eyewitness identification procedures: Recommendations for lineups and photo spreads. *Law and Human Behavior, 22,* 603–647.

Wrightsman, L.S. (2001). *Forensic psychology.* Belmont, CA: Wadsworth.

8

Interviewing Suspects

Historically, questioning suspects in a crime has been referred to as *interrogation*, while the term *interview* has been reserved for questioning victims and witnesses. More recently, as part of the professionalization of law enforcement, the term interrogation tends to be avoided because it connotes counterproductive attitudes and questionable methods. This shift in terminology is not simply based on political correctness but on sound psychological principles, summed up in one statement: Human beings, no matter who they are, are more likely to respond to respect, empathy, and helpfulness than to browbeating, deceit, and coercion. The trend is also based on legal and ethical considerations, which often were not considered in the days of third-degree interrogations.

How officers interview suspects and how confessions are obtained have become topics of great interest and concern. DNA analysis has increasingly demonstrated that many people who had been convicted of crimes and spent years in prison were, in fact, not guilty. This concern is clearly reflected in Kassin's (1997) statement:

> Basic questions are raised concerning police interrogations, the risk of false confessions, and the impact that such evidence has on a jury. On the basis of available research, it was concluded that the criminal justice system currently does not afford adequate protection to innocent people branded as suspects and that there are serious dangers associated with confession evidence. The specific problems are threefold: (a) The police routinely use deception, trickery, and psychologically coercive methods of interrogation; (b) these methods may, at times, cause innocent people to confess to crimes they did not commit; and (c) when coerced self-incrimination statements are presented in the courtroom, juries do not sufficiently discount the evidence in reaching a verdict. (p. 221)

Today, the courts are interested in how confessions are obtained and increasingly ready to rule confessions inadmissible that would have sent guilty and innocent suspects to life in prison or to their deaths a quarter century ago.

Society also is becoming more aware that innocent people have been convicted of major crimes and sent to prison, including death row. Consequently, the theme of questioning suspects in professional law enforcement is changing from one of extracting confessions to one of information gathering. The differences in these themes are not merely semantic but real, because the attitudes and behaviors that flow from each are often quite different.

Rather than simply aiming at extracting confessions, today interviewing suspects provides opportunities to

- Discover the truth, whether or not it leads to an arrest
- Clear innocent people
- Locate physical evidence
- Establish witnesses that will clear or convict the suspect
- Locate new witnesses
- Develop suspects in other crimes
- Develop informants
- Obtain a valid confession
- Recognize a false confession
- Develop rapport so that the suspect, guilty or innocent, will feel free to contact officers with helpful information in the future

This chapter will deal with seven issues: the officer's attitude, preparing for the interview, questioning the suspect, avoiding false assumptions, interview tactics, false confessions, and behavioral analysis. The strictly legal issues that pertain to interviewing suspects will be left to other sources.

THE OFFICER'S ATTITUDE

As is true of interviewing witnesses, who officers *are* will largely determine what they *do* when interviewing suspects. The officers' cognitions, beliefs, and values will directly affect how they approach their role as an interviewer. Constructive, reality-based attitudes are likely to be translated into professional, legal, ethical, and productive interviews, whereas destructive, myth-based attitudes are likely to result in the opposite. The following points reflect officers' attitudes toward making an arrest, as well as their view of themselves and the suspect.

Arrest as a Priority

Professional officers realize that arresting a suspect, even in high-profile cases, is not the highest value in law enforcement. Maintaining the integrity of law enforcement and its officers is the highest value because everything else rests on that. They recognize that all is *not* fair in the war on crime and that the ends do *not* justify all means. They also accept the fact that the only suspects who deserve to go to prison are the ones guilty of the crime in question, not those who are innocent of the crime under investigation but who have committed other crimes for which they have yet to be apprehended or punished.

It is not officers' responsibility to punish suspects mentally or physically for their lifestyles or crimes. Professional officers understand that their sole objectives are to gather evidence and, in the case of a guilty suspect, obtain a confession, make an arrest, and forward a report to the prosecutor. It is the responsibility of the judicial system to convict and punish.

Understanding the difference between actual and legal guilt is also important when dealing with suspects. Actual guilt means that the suspect did, in fact, commit the crime. Legal guilt means having sufficient evidence gathered in ethical and legal ways that prove beyond a reasonable doubt in court that the suspect committed the crime. At times, there can be a strong temptation to "strengthen the evidence" by questionable means when officers *know* the suspect is guilty but cannot quite garner sufficient evidence to prove it in court. Professional officers resist this temptation, even if it means a delay in prosecution until more evidence is gathered.

Professional law enforcement officers also believe that clearing innocent suspects is as important as, if not more important than, arresting guilty ones. Unfortunately, when pressure to make an arrest is great, clearing an innocent person is more likely to cause a feeling of disappointment than one of success, although the latter would be more appropriate. Moreover, officers who make an arrest as a result of interviewing are likely to be rewarded by their agency and society, whereas officers who clear a prime suspect as a result of an outstanding interview are unlikely to be rewarded by anyone.

Realistic View of Self

Professional law enforcement officers have a realistic estimate of their accuracy rate in detecting truth and falsehood in suspects' statements. As research indicates, despite their high level of confidence, officers' ability to detect truth or deceit in people is not much better than chance and no better than that of college students (Ekman & O'Sullivan, 1991). Selective memory allows some officers to have a misplaced confidence in their ability because they clearly remember the times they were correct but fail to remember instances in which they were incorrect. A realistic attitude in this regard will reduce the number of mistakes that arise when officers are "certain" a suspect is lying or telling the truth.

Effective officers have a pressure-resistant attitude; that is, they recognize when they are under great internal and external pressure to make an arrest and do not permit this pressure to short-circuit their decision-making processes. Pressure often leads to premature decisions that are based much more on hope than reality and eventually cause problems for everyone.

Pressure can also lead to the "bloodhound syndrome," which occurs when officers are so hot on the trail of a suspect that they develop tunnel vision and become blind to all the indications that the suspect may be innocent or that others may be guilty. Officers must always be open to the possibility, even when it is a faint one, that they could be wrong.

Respect for the Suspect

Professional officers treat all suspects with respect, regardless of how repulsive they are or how heinous their crime. They treat suspects with respect because it is the right thing to do and because it is more likely than disrespect to elicit cooperation. Because officers respect themselves and their profession, they do not attempt to out-macho, out-shout, out-flex, out-curse, or out-intimidate suspects, no matter how tempted they may be at times to do so.

Officers can recognize that the term *suspect*, or even *prime suspect*, is not necessarily synonymous with *guilty suspect*, and the term *innocent suspect* is not an oxymoron, but one that describes many suspects. They realize that, even in examining their own track record, at least some of their "slam dunk" suspects ended up being slammed but not dunked because they were eventually found to be innocent. This realization leads to a more prudent assessment of suspects' guilt or innocence.

Professional law enforcement officers have an attitude of healthy skepticism for confessions that "come too easy or too hard." As will be seen later in this chapter, walk-in, voluntary confessions should always be met with a certain degree of skepticism rather than embraced with enthusiasm because they are not always valid. On the other hand, confessions extracted after long, uninterrupted hours of interviewing, especially if coercion and deceit are used, also may be suspect. This does not mean that either of these types of confession automatically must be invalid, but it does indicate that these confessions tend to be false more than those that fall in the middle between too easy and too hard.

Effective officers recognize the differences between an interview and an inquisition. They perceive interviewing as a graduated process that begins with the soft approach (being respectful, straightforward, receptive, helpful). When this method is unproductive, they proceed to a moderate approach (becoming more incisive, focused, confrontational, but still maintaining the characteristics of the soft approach). Only if several efforts at this approach fail do they proceed to the hard approach (employing deceit and coercion within legal and ethical boundaries). They do not begin their interviews with the hard approach but use it only as a last resort and never participate in "third degree" tactics of physical threat or assault.

Personal Reflections _____

1. What is your accuracy rate in distinguishing true statements from false ones with respect to the people with whom you relate daily?

2. When you hear that a prime suspect in a serious crime has been declared innocent, are you as happy as if he were found guilty? Why?

3. How pressure-proof are you? If your bosses or friends are placing great pressure on you to do something you are not ready to do, how do you deal with it?

PREPARING FOR THE INTERVIEW

The more thoroughly officers prepare for their interviews, the more successful they are likely to be. The following questions can be asked in order to set the stage for an interview.

What Was the Specific Nature of the Crime?

Before interviewing suspects, it is important to have a detailed understanding of the crime whenever possible. This understanding is achieved by reading investigative reports, visiting the crime scene, interviewing witnesses, and canvassing the neighborhood, and should be done even in cases in which there is a prime suspect. The information can be used for a number of purposes:

- To instill confidence in officers that they are armed with as many details as possible going into the interview and know about as much as the perpetrators
- To demonstrate to suspects that the officers know exactly what they are doing and therefore are not likely to be fooled
- To give officers material to ask "the right questions," which are more likely to elicit "the right answers," in contrast to asking unfocused or meaningless questions
- To help officers measure the suspect's story against the known facts of the crime
- To help officers anticipate and prepare for the suspect's denials, deceit, deflections, and alibis
- To help officers develop a clear interview objective, in contrast to embarking on fishing expeditions that accomplish nothing, except to communicate to the suspect that "the cops got nothing"

How Did the Suspect Come to the Attention of Officers?

It is important to know whether the victims and witnesses are "certain" about the identity of the suspect, or only "pretty certain" or "kind of certain." The motives of the victims and witnesses also enter the situation because it is necessary to know whether their motives are pure, or if they are tainted with other agendas, such as revenge. Officers need to know whether the victims and witnesses are willing to get involved in the investigative process, identify suspects, and appear in court, or if they are likely to bail out before they can really help the case. This information helps officers gauge whether they have a strong or weak case and how reliable the victims or witnesses are likely to be.

What Kind of Person Is the Suspect?

It is better to know the suspect as a unique individual rather than merely as "a suspect." When officers can convey the message, even in a nice way: "I know who you are, where you've been, and what you're likely to tell me," it can have an unsettling effect on the suspect ("What do they know about me?"). This could lead suspects to divulge information they otherwise might not volunteer. The more information officers have, the more they will be able to tailor their questions to the suspect. The information can include

- Age, race, religion, marital status, education, finances
- Criminal history and other experiences with the criminal justice system
- Psychological makeup (disorders or dysfunction), medical history (disabilities, illnesses, addictions), social sphere (family, friends, enemies)
- Strengths and weaknesses likely to be demonstrated in the interview
- Attitudes toward law enforcement
- Level of desperation, violence potential, including suicide potential
- Nature of possible denials, excuses, alibis
- Inducements that might lead to a confession
- Possible motives for committing the crime
- Elements that could clear the suspect

Equipped with this kind of information, officers can develop a strategy (an overall plan for the interview) and tactics (methods to implement the plan). For example, the officer's strategy might be to surround the suspect with a phalanx of evidence, and the tactic may be to express the futility of the suspect even trying to deny his guilt.

Personal Reflections

1. What are the best attitude and the worst attitude an officer can have in approaching a suspect interview?
2. Do you believe that most officers agree it is just as important to clear as it is to convict a suspect? If so, why? If not, why not?
3. Respond to the statement: "It's all well and good to be respectful in dealing with white collar criminals, but respecting criminals in gang-infested neighborhoods is viewed as a weakness that could have tragic results."

QUESTIONING THE SUSPECT

When officers have a proper attitude and good preparation, the questioning of the suspect can begin. Questioning is a highly dynamic and variable process that resembles the map of a high desert because no two officers, suspects, crimes, and situations are alike. To a novice explorer, a map may indicate a "clear shot" through the desert from one point to the next. But people familiar with deserts realize that nothing could be further from the truth. There can be clearly marked roads, back roads, unmarked roads, dangerous rock formations and precipices, pure or contaminated water, dead ends, optical illusions, mirages, and quicksand. Just as people can chase mirages and die in quicksand, officers can chase the wrong suspects and die in their investigations. Therefore, it is important to realize that no map exists to lead officers, step by step, through every interview process. However, the following guidelines can be helpful.

Creating a Facilitative Environment

Officers are fond of telling suspects: "We can do this the easy way or the hard way. Which way do you want to go?" However, officers themselves need to realize that they can go the easy way or the hard way in interviews, depending on the relationship they choose to have with the suspect. In other words, if mutual cooperation is ever going to occur, it is far more likely to be in a facilitative environment than in an intimidating one.

Establishing rapport creates a facilitative environment. As applied to questioning suspects, rapport will be different than establishing rapport in a job interview: "So, tell us something about yourself. Do you have any hobbies?" Establishing rapport does not mean being chummy with the suspect, but does mean treating the suspect with respect, straightforwardly explaining the reason for the interview, listening fully to what the suspect has to say, and communicating a helpful attitude. This is in contrast to beginning the first interview with intimidation ("You'd better confess now, or I'll make your life miserable"), contempt ("How can a creep like you live with yourself?"), or emotionally charged language ("I brought you in because I think you raped your 12-year-old stepdaughter").

The following is an example, not a script, of how rapport building can begin.

> Hello, Mr. Smith. I appreciate your coming in today. I wanted to speak with you because your name happened to come up in an investigation. So, I'd like to ask you a few simple questions, get a few honest answers, and see where it takes us.
>
> In a sense, we're in the same boat: I need your help to find out if you know anything about an incident that involved one of your sixth-grade female students in order to either clear you or help you get a fair shake today, before it's too late. You need my help because I'm the only person in the world who can clear you or, if you're involved, see to it that we get the fairest deal we can for you. Does this sound like a plan? If not, tell me how you think we can help each other.

In this type of statement, which would take only 20 seconds to make, the officer clearly:

- Demonstrates respect and appreciation toward the suspect
- Is low-keyed, nonaccusatory, just information gathering
- Suggests a partnership, rather than an adversarial relationship
- Avoids emotionally charged language
- Implies that his help is contingent on being told the truth, a one-time offer
- Invites the suspect to commit to the plan by his own free choice
- Makes no guarantees and states only that the officer will be helpful and the suspect will be treated fairly

Of course, it can be said that while officers could begin a relationship with a schoolteacher this way, it would not work with hardened criminals. Yet, as a matter of fact, with a few minor modifications, it can and does.

AVOIDING FALSE ASSUMPTIONS

False assumptions abound in the field of questioning suspects, most from police lore. Like faulty maps, false assumptions eventually land officers in places far from where they want to be. Following are some common false assumptions, false because they are outright wrong or because their absoluteness fails to allow for the many exceptions to them.

- If suspects lie about one thing, they are likely lying about others and, therefore, are probably guilty. Suspects, including innocent ones, can lie for many reasons during questioning, including giving false alibis, but this does not necessarily mean they are guilty of the crime under investigation.
- If suspects have a bad attitude, they must be guilty. This is no more true than the assumption that if investigators have a bad attitude, they must not have a strong case.
- If suspects have a criminal history, especially one related to the crime under investigation, they are likely to be guilty of the current crime. Absent corroborating evidence, "likely" should be reduced to "possibly," a change that should widen the focus of the investigation.
- If suspects act guilty, they probably are. What exactly is "acting guilty"? It often means "acting petrified," which is seen more in innocent suspects than career criminals during interviews.
- If suspects keep changing their story, they must be guilty. In truth, suspects can change their story many times for many reasons, only one of which is that they are guilty of the crime. For example, the stress of an interview can constrict the memory of suspects but later, in more

relaxed circumstances, they may remember things differently than they did during questioning.

- If suspects fail to answer phone messages from officers, cancel appointments, or simply fail to appear at a scheduled interview, they must be guilty. In fact, for some people casualness regarding appointments is a personality trait and not solely a response to the interview situation. Other people may view the interviews as so distressing that they want to avoid them, even though they are innocent.

- If suspects brag to friends or cellmates that they committed the crime under investigation, they must have committed it. In fact, it is not uncommon for people seeking a claim to fame to announce that they committed a crime that they did not commit.

- If suspects are intensely interested when officers offer them deals to confess, they must be guilty. Innocent suspects in a no-win situation concocted by officers may well listen intently to the officer's lesser-of-two-evils offer.

Personal Reflections _____

1. Of the eight false assumptions discussed, what two do you think are the most common? Why do you think this is the case?

2. Respond to this officer's statement: "When you *know* a suspect is guilty of a crime, why waste time looking for other leads?"

INTERVIEW TACTICS

When suspects resist giving information about a crime or deny guilt, officers may need to use special tactics in their attempts to arrive at the truth. These tactics should seldom be the first approach but used only when it becomes clear that more forthright methods are ineffective. Tactics typically involve at least some degree of trickery, deceit, and coercion, which tends to raise suspicion in the judiciary and society at large that something improper may have occurred. Arrigo (2000) addresses this concern:

> No other piece of evidence is more damaging to a criminal than a stated confession. Throughout history, confessions have been obtained in a number of ways. Due process specifically states that interrogators may use certain tactics to obtain confessions from an accused, provided that the confession is voluntary and a product of an essentially free and unhindered person. However, many tactics employed by interrogators do not fall within these guidelines and are therefore considered "coerced." (pp. 23–24)

In an ideal world, interview tactics would be unnecessary because no crime would ever occur and, if it did, the suspects would immediately and voluntarily confess. In the real world, however, what is "nice" sometimes has to be sacrificed for what is "necessary" to protect society. The constant caution to be exercised when using interviewing tactics is that they might induce innocent people to confess to a crime. However, if officers are primarily motivated by professional values and not by increasing their clearance rate, this should never happen or should be rectified quickly if it does.

Another issue to be kept in mind is that of individual differences. Tactics must be tailored to the individual suspect and not applied simply as a matter of routine or based on a whim. The wrong tactics with the wrong suspect at the wrong time can backfire in a way that the officer loses not only the suspect but also the entire case. The use of tactics is not for amateurs; it requires a quick mind, facile verbal skills, and acting ability. New officers need to shadow veteran officers in their interviews to see how it is done. Finally, tactics are not likely to work well with suspects who are intellectually bright or those who have had so many tactics tried on them in their life of crime that they know them better than the officers do. With these thoughts in mind, it can be helpful to discuss several interviewing tactics.

Basic Interview Tactics

Minimization.   Officers reduce the seriousness of the crime. Their attitude is that whatever the suspect did, from mayhem to murder, is "no big deal." "So you killed some low life who needed to be killed—you did us a favor. Just write a little statement so I can spend my time going after some really bad guys."

Maximization.   Officers exaggerate the seriousness of the crime with the hope that suspects will correct the exaggeration, thus implicating themselves: "You embezzled over $100,000 from the bank, which means that we have to get the FBI and the federal prosecutors involved. Under $50,000 we could deal with it on the local level and maybe help you out, but we're afraid you're a little over the limit." The hope is that the suspect will confess to embezzling the $45,000 she actually took.

Rationalization.   Officers provide excuses to the suspects to mitigate their guilt: "Look, you deeply love your wife; she's everything in the world to you, and you come home, find her in bed with some creep and stab him. Anyone who ever loved somebody could understand what you did in the heat of the moment."

Projection.   Officers remove blame from the suspect by projecting it onto the suspect's accomplices: "I can see you're not the kind of guy who would choose to beat a guy within an inch of his life, but with all that pressure from the rest of your crew, you were forced to do it; you really had no choice. Actually, *they're* more responsible for this thing than *you* are."

Bluffing.   Officers pretend that they can get evidence possibly linking the suspect to the crime, when, in fact, they cannot. For example, in a case in which fingerprints are unavailable, an officer might say: "I'm going to process the fingerprints later today, but it may be helpful to both of us if you can tell me whether I'm going to find your prints at the scene."

Baiting questions.   Officers ask questions with a hook in them: "If you say you weren't near the park last night, that's good enough for me, but who was driving your car in the vicinity? Because someone took down your license plate number." In fact, no one saw the car; the hope is the suspect will believe this bluff and confess.

Good cop—bad cop.   Officers who are partners play these roles. One officer plays the role of the kind, caring, helpful cop, while the other one is the mean, hostile, intimidating cop. The good cop tells the suspect: "Look, between you and me, my partner is crazy, but he sends guys like you away for a long time. Why don't you let me help you before he gets back from lunch, so we can tidy this all up and save you a lot of grief." The hope is that the suspect will confess to the officer who understands him.

Compassion.   Officers feign understanding and sympathy with respect to the suspect's situation: "I can easily see how you ended up having sex with that 13-year-old girl. She looks 20 and acts 40, and she clearly seduced you. Believe me, I could have found myself in the same situation, so let's help each other out here, so that you get a fair shake." Some officers feel uncomfortable placing themselves on the same level as suspects of particularly heinous crimes, even when they are just pretending, but are willing to do so to obtain a confession.

Admiration.   Officers pretend that they admire, even respect, a suspect who committed a well-executed crime: "I have to tell you, you're one smart guy the way you planned and carried that off. For the life of me, I still can't figure out how you defeated the alarm system." The hope is that the suspect, who was smart enough to commit the near perfect crime, will be stupid enough to fall for this tactic.

Playing one suspect against another.   Officers tell one suspect in a crime that the other one confessed and fully implicated him: "Well, I guess the old saying that 'there's no honor among thieves' is right. Your best buddy just ratted you out and cut a nice deal for himself." The hope is that the first suspect will get smart and seek to save his own skin by blaming his accomplice for the crime.

Underestimating.   Officers denigrate the intelligence of the suspect: "I don't know *why* my partner thinks you're good for the crime. Whoever did the crime had a lot of savvy and, no offense, but that description doesn't exactly fit you."

The hope is the suspect will rise to the bait: "Oh, yeah! Well, I *do* have the savvy to commit the crime, and I'll *prove* it to you."

Guilt induction. Officers attempt to make a suspect feel guilty about the crime: "Look, I know, deep down, you're really a good person and ordinarily wouldn't harm a fly. But as long as you hide this baby that doesn't belong to you, you are causing the parents deep pain and sorrow. All they want is to get their baby back, and I'm sure they'd be willing to forget the whole thing." The hope is that the suspect will become conscience stricken, confess, and return the baby.

Forgiveness. Officers attempt to lead suspects to believe that the victims of their crime are willing to forgive them: "You're a lucky lady because the people you stole from are willing to forgive you, but you have to give them a reason to forgive you. All they want are their possessions and an apology." The hope is that the suspect will interpret "forgiveness" as not pressing charges and confess to the crime.

The Good Samaritan. Officers use this solo version of "good cop—bad cop" to earn the confidence of suspects: "Look, I didn't become a cop to throw people in jail to rot for the rest of their lives. I became a cop to help people, but I can't help you until you give me something to work with." The hope is that the suspect believes this story and confesses the crime to "his friend"—the cop.

Psychologizing. Officers offer the suspect mental health reasons for the crime: "Let's face it; you've got some very serious psychological problems, probably due to an abusive childhood and being misunderstood by everybody. You went crazy for a few minutes, and now that you're back in reality, you obviously feel a deep sense of remorse. Nowadays, people are going to understand that and get you some help."

Reciprocity. Officers lead suspects to believe that each can help the other: "This is the way it is. If I crack this case, I get a promotion, and if you confess, I might be able to get you out of this jam. What do you say we work as a team and each profit from this?"

Indifference. Officers lead suspects to believe that they do not care whether the suspect confesses or not: "I've got more important fish to fry. Do you want to tell me what really happened so I might be able to help, or do you want to go all by your lonesome on this? Either way suits me fine." The hope is that the suspect will jump at this fleeting chance to cut a deal.

Futility.   Officers lead suspects to believe there is an avalanche of evidence against them when, in fact, there is not: "People are waiting in line to make you good for the crime. Why don't you open your eyes, recognize that it's all over, and give it up, so I can help you out?"

Stumped.   Officers pretend to have reached a dead end in the investigation. "Look, I'll be completely honest. You've convinced me you're not the guy we're looking for, but you're obviously a smart guy. Help me out. How would *you* go about finding out who did this? Where did the perpetrator screw up?" The hope is that the suspect will not be able to resist the temptation to show that he is smarter than the cops.

Problematic Tactics

Distinguishing between conventional and true wisdom is important in interviewing suspects. Conventional wisdom holds that the more the interviewers can squeeze suspects by intimidation, ridicule, threat, coercion, deceit, embarrassment, tricks, and "the color of authority," the more the suspects will be likely to choke up useful information and a confession. Three problems result from this belief. First, intimidation typically causes a "fight–flight" dynamic; that is, the suspect fights (digs in and attacks) or flees (retreats and hides psychologically and/or geographically). Second, if these tactics do produce a confession, the question of voluntariness will likely be raised in court and create the risk of losing what otherwise may have been a solid case. Third, confessions that are *extracted* (in the way teeth are extracted) are far more likely to lead to recanted confessions than those that were *educed* (coaxed out of the suspect). Sometimes forceful tactics are a necessary evil but, overall, they should be avoided because increasingly juries seem to perceive deceit and trickery as unfair and underhanded and may acquit on the basis of jury nullification.

Six interview tactics in particular lend themselves to judicial scrutiny: physical coercion, psychological coercion, manipulating the emotions of a suspect, taking advantage of an intellectually or psychologically impaired suspect, making promises, and using deception. These tactics can create ethical problems and concern in judges and juries because they raise two serious questions: Could the tactics induce an innocent person to confess to a crime? Do they violate due process, which guarantees fair and impartial treatment for all people, regardless of their crime? As Wrightsman (2001, pp. 150–158) indicates, the courts have made the following rulings on these six tactics.

Physical coercion.   Torture, as well as any other kind of physical force, is illegal. Also illegal are depriving a suspect of food, sleep, or the use of a restroom for prolonged periods of time and making explicit or implicit threats of physical force if the suspect refuses to cooperate.

Psychological coercion. Profound psychological coercion—for example, threatening to arrest a suspect's family members if he refuses to confess—is illegal. Lesser forms of psychological coercion—for example, telling a suspect he should be ashamed of himself for "laying the rap on your girlfriend"—probably would be viewed as legal.

Manipulating the emotions of a suspect. It is generally legal to play on the suspect's emotions as long as it does not cross the line into undue coercion or threat. For example, it would likely be permissible for officers to pretend to befriend the suspect, express compassion for him, induce him to feel guilty, or play on his superstitions.

Taking advantage of an intellectually or psychologically impaired suspect. If taking advantage of the impairment would increase the possibility of an innocent person confessing, the action would likely be ruled illegal.

Making promises. Officers' statements that promise a guaranteed result are likely to be illegal, especially if they pertain to special treatment, for example, a reduced sentence if the suspect confesses. A promise to speak with a prosecutor on behalf of the suspect is likely to be legal if it is clear that there are no guarantees that such efforts will be successful.

Using deception. In general, deception, with the exception of threatening harm, taking advantage of an intellectually or psychologically impaired suspect, or making promises of leniency, is likely to be legal. For example, falsely telling a suspect that there is physical or eyewitness evidence linking her to the crime, that a codefendant "rolled over" on her, that the crime committed was "not such a big deal" would all likely be viewed as legal.

Ethical Issues

Everything that is legal is not necessarily ethical and vice versa. Two basic ethical theories can be applied to deceit and coercion. The absolutist theory holds that one should *never* use deceit or coercion to obtain anything, including a police confession, because no moral good ever results from immoral means.

On the other hand, utilitarianism holds that people have a moral obligation to choose the act that will create the greatest good, for example, justice, for the greatest number of people. This is determined by a cost-benefit analysis, for example: Does the moral cost of using deceit and coercion outweigh the moral benefit of convicting a suspect of the crime he committed? So, although officers, using this moral calculation, may choose not to use deceit and coercion to obtain a confession from a juvenile who stole a bike, they may use them to obtain a confession from an adult who has been molesting children. In other words, is it more morally evil to use deceit and coercion in this case, or more morally evil to allow the man to go free to molest more children? Although these cases present relatively clear alternatives, in many cases the answer is not as clear and the ethical dilemma far more complex.

A second justification for using deceit and coercion to obtain a confession is that society gives law enforcement the right to use lethal force to maintain justice in special circumstances, for example, when an armed person is threatening innocent people, including officers. It can be logically deduced that this right extends to using deceit and coercion in certain situations to arrive at justice, because these acts fall far short of lethal force.

However, three serious, unintended consequences can result when officers use deceit and coercion. First, an innocent person may be arrested and convicted, creating a situation in which a moral evil (deceit and coercion) causes an even greater moral evil (the conviction of an innocent person). Second, such behaviors often create a slippery slope in which perceived "lesser of evils" include perjury and tampering with evidence—acts that, whatever their ethical standing, would be considered illegal. Last, but not least, public confidence in law enforcement can be seriously compromised. As Skolnick and Leo (1998) state:

> Rarely do advocates of greater latitude for police to interrogate consider the effects of systematic lying on law enforcement's reputation for veracity. Police lying might not have mattered so much to police work in other times and places in American history. But today, when urban juries are increasingly composed of jurors disposed to be distrustful of police, deception by police during interrogation offers yet another reason for disbelieving law enforcement witnesses when they take the stand, thus reducing police effectiveness as controllers of crime. (p. 119)

Failure to advise suspects properly of their *Miranda* warnings to remain silent and obtain counsel can also result in an inadmissible confession. The key word is *properly*. *Miranda* warnings can be read in ways that cast doubt on the validity of the admonishment. They can be read so fast that suspects do not have the slightest idea what they are being told, or in a tone of voice that clearly suggests: "You'd better not be so stupid as to invoke these rights," or "Because you claim to be innocent, invoking your right to silence would be an obvious admission of guilt." This is to say nothing of what *Miranda* warnings may mean to a suspect with limited education or intelligence, or one who is psychologically impaired or intoxicated, or for whom English is a second language. An outright deception that is sometimes used regarding these warnings is to tell suspects that they are free to leave at any time even though in fact they had better not try it. By making this statement, officers falsely create a noncustodial situation, so that they are not required to Mirandize the suspect. Of course, a good defense attorney will have a field day in court with this situation. The point is that reading *Miranda* warnings is not necessarily a challenge-proof preface to a confession.

Although some officers may feel that deceit and coercion are often a necessary part of interviewing uncooperative suspects, in fact this is not true. Deceit, trickery, and undue pressure are illegal in England and Wales and, if used, make a confession inadmissible. Moreover, all interviews done in police buildings must be at least audiotaped, and all vulnerable suspects, for example, the mentally challenged, must have a third party present to protect the suspects' rights. These restrictions, which have been in place since 1986, have not seemed to reduce the number of confessions or convictions in England (Moston & Stephenson, 1993, p. 113).

A good example of both confirmation bias and a deceitful tactic gone embarrassingly and expensively wrong is the case of Richard Jewell, the original suspect in the 1996 Atlanta Olympic Games bombing. Jewell was working as a security guard when he discovered a bomb hidden in an abandoned knapsack. He alerted authorities and began clearing the area when the bomb exploded, killing 1 person and injuring 111. Jewell was hailed as a hero and basked in the international limelight for three days.

Because the bombing was viewed by a large, international television audience and the games were still in progress, crushing pressure fell on law enforcement to identify and apprehend the bomber. Because Jewell found the bomb, "fit the profile" of a terrorist bomber, and was involved in some behaviors at the scene that were viewed as suspicious, he went overnight from being "the Olympic hero" to being "the Olympic bomber," even though there was no forensic evidence, eyewitness testimony, or confession linking him to the event. He was such a "slam dunk" suspect that officers limited their investigation to him and his possible accomplices. This remained the case for months, until investigators gradually began to realize that Jewell probably was not a viable suspect.

When word leaked out that Jewell was the prime suspect, he spent 88 days being hounded by law enforcement and the media, literally 24 hours a day. Both he and his mother, with whom he lived, were vilified, ridiculed, threatened, and shunned. Jewell said that, throughout the three months, he constantly "worried about being put in the electric chair." At the end of three months, the Justice Department sent Jewell, through his lawyer, a terse, two-sentence letter. The first sentence stated that Jewell was no longer "considered a target" of the investigation. The second sentence asked that he "provide further cooperation as a witness." Jewell later became a police officer, rose to the rank of sergeant, and another person became the target of the investigation.

In their attempts to obtain some direct evidence of Jewell's guilt, investigators used a ruse. Knowing that Jewell was interested in a law enforcement career, investigators befriended him and asked if he would help them put together a training film on how to interrogate suspects of terrorist bombings. Jewell willingly agreed to participate in the project, which was, in fact, a ruse to get him to confess that he was the bomber. He was asked to play the role of a terrorist bomber who was being interrogated by investigators (who were the actual investigators of the Atlanta bombing). During the taped interview, Jewell was Mirandized and waived his rights; otherwise, the film should have stopped at that point. Actually, both Jewell and the investigators were fortunate that the bogus interview turned out the way it did. If Jewell had said something that seemed to incriminate him, he likely would have been arrested on the spot, a move that would have caused investigators even more grief than they were about to experience.

The collateral damage resulting from the confirmation bias was that months were lost that could have been spent on concerted efforts to develop others suspects. With respect to the "interview" and leaks to the media, American law enforcement was severely embarrassed around the world, and Jewell successfully sued law enforcement and the media for millions of dollars.

Although one can certainly empathize with the investigators who were obviously under unbearable pressure from all sides, objectivity requires that some critical thinking be applied to the situation.

- Did agency top executives sufficiently modulate the pressure, so it would not cause tunnel vision and premature conclusions on the part of first-line supervisors and investigators?
- Was there an arrogant attitude present among investigators, leading them to believe they were more intelligent, clever, and sophisticated than the results indicate they were?
- Was "the end justifies all means" ethic present, especially with respect to subverting the *Miranda* warnings by misleading Jewell into thinking he was not a suspect and was not really being interrogated with respect to the bombing?
- How much critical thinking went into the expectation that, if Jewell *were* the perpetrator and gave evidence or confessed during the bogus interview, the courts would uphold the legality of the interview and not dismiss the entire case?

Personal Reflections

1. How would you feel if you were innocent of a crime, but officers believed you were guilty and so used the tactics just discussed to get you to confess?
2. Which tactics, if any, would you *not* use because you would feel uncomfortable using them or believe they would never work?
3. At what point do you think that physical coercion becomes unethical and/or illegal?
4. At what point do you think that psychological coercion becomes unethical and/or illegal?

FALSE CONFESSIONS

False confessions occur when people confess to a crime they did not commit. Although some false confessions are beyond the control of officers, many are the result of poor, if not unethical or illegal, interviewing procedures. Even when false confessions are beyond the control of officers, they have the responsibility to scrutinize these confessions to the degree that they do not result in an indictment, much less a conviction.

While there is no way of knowing how many false confessions are made each year, research sheds some light on the question. Huff, Rattner, and Sagarin (1986) analyzed 205 cases of wrongful convictions and found that 16 (8 percent) were the result of false confessions. Scheck, Neufeld, and Dwyer (2000) examined 62 cases of wrongful convictions in the United States involving serious crimes and found that 24 percent of them involved, among other irregularities, false confessions.

A classic case of false confession that originally resulted in life prison sentences is that of the Guildford Four, which took place in England in 1974 (Frankel, 1989). Four members of the Irish Republican Army were accused of bombing a pub in England, killing 4 people and injuring 57. While in custody, all 4 men confessed to the crime but later recanted, claiming they had falsely confessed in response to intense and unrelenting police pressure, coercion, and torture.

Police accepted the confessions as valid, despite the fact that virtually no evidence linked the suspects to the crime. There were 140 inconsistencies between the statements of the four suspects, and one of the suspects had a verified alibi. The case went to trial in September 1975, and all four defendants were sentenced to life in prison. In 1977, two other men admitted to being the bombers and claimed the four who had been convicted of the crime were innocent. These confessions, added to the uncovering of fabricated evidence, moved the court of appeals to free the four suspects in October 1989, after each had served approximately 15 years in prison.

Today, evidence rebuts the age-old law enforcement axiom: People do not confess to crimes they did not commit.

False confessions serve no one well. If they are accepted or coerced by officers, they place a black eye on the face of law enforcement, a sign of incompetence, if not unethical and/or illegal conduct. False confessions also ensure that the true perpetrator will not be apprehended, putting the victims of the crime and society at large at risk. False confessions also do not serve well the people who make them, or their families. Therefore, it is imperative for officers to understand the nature of false confessions so that they do not volitionally or unwittingly become part of a procedure that elicits them. There are three types of false confession: voluntary, coerced compliant, and coerced internalized (Kassin, 1997).

Voluntary False Confessions

In this type of false confession, people volunteer to confess to a crime they did not commit. The following are some motives that underlie this behavior.

To achieve notoriety.   People who confess to a crime in a high-profile case often receive national, if not international, attention. Some people have a pathological need for attention, to be in the limelight, to be somebody. After studying the crime from media reports, they walk into a law enforcement agency and confess, often in great detail, to a crime they did not commit.

To escape stress.   Some people possess very low stress tolerance; even the slightest bit of stress is very unsettling. For them, the stress involved in even the most low-key interview is too much to bear. People with limited intelligence and those who are psychologically fragile are especially prone to wilting under the stress of even the most benign interview. This includes children who are, by nature, cognitively immature and psychologically fragile. Children may confess to anything to escape the stress of an interview.

To protect someone else.   Some people voluntarily confess to a crime to protect a loved one who they know committed the crime, a spouse, child, parent, or friend. They would rather sacrifice themselves and go to prison than stand by and watch a loved one go to prison. A more sinister variation of this attitude is the person who "takes the rap" out of fear or as proof of loyalty to a gang or the mob.

To cover up illicit behavior.   These people would rather be arrested for a relatively minor crime they did not commit than be "killed" by a loved one for an indiscretion they did commit. For example, a married man's valid alibi is that he was with his girlfriend at the time of the purse snatching. He falsely confesses, preferring to take his chances with the justice system rather than with his wife.

To atone for unrelated guilt.   Some people harbor deep, abiding guilt for some unrelated past behavior for which they were never caught. Their consciences have tormented them for a long time, the guilt increasing rather than decreasing over the years. For example, a man sexually molested a child many years prior but never got caught. He is called in for questioning about a child molestation that occurred in his apartment complex but in which he was not involved. This event unleashes the guilt he has tried to suppress for years, and he confesses to the crime to relieve this guilt. In other words, he confesses to the wrong crime to relieve his guilt over another crime.

Although these confessions are not common, they also are not rare, especially in large urban areas, which have proportionately more people with problems that lead to false confessions. When the Lindbergh baby was kidnapped in 1932, more than 200 people falsely confessed to the crime, and ironically later research suggests that the man who was convicted and sentenced to death for the crime may not have committed it.

More recently, in the 1980s, Henry Lee Lucas voluntarily and falsely confessed to over 600 murders, in addition to the 3 he apparently did commit. One confession that probably was false (there was no forensic or circumstantial evidence, and he had a verified alibi, which was that he was at work, 1,300 miles away from the murder scene) ironically earned him the only death sentence he received. Commenting on this case, Gudjonsson (1999) states: "The fact that Mr. Lucas may well be executed for his [false] confessions shows how reluctant judges in the USA are to accept that false confessions can and do on occasion happen. Indeed, there seems to be a cultural reluctance in the USA to recognize the existence of false confessions . . . " (p. 425). Lucas's sentence was later commuted to life imprisonment.

Officers cannot prevent this type of false confession because it is generated by the person making it. Yet officers can do a great deal to test the validity of the confession before reflexively filing charges, as tempting as it may be to clear the case.

Coerced-compliant False Confessions

Coerced confessions, athough not common, occur in a number sufficient to create concern in the law enforcement and legal communities, as well as alarm in society at large. Coerced-compliant confessions are extracted when officers use coercion. The suspects know they did not commit the crimes, but confess for the following reasons.

To escape harm. In some cases, interviews can be highly aggressive and intimidating, both physically and psychologically. Interviews can be physically coercive when interrogators use third-degree tactics. Examples of physical coercion include slapping, punching, kicking, or spraying suspects with chemical agents; forcing suspects to remain handcuffed to chairs for prolonged periods of time; hitting them with batons, rolled-up newspapers, or telephone books; pointing guns at them; not permitting them to use restrooms; and allowing drug addicts to go through painful and medically dangerous withdrawal until they confess. Examples of psychological coercion ("fourth-degree" interrogations) include shouting in the face of suspects, calling them derogatory names, ridiculing them, pounding on tables, throwing objects, kicking walls and lockers, isolating suspects by holding them incommunicado for long periods of time, interviewing suspects without interruption for long hours, threatening dire consequences to the suspect and his family if he does not confess, and threatening to spread malicious rumors about the suspect to his family, friends, and cohorts in crime.

To identify with the aggressor. Identification with the aggressor is the psychological equivalent of this axiom: If you can't beat them, join them. Under great intimidation, some suspects identify with their interviewer; that is, they want what the interviewers want. To please the officers, to be on their side, to avoid their wrath, these suspects "willingly" confess to the crime. They become buddies with the officers. The suspects may even defend the coercive tactics of the officers if they come under scrutiny (battered witness syndrome).

To receive a lighter sentence.   Some suspects confess to a crime they did not commit because officers lead them to believe there is an overwhelming amount of evidence against them, including victim or witness identification. Suspects are told that, if they are smart, they will confess to the crime and receive a lighter sentence than if they force everyone to go through a lengthy, expensive legal process. This places innocent people in a no-win situation. They can falsely confess and receive a sentence of, for example, five years, or face conviction at trial and a sentence of twenty years. It does not take much time for a suspect, especially one with limited intellectual, psychological, economic, and social resources, to accept this as "a good deal."

To control collateral damage.   Some suspects have skeletons in their closet. Some years prior to the crime, they may have been accused of, or arrested for, rape, child molestation, securities fraud, homosexual conduct, embezzlement, and so forth. Since that time, they have kept out of trouble and begun a new life. When someone commits a crime similar to the one in which they were involved, they become a suspect, even though they had nothing to do with it. They are called in for questioning, and officers want to strike a deal: "Confess to the crime, and we'll keep this out of the media and forget about your past troubles. Refuse to confess, and we have to open up your past to everybody. It's your call." Because this is not much of a choice, the person confesses and hopes the interviewers keep their promise.

Coerced-internalized Confessions

Coerced-internalized confessions result when officers use persuasion and manipulation to convince people they actually committed the crime, even though they have no memory of it (because they did not commit it). People susceptible to this kind of coercion tend to have one or more of the following traits.

High suggestibility.   As discussed in the sections on hypnosis and eyewitness testimony, some people are very vulnerable to suggestion. They are easily influenced to think, feel, and act in ways that another person wants. Analogously, suggestible people resemble clay that easily can be shaped in ways the sculptor wishes.

Weak self-identity.   These individuals lack a clear sense of who they are, what they want, how they got where they are, why they are doing what they are doing, or where they are going. Their theme in life is this: I don't know who I am—do you?

Strong need to please.   These people have learned that the best way to get good things and avoid bad things in life is to please people. This compulsive pleasing includes pleasing people who are nice, mean, powerful, weak, and, of course, especially pleasing law enforcement officers.

Strong dependency needs.   People with strong dependency needs inordinately rely on others for self-worth, affirmation, attention, and support. Their theme in life is: "If you meet my needs, I'll do whatever you want."

Understanding the dynamics that lead to false confessions can help officers debunk them before they reach the prosecutor's office or the courtroom. When the motives for false confessions are dissected, it is easy to see where interviewers could have matched the evidence (or lack of evidence) of the crime with the suspect's story and ascertained that the suspect could not have committed the crime. A false confession that results in arrest and, even worse, conviction and imprisonment, is always a sign of serious failure because, at the very least, it indicates officers did less than a thorough job in the investigation.

Personal Reflections _____

1. After people hear that someone made a false confession, they typically say: "I'd never be so stupid as to confess to a crime I didn't commit." After reading the reasons why people make false confessions, how would you respond to this statement?
2. Of the five reasons for making false confessions, which one is likely to be the most common and why?
3. How do you think it happens that officers and prosecutors allow a person who made a false confession to get to trial?

BEHAVIOR ANALYSIS

The term *behavior analysis* relates to analyzing suspects' behavior to determine whether they are telling the truth or lying. The behavior that is analyzed is both verbal (words, sounds, silences) and nonverbal (body language—posture, movements, facial expression).

Indicators of Deceit

The law enforcement literature is replete with books, articles, training manuals, and videotapes purporting to teach methods officers can use to detect deceit. These presentations typically begin with a major premise: All behavior is meaningful (which is inarguable). They quickly proceed to the next premise: With proper training and skills, officers will be able to interpret behavior so they can detect whether suspects are lying or telling the truth (which is arguable). Some examples of behaviors purported to be "excellent," "probable," or "good" indicators of deception are the following:

Verbal	Nonverbal
Makes slips of the tongue	Holds head down
Evades questions	Exhibits impatience
Stammers	Avoids eye contact
Gives vague answers	Blinks eyes rapidly
Changes the subject	Tilts head to the side
Contradicts self	Fidgets
Speaks rapidly	Taps fingers, feet
Speaks slowly	Slides chair backwards
Talks gibberish	Crosses arms across chest
Asks that questions be repeated	Slouches in chair
Has lengthy response times	Sits rigidly
Has rapid response times	Covers mouth
Ignores questions	Forgets details
Shifts focus to officers	Flinches
Emits deep sighs	Smiles, laughs inappropriately
Offers unsolicited comments	Stares into space
Gives premature denials	Stares at interviewer
Does not complete sentences	Grimaces
Lapses into silences	Clenches fists
Fails to understand question	Turns red, perspires
Protests too much	Paces floor
Offers vague threats	Supports answers by swearing on mother's grave
Asks for friend, attorney	Has a dry mouth
Invokes *Miranda* warnings	Exhibits shortness of breath
Acts too friendly	Points foot toward interviewer
Acts too unfriendly	

Behavior analysis presentations often offer a caveat in their introductions and summaries stating that no single behavior or pattern of behavior *necessarily* indicates truth or deception; however, the body and bulk of the presentations often suggest the opposite. Mosten and Stephenson (1993), commenting on the accuracy of detecting deception by observing nonverbal behavior, state: "Even though the detection of deception through observations of non-verbal cues is an almost entirely unreliable process, it is still a popular belief amongst police interviewers that the ability to spot deception is an essential aspect of interviewing competency" (p. 107).

Difficulties in Detecting Truth

Several variables make it difficult, if not impossible, to reliably detect the truth or deception in suspects', victims', and witnesses' verbal and nonverbal behaviors.

Causality and symptoms.   There is an analogous problem between detecting deception in interviews and in polygraph testing. The polygraph does not measure lies but rather affective arousal. In the same way, the behavioral cues just listed could well be symptoms of affective arousal (fear, anxiety, confusion, guilt, anger, and so on) but have nothing to do with a suspect's guilt or innocence. In fact, an innocent person who is the prime suspect in a capital crime is far more likely to exhibit affective arousal than is a habitual offender with an antisocial personality or one who is "brain dead" due to substance abuse.

Basal rate.   In order to assess the meaning of suspects' behavior accurately, officers should know the suspects' basal rates, that is, how the suspects behave when officers are not interviewing them. In other words, a suspect may *always* cover her mouth (avert her eyes, fidget), whether she is in enjoyable situations, ordinary stressful situations, or police interviews.

Cultural and social differences.   The differences in communication styles between social groups are often overlooked in deceit detection, sometimes causing innocent people to be perceived as guilty. It is natural, for example, for white officers to expect *everyone* to communicate as they do, especially if they have not been exposed to the communication styles of other ethnic groups. But research (Vrij, 1998) indicates that this is not the case. Cross-racial studies indicate several differences in the communication styles of blacks and whites. For example, black people tend to have more gaze aversion and move their bodies more than white people do, behaviors that may well be interpreted as indicators of deception when they are not.

Some ethnic groups tend to be obsequious in the presence of authority, while others are inclined to be aggressive, and still others tend to be more moderate in their behavior. Less educated people and those whose second language is English often respond to personal questions with "Who, me?" even when they are the only other person in the room. Officers typically perceive this as a "stall tactic," which it often is, but it is not necessarily a "lie tactic." The individual is often stalling in order to process what exactly is being asked and how best to respond. Adolescents and elderly people also tend to have different communication styles, as do educated and uneducated people, males and females, southerners and northerners, and so on.

No-win situation.   Many of the above indexes of deception place innocent suspects in a no-win situation (or guilty–guilty situation). The probability of deception will be registered if suspects

- Try to convince officers of their innocence or do not try to convince officers of their innocence.
- Sit rigid in a chair or slouch in a chair
- Speak rapidly or speak slowly
- Take a long time to respond to questions or answer them too quickly
- Make unsolicited comments or do not make unsolicited comments
- Immediately deny involvement in the crime or do not immediately deny involvement in the crime
- Protest too much or protest too little
- Avoid eye contact with officers or stare at them

This use of behavior analysis presents a particularly grave problem because innocent suspects can be perceived as "obviously lying" by overzealous officers. As Bartol and Bartol (1994) state:

> It is not wise . . . to make assumptions about truthfulness or deception strictly on the basis of nonverbal cues. It is especially foolhardy to accept the prevailing folklore in the area. If anything, the cues associated with deception may be better behavioral indicators of stress and anxiety than they are signs of lying. (p. 256)

Human behavior is simply too complex and the inadequacies of human observation too great to possess high confidence in any person's ability to differentiate between truth and falsehood with a significant degree of consistent accuracy, especially when dealing with strangers. Moreover, even trained observers have difficulty detecting lies. The emotional "microexpressions" that can accompany lies frequently last only 1/25 of a second, a cue that could be lost to observers if they even blink (Ekman & O'Sullivan, 1991).

Contrary to what might be expected, law enforcement officers in general are no better than any other group in detecting deceit. In one study (Ekman & O'Sullivan, 1991), members of the U.S. Secret Service, CIA, FBI, National Security Agency, Drug Enforcement Agency, police officers, judges, psychiatrists, college students, and working people did not, in general, detect deception in subjects based on their verbal and nonverbal behavior. The average accuracy rate for the Secret Service was approximately 65 percent and was significantly higher than that of all the other groups, which ranged in accuracy from 53 percent to 56 percent, slightly better than chance or the flip of a coin.

These results are troublesome, but even more troublesome is the fact that these studies are not new but have spanned the last quarter century. Yet, a summary of 33 other studies across the same time span indicates that many law enforcement officers continue to cling to the stereotyped indices of deception, such as a high-pitched voice, averted eyes, shifting position, and so on (Vrij, 1998, pp. 44–46). It appears that beliefs die hard, even in the face of contradictory empirical evidence.

Paradoxically, while the accuracy of law enforcement officers in detecting truth or deceit is generally unimpressive, they tend to remain highly confident in their assessments (DePaulo & Pfeifer, 1986). Therefore, officers need to be cautious in applying these indices of deception to all suspects.

Practical Implications

Officers should exercise great caution in deceit assessment, and their training should stress caution, not just perfunctorily but continually. Also, larger law enforcement agencies have the resources to do good research. Because studies are lacking in regard to the relationship between suspect behavior and deception in real police interviews, this would be a fertile ground for research.

It would be relatively easy for organizations that offer workshops on deceit assessment to compare the accuracy rates of their graduates to those of a control group of officers who did not take the workshop and another control group of average citizens (or college students). Results assessment should always be a part of any workshop dealing with important issues.

Workshops in deceit assessment should include scenarios in which both instructors and students interview "suspects" to test the interviewer's skills, and no one, including the instructor, would know which subjects are lying and which are telling the truth, then compare and analyze the results.

Officers can realize that indexes of deception may or may not indicate deception. Many other variables can account for innocent people manifesting deceptive cues: high anxiety, limited intelligence, lack of social skills, use of licit or illicit drugs, psychological disturbance, physical ailments, limited language skills, exhaustion, shock, distraction, anger, immaturity, or insecurity.

The question is not whether officers should participate in deceit assessment; they always have and always will. Professional law enforcement officers understand and accept the fact that deceit assessment is an art, not a science, and must be practiced with prudence, sensitivity, integrity, respect, and, perhaps most importantly, with humility, in that the officers must accept their limitations, admit their mistakes, and learn from them.

Personal Reflections _____

1. How would you react if you were informed that you failed a job interview because you didn't look the interviewers in the eye, fidgeted, or took too long to answer questions, so they concluded you were not being truthful?

2. What is your "success rate" in assessing whether family and friends are lying or telling you the truth?

*S*ummary

Interviewing suspects is one of the more important and challenging tasks that officers face. Because human behavior is so complex, there is a great deal of room for officers to make mistakes. A suspect can look "as guilty as sin," and be innocent, and another can look "as innocent as a saint" and be as guilty as sin. Professional officers appreciate this fact and progress carefully and slowly through the interview process. They are comfortable in gray areas and willing to let the suspect's true colors eventually show through as a result of skilled interviewing. Other officers, however, think they can immediately tell when a suspect is guilty, are allergic to gray areas, and through a process of confirmation bias and tunnel vision, prematurely declare the suspect guilty. This dynamic has made *rush to judgment* a household phrase.

Interviewing suspects is also challenging because courts and juries have become increasingly skeptical of the investigative competence and integrity of law enforcement. Unfortunately, law enforcement has brought much of this on itself by shoddy, if not illegal and unethical, work in some high-profile cases. As a result, courts and juries are less likely to give investigators the benefit of the doubt when questionable practices come to light. Therefore, when interviewing suspects, officers should assume that every move they make and every word they utter will be placed under a microscope and act accordingly.

A final reason that interviewing suspects is important and challenging is that innocent people who are arrested, convicted, and/or imprisoned often have their lives and those of their loved ones irreparably damaged. This is a serious moral and legal issue. Morally, officers who enter law enforcement to help people and give back to the community may end up being responsible for virtually destroying the lives of innocent people, which should never be considered "acceptable collateral damage" in the war against crime. Individual officers and their supervisors are increasingly being held accountable, both legally and civilly, for unprofessional and illegal conduct during the course of their investigations.

For these reasons, officers should view interviewing suspects in the same ways that physicians view performing surgery: Make sure you have the right patient, the right laboratory results, the right instruments, and the right procedures because an error in any one of these elements could have catastrophic consequences for both the patient and the surgeon.

*R*eferences

Arrigo, B.A. (2000). *Introduction to forensic psychology: Issues and controversies in crime and justice.* New York: Academic Press.

Bartol, C.R., & Bartol, A.M. (1994). *Psychology and law: Research and application* (2nd ed.). Pacific Grove, CA: Brooks/Cole.

Brenner, M. (1997, February). American nightmare—The ballad of Richard Jewell, *Vanity Fair.* Retrieved November 2, 2002 from the World Wide Web: http://www.mariebrenner.com/articles/nightmare/nightmare2.html.

Collins, J. (1996, November 11). The strange saga of Richard Jewell. *Time, 148* (22). Retrieved October 12, 2002 from the World Wide Web: http://time-proxy.yaga.com/time/magazine/article/qpass/0,10987,1101961111-135001,00.htm.

DePaulo, B.M., & Pfeifer, R.L. (1986). On-the-job experience and skill at detecting deception. *Journal of Applied Social Psychology, 16,* 249–267.

Ekman, P., & O'Sullivan, M. (1991). Who can catch a liar? *American Psychologist, 46,* 913–920.

Frankel, G. (1989, October 20). British court overturns convictions in IRA case. *Wasington Post*, A36.

Gudjonsson, G. (1999). The making of a serial false confessor: The confessions of Henry Lee Lucas. *The Journal of Forensic Psychiatry, 10,* 416–426.

Huff, C.R., Rattner, A., & Sagarin, E. (1986). Guilty until proven innocent: Wrongful conviction and public policy. *Crime and Delinquency, 32,* 518–544.

Kalbfleisch, P.J. (1994). The language of detecting deceit. *Journal of Language and Social Psychology, 13,* 469–496.

Kassin, S.M. (1997). The psychology of confession evidence. *American Psychologist, 52,* 221–233.

Moston, S., & Stephenson, G.M. (1993). The changing face of police interrogation. *Journal of Community and Applied Social Psychology, 3,* 101–115.

Scheck, B., Neufeld, P., & Dwyer, J. (2000). *Actual innocence.* New York: Doubleday.

Skolnick J.H., & Leo, R.A. (1998). The ethics of deceptive interrogation. In M.C. Braswell, B.R. McCarthy, & B.J. McCarthy (Eds.), *Justice, Crime and Ethics* (3rd ed.) (pp. 109–123). Cincinnati, OH: Anderson Publishing.

Vrij, A. (1998). Nonverbal communication and credibility. In A. Memon, A. Vrij, & R. Bull (Eds.), *Psychology and law: Truthfulness, accuracy and credibility* (pp. 32–58). New York: McGraw-Hill.

Wrightsman, L.S. (2001). *Forensic psychology.* Belmont, CA: Wadsworth.

9

Investigative Techniques

L aw enforcement has two fundamental purposes: crime prevention and crime solution. Because crime prevention is difficult to quantify, clearance rates are the only quantifiable measure of an agency's success or failure. Therefore, after all the various services provided by a law enforcement agency are touted to the public, everything boils down to one question: What was your clearance rate for major crimes last year? The answer to this question will justify or fail to justify the existence of an agency, or at least the existence of its executives, whether or not it should.

With the exception of homicide, which nationally has about a 63 percent clearance rate, the clearance rate for other serious crimes averages less than 30 percent (Federal Bureau of Investigation, 2002). There are several reasons for low clearance rates, one of them being that investigative techniques are sometimes not as effective or accurate as the people who use them believe them to be.

Investigative techniques are tools, so it is important to understand something about their nature. Some tools are worthless, and no matter how much people pay for them and follow the directions, they will never achieve their manufacturers' claims. Other tools are well made, but their worth derives from the skills of the people who use them, which run the gamut from great skill to no skill. Inherently worthless tools or those used by unskilled people can harm the people who attempt to use them and others involved in the project. For example, whatever the worth of a polygraph machine, when operators come up with false positives (declare people are lying when this is not the case) or false negatives (declare people are truthful when they are not), great harm can result.

The purpose of this chapter is to present what the forensic and behavioral sciences have learned about some of the more common investigative techniques: polygraph testing, voice stress analysis, forensic hypnosis, criminal profiling, as well as the use of expert witnesses. Officers can use this knowledge to develop a healthily critical assessment of these techniques and the competence to use them more effectively.

THE POLYGRAPH EXAMINATION

The polygraph was invented around 1917, the term meaning "many writings." The polygraph typically has three channels of measurement: the pneumograph, which measures respiration; the galvanograph, which measures electrical resistance of the skin; and the cardiosphygmograph, which measures blood pressure and pulse. These measures, which appear on a computer screen, reflect only one phenomenon: *emotional arousal*, caused by heightened feelings of fear, anger, guilt, excitement, frustration, embarrassment, and so on. Therefore, polygraphs are not "lie detectors" but "emotion detectors," and, for this reason, officers are advised to use the term *polygraph* rather than *lie detector* in court and other formal situations.

The basic assumption underlying the use of polygraphs is that emotional arousal during polygraph testing is caused by anxiety due to lying. Therefore, people who lie will manifest stronger emotional responses and, hence, more remarkable polygraph readings than those who tell the truth. Although polygraphs are widely used by the government, insurance companies, and in civil cases, this section will limit its discussion to the polygraph in law enforcement, in which the polygraph should be used only when all available leads have been exhausted. This is so because the procedure is costly and, more important, may lead to the premature inclusion or exclusion of suspects to a crime, thus precluding a more open-minded investigation. In other words, it should be used as only a last resort.

It is important for all law enforcement officers to be at least generally familiar with the basics of polygraph testing for a number of reasons. First, approximately 67,000 law enforcement candidates are administered a polygraph each year by 600 law enforcement agencies, which reject 22 percent of these candidates based on polygraph results alone (Horvath, 1993). Moreover, law enforcement officers can be required to take a polygraph examination when they transfer from one agency to another, are promoted to positions of higher security, or are subjects of an internal affairs investigation.

Law enforcement officers also will be directly or indirectly involved with polygraphs because their use is widespread, especially in major crimes, to establish investigative leads, encourage confessions, and develop suspects. Two types of polygraph methods will be addressed: the Controlled Question Test and the Guilty Knowledge Test.

Controlled Question Test

The Controlled Question Test (CQT) is the test most used in the United States (Lykken, 1998, p. 115). There are several versions of the CQT and different methods of administering the same version. The description here offers a typical method of administering the CQT.

Pretest interview.   This is the critical part of the process because it sets the stage for distinguishing truthful subjects from deceptive ones. These interviews generally last from 30 to 60 minutes, depending on the nature of the subject and the crime under investigation. This interview has five purposes:

- To introduce subjects to the examiner, the machine, and the general procedures, so that their reactions during the actual test will not be contaminated by confusion, distractions, or anxiety stemming from unfamiliarity with the situation.
- To review the questions that the examiner will ask in the actual test, in order to build up anxiety around questions that may evoke heightened emotional responses. Typically, there are 10 questions in the actual test, which are carefully distilled from a good deal of information about the crime and the suspect.
- To create a psychological set in subjects that will prime them for the test. This is accomplished by the examiner selling the subject on two ideas: The polygraph is infallible, and the slightest bit of deceit by the subject on any question will make him the kind of person who committed the crime under investigation, thus causing him to fail the test. Of course, neither of these claims is true, but it is important for the subject to believe them if the test is to work.
- To explain that subjects must answer either "yes" or "no" to each question. They will have the opportunity to explain and elaborate on their responses in the posttest interview.
- To ask neutral questions ("Is your name John Smith?" "Were you born in this city?") to obtain a baseline against which to compare responses to evocative (control and relevant questions) that will be asked in the next stage. In other words, it is important to know whether a subject is normally calm, anxious by nature, or anxious only when faced with evocative questions.

Actual test.   After the pretest interview, the actual test begins, which includes the examiner asking neutral, relevant, and control questions.

A *neutral question* is often asked first to reestablish a baseline that may be more elevated once the test begins.

A *relevant question* is asked next, which directly relates to the crime under investigation. For example, if the victim, Mary Jones, was raped, then murdered, the relevant questions might be: "Do you know Mary Jones?" "Were you with Mary Jones within the last week?" "Did you rape Mary Jones?" "Did you murder Mary Jones?" The purpose of the relevant questions is to evoke a heightened state of emotional arousal, which registers as a large blip on the chart in guilty subjects when they answer "no," but little or no arousal in innocent subjects when they answer "no."

A *control question* is then asked, which is only indirectly related to the crime: "Did you ever have a sexual thought you wouldn't want anyone else to know you had?" "Did you every feel like hurting someone?" "Have you ever done anything that you hoped no one would ever find out about?" The assumption underlying control questions is that *everyone* has experienced these thoughts, feelings, and behaviors at some point in their lives, so that to answer "no" would register as deception. This is meant to place innocent subjects in a tense, no-win situation. If they answer "yes," they are told this makes them the kind of person who committed the crime, and if they answer "no," the infallible polygraph will detect their deceit and make them the likely perpetrator. The expectation is that innocent subjects will choose the lesser-of-two-evils path, taking a chance on lying and hoping the polygraph fails to detect it, rather than openly admitting they are the kind of person who committed the crime. Guilty subjects are also likely to answer "no" to the control questions, causing the machine to register deceit, the size of which will be measured against the size of the blip registered to their expected "no" response to the relevant questions.

The rationale underlying this sequence is that both innocent and guilty subjects will register a blip when they answer "no" to control questions because they are being deceitful, but only the guilty subjects will register a blip on the relevant questions when they answer "no" because they are being deceitful, whereas innocent subjects are being truthful.

After this round of 10 questions, another two rounds follow, the questions remaining the same to test for reliability, but the sequence is altered to avoid the prediction of the next question and the subject tailoring a response to fit it.

Posttest.   After the actual test, examiners clear up any confusion and give the subjects the opportunity to explain their answers. In some cases, especially when quantitative scoring is used, the test is ended at this point. In other cases, especially when global scoring is used, examiners, especially if they are officers, may give the subject the results. In cases in which the subject "failed" the test, the officer may exhort the subject to confess in light of "the over-whelming evidence" of his guilt. Sometimes, even when a subject who officers believe is guilty passes the test, they will tell him that he "failed miserably" and give him the "opportunity to come clean" while there is still time for the officers to put in a good word for him with the prosecutor's officer. These ploys, surprisingly, can get subjects to confess but, unfortunately, they can pressure both guilty *and* innocent subjects to confess, the latter to a crime they did not commit.

Scoring and interpretation.   The final step in the process is scoring and interpreting the test. Two kinds of analysis can be used: a global approach and a quantitative approach. In the global approach, the examiner develops a general impression of the truthfulness or deceptiveness of the subject from four sources: the psychophysiological readings on the chart, information about the case, knowledge of the subject's history and statements to officers, and the subject's verbal and nonverbal behavior during the test. The examiner takes each of these pieces of the puzzle and constructs a picture of a truthful or deceitful subject.

In the quantitative approach, the examiner mathematically compares the psychophysiological responses to the relevant and control questions (zone of comparison). When a subject's reaction to a relevant question is stronger than that to a control question, a negative score is assigned. For example, a "noticeable difference" would be scored a –1, a "strong difference" a –2, and a "dramatic difference" a –3.

When a subject's reaction to a relevant question is weaker than that to a control question, a positive score is assigned. Thus, a "noticeable difference" would be scored a +1, a "strong difference" a +2, and a "dramatic difference" a +3. A total score is obtained by adding the scores across all three channels and all three rounds of questions. This will result in one of three conclusions: The subject was being deceptive and thus is presumed guilty of the crime for purposes of the investigation; the subject was being truthful and thus is presumed to be innocent of the crime for purposes of the investigation; or the subject's responses were so weak in either direction that the results are inconclusive or indeterminate.

Critique of CQT.   The following are four criticisms of the CQT.

- *Faulty basic assumption.* The basic assumption underlying the test is that innocent subjects will not experience a state of emotional arousal when asked relevant questions, but guilty subjects will. However, this assumption is not necessarily valid. For example, when an older woman who has lived a sheltered life is asked a relevant question: "While you were employed as a pre-kindergarten teacher, did you touch Jimmy Smith's penis?" her emotional arousal may go off the chart, not because she is lying, but because she is shocked and embarrassed by the question. In other words, she registers a false positive response and appears to be lying.

    The other side of the assumption is equally problematic; namely, that when people lie they will manifest a heightened emotional reaction. In fact, people with antisocial personalities and other disorders typically do not experience guilt about their misconduct, which includes lying. These individuals may lie but experience no emotional arousal when asked about their misconduct as part of a polygraph examination. As a result, they register a false negative on the test, indicating they were not lying. In other words, some people can lie, feel no guilt, and pass the test while others may tell the truth, experience significant anxiety, and fail the test.

- *Subjective analysis.* The CQT can have a significant subjective component, which could contaminate the results. Typically, examiners have extrapolygraphic knowledge of the suspect and the crime from case files, the media, and investigators, as well as from observing the subject's behavior at the time of testing. This information could, consciously or unconsciously, cause examiners to be biased in the direction of the subject's guilt or innocence, thus influencing questions and scoring, especially if the global approach is used because it is based on the examiner's subjective impressions. Subjectivity can also enter the quantitative approach to scoring because there is a lack of standardized, validated criteria for designating what constitutes "noticeable," "strong," and "dramatic" differences in scores, or what constitutes discrete differences within those categories. Therefore, examiners use their own subjective criteria to make these distinctions.

- *Vulnerability to countermeasures.* Two kinds of countermeasures can be used to defeat the test: physical and psychological. Physical countermeasures occur when subjects purposely alter their normal physiological functioning to defeat the polygraph; for example, they can bite their tongue, squeeze their thighs together, press their toes against the floor, or increase or decrease their respirations. Psychological countermeasures are techniques that dissociate the subject's mind from the questions and their implications. Examples of psychological countermeasures are mentally counting backward, doing math problems, and imagining peaceful or terrifying scenarios. Guilty subjects can use countermeasures to increase emotional responsivity during control questions and suppress physiological responsivity during relevant questions. Research indicates that subjects trained even for a brief period of time can learn to defeat the polygraph 50 percent of the time (Iacono and Patrick, 1999). Usually, countermeasures will result in inconclusive results, not results that indicate innocence.

- *Variable accuracy of CQT.* The accuracy of the polygraph can be scientifically measured in two ways: in a laboratory, using volunteer subjects responding to polygraph questions regarding a mock crime, and in the field, using subjects responding to polygraph questions regarding real crimes for which they are suspects. Each measure has its advantages and disadvantages.

Polygraph charts also can be read in two ways: by "blind examiners," those with no extrapolygraphic knowledge of the subject, and by "original examiners," those who possess a typical amount of pretest information on the person gathered from case files, investigators, and the media.

The studies referred to in this section were chosen by Vrij (1998, pp. 90–94) from many studies by researchers because they meet the criteria for proper scientific controls and thoroughness.

In laboratory studies using blind examiners:

- 75 percent of *guilty* subjects were classified as guilty.
- 9 percent were incorrectly classified as innocent.

- 16 percent were classified as inconclusive.
- 67 percent of *innocent* subjects were correctly classified as innocent.
- 13 percent were incorrectly classified as guilty.
- 20 percent were classified as inconclusive.

As can be seen, the CQT does about equally well in detecting guilty and innocent subjects. However, the false positive rate—that is, innocent people being classified as guilty—is disturbingly high (12 percent). In addition, the fact that 18 percent of innocent subjects' results are inconclusive is not unimportant. Almost one in five innocent people who volunteer to take a polygraph to attest to a life of integrity (for example, a law enforcement candidate) or to clear themselves of a crime could be suspected of having a shady, if not criminal, past because of these results. This, added to the 12 percent incorrectly classified as guilty, means that over one-third of innocent people may not be classified correctly as innocent.

In field studies using blind examiners:

- 89 percent of *guilty* subjects were correctly classified as guilty.
- 8 percent were incorrectly classified as innocent.
- 3 percent were classified as inconclusive.
- 60 percent of *innocent* subjects were correctly classified as innocent.
- 18 percent were incorrectly classified as guilty.
- 22 percent were classified as inconclusive.

Again, the false positive rate is disturbingly high (18 percent). Added to the inconclusive rate (22 percent), this indicates that 40 percent of innocent people were not correctly classified.

In field studies using original examiners:

- 87 percent of *guilty* subjects were correctly classified as guilty.
- 4 percent were incorrectly classified as innocent.
- 9 percent were classified as inconclusive.
- 82 percent of *innocent* subjects were correctly classified as innocent.
- 3 percent were incorrectly classified as guilty.
- 15 percent were classified as inconclusive.

In these studies, false positive errors are significantly reduced from about 18 percent in the blind examiner studies to 3 percent in the original examiner studies. However, adding the 3 percent incorrect classifications to the 15 percent inconclusive rate still means that a significant percentage (18 percent) of innocent subjects were not correctly classified as innocent.

The fact that original examiner studies yielded more accurate results in correctly classifying innocent subjects can be used to buttress each side in the debate as to whether the polygraph is accurate. Proponents argue that when polygraphs are used properly, that is, operated by trained examiners, the results are quite accurate. Those who doubt the accuracy of the polygraph argue that it is not the polygraph itself that is accurate, but the skills of the examiner that make the polygraph machine more or less accurate. This creates the unpredictable situation in which polygraph results are largely dependent on the skills of the examiner. If the examiner happens to be highly skilled, the innocent subject is in luck (and the guilty subject out of luck). However, if the examiner is less than highly skilled, the innocent subject may be out of luck (and the guilty subject in luck).

Guilty Knowledge Test

The Guilty Knowledge Test (GKT), which is used less frequently than the CQT in the United States, does not determine whether a subject is being truthful or deceitful, as does the CQT, but rather determines whether the subject *possesses knowledge* indicative of having been involved in a crime. The questions are multiple choice and include information known only to the victim and the perpetrator. This information needs to be closely guarded for this test to be effective, so that innocent subjects will have no knowledge of the facts surrounding the case. The assumption underlying the GKT is that when guilty people are presented with stimuli connected to the crime, they will manifest a greater emotional arousal than will innocent people, for whom the stimulus has no meaning.

A sample question in a rape case might be this: Was the victim wearing: (a) red underpants, (b) yellow underpants, (c) pink underpants, (d) purple underpants, (e) no underpants?

Like this example, each multiple-choice question has five alternatives, and the subjects are instructed they *must* answer "no" to each alternative, which means a guilty subject will be afforded the opportunity to lie on one alternative for each question. In the above example, the theory is that, if the victim's underpants were pink, the guilty subject would manifest a stronger emotional response to item "c" than would an innocent subject who has no idea of the color the victim's underpants.

Great care must be taken in constructing the alternatives for each question, making certain that their potential to evoke an emotional response is equal throughout all five alternatives. For example, consider this statement: "The victim of the murder was: (a) beaten, (b) shot, (c) disemboweled, (d) strangled, (e) drowned." It is likely that the term and mental image of *disemboweled* could evoke a heightened emotional reaction even in innocent people.

Critique of GKT.   It is often difficult for officers to keep even the most sensitive information concerning a crime from the public. Leaks reach the media from officers and other agency personnel, the prosecutor's office, defense attorneys, witnesses, and even the victim and the victim's family. The more this "protected information" is unprotected, the less valid the GKT will be. This is one main reason that the GKT is not used a great deal in the United States in contrast to Europe, where laws allow sensitive information to be better protected.

Several difficulties exist with the assumptions underlying the GKT. One difficulty, which is also present in the CQT, is that some subjects—for example, those with antisocial personalities—may not manifest a heightened emotional arousal to stimuli that would cause such arousal in a normal, guilty subject. Moreover, innocent people can manifest emotional arousal to stimuli that they find embarrassing or particularly disturbing. For example, in the sample question in the rape case example, an innocent subject may react to alternative "e" (no underpants) because it is terribly embarrassing or shocking to that particular subject.

Another problem is that the GKT assumes each perpetrator shares equally in the knowledge of the crime's minutiae. In a gang rape perpetrated by four men, some of them may have little or no knowledge about particulars. For example, the last man to rape the victim may have no idea of the color of the victim's underpants. A variation of this difficulty is that a guilty subject may have been so crazed or impaired at the time of the crime—overcome by passion, alcohol, drugs, psychopathology, or neurological dysfunction—that he has no knowledge or recollection of the more subtle details of the crime. In fact, he could have partial or total amnesia regarding it.

An innocent subject who has gained knowledge of the crime from a perpetrator or the media may manifest a heightened emotional reaction to a question that reflects this knowledge. On the other hand, a guilty subject who does poorly on the GKT can claim that he learned all the information about the crime from the perpetrators, whom he refuses to identify. Finally, countermeasures can also be used with the GKT, but they are more difficult to use with this test than with the CQT.

Accuracy of GKT.   The results from a review (Vrij, 1998, pp. 87–91) of three *laboratory* studies on the GKT indicate that 80 percent of *guilty subjects* were correctly classified as guilty, and 17 percent were incorrectly classified as innocent. With respect to *innocent subjects*, 96 percent were correctly classified as innocent and 4 percent were incorrectly identified as guilty. These results indicate that the GKT is best at clearing innocent subjects and far less accurate for detecting guilty ones. The GKT does not have an "inconclusive" category.

Apparently only two *field* studies have been published regarding the GKT. In these studies, an average of 96 percent of *innocent subjects* was correctly classified as innocent, and 59 percent of the *guilty subjects* were correctly classified as guilty. As was the case with the laboratory studies, the field studies indicate the GKT is very accurate in correctly classifying innocent subjects but far less accurate at correctly classifying guilty ones, creating a high false negative rate.

The Polygraph in Court

Through the years, there were times when polygraph results were allowed as testimony in court, then not allowed; currently, they are allowed in some courts but not in others.

In some states, polygraphs can be used by defendants who pass them to prove their innocence in court. These are referred to as "friendly" tests because the examiner is paid by the defense, and the results are protected by the attorney – client privilege. Defendants have little to lose by taking these polygraphs. If they pass the test, they may be able to use it in court as exculpatory evidence; if they fail it no one has to know. Because of this friendly atmosphere, much of the anxiety that is important for test validity is significantly reduced.

Polygraphs also can be administered or commissioned by law enforcement agencies to help ascertain a suspect's guilt or innocence. These tests are called "adversarial" (in contrast to "friendly"), because a law enforcement officer or an outside examiner administers polygraph tests to real suspects in serious crimes; and the results may be presented in court in states in which such evidence is admissible. Therefore, the stakes are much higher and the process more anxiety producing.

The decision as to whether polygraph results can be introduced in criminal trials is made on a state-by-state basis. In two states, Massachusetts and New Mexico, polygraph results are freely admitted. In about twenty states, polygraph evidence is allowed into court if the prosecution and defense agree to its admissibility. Some of these states require a pretrial hearing to ascertain whether the test meets certain scientific standards (see Expert Witnesses on page 253). The remaining states prohibit the use of polygraph evidence at trial. It appears that when polygraph results are introduced at trial, jurors are likely to give significant weight to these results, especially when expert witnesses claim the test is 80 percent to 90 percent accurate.

Marked disagreement exists between some law enforcement personnel and the scientific community with respect to the accuracy and admissibility of polygraph testing. Some law enforcement officers, especially those who administer polygraphs, tend to believe that the results are highly accurate. Scientists, however, tend to think that although polygraph results may be accurate at one time or another, the results are too dependent on uncontrollable variables to be relied upon with a high degree of confidence. For example, a study by Iacono and Lykken (1997) was conducted on a random sample of members of the Society of Psychophysiological Research, who would have a sound knowledge of the nature of the polygraph and relevant research. The respondents were presented with several statements about the polygraph and asked if they agreed with them. Following is a small sample of these statements and the agreement rates.

Statement	Percent Agree
CQT is based on scientifically sound theory.	36
GKT is based on scientifically sound theory.	77
Would advocate admitting failed CQTs as evidence in court.	24
Would advocate admitting passed CQTs as evidence in court.	27
CQT can be beaten by augmenting one's response to the control questions [countermeasures].	99

The courts use this kind of input based on theory and research to help them decide whether polygraph results are sufficiently valid and reliable enough to be admitted in court.

Conclusion

Although the scientific validity and reliability of the polygraph remain questionable, it can be a valuable investigative tool. Guilty suspects sometimes confess to crimes as soon as the word *polygraph* is mentioned or even in the middle of a polygraph examination. Polygraphs are also useful in screening suspects, eliminating those whom the polygraph classifies as innocent, and doing follow-up investigations on those classified guilty or whose results are inconclusive. Polygraphs also can give some indication as to whether victims and witnesses are telling the truth or at least the whole truth. However, it is too large a step to go from investigative to accusatory use to convict a person. The science and data simply are not yet at a point to justify this leap. As Vrij (1998) states:

> Taking into account the accuracy rates of blind examiners in field studies, we believe that polygraph evidence in criminal cases is undesirable, because too many mistakes are made to justify polygraph evidence. However, we acknowledge that polygraph interrogation may give valuable insight concerning whether or not a suspect is lying. We therefore believe that polygraph interrogation may be a useful tool in police investigations, for instance, to eliminate potential suspects, to check the truthfulness of informants or to examine contradicting statements of witnesses and suspects. (p. 96)

In this regard, Lykken (1998) cautions:

> The great problem in police polygraphy is in restraining the enthusiasm and credulity that these methods inspire in many police officers. . . . But if police polygraphy is not to be abused, then police officers must learn to accept that the lie test is never certain either, that some villains pass, that many who fail will turn out to be innocent, that not even a confession should be accepted without verification. (p. 271)

Personal Reflections _____

1. If you were an innocent suspect in a serious crime, would you volunteer to take a polygraph test?

2. If you were a police officer accused of serious misconduct of which you were innocent, would you be relieved or anxious about being required to take a polygraph test?

3. If someone you loved was falsely accused of embezzling money at work, would you encourage or discourage her with respect to taking a polygraph test?

VOICE STRESS ANALYZERS

In addition to the polygraph, voice stress analyzers (VSAs) also claim to detect deception. There are several types of VSA, but all are based on the same three-fold theory as the polygraph:

1. The experience of stress causes the body to react in measurably different ways than when it is at rest.

2. Lying causes stress, which will be reflected in an identifiable pattern of physiological responses.

3. This identifiable pattern of responses indicates the subject is lying.

In the case of VSAs, the physiological measurements are limited to fluctuations in the voice, whereas the polygraph typically measures at least three of the following variables: pulse rate, blood pressure, breathing, and galvanic skin responses.

The physiological theory underlying VSAs holds that when people lie, they experience stress and this stress tightens muscles, including the laryngeal muscles that control voice. Laryngeal muscles, like all working muscles, produce microvibrations, which seem to diminish when the muscles are under stress. Microvibrations create both frequency and amplitude modulations in the voice that are usually inaudible and can only be detected with sensitive electrical instruments. VSAs work by detecting low-frequency amplitude vibrations in the voice, which are reflected in an oscilliscopic pattern on a computer screen and interpreted by trained analysts to determine truth or deception. A truthful pattern resembles a slightly saw-toothed pyramid, whereas a deceptive one has a large, saw-tooth pattern that is broader in width with a flattened top.

When a VSA recording is made in a formal interview, the format is much the same as that used by polygraph examiners. A stress baseline is established, followed by interspersed relevant, irrelevant, and control questions, and differences in physiological responses are recorded.

Voice stress analyzers are easier to operate than polygraphs because the instruments are simply laptop computers with an attached microphone. Measurements can be made from in-person formal interviews or covert recordings, as well as from telephone, radio, or television recordings. The instruments are nonintrusive because they are not attached to the subject's body. With respect to expense, the cost of the instruments, including approximately one week of training, ranges from $6,000 to $12,000. This is in contrast to purchasing a polygraph along with an eight-week training course, which costs approximately $30,000. According to the leading VSA manufacturer (National Institute for Truth Verification, 2002), over 1,000 police departments have purchased these instruments and perhaps as many as 6,000 operators have received formal training in their use.

Accuracy of VSAs

While some controversy surrounds the accuracy of polygraph machines, there is more surrounding the use of VSAs in law enforcement. After all the explanations of theory, hardware, operation, and analysis, only two points of scientific interest remain with respect to instruments claiming to measure deception:

1. How accurately do they measure deception? (This is an entirely different question than "How accurately do they measure physiological changes due to stress?")
2. How reliable are the judgments of examiners as to truth or deception based on the instrument's recordings?

Depending on who is answering these questions, the answers are very different. Proponents of VSAs claim that they have a 98 percent accuracy rate, but company representatives concede this estimate stems from anecdotal evidence from customers and not from independent research (Wylie, 2001).

On its official Web site, the leading VSA manufacturer (National Institute for Truth Verification, 2002) claims:

> . . . [The instrument] is effective in all investigative situations such as homicide, sex crimes, robbery, white collar crimes, and internal affairs investigations, as well as pre-employment examinations for background investigators. . . . The system has also proven itself a very reliable tool for verifying statements of witnesses, denials of suspects, and for determining the validity of allegations made against police officers. [It] gets to the truth and accurately identifies deception, or validates statements in the shortest time possible (average exam time is 40 minutes).

On the other side of the issue, critics believe that the VSA does not detect deception beyond the level of chance. This position is described by Cestaro (2001), who completed four studies of the most popular VSA instrument for the U.S. Department of Defense Polygraph Institute over a period of approximately three years. In his testimony before the Texas legislature regarding the validity and reliability of the instrument, Cestaro (2001) stated: "I was unable to establish that the instrument could detect differential levels of stress, or provide any indication that the respondents were being truthful or deceptive." Commenting on a separate study on the same instrument done at Walter Reed Army Institute of Research, Cestaro (2001) states:

> . . . There was very little agreement among the examiners, indicating very poor scoring reliability—making the validity issues extremely questionable. . . . However, the utility of other voice stress analytic technologies was not ruled out. I am not aware of any published controlled studies using other voice stress equipment or technologies.

Based on Cestaro's findings, the Department of Defense, the Central Intelligence Agency, and the Federal Bureau of Investigation do not use voice stress tests (Wylie, 2001).

It seems that much anecdotal support for VSA comes from officers who have used it to obtain a confession and therefore are pleased with it. But these questions arise: Did the VSA establish in a scientifically valid and reliable manner that the subjects were deceitful about a crime they committed? And, based on these findings and other corroborating evidence, was an arrest made, or was the VSA used simply as a ploy to get suspects to confess to crimes they may or may not have committed? One infamous case demonstrating the latter is that of Michael Crowe, in which a VSA was used to help elicit confessions from 14-year-old Michael Crowe and two of his teenage friends in the 1998 stabbing murder of Crowe's 12-year-old sister. On the day before their trial, the victim's blood was found on the clothing of a transient who had been seen pounding on doors in the neighborhood the night of the murder, and the defendants were released. Crowe's parents initiated civil rights suits against everyone involved in the prosecution of the case, as well as the manufacturer of the VSA. These suits are still pending (Wylie, 2001, p. 3).

In the final analysis, each law enforcement agency must decide whether VSA or any other technique will be a cost-effective addition to its battery of techniques aimed at investigating and solving crimes. However, it is important for agencies to make informed decisions and not be swept up in advertising claims or the testimonials of officers that may focus more on cases in which the VSA was somehow related to an arrest and less on those in which the VSA was not helpful.

Personal Reflections _____

1. What is your assessment of the theory that underlies the use of VSA (and polygraphs)?

2. If you were required to take either a polygraph examination or a VSA as part of an investigation of a crime of which you were innocent, which would you choose?

3. If you were the director of a law enforcement agency, would you purchase a polygraph, a VSA, both, or neither? What is the reason for your answer?

4. Why do you think so many agencies have purchased VSA in light of the research questioning its accuracy?

FORENSIC HYPNOSIS

The term *forensic hypnosis* refers to the use of hypnosis in a legal setting. Officers should have a basic understanding of forensic hypnosis because its use is increasing as an investigative tool in law enforcement. Simply defined, hypnosis is a technique that places people in an unusual state of awareness in which they respond to suggestions that cause changes in sensation, perception, memory, thought, feeling, and action.

Hypnotized people often experience most, if not all, of the following reactions: absorption in internal or external stimuli, susceptibility, willingness to obey directions, suspension of logic and judgment, dissociation from current reality, a state of relaxation, the ability to transport themselves back in time, and the transference of their will and decision making to the hypnotist.

As can be seen by these reactions, hypnosis can be a two-edged sword. It can facilitate the lowering of anxiety, distractions, and defenses to such a degree that people can, among other things, retrieve and refresh memories. On the other hand, these reactions clearly reflect how vulnerable the hypnotized person is to the power and control of the hypnotist.

At this intersection experts take different paths. Those on one path believe that, if hypnosis is done professionally and effectively, it can be an instrument to find truth and retrieve and enhance memories. Those on the opposite path believe that no matter how competent the hypnotist, hypnosis may elicit memories that are contaminated, not only by the hypnotist's conscious and unconscious biases but also by the subject's conscious and unconscious motives, needs, thoughts, fantasies, and feelings. These experts conclude that it is impossible to distinguish accurate from contaminated memories as they are elicited through hypnosis. This debate has resulted in courts being hesitant to allow testimony aided by hypnosis to be presented at trial.

Relevant Issues

Situations for use.   There are two situations in which forensic hypnosis is used in law enforcement: memory retrieval and memory enhancement. Memory retrieval is used to recover memories that have been lost due to amnesia caused by psychological trauma. Memory enhancement is used to refresh memories that are weak because they are based on fleeting perceptions or have decayed over time.

Hypnotizability.   People cannot be hypnotized unless they are hypnotizable. Hypnotizability seems to be a relatively stable personality characteristic that begins around five years of age, peaks in late childhood, and declines slightly later in life. Several rating scales can measure hypnotizability, indicating whether people are highly, moderately, or minimally susceptible to hypnosis.

Approximately 15 percent to 20 percent of people are highly hypnotizable, about 10 percent have minimal or no hypnotizability, and the rest fall somewhere in between (Hess & Weiner, 1999, p. 486). Hypnosis should not be attempted on people whose test results indicate that they are minimally hypnotizable because it is unlikely to work and may nullify their ability to testify in court, because even the attempt at hypnosis may contaminate their memories, making them legally ineligible as witnesses.

Techniques. The hypnotic technique most used in law enforcement is the screen method, which means subjects are asked to imagine they are watching the event unfold on a movie screen. The subjects describe what they see on the screen, along with what they hear and feel. The hypnotist acts like a director, gently leading subjects to focus and expand on certain elements of the event. In their hypnotic state, subjects see, hear, feel, even smell or taste things that had previously been cloudy or lost.

Cautions. Forensic hypnosis is not necessarily a risk-free endeavor. Memories are often repressed for good reasons. The traumatic event may have caused a power surge, triggering the memory's circuit breaker and shutting down its normal processing. Hypnosis attempts to sneak into the memory storage area and retrieve the lost memory. If this attempt is successful, the traumatic memory may resurface abruptly and be as traumatic as the original event. People who either are vulnerable by nature or have been the victim of, or witness to, a heinous crime, may exhibit acute distress when the memory is retrieved. Although this reaction is rare, it does occur, and officers should be aware of this possibility.

Difficulties with Hypnosis

Uncontrollable by officers. Several difficulties regarding hypnosis can occur outside the control of officers. Memory, by itself, is a complicated process. Add hypnosis, which is also complicated, and the issue becomes even more challenging. All the short circuiting that can occur in the memory process, especially when it deals with stressful events, can be minimized *or* maximized by hypnosis. Therefore, hypnosis does not operate cleanly on a blank slate but on one containing many types of messages.

People can seek hypnosis before, during, or after their meeting with officers, with or without the officers' knowledge, thus contaminating the process. People can be hypnotized by psychotherapists, stage hypnotists, friends, audiotapes, and even by self-hypnosis. Officers should be aware of these possibilities and take appropriate precautions.

People can pretend that they are being successfully hypnotized when, in fact, they are using it to serve their own purposes. For example, defendants can "recall memories" to clear themselves of a crime. Suspects who exhibit signs of being hypnotized have fooled even experienced, professional hypnotists, because the suspects studied hypnotism before meeting with the hypnotist.

Controllable by officers. Other difficulties with hypnosis can occur within the officer's control. When an overzealous hypnotist hypnotizes a highly suggestible person, the chances for memory contamination are high. By examining the list of reactions people experience under hypnosis (increased susceptibility, willingness to obey directions, the ability to suspend logic and judgment, inclination to hand one's will to the hypnotist), it is clear just how vulnerable hypnotized people can be. Even ethical, well-intentioned hypnotists can unconsciously shape the subject's memories to fit their theory, rather than the reality, of the crime.

Hypnotists can overestimate the accuracy of memories elicited by hypnosis if they perceive hypnosis as possessing near magical properties and interpret the subject's high confidence in his or her memories as proof they are accurate. As a consequence of this perception, the wrong person can be arrested and the real criminal can remain at large.

Hypnotists also can unduly influence subjects in their prehypnotic briefing. For example, the hypnotist can, in the spirit of encouragement, assure the subject that, as a result of being hypnotized, she will have a clearer memory of the crime and the identity of the perpetrator. In her need to please the hypnotist, the subject may stretch a hazy memory into an artificially clear one and give a detailed description of the suspect to the hypnotist.

Admissibility in Court

The complex nature of forensic hypnosis is directly reflected in the laws governing its admissibility in court. The courts have taken three positions on this issue: prohibit it, admit it with safeguards, and admit it unconditionally (Brown, Scheflin, & Hammond, 1998, pp. 637–662).

Per se exclusion.   The first is the per se exclusionary position, which prohibits admitting hypnotically aided testimony in court. Courts may allow documented prehypnosis testimony, but not posthypnotic testimony or posthypnotic identification of a suspect from a lineup.

Admissibility with safeguards.   The second position is called the admissibility with safeguards test, or the totality of the circumstances test. This position holds that, in cases in which hypnosis is used or attempted, a pretrial hearing must be held to determine whether rigorous safeguards were used. Typically, these safeguards are

- Hypnosis must be administered by a psychologist or psychiatrist with special certification in hypnosis.
- The hypnotist must be an independent practitioner; that is, one who owes no allegiance to either the prosecution or the defense.
- Prehypnotic testimony must be documented in order to compare it to posthypnotic testimony and other witness accounts.
- The hypnotic session(s) must be electronically recorded, preferably by videotaping.
- Only the hypnotist and the subject are to be present in the room during hypnosis.

The more that forensic hypnosis deviates from these safeguards, the more likely courts will disallow it.

Open admissibility. The third position, open admissibility, holds that all hypnotically aided testimony can be admitted, and it is left to the judge and jury to decide its veracity.

About two-thirds of states have adopted the *per se exclusionary* rule and about one-third have adopted the *admissibility with safeguards* rule, with only a very small number having adopted the *open admissibility* rule. Because these positions differ from state to state and even within federal jurisdictions, officers need to be familiar with the laws in their jurisdiction.

There are three general reasons that hypnotized subjects are not allowed to testify in many courtrooms. First, they may have been suggestible to the conscious or unconscious memory shaping of the hypnotist, which interferes with the accuracy of the memories. Second, these subjects are often unable to distinguish between their true memories of the actual event and their hypnotized memories, so that the commingling of memories may generate distorted testimony. Finally, hypnotized subjects may become even more confident in their memories of an event after their memory has been "refreshed" during hypnosis, a phenomenon called "memory hardening." This confidence, even when it stems from distorted memories, makes these subjects more capable of standing up under cross-examination and of convincing jurors of the supposed accuracy of their testimony.

Wrightsman, Nietzel, and Fortune (1998) summarize the situation:

> Few professionals find fault with forensic hypnosis when it is restricted to generating new leads for a police investigation that has stalled. However, the situation is different when hypnosis is used to help a witness recall details that may later be testified to in court or when hypnosis is used to help witnesses choose between conflicting versions of events that they have provided on different occasions. In these situations, many hypnosis researchers contend the technique is fraught with so many problems and potential abuses that its use to refresh memories of witnesses should be allowed only under the strictest safeguards or should be banned altogether. (p. 183)

McConkey and Sheehan (1995) issue a final, practical caution:

> Case and experimental data considered together suggest that the most substantial risk to using hypnosis lies perhaps not so much in the tendency to misreport, although that is substantial, as in the tendency for hypnotized persons to be overconfident in their reporting. This confidence effect is pervasive enough in itself that it offers sufficient grounds for limiting the use of hypnosis in the forensic setting. Confidence can create a witness who may resist the normal impact of cross-examination. (p. 212)

Personal Reflections _____

1. If you were falsely accused of a crime, would you agree to be hypnotized to get at the truth?
2. Would you want to be hypnotized under any circumstances?
3. If a good friend were accused of a crime and you really did not know if he did it, would you accept as "truth" your friend's admission under hypnosis that he committed the crime?

CRIMINAL PROFILING

Criminal profiling—also called psychological, sociopsychological, or offender profiling—is a procedure aimed at developing a composite of the physical and psychological characteristics of the kind of person likely to have committed a crime in cases wherein the actual offender is unknown. Although a profile can be based on a single crime, it is generally reserved for multiple crimes that have a good deal in common. The reason for this is that the more crimes are committed by what appears to be the same person (serial rape, murder, arson), the more forensic and behavioral evidence there is on which to base a profile; and the more appropriate it is to allocate funds for profiling, which often requires a prodigious amount of time and resources.

Purposes

The purposes of criminal profiling are fourfold:

- To narrow down an investigation from a large pool of possible suspects to one or a few kinds of people whose modus operandi (method of committing the crime) and personality match the profile for the purposes of apprehension and prosecution of the actual perpetrator. The purpose of criminal profiling is not to identify a specific suspect but to identify the kind of person who could commit the crime in question.
- To accumulate as much information as possible on the profiled suspect in order to augment in-depth interviews with suspects who will be detained in connection with the crime.
- To develop personal, demographic, forensic, and psychological information on the kinds of offenders who commit serial crimes so that it can be applied to future investigations of similar crimes wherein the suspects are unknown; for example, information about one serial rapist may be applied to others at a future date.
- To distribute the profile to the media in the hope that people will relate the profile to someone they know and notify authorities.

As is true with all investigative techniques, criminal profiling was never meant to be a panacea for solving crimes but only one of many tools to help compile information.

Methods

Two basic methods are used in criminal profiling: the inductive and the deductive method.

Inductive method. The inductive method, also called the statistical method, begins by gathering a great deal of information about the kinds of people who committed serial crimes in the past and developing profiles of "typical offenders." For purposes of clarity, serial arson will be used as an example. Generally, a profile is based on five primary sources of information: studies of known serial arsonists from which a good deal of information is recorded and analyzed, media accounts of serial arsonists, computer databases that hold a great deal of information supplied by law enforcement agencies on serial arsonists, professional literature and workshops on serial arsonists, and the professional experience of arson investigators. This information is carefully analyzed, often using statistical methods (80 percent of serial arsonists were fascinated with fire even in early childhood) to develop a portrait of the kind of person who could be a serial arsonist.

One advantage of this method is that it is relatively simple to use, especially once a profile of a suspect is completed. In other words, while a completed profile of a serial arsonist may be adjusted as new information arises, it does not have to be developed from scratch every time a serial arson is suspected. In addition, the use of this profile requires no special education or training.

A disadvantage of the inductive method is that a profile, such as that of a serial arsonist, provides only a general description of a suspect and is not tailored to any specific act of arson. Therefore, like an off-the-rack suit, the profile may be too small or too large to fit a particular unknown suspect for which the agency is looking. Moreover, the data on which the profile is based are quite limited, stemming mainly from a small group of criminals who have been caught and whose accounts may or may not be true. The question becomes this: How well will a profile based on a small number of unsuccessful criminals match that of successful, not yet apprehended criminals?

Deductive method. The deductive method, also called behavioral evidence analysis, begins with a present crime, analyzing it thoroughly and using this information to deduce the kind of person who could have committed the crime. The three basic dimensions of this method are

- Forensic analysis: finger, foot, tire prints, blood spatter, body fluids; hair, cloth, rug, soil samples; the instruments of the crime and how they were used; the type, location, and extent of injuries; the time element and the original site of the crime; the sequence of the crime, the victims' reactions, the level of risk; crime scene photos, witness accounts, police report; toxicology, DNA, ballistic, trace evidence; and autopsy results. The analysis also includes evidence of planning the crime and precautionary acts as well as crime signatures (acts unique to the criminal that were not necessary to commit the crime).

- Offender and victim characteristics (victimology): sex, race, physique, hair color, dress, jewelry; distinguishing characteristics, as well as possible educational and socioeconomic levels; marital, employment, criminal status and history; social contacts including relatives, friends, associates, and religious and political affiliations. Offender characteristics likely to be the least reliable are sex, age, and intelligence because, as it is now well recognized, women, children, and adolescents can commit crimes equal in violence to men and adults; some intelligent people can commit some very stupid crimes, and some unintelligent people can commit very sophisticated crimes. Therefore, unless good evidence points to these offender characteristics, they should ordinarily be excluded from profiles.
- Behavioral analysis of how the offenders
- Perceive themselves, life, and others, especially the victim; for example, if the offenders perceive themselves as morally righteous and called upon to rid the world of sinners, especially prostitutes.
- Feel about themselves, life, and others, especially the kind of people the victims were; for example, the offenders hate people who threaten their sexuality, especially gay men.
- Relate to people socially, including if they are comfortable, aloof, aggressive, exploitive, or shy.
- Handle their sexual and aggressive impulses; for example, if they repress them, generally handle them well, or occasionally or frequently erupt in aggression or sexual violence.
- Maintain a façade that allows them to go undetected; for example, if they go out of their way to be solicitous to neighbors.
- Meet victims and arrange to be alone with them, including whether they meet their victims in bars, at church, through work, on the Internet, at recreational activities, through newspaper ads; or if they were in a relationship with the victims or knew them in some other way.
- Avoid feeling anxiety and guilt about their crimes, such as by simply suppressing them or dulling their conscience with alcohol, drugs, or sex.
- Time the sequence of their crimes, including whether they are meticulously planned or are crimes of opportunity or passion, or if the offenders are crime free until something sets them off.
- Derive satisfaction from their crimes. This includes having motives such as power, control, hostility, jealousy, sex, revenge, financial gain, or seeking

to gain notoriety, outwit law enforcement, make a political statement, or become a hero.

- Create a safe environment in which they can commit the crime undetected.

This and similar information derived from the deductive method comprises the profile of the offender.

An advantage of the deductive method is that it produces a specific profile, tailored to the crime under investigation. It focuses officers on the present crime without being influenced by theories based on statistical data derived from past crimes. A disadvantage is that it requires a great deal of education, training, personnel, time, effort, and money, and entails investigators becoming more emotionally involved in the crimes, which can take its toll over time.

In reality, the two methods are not mutually exclusive but can be used together, which may simplify or complicate matters, depending on the nature of the crimes and the investigators attempting to solve them.

Challenges

In addition to its positive aspects, criminal profiling also has some challenges. Some of the basic ones follow:

Different approaches.   Different disciplines work from diverse theoretical foundations, which, in turn, lead to different practical approaches to profiling. For example, forensic scientists, detectives, profilers, and behavioral scientists all view a crime from different perspectives. Even within the same group of experts, for example, profilers, there are varying theoretical and practical models that further complicate the issue. Difficulties can result with respect to communication and arriving at a consensus as to what profiling is, as well as what a specific profile should include. Because of these factors, it is necessary to distinguish one method of criminal profiling from the other when discussing issues such as validity, reliability, and utility.

Underlying psychology.   A good deal of the psychology that underlies criminal profiling is controversial, although it is often presented as being universally accepted. Whether or not profilers realize it, the psychological dimension of their profiles tends to be based largely on psychoanalytic (Freudian) theory, much of which is of great historical interest but lacks the empirical validation of more contemporary theories. For example, to draw a direct link between a rapist's relationship with his mother and his adult sexual behavior is tenuous at best. Although it is likely, for example, that some serial rapists had seductive and domineering mothers, it is much more likely that the majority of men from such backgrounds are not rapists, much less serial rapists, and the vast majority of men who do rape do not come from that particular background. There is no room for unexamined theories or armchair psychology in professional profiling because the stakes are too high.

Individual differences. The phenomenon of individual differences creates problems in two ways. First, serial rapists, for example, may be as different from one another as they are alike, which makes it difficult to construct a sound "serial rapist profile." Second, a specific serial rapist could behave differently from one crime to another; the rapist may be solicitous toward one victim and humiliate the next. In other words, although adult behavior tends to be reasonably consistent, many exceptions to this principle exist, especially among psychologically disturbed people, making it somewhat difficult to create a highly valid profile for a specific serial rapist, much less serial rapists in general.

Absence of standards. Criminal profiling is serious business because its effects can be instrumental in the destruction of people's reputations, if not their lives, if they are falsely accused and arrested based at least partially on a profile they purportedly match. This highlights the fact that the field of profiling currently lacks professional and ethical standards that address the use of theories, research, and methods of profiling, as well as the professional qualifications and claims of profilers, as do, for example, the strict ethical guidelines psychologists have for the use of psychological testing. In an attempt to develop these guidelines, the Academy of Behavioral Profiling has developed a set of Ethical Guidelines for Professional Conduct for its members in order to arrive at a standard that could be used by all profilers to further professionalize the field (see Box 9.1).

Box 9.1

Ethical Guidelines for Professional Conduct

Applicants, Students, Affiliates, and Members of the ABP shall:

- Maintain an attitude of professionalism and integrity.
- Conduct all research in a generally accepted scientific manner.
- Assign appropriate credit for the ideas of others that are used.
- Treat all information (not in the public domain) from a client or agency in a confidential manner, unless specific permission to disseminate information is obtained.
- Maintain an attitude of independence and impartiality in order to ensure an unbiased analysis and interpretation of the evidence.
- Strive to avoid preconceived ideas or biases regarding potential suspects or offenders from influencing a final profile or crime analysis when appropriate.
- Render opinions and conclusions strictly in accordance with the evidence in the case.

- Not exaggerate, embellish, or otherwise misrepresent qualifications when testifying, or at any other time, in any form.
- Testify in an honest, straightforward manner and refuse to extend their opinion beyond their field of competence, phrasing testimony in a manner intended to avoid misinterpretation of their opinion.
- Not use a profile or crime analysis (the inference of Offender or Crime Scene Characteristics) for the purposes of suggesting the guilt or innocence of a particular individual for a particular crime.
- Make efforts to inform the court of the nature and implications of pertinent evidence if reasonably assured that this information will not be disclosed in court.
- Maintain the quality and standards of the professional community by reporting unethical conduct to the appropriate authorities or professional organizations. (Turvey, 2002, p. 586)

Confirmation bias.   Some profilers may view the evidence through the prism of their personal theory of profiling and the crime rather than on an objective analysis of the evidence. As a result, they will look only for things that confirm their theory and may possibly overlook other important leads. For example, a profiler may be deeply committed to her theory that a serial sniper is a lone white male and hence ignore the possibility that the suspects could be two black males who committed a series of sniper incidents in the past. This would open up a whole new vista for investigation. In other words, the profile must first fit the evidence and secondarily the personal theories of the profiler. Profilers can have such confidence in their profiles that they lock into them and ignore other possibilities, thus causing investigators to spend priceless hours looking for the wrong person while the real criminal eludes them.

Misplaced confidence.   The same people who correctly state that criminal profiling is in its infancy and is more art than science are often the same ones who express as much confidence in it as they do in a science like medicine. Proponents of profiling cannot have it both ways: Profiling is either a discipline in its infancy and is more art than science, in which case its effectiveness is understandably quite limited, or it can do marvelous things, in which case it is a mature science that can stand up to rigorous empirical testing.

Interdisciplinary conflicts.   Unfortunately, as is true in most professional endeavors, there are turf battles between disciplines: forensic scientists, detectives, profilers, criminologists, sociologists, psychologists, and psychiatrists. While reason would suggest that all of these disciplines have an integral part to play in a multidisciplinary approach to criminal profiling, members of certain disciplines tend to believe they are the best suited to do profiling and thus dismiss the input of those in other disciplines whom they see as lacking the experience or expertise to make a significant contribution.

Incomplete data.   Criminal profiles, contrary to what most people think, are typically only a page or two in length. This may be one of the reasons that claims are often made with no rationale given to explain them. For example, a profiler may write, "Unconsciously, this subject wishes to be caught and likely will be caught soon," without further comment. It would be a great help for the investigators to know the basis on which this claim is made so they can assess its cogency and, if called for, modify their investigation accordingly.

Ethnic profiling.   A controversial use of profiling is ethnic profiling, which means that ethnicity is the overriding factor in looking for suspects. For example, it can be counterproductive to detain and question Middle Eastern males based solely on a profile that describes Middle Eastern males as likely perpetrators of future terrorism. Although ethnicity is a legitimate part of profiling, it is not meant to be an overriding variable, but to be considered only in conjunction with other relevant factors.

Criminal profiling may have its place in investigations as an ancillary tool, meaning that it may be helpful in narrowing down a pool of suspects, raising issues to be covered in interviewing suspects, developing information to be used in similar crimes, and eliciting public support in apprehending and prosecuting suspects. However, profiling should be only one factor in the investigation and never be used as the sole, or even a major, basis of probable cause to make an arrest. Turvey (2002), a forensic scientist and criminal profiler, is deeply concerned about what he refers to as "the rapid de-professionalism of criminal profiling." He states:

> The time for isolationism and for sectionalism is over. The time for politics is also over. The criminal profiling community cannot continue to play to the images portrayed in the popular media and expect to achieve professional credibility, or maintain professional integrity. The criminal profiling community must begin to communicate and agree upon standards, practices, terminology and methods. It must move away from reliance upon subjective expertise and more toward a more professional, more scientific approach if it wishes to carry through into the next century. The human price for not meeting this challenge is simply too high. (p. xx)

Personal Reflections

1. How closely do the Hollywood and television versions of criminal profiling resemble the real thing? What are the differences?

2. Which method of criminal profiling, inductive or deductive, do you believe would generally be more accurate? Why?

3. Of the nine challenges related to criminal profiling, which three do you believe are the most problematic? Why?

4. Do you think that, in general, criminal profiling is worth the time and expense it requires? What is the reason for your answer?

EXPERT WITNESSES

Before enlisting the assistance of people who have scientific, technical, or special knowledge—for example, polygraphers, voice analysts, forensic hypnotists, or criminal profilers—agencies should have three questions in mind.

1. Do these individuals have a documented and verifiable history of success in performing the specific tasks they will perform for the agency?

2. Considering the magnitude of the case, will the amount of resources these individuals require to do their job well be cost effective?

3. Will these individuals be put forth as expert witnesses at trial, and, if so, will they meet the legal standards for admission as an expert witness?

It should be noted that the term *expert witness* applies not only to those in the professions but also to anyone, including officers, who gives testimony based on specialized knowledge or training; for example, an officer with special training in defensive tactics may testify in an excessive force case.

Prior to 1923, almost anyone could be considered an expert witness because there were no standards to meet. It was left up to the jury to decide whether they chose to accept or reject the "expert" witness's testimony. However, in 1923, the defense in a murder trial attempted to introduce the results of a blood pressure test as evidence that the defendant (Frye) told the truth when he claimed he was not the murderer. The Court of Appeals for the District of Columbia (*Frye* v. *United States,* 1923) ruled the blood pressure test lacked sufficient acceptance by the scientific community as an accurate measure of whether a person is telling the truth. This case produced the *Frye* standard, which holds that the threshold test of admissibility of expert testimony in federal courts is the general acceptance by the relevant scientific community of the methodologies employed to support the expert's claim. The assumption underlying this standard is that the scientific community would not accept invalid methodologies. For this reason, the *Frye* standard is known as the "general acceptance" standard. Many state courts also adopted the *Frye* standard, which remained the basis for admissibility of expert witness testimony for the next 70 years.

In 1993, the plaintiff in a civil suit claimed that a medication she took for morning sickness during her pregnancy caused a birth defect in her baby. Her family sued the manufacturer of the medication (*Daubert* v. *Merrell Dow Pharmaceuticals,* 1993) and presented eight prospective expert witnesses to support the claim that the medication could cause birth defects in pregnant women.

Because animal studies were used to support this claim, the judge disallowed the testimony as irrelevant and ruled that the methodology did not meet the general acceptance standard of the field of epidemiology. The judge ruled that the Federal Rules of Evidence (1975) in general, and specifically Rule 702, replaced the *Frye* standard in federal courts. Adding its own thoughts to the Federal Rules of Evidence, the court concluded that expert testimony must be grounded in scientific knowledge and introduced two basic standards: It must be *relevant* to the case at hand, and it must be *reliable*, that is, based on scientifically valid principles and methodologies. In the pretrial hearing, judges may concern themselves only with the soundness of the methods used to arrive at and support the prospective expert witness's claim. They may not question the interpretations or conclusions based on those methods. However, if the witness is accepted as "an expert" by the judge and renders interpretations and conclusions during the trial that the judge does not believe are merited by the results of the methodology, the judge can order the jury to disregard the testimony.

Judges can ask prospective expert witnesses the following questions to help decide whether their testimony is relevant and reliable:

1. Is the claim being advanced by the prospective expert witness based on a theory that has been tested by sound scientific methods in ways that could refute the theory and prove that it is false (the principles of falsifiability and refutability)?

2. Has the claim been subjected to the scrutiny of the relevant scientific community through peer review and publication?

3. What is the potential error rate of the claim; in other words, is the accuracy rate 100 percent or only 70 percent?

4. Is there widespread acceptance of the theory by the relevant scientific community?

5. Will the testimony of the prospective expert witness help the trier of fact (judge and/or jury) better understand the material issues because it is beyond the common knowledge of jurors, or is it information jurors can understand on their own and will be brought out naturally in the course of the trial?

6. Does the probative value (whether it points to guilt or innocence) of the testimony substantially outweigh the prejudicial effect it may have on a jury?

These questions are simply meant to be guidelines to help judges decide whether to accept or reject a prospective expert witness. During pretrial hearings each side typically presents prospective expert witnesses, and the opposing side challenges their expertise during cross-examination. Judges alone are the gatekeepers as to who qualifies as expert witnesses. They have a wide range of discretion, and a good deal of subjectivity is involved in this decision. However, once a judge makes the decision, it will not likely be overturned on appeal unless the ruling was clearly in error or an abuse of discretion.

Today, all federal courts apply the "scientific knowledge" standard of *Daubert*, while approximately half the states also use the *Daubert* standard and the other half use the *Frye* standard. Therefore, it is important for agencies to know what standard is used in the court in which their case will be tried.

This information is not simply of theoretical interest. Law enforcement officials have lost more than a few cases because they placed all their hopes in prospective expert witnesses from within or outside of their agency, only to have the witnesses disallowed because they did not meet the local standard for admitting expert witness testimony. Therefore, it is prudent for officers to consult with the prosecutor's office before enlisting the help of people who may later testify as expert witnesses.

*S*ummary

The value of polygraph testing, voice stress analysis, forensic hypnosis, and criminal profiling must be honestly and accurately addressed and acknowledged. To many, each of these methods of seeking truth has strengths and weaknesses. To overemphasize the strengths and deemphasize the weaknesses, or vice versa, does a disservice to the methods themselves, the truth, and law enforcement in general. All four methods may have something to offer law enforcement, but their validity and reliability need to be further researched and increased. With more research and informed practice, the day may come when these methods, and those not yet discovered, will be accepted as consistently trustworthy by the scientific and legal communities.

*R*eferences

Brown, D., Scheflin, A.W., & Hammond, D.C. (1998). *Memory, trauma treatment, and the law.* New York: W.W. Norton.

Cestaro, V.L. (1995). *A comparison between decision accuracy rates obtained using the polygraph instrument and the computer voice stress analyzer (CVSA).* (Report No. DODP195-R-0002). Fort McClellan, AL: U.S. Department of Defense Polygraph Institute.

Cestaro, V.L. (1996). *A comparison of accuracy rates between detection of deception examinations using the polygraph and the computer voice stress analyzer in a mock crime scenario.* (Report No. DODP195-R-0004). Fort McClellan, AL: U.S. Department of Defense Polygraph Institute.

Cestaro, V.L. (2001, March 7). *A summary of the testimony before the Texas legislature regarding the reliability and validity of the Computer Voice Stress Analyzer.* Retrieved July 5, 2002, from the World Wide Web: http://www.voicestress.org/ summary_of_the_testimony.htm.

Cestaro, V.L., & Dollins, A.B. (1994). *An analysis of voice responses for the detection of deception.* (Report No. DODPI94-R-0001). Fort McClellan, AL: U.S. Department of Defense Polygraph Institute.

Daubert v. Merrell Dow Pharmaceuticals, Inc. (1993). 113 S. Ct. 2786.

Doll, R.E., Law, J.G., Jr., & Piotrowski, C.A. (1990). *A literature review of cross-cultural factors affecting polygraph testing.* (Report No. DODP190-R-0004). Ft. MClellan, AL: U.S. Department of Defense Polygraph Institute.

Dollins, A.B., Krapohl, D.J., & Dutton, D.W. (1999). *A comparison of computer programs designed to evaluate psychological detection of deception examinations: Bakeoff 1.* (Report No. DODPI99-R-0001). Ft. Jackson, SC: U.S. Department of Defense Polygraph Institute.

Federal Bureau of Investigation (2002). *Crime in the United States 2000: Uniform crime reports.* Washington, DC: U.S. Department of Justice.

Ford, C.V. (1965). *Lies! lies!! lies!!!: The psychology of deceit.* Washington, DC: American Psychiatric Association.

Frye v. *United States* (1923). 293 F. 1013 (D.C. Cir. 1923).

Gladwell, M. (2002, August 5). The naked face. *The New Yorker*, 38–49.

Hansen, M. (1999). Truth sleuth or faulty detector? *ABA Journal, 85* (5) 16.

Hess, A.K., & Weiner, I.B. (1999). *The handbook of forensic psychology.* New York: John Wiley.

Horvath, F. (1978). An experimental comparison of the Psychological Stress Evaluator and the galvanic skin response in detection of deception. *Journal of Applied Psychology, 63*, 338–344.

Horvath, F. (1993). Polygraph screening of candidates for police work in large police agencies in the United States: A survey of practices, policies, and evaluative comments. *American Journal of Police, 12*, 67–86.

Iacono, W.G., & Lykken, D.T. (1997). The validity of the lie detector: Two surveys of scientific opinion. *Journal of Applied Psychology, 82*, 426–433.

Iacono, W.G., & Patrick, C.J. (1999). Polygraph ("lie detector") testing: The state of the art. In A.K. Hess & I.B. Weiner (Eds.), *The handbook of forensic psychology* (2nd ed.) (pp. 441–473). New York: John Wiley.

Janniro, M.J., & Cestaro, V.L. (1996). *Effectiveness of detection of deception examinations using the computer voice stress analyzer.* (Report No. DODPI96-R-0005). Fort McClellan, AL: U.S. Department of Defense Polygraph Institute.

Kalbfleisch, P.J. (1994, December). The language of detecting deceit. *Journal of Language and Social Psychology, 13* (4), 1–25.

Kassin, S.M. (1997, March). The psychology of confession evidence. *American Psychologist, 52*, 221–233.

Lykken, D.T. (1998). *A tremor in the blood: Uses and abuses of the lie detector.* New York: Plenum.

McConkey, K.M., & Sheehan, P.W. (1995). *Hypnosis, memory and behavior in criminal investigation.* New York: Guilford Press.

National Institute for Truth Verification (2002). CVSA perfects crime-fighting technology. *Official Web site of the National Institute for Truth Verification.* Retrieved, July 4, 2002, from the World Wide Web: http://www.cvsal.com/product/php.

Palmatier, J. (1999). *The validity and comparative accuracy of voice stress analysis as measured by the CVSA: A field study conducted in a psychophysiological context.* A federally funded study conducted by Dr. Palmatier in cooperation with the Michigan State Police. Retrieved July 5, 2002, from the World Wide Web: http://www.voicestress. org/palmatier_study.htm.

Rubinkam, M. (2002, February 10). Police using voice stress analysis to detect lies. *Jefferson City News Tribune, Online Edition.* Retrieved September 12, 2002 from the World Wide Web: http://www.newstribune.com/stories/021001/ wor_0210020524.asp.

Turvey, Brent. (2002). *Criminal profiling: An introduction to behavioral evidence analysis* (2nd ed.). San Diego, CA: Academic Press.

U.S. Department of Defense Polygraph Institute Staff, Meyerhoff, J.L., Saviolakis, G.A., Koening, M.L., & Yurick, D.L. (2001). *Physiological and biochemical measures of stress compared to voice stress analysis using the computer voice stress analyzer (CVSA).* (Report No. DODP101-R-0001). Fort Jackson, SC: U.S. Department of Defense Polygraph Institute and Washington, DC: Walter Reed Army Institute of Research.

Vrij, A. (1998). Physiological parameters and credibility: The polygraph. In A. Memon, A. Vrij, & R. Bull (Eds.), *Psychology and law: Truthfulness, accuracy and credibility* (pp. 77–101). New York: McGraw-Hill.

Wells, G.L. (1993, May). What do we know about eyewitness identification? *American Psychologist, 48,* 553–571.

Wrightsman, L.S., Nietzel, M.T., & Fortune, W.H. (1998). *Psychology and the legal system* (4th ed.). Pacific Grove, CA: Brooks/Cole.

Wylie, M. (2001). Police use of voice stress analysis generates controversy. Newhouse News Service. Retrieved July 5, 2002, from the World Wide Web: http://www.newhouse.com/archive/story1010501.html.

10

Responding to Violence and Death

Responding to violence and death is part of most officers' daily responsibilities and challenges. These situations are generally volatile, complex, and depressing; therefore, they require substantial education and training if officers are to respond in a professional manner.

Unfortunately, while training academies teach the legal aspects involved in various acts of violence and death, they seldom prepare officers for the equally important psychosocial dimensions of responding to the victims. Therefore, this chapter focuses on the immediate reactions of the victims and co-victims of violence and death, as well as the reactions of the officers themselves. This is important because helping people in crisis is not only the right thing to do but also the prudent thing to do because the more that officers can calm victims and co-victims of violence and death, the better witnesses they will be. To this end, the following topics will be discussed: child maltreatment, domestic violence, sexual assault, elder abuse, and unexpected death.

CHILD MALTREATMENT

Child maltreatment, which has replaced the term *child abuse* because the latter tends to connote only physical abuse, is a complex, sensitive issue that requires special training for officers. However, many officers have not had the opportunity for such training, yet are often the most critical part of the investigative process. These officers set the stage for the investigation by establishing a relationship with the child, the parents, and other directly involved parties. This relationship will be either facilitative, meaning one that will make the investigation easier, or antagonistic, meaning that the investigation may never get off the ground because of resistance by the child and/or the other parties.

The Office for Victims of Crime of the U.S. Department of Justice produced the guide *Law Enforcement Response to Child Abuse* (2001b), which clearly underscores the importance of the officers' role in responding to child maltreatment calls:

> With their legal authority to investigate violations of the law, law enforcement officers are vital members of a community's child protection team. Failure to respond properly to child abuse cases from the outset . . . can result in cases being dismissed in court or, in some cases, in innocent people being falsely accused. (p. 4)

Forms of Child Maltreatment

Child maltreatment can include the following:

- *Physical abuse, nonsexual in nature:* inflicting physical damage on a child using one's hands, feet, mouth, or an object
- *Physical abuse, sexual in nature:* engaging a child in sexual acts that involve kissing, touching, oral or anal sex, or sexual intercourse
- *Physical neglect:* failure to properly feed, clothe, bathe, shelter, educate, or medicate a child
- *Psychological abuse:* treating the child in demeaning ways by continuous yelling, ridiculing, threatening, embarrassing, bullying, tormenting, criticizing, isolating the child from family and friends

It is important to realize that some of these behaviors may not be crimes; for example, some types of psychological abuse and neglect, while others may be crimes in some states but not in others. For this reason, officers must be familiar with the laws in their state, federal laws, and the policies emanating from their prosecutor's office and their agency.

Relevant Issues

The following are some points that officers can keep in mind when responding to child maltreatment.

Privacy.   It is generally better to interview the child alone because the presence of family members or other caretakers may have a chilling effect on the child's spontaneity. If the child wishes to be near parents, officers can assure the child that the parents are in the next room and can be reached by simply calling them.

Fear.   Often children who are victims are frightened. They are frightened of the people who maltreat them and frightened to do anything that will cause increased maltreatment after the officers leave. They may also be frightened of the officers, whom they sometimes perceive more as threats than rescuers. The first task for officers is to establish rapport with children, engaging them in positive conversation until they feel safe in the officers' presence.

Shame.   Maltreated children often feel a sense of shame that they are the cause of consternation in the home. They feel that, because they are targets of serious discussion, they must have done something wrong. Their whole demeanor, from their facial expression, to their voice, to their posture reflects shame. Therefore, one of the first things officers should do is deal with the shame, but not by telling children they have nothing to be ashamed about, which only confirms that shame is an issue. It is better to encourage children to discuss some positive things about themselves—who they are and what they have done—and thus elicit a sense of pride that may balance the shame.

Sensitivity.   Ordinarily, children are very sensitive, even those who appear to be tough. They are particularly sensitive to anyone thinking negatively of them or their family, even when the family is abusing them. Therefore, officers should gently approach children with an attitude that communicates: "We're sure you and your family are good people. We're just here to see if we can understand some things."

Communication.   The vocabulary officers use is important. Officers need to keep in mind that two-, four-, six-, or eight-year-old children use and understand a very different vocabulary than officers do. In addition, it is important to refrain from using emotionally laden words. For example, instead of asking: "Does your dad ever beat (hit, knock you down, whip) you?" officers can ask: "Does your dad sometimes do things to you that make you feel bad (sad, scared, like crying) even though maybe he doesn't mean to?"

Blame.   Victimized children are often in a double bind in many ways. For example, when blame enters the picture, the children usually have only two choices: to blame either themselves or the person maltreating them. Often children will blame themselves because they are fearful of retribution if they blame the abuser, a fear that is often realistic. For this reason, blame should not be an issue when talking to children. An attitude of "We're just trying to understand some things so we can help everyone" is likely to elicit more meaningful information than an attitude of "We're here to find out who's to blame for this."

Suggestibility.   Children are very suggestible, meaning they tend to sense what adults want and give it to them. Perhaps the biggest danger in interviewing children lies in asking leading questions: "Did your uncle touch you down there?" which is likely to elicit an affirmative response if the child likes the officers and wishes to please them. A better prompt is this: "Tell me all the things you and your uncle did when he took you to the park."

Patience.   Young children's minds are such that they have difficulty focusing and sticking with a train of thought. Their minds meander through a myriad of topics completely unrelated to what officers want to discuss. This does not necessarily mean that the children avoid admitting to maltreatment; it may simply be a manifestation of the way children typically think and communicate. Therefore, officers should not adopt a "just the facts" attitude when dealing with children, but should exercise great patience, gently bringing the child back to the topic after each short excursion until a coherent picture begins to develop.

Crying.   Children often cry during interviews with officers because they feel afraid, confused, and alone. Although officers may be inclined to exhort the child not to cry, doing so is seldom effective. It is better to let the child cry it all out and reduce pent-up tension, which may result in a more coherent picture of what happened.

Perspective.   Officers need to keep a broad perspective when dealing with child maltreatment, which does not commonly occur in a vacuum but is often related to other factors, such as domestic violence, substance abuse, and the involvement of more than one child. So, while one child may be the designated victim, several other child and adult victims may be involved. For this reason, officers need to focus on these situations using a wide-angle lens in order to get a fuller picture.

Sexuality.   In cases of sexual abuse, it is important that officers feel comfortable discussing sexual issues in the child's language. Any officers' discomfort will be communicated to the child, who will perceive it as a sign that dangerous territory is being embarked upon and will likely become mute as the best way to avoid as much danger as possible. When officers can assume a matter-of-fact, casual demeanor, their "This is no big deal" attitude will be transmitted to the child, who will likely feel more comfortable in the situation.

Overzealousness.   Child maltreatment, especially if sexual abuse is involved, inflames many people, including officers, particularly those who have children of their own. The danger is that officers will want to crucify the people who allegedly maltreated the child. This reaction may interfere with the officers' judgment, causing them to ignore comments that contradict their theory of the crime and focusing on those that support it. Child maltreatment is a terrible thing, but accusing the wrong person of a heinous crime or losing a good case in court because of a "rush to judgment" also is a terrible thing. Officers need to remain dispassionate, following the evidence and not their vengeful feelings, which may lead them into a good deal of trouble.

Process.   Disclosing details of a crime is a process and not an event, meaning that the first meeting is only one piece of a puzzle that likely has many pieces that are not visible on even the second or third meeting with the child and the family. Officers should not feel pressure to wrap up a case by the end of the first contact. Usually responding officers simply lay the foundation for more experienced investigators to complete the investigation.

Attachment.   Officers can realize that children who are victims of maltreatment are often psychologically attached to their abusers and perceive them as good people. Therefore, officers should avoid speaking, even by insinuation, in terms of "good" ("good touches") or "bad" ("bad touches"), because anything done by a person perceived to be "good" is seen as good by the child and cannot be bad. Officers need to speak only in terms of "goods": "Your daddy sounds like a really good daddy. You said he gives you your bath. I bet he does lots of things to help you get clean. What kinds of things does he do?"

Responding to child maltreatment often requires officers to consider all of these issues—sometimes simultaneously. They must keep in mind that children are not simply small adults, but that they think, perceive, feel, and communicate in ways that are very different from adults. Therefore, officers must try to place themselves in the position of the children, seeing events through their eyes as much as possible.

Children who are victims of maltreatment often are at a fulcrum point. How officers approach them will begin a process that can make things much better or much worse for the child and everyone concerned.

Personal Reflections

1. What do you think the most common type of child maltreatment is, and why do you think it occurs?

2. What are your reactions to child maltreatment? How do you think these reactions could interfere with your interviewing the suspect in a child maltreatment case?

3. What do you believe is the worst kind of child maltreatment? Why do you think this?

4. Do you think you can tell if children are telling the truth or simply giving you the answer they think you want to hear? If so, how can you tell this?

5. What percentage of the time do you think making arrests in cases of child maltreatment stops the maltreatment?

6. What do you think drives parents or caregivers to maltreat children?

DOMESTIC VIOLENCE

Until a few years ago, officers generally viewed domestic disturbance as "a family matter" best handled within the family and with professional counseling. For the most part, this has changed. Increasingly, domestic violence is perceived as a law enforcement issue because a crime, often a felony, has been committed. The Office for Victims of Crime of the U.S. Department of Justice (2001a) makes this clear in its document *First Response to Victims of Crime:*

> Domestic violence is a crime, not a family matter, and should be approached as such by law enforcement. U.S. Department of Justice statistics indicate that approximately 20 percent of homicides are committed within families or within intimate relationships, and one out of three female homicide victims is killed by an intimate. Furthermore, approximately 28 percent of violent crimes against females are committed by husbands or boyfriends. Finally, approximately 50 percent of domestic violence occurs between married partners and 25 percent between nonmarried partners living together, both involving mainly male assailants and female victims.
>
> The three primary responsibilities of law enforcement in domestic violence cases are to (1) provide physical safety and security of victims, (2) assist victims by coordinating their referral to support services, and (3) make arrests of domestic violence perpetrators as required by law. (p. 15)

Domestic disturbance calls are among the most challenging officers face because they often represent a classic no-win situation: If officers effect an arrest, they open themselves to physical attack, not only by the assailant but also by the victim and everyone else at the scene. Moreover, they may be accused of all sorts of things, including excessive force and traumatizing the children present at the scene, resulting in citizen complaints and lawsuits. If the officers do not arrest, they can be accused of not taking the situation seriously or taking the assailant's side. If the situation erupts again, even days or weeks later, their decision not to arrest will be questioned, not only by the parties but the officers' agency as well.

Another challenge is that the cost-benefit ratio for officers (and society) is often poor, meaning that officers spend many hours and often many days on the case: follow-up investigations, reports, interviewing witnesses, meetings with the prosecutor's office, and possible court appearances. The outcome is rarely to the officer's satisfaction—the assailant receives a "slap on the wrist" (diversion counseling that he will not attend, a restraining order that is likely to be violated, a fine that will never be paid) or the victim and witnesses recant. Little wonder officers dread responding to domestic disturbance calls.

These issues are not just theoretical but spawn corresponding attitudes in officers that can best be described as a "Let's get in and get out of there as quickly as possible" attitude toward domestic disturbance calls. This means giving the call short shrift, as is seen in the catch-all admonition: "You'd better calm down right now, because if we have to come back, one or both of you are going to jail." The problem with this "intervention strategy" is that officers do not address the real issues and offer no resources to deal with the problem. As a result, violence will erupt again, but the parties will be reluctant to call for help because they fear being arrested.

Therefore, officers should develop a strategy that addresses the three primary responsibilities indicated in the U.S. Department of Justice document just quoted without spending so much time and energy on the situation that other equally valid demands are left unaddressed. The manner in which officers at the scene respond to domestic disturbances often significantly affects the dynamics of the situation. Officers are in the position to deal with a situation in ways that bring about the best results under the circumstances, or cause the situation to deteriorate even more, escalating the problem and the danger for both the parties and the officers.

Misconceptions about Domestic Violence

The following are some common misconceptions held by officers that can preclude them from being as effective as possible in domestic violence situations.

Misconception 1: Domestic disturbance calls are the most dangerous ones that officers face.   The fact is that Federal Bureau of Investigation statistics indicate only 5.7 percent of all officers' deaths result from responding to domestic disturbance calls (Garner & Clemmer, 1986). Although officers should always be vigilant on these calls, this misconception often causes hypervigilance and anxiety in officers that significantly interfere with their ability to do a good job: being able to listen attentively, think rationally, focus sharply, exercise patience, act calmly, and decide fairly.

Misconception 2: It does no good to make an arrest because these people are out of jail in a few hours and commit the same violent acts again.   Debate exists as to whether arrest in itself deters future domestic violence. Whether or not it does is an issue for criminologists and not officers, who must do the right thing at the scene. If there is probable cause for arrest, an arrest should be made, and other people (the prosecutor's office, the probation department, mental health professionals, and the courts) can subsequently decide on the proper course of action after considering all the factors of the case.

Misconception 3: Repeat domestic disturbance calls should not have a high priority because if the parties were going to seriously hurt each other, they would have done so already.   Research by the Office of Victims of Crimes, Office of Justice Programs (2000a) indicates that two years before an assault or homicide occurred officers had responded to the scene at least once in 85 percent of the cases and five times in approximately 50 percent of the cases. In addition, serious threats had preceded the violence in over 50 percent of the cases. This means that multiple calls from the same residence tend to indicate the risk for violence is increasing rather than decreasing. Therefore, all cases should be taken seriously for both the protection of the victim and the legal protection of the officers and agency. In the landmark case of *Thurman* v. *City of Torrington* (1984), a brutally beaten victim won a $2.3 million judgment because, although she had made repeated calls for help and police promised to respond, they did not.

Misconception 4: Officers do not like to make arrests because they regard domestic disturbance calls as primarily private family matters or because male officers take the side of the assailant, who is usually a male. Today, when officers do not want to make an arrest, it is less because of these reasons, and more because the law and/or their agency guidelines are unclear. The officers fear they will not be supported by the prosecutor's office or their agency should complaints or lawsuits arise from an arrest. Many officers operate on this axiom: "You can get in less trouble not making an arrest than making one." In fact, however, lawsuits have been brought against officers and their agencies in cases wherein officers failed to arrest when there was probable cause and the assailant later seriously injured or murdered the victim (Bangham, 1986). The antidote to this lies with the prosecutor's office and the agency, which must offer clear guidelines and, when they are followed, fully support the officers and their actions.

Misconception 5: Once an arrest is made, the officer's work is finished. Arrest represents only one part of the intervention. In addition to gathering evidence and information, officers need to ascertain whether the victim needs medical or psychological help, as well as make the appropriate referrals with regard to counseling, domestic violence classes, legal resources, hot lines, shelters, social service agencies, and emergency protective orders.

Misconception 6: All the factors present in a domestic disturbance must be weighed before an arrest is made. Officers generally have neither the competence nor the time to grasp and evaluate the countless extralegal (psychological, social, cultural) factors involved in domestic disturbance calls. During the time it takes to consider and weigh all these variables, serious problems can arise. There may be something to be said for a "holistic approach to intervention," which includes several disciplines and agencies, but nothing to be said for a "holistic approach to arrest." The safest course of action, both legally and physically, is to arrest when probable cause exists and remove the assailant from the scene. It is only after this occurs that a holistic intervention may be considered by those processing the case.

Misconception 7: Mandatory arrest laws take discretion away from the officers at the scene. Mandatory arrest laws limit, but do not eliminate, officer discretion. Officers still need to make critical decisions: Are there visible signs of abuse? Are they sufficiently fresh as to be recently inflicted? Is the situation simply a "he says–she says" one, or are there corroborating witnesses that add to or detract from probable cause? Who was the primary aggressor? Was the injury willfully inflicted? Should an arrest be made at the scene or charges filed later with the prosecutor's office? The answers to these questions lie at the heart of whatever enforcement action officers will take and are critical elements in officer discretion.

Misconception 8: Officers should try mediation and counseling techniques at the scene, and arrest should only be a last resort.   There are places for mediation and counseling in law enforcement but not in the midst of domestic violence situations in which a felony is likely to have been committed, the parties are highly agitated and combative, and arrest is a distinct possibility. To attempt mediation and counseling is likely to do more harm than good, escalate and prolong the situation, and make it increasingly more volatile and dangerous. Whatever action officers take must be "short and sweet"; that is, taken as quickly and professionally as possible.

Responding to Domestic Violence Calls

In addition to officer safety, the following issues should be considered when officers respond to domestic disturbance calls.

Remain calm.   The parties' hostility should not be contagious and allowed to infect the officers. Sometimes, officers can become angrier at the parties than the parties are at each other. This is a formula for disaster.

Remain objective.   Officers should not allow personal prejudices to short-circuit a rational, dispassionate approach to resolving the situation. Officers are human beings, have their own ideas and feelings about domestic issues, and may be inclined to inject them into the situation. Officers will do better if they deal only with the facts of the situation and check their personal thoughts and feelings at the door.

Be present focused.   Officers should realize that what is occurring between the parties is often just the tip of the iceberg, which may have many years of toxic waste beneath the surface. Officers should avoid becoming immersed in discussions about who the saint and the sinner are because these roles often change from one hour to the next. The focus must remain on the present: We have a problem right now, and we have to solve it right now.

Be succinct.   Officers should come to the point, use words well but sparingly, make every word count, and seldom repeat anything more than twice. Many officers have a tendency to talk too much in these situations, repeating the same thing over and over again as if it will sink in the tenth time, and lecturing and threatening the parties with dire consequences. As soon as officers have a reasonably clear picture of the situation, which may take only minutes and ordinarily should not take more than 10 minutes, their message is clear: "Thank you for giving us all the information we need to make a decision as to how to best resolve this situation, at least temporarily. Here's what we need to do now, and here's how we need to do it."

Be civil.　Officers should treat the involved parties civilly, even in cases in which an arrest must be made. Berating or ridiculing the parties only further inflames the situation and can harm the parties, the officers, and the reputation of law enforcement in general. People involved in domestic disputes do not need to feel worse about themselves or each other, or have their fuses reignited by being humiliated, especially in front of others.

Monitor advice.　Officers should be cautious about offering psychological and legal advice and referring the parties to attorneys, mental health practitioners, and clinics that have not been authorized by their agency. Potential liability exists for the officers and their agency if further harm, or perceived harm, befalls the parties when they follow the advice. Agencies should provide domestic disturbance packets that can be reviewed with the parties and left with them. This ensures that appropriate information is given to the individuals who can consider it when they have calmed down.

Be sensitive.　Officers should be sensitive to the presence of children, who can sometimes be more traumatized by the presence of officers than by the disturbance to which they may have become accustomed. Whenever possible, officers should arrange for children to remain with neighbors, family, or friends, while the officers resolve the situation.

Record the situation.　Officers should use pocket tape recorders to memorialize what occurred at the scene because these situations have great potential to end up in civilian complaints, if not lawsuits.

　　While all these ideas should be helpful in developing a professional framework within which to address domestic violence in general, like all things in law enforcement, no two situations are ever exactly the same, so variations within the framework must be devised to meet the needs of each situation.

Personal Reflections _____

1. Why do you think that, until relatively recently, law enforcement generally viewed domestic violence as a family matter and not a legal one?
2. What do you think is the single most challenging part of a domestic disturbance call for officers?

3. What is your attitude toward domestic disturbance? How do you think it would influence your intervention in such calls?

4. Do you believe mandatory arrest laws are good or bad? Explain your answer.

5. How would you determine who the "primary aggressor" is in a domestic violence situation?

6. Do you think there are preconceived gender biases in domestic disturbance calls with regard to who the primary aggressor is?

SEXUAL ASSAULT

Sexual assault, which includes but is not limited to rape, occurs when a person commits a sexual act on a child or adult, male or female, heterosexual or homosexual, against the person's will. Officers can be aware of some basic issues relevant to responding professionally and effectively to situations involving sexual assault. Some of the basic considerations follow:

Victim Concerns

In order to be effective when responding to sexual assault calls, officers should first understand the concerns of the victim. In some cases, victims think officers will not take their situation seriously. Heterosexual males, homosexual males and females, intoxicated individuals, the mentally ill or retarded, and the elderly may fear that their claims will be ignored or minimized because of their status. Victims without visible physical injury may feel their report will be minimized, even though there are no physical injuries in the vast majority of sexual assault cases. People with a promiscuous sexual history are often concerned that they will be considered less victimized or as having "asked for it." Victims who were traumatized and do not report the crime for days or weeks afterward fear that their veracity will be questioned.

Officers, as human beings, may harbor their own biases against victims of sexual assault, being skeptical and unhelpful in cases in which the victim is male, homosexual, seductive, promiscuous, uneducated, poor, homeless, or a member of a different ethnic group. Officers need to be aware of their biases and leave them at the door when investigating any crime, including that of sexual assault. It is not the officer's role to question the assault or judge whether victims are "100 percent victims" or only "50 percent victims." The officer's role is to investigate the case fully and objectively, write a thorough report, and let prosecutors, judges, and juries decide degrees of culpability.

Difficulties for Officers

From the point of view of officers, sexual assault cases can be very difficult for several reasons.

First, officers may feel uncomfortable discussing intimate sexual matters in general and even more so with strangers. Training can help officers in this regard, especially when they can role-play with same-sex and opposite-sex "victims," becoming more comfortable discussing sensitive topics. Officers also may have been on the receiving end of sexual double messages and game playing during their dating experiences and have a certain antagonism toward the victim and sympathy for the assailant. Both honest introspection and training can help officers dissociate their personal from their professional lives.

Another difficulty for officers occurs when victims of sexual assault are reluctant witnesses, often for good reasons. They do not want their family or friends to know about the assault; they do not want their case to reach the media; they do not want to suffer retaliation at the hands of the assailant. They just want to put the event behind them and move on. Often officers must spend a great deal of time and effort maintaining the motivation of the victim. Reluctant witnesses require great patience, understanding, and a deep commitment to help them remain strong enough to testify in court.

A third difficulty arises if the victim recants, often after many months of investigation and immediately before the case goes to trial. This is frustrating and, unfortunately, officers sometimes can do little to change the situation. They can do only the best they can, knowing that if the victim recants, there still remains a good deal of documentation, including the 911 tape if there is one, that can be used at trial to impeach a recanting witness or used when the assailant attacks again, which is likely in cases of recantation.

Fourth, family and friends of the victim often become involved in the situation, exerting great pressure on officers to arrest the alleged assailant immediately. In the heat of passion, these people are often impatient with officers who must deal with the elements of probable cause before making an arrest. Again, officers who are understanding and place themselves in the position of the co-victims of sexual assault can maintain their patience and sense of compassion.

Finally, sexual assault victims sometimes have a psychological bond with their assailants. They vacillate from hating, to feeling sorry for, to loving them. These vacillations are reflected in the ebb and flow of the victim's motivation to prosecute the assailant. Officers must strike a balance between exerting too much pressure on victims to remain committed to the prosecution, which may backfire in a recantation, and deferring too easily to the victims' reservations, which may cause them to recant when concentrated support from officers may have given them the motivation to stay the course.

As can be seen, sexual assault cases are often difficult for officers as well as victims, to say nothing of the difficulties for prosecutors, juries, and judges. Therefore, officers who act professionally must be prepared to bring more psychological and legal resources to sexual assault cases than they do for most cases, keeping in mind that the results of a well-investigated case can be well worth the time and effort because it may remove a dangerous person from the streets for some time.

Victim Responses

Officers should be aware of the following reactions they are likely to encounter when responding to victims of sexual assault.

Shock.   Sexual assault is an assault not only on victims' sexuality but also on all the dimensions of their being: mental, emotional, social, moral, and spiritual. Because this is often the case, victims of sexual assault are typically in shock, not only for hours after the assault but sometimes for days, if not weeks later. Shock protects the victim from experiencing the full psychological brunt of the trauma all at once and gives the victim time gradually to absorb and adjust to what happened. Therefore, officers should realize that the victim's reaction to the assault often is not what people might expect. The victim may appear almost casual about the assault, which may cause officers to think that the situation need not be taken too seriously.

Interviewing victims in shock requires patience, especially because many of the facts of the assault that officers need to know are often the same ones that the victims need to block out. The questioning needs to be done with surgical precision, sufficiently probing so that critical information is gained but not so invasive that the victim reexperiences the trauma and withdraws. For this reason, officers must decide what information is absolutely necessary to obtain in the first contact, and what can be left to more experienced investigators and mental health professionals for later follow-up.

Shame.   Victims of sexual assault often feel ashamed because society tends to look upon victims of sexual assault as somehow tainted. Officers need to be aware of this response because it can significantly interfere with a free flow of information between victims and officers. Telling victims they should not feel ashamed is likely to be unhelpful for two reasons. First, victims are not going to stop feeling ashamed simply because officers admonish them to do so. Second, victims may well perceive the officers' response as proof that they do not understand what the victims have endured and how their family and friends will react to them. The best approach is for officers to treat victims with respect, patience, and compassion, sending this message: "Whatever you feel about yourself or others feel about you, we have nothing but the greatest respect for you and want to help you in any way we can."

Distrust.   Victims of sexual assault often feel an abiding sense of distrust, especially if they knew and trusted their assailant. This is perhaps the worst and most enduring feeling that results from sexual assault. Victim accounts are often interspersed with comments such as "How could he have done this to me?" a question that is often meant to be rhetorical and not to be answered by officers. A practical ramification of victim distrust is that it may also be transferred to officers. Victims may place distance between themselves and the officers, be reluctant to share information, especially of an intimate nature, and question the motives of officers who ask intimate questions. It is sometimes suggested that only female officers interview female victims of sexual assault because somehow there will be more compatibility between the officer and victim. However, because the vast majority of officers are male and no empirical evidence suggests female officers do a better job in these situations, there need not be a reluctance or an apology for sending male officers to the scene of a sexual assault.

Whatever the sex of the responding officers, they need to be aware that deep distrust may be an issue that creates distance between them and the victim, and not perceive this as personal or volitionally obstructive behavior. Officers can respect both the physical and psychological distance the victim wants to maintain and still do the best they can to elicit important information.

Control.   Sexual assault victims may feel a loss of control because, as has been pointed out, sexual assaults often attack victims' entire beings, causing them to feel helpless. Loss of control, along with hurt and distrust, are likely to remain with the victim far longer than any physical injuries. The loss of control may be manifested by the victim wanting to defer all decisions to the officers—a gesture that officers must decline. Victims should maintain some control over the entire investigation, so that they can rightly feel they are partners in the process and control something that may well affect the rest of their lives. Because many victims feel helpless, well-intentioned officers are tempted to take over for them, further adding to their feelings of helplessness.

Rage.   Sometimes rage is the predominant feeling that results from sexual assault. In one sense this response is good because it indicates the victim is grounded in reality and does not feel helpless. On the other hand, rage creates problems in a number of areas. Victims may want to track down assailants and murder or at least do serious damage to them. Although this sentiment is understandable, it only creates more problems for the victims and officers. If the victim's family adopts this rage, an entire family may place itself in serious physical and legal jeopardy, creating infinitely more difficulties for them and distractions for officers.

Sometimes, a female victim's anger is directed at male officers. This is a difficult situation because the officers may be nice people who only want to help the victim. Once again, however, professional officers transcend the trauma, recognize the dynamics in the situation, psychologically step to the side as they would react to a physical attack, and respond with patience and understanding. The worst response is for officers to take the attack personally and respond in kind.

Grief. Victims of sexual assault may react with grief because they feel that they have lost something precious to them, namely the right to share their body and being only with people they choose. This grief is compounded when they think of the people they may be presently sharing themselves with (husband, boyfriend) or will share themselves with in the future. This grief may result in depression that deadens their being and is manifested in their sad eyes, weak voice, and slumped posture. This represents a particularly difficult challenge for officers because the victim appears unwilling or unable to cooperate. The victim's attitude is this: Something's been taken from me that I can never replace, so nothing else matters to me right now. Officers can ask for the victim's cooperation, so that the assailant will never hurt anyone else again. This can create some energy in the victims that will move them to cooperate, maybe not for their own sake, but for the sake of other potential victims. In some cases, depression can become so acute that the victim considers suicide. In these cases, officers have the responsibility to do a mental health assessment and take the appropriate action; leaving these victims alone when officers depart is ill advised.

Confusion. Victims may experience a deep sense of confusion. They frequently ask questions such as these, often to no one in particular: Why did this happen to me? Could I have done something to prevent or stop it? How could someone do this to me? What will my family and friends think? How will this affect me in the future?

These questions are usually meant to be rhetorical. Officers need not take the questions literally and try to answer them because their answers will likely further confuse and complicate the situation. The best approach is to acknowledge that these questions are normal and the answers will likely come slowly over time as the victim discusses the assault with loved ones and counselors.

The challenges of sexual assault cases are far less daunting when officers are adequately educated and trained to address them. Awareness and sensitivity to the unique aspects of each case can help officers respond in a manner that provides support for the victims and establishes a sound legal basis for prosecution.

Personal Reflections

1. Do you believe male and female officers respond differently to female victims of sexual assault? Explain your answer.

2. How would you know if a victim of a sexual assault, or of any trauma, is in shock or actually is not that concerned about it?

3. How do you feel when you are ashamed of something, and someone tells you that you should not be, or you are terribly upset about something, and someone tells you to calm down?

4. What temptations would you have to resist in comforting the victim of a sexual assault or any other trauma?

ELDER ABUSE

Elder abuse can be defined as harming a person over the age of 65 psychologic-ally, physically, or financially, although the elements of the crime differ from state to state. Whether or not elder abuse has increased over the past two decades, reports of it certainly have. Estimates show a 150 percent increase in reported cases nationwide since 1986 (Davis & Media-Ariza, 2001). Because there are approximately 35 million people over the age of 65 in the United States, offi-cers will be responding to increased reports of elder abuse in the future.

One study (Klaus, 2000) reports the kinds and number of crimes perpet-rated against elderly people each year from 1992 to 1997:

- Property crimes (residential burglary and theft, motor vehicle theft): 2.5 million
- Purse snatching and pickpocketing: 46,090
- Nonlethal violent crimes (robbery, rape, assaults): 165,330
- Homicides: 1,000

Four categories of elder abuse can be distinguished:

- *Psychological abuse:* verbal intimidation, humiliation, berating, isolating, ignoring, threatening, or withholding affection and emotional support
- *Physical abuse:* assault and battery as manifested by shaking, slapping, punching, whipping, squeezing, kicking, pushing, tying up, or sexual assault
- *Physical neglect:* failure to see to it that the person is properly bathed, fed, dressed, housed, medicated
- *Financial abuse:* loss of money due to purse snatching, pickpocketing, for-gery, burglary, credit card and check theft, telephone, mail and television fraud, embezzlement

When elderly people are victims of violence, they often suffer greater and more lasting physical and psychological trauma than do younger people because elders tend to be fragile in these areas. In many cases elderly people never fully recover from the trauma because their healing processes are slow and their social supports few. Moreover, because many elderly people live on a fixed income, they often lack the financial resources to obtain adequate medical and psychological care.

Elderly people have characteristics that define their stage in life, just as children, young adults, and middle-aged people do, but caution should be taken not to stereotype them. While it is true that some people in their seventies and eighties do not see or hear well or think clearly, it is also true that others see, hear, and think as well as the officers at the scene. Therefore, it is always better to begin the encounter assuming that the victim has the same faculties as the officers and only modify this assumption when it becomes clear that such is not the case.

Traits of Elderly Victims

When interviewing elderly victims of crime, officers can be mindful of the following points.

Senses. Officers need to realize that as people age, their senses often become less acute, meaning their eyesight may be poor, their hearing impaired, and their sense of pain diminished. The aging process has three ramifications. First, officers should exercise great patience when interviewing elderly victims because they may not be as cogent as officers would like, and this can cause frustration. Second, hearing impaired people sometimes pretend to hear what people are saying and therefore may respond with inaccurate information. Officers need to be certain that the elderly victim understands what they are asking before listening to the answer. Third, elderly victims may not realize they have sustained injuries because they cannot see or feel them. Officers should physically assess these victims or have medical personnel do so in order to ascertain the full extent of injuries.

Memory. The memory of elderly people is often not as sharp as it was in earlier years. Even when the crime was committed only minutes prior to the arrival of officers, elderly people may have forgotten some key elements. For this reason, officers can interview these victims in short segments, for example, interview for five or ten minutes, take a break, and return to the interview because recall is often better when there is not concentrated pressure to remember things.

In some ways, the cognitive processes of elderly people resemble those of young children. For example, part of elderly persons' statements can be surprisingly lucid and accurate, but seconds later they may lapse into an improbable rendition of events. In addition, when the elderly cannot honestly recall something, they may confabulate, meaning they simply make up something to fill in memory gaps. This is another reason for doing interviews in segments, with several "time-outs," so that officers can hear the story on several occasions to check for reliability. One way to do this is to say "Let's go over this again because I want to make sure I'm getting everything down" in contrast to "You said you think they drove away in a green pickup truck—is that correct?" The latter question gives the victim an answer, whether or not it is the correct one.

Irritability. Sometimes elderly people, especially when under stress, become irritable as a defense against their deep fears, confusion, and feelings of vulnerability. Victims may be irritable and sometimes even belligerent with officers as a way of exercising control when, deep down, they feel as though they have no control. Officers can understand that the victims' irritability and anger are not directed at them personally, simply sidestep it, and proceed with the interview with kindness and patience. The worst thing officers can do is take the victims' irritability as a personal and professional affront and respond in kind.

Suggestibility. Elderly people are of a generation that generally has great respect for law enforcement and wants to help officers. In addition, the elderly may doubt their ability to be good witnesses and thus be inclined to go along with the officer's proposed version of events rather than their own. Elderly victims may respond: "Well, officer, I can't honestly say that happened because I was so scared, but you're probably right—it did happen that way." These prompted statements can create problems later when these witnesses are cross-examined in court.

Fears. Elderly victims often have a unique set of fears. They fear they will let the officers down; family members will think they need to be placed in residential care as a result of the crime; and the abuser will return to harm them. This situation is particularly difficult for officers because these possibilities are beyond their control. What officers *can* do is affirm the victim's efforts to help, offer to speak with relatives to assuage the victim's fears, and relate their experiences with repeat crimes: "Although I can't promise anything, I know that in 99 percent of the cases I've investigated, the bad guys never returned to the scene."

Guilt. Elderly people often feel guilt as a result of being victimized. They wonder how they could have been "so stupid" as to have contributed in some way to the situation, feel bad that loved ones must minister to them, and are concerned that officers must take time from "more important" duties to investigate the crime. Officers can assure these individuals that one of the critical roles of family and law enforcement is to help someone in need, just as the victim would gladly help someone in a similar situation.

Hurt. Because the vast majority of elder abuse victims have been harmed by intimates (spouse, adult children, or trusted caretakers), an element of deep hurt is involved in their reaction to the incident. Often this hurt is more damaging than the physical or financial abuse they suffered. Officers can only listen to the victims' hurt and support them as best they can.

Denial. Because the survival of many elder abuse victims is dependent on the same people who are abusing them, the elderly may deny they are being abused. They are frequently in a double bind: Victims who name their abusers may be in danger of even more abuse, and those who deny being abused will likely continue to be abused. Therefore, when officers suspect that denial is covering up abuse, they can encourage victims to discuss their fears, consider the pros and cons of admitting that they are being abused, and help them arrive at a good decision.

Attitudes of Officers

When younger people, including officers, relate with elderly people, they are tempted to do the following:

- Treat them like children, talking to them as if they were three years old and being condescendingly solicitous. Elderly people typically resent this attitude and want to be treated like any other adult in similar circumstances.
- Shout at them, assuming everyone over 65 must be hearing impaired. Officers should speak in normal tones until it becomes clear the victim is not hearing everything they say.
- Believe everything they say. Elderly crime victims, as is true of all crime victims, can be mistaken in their perceptions or say things they know are not true to get attention or retaliate against family members they do not like.
- Take all matters out of the hands of elderly victims as a way of lightening their burden. Although the officers' actions are well intentioned, the victims are left feeling that they have no control over what is happening to them.
- Interpret and finish sentences for the victims who often speak in slow, halting ways. Patience is the basic requirement for relating well with elderly victims.

Society, including officers, tends to discount elderly people, underestimating their intelligence, doubting the accuracy of their perceptions, humoring them, and, in general, treating them like children who are simply imagining slights and seeking attention. Perhaps the best approach is for officers to imagine that elderly victims are their own parents or grandparents, thus engendering a deeper sense of respect and concern for their welfare.

Personal Reflections

1. Can you envision a situation in which it is understandable, although not permissible, for someone to abuse an elderly person?
2. What do you think would be the greatest challenge for you with respect to dealing with elderly people?
3. Why do you think one of the common responses of elderly people when they are upset is to be irritable with the very people who are trying to help them? How would you react to this irritability?
4. How do you respond to an elderly woman who was just thrown to the ground by her 40-year-old daughter? How do you respond to the daughter?

GENERAL CONSIDERATIONS

Officers often spend a good deal of time responding to victims of violent crime. Although it is true that each victim of a specific violent crime, for example, domestic violence, has different reactions, and it is also true that victims of different kinds of violent crimes have different reactions, all victims tend to share some qualities in common. This section addresses ways in which officers can help victims and gather the information needed to solve and prosecute any crime that may have occurred.

Creating an Atmosphere

Officers have four basic goals when responding to victims of violent crime: to calm them down, ascertain whether they need medical or psychological help, gather pertinent information from them, and make appropriate referrals. While these goals appear to be modest, they are, in fact, often challenging. Therefore, officers should create an atmosphere within which victims feel safe, cared about, and understood. This is the opposite of an atmosphere that denotes the officer is inept, does not care about the victim as a person but only as a witness, and seems to be on a different wavelength than the victim.

The officers' demeanor immediately establishes an atmosphere created by their posture, facial expression, tone of voice, mannerisms, and words. Often, by the time the officer and victim sit down to talk, the victim is well on the way to feeling comfortable or uncomfortable in the presence of the officer.

Officer Behaviors

The following behaviors can foster a positive atmosphere within which the officers' goals are likely to be attained.

Privacy.   It is important that the privacy of the victims be respected. Often, well-intentioned relatives, friends, and neighbors thrust themselves into the situation, precluding any hope of privacy. To ensure privacy, officers can politely ask *everyone* except the victims to step outside, unless the victims insist that one or two people remain for support.

Assurances.   Victims typically need to be assured about a number of issues: They need to be encouraged that they are now safe, are not to blame for the situation, and that their reactions are normal for anyone faced with what they have experienced.

Deference.   Officers should ordinarily defer to the needs and wishes of the victim. The officers' attitude should be this: How can we be of the most help to you right now, and what do *you* want to see happen next? This gives the victims some control over the situation and respects the fact that they are the principal people in the situation, not their relatives or the officers.

Sensitivity.   Officers need to be sensitive to the fragile state of victims. Often their nerves are raw so that even normal comments and questions can be irritating or hurtful. A question such as "Why didn't you leave the house when you saw your husband was losing his temper?" may be appropriate in itself, but to a woman who has just been beaten by her husband, it becomes an accusation: "If only you had left the house when you saw your husband was losing his temper, you could have prevented this whole situation."

Focus.   Officers should focus primarily on victims as human beings who have just suffered a trauma they will never forget and not merely as the means to help the officers develop a strong case. The more that victims gradually become comfortable with officers, the better witnesses they will be. In other words, officers should take care of the victim first and the case second because it is the right thing to do and will, incidentally, strengthen their case.

Interpretations.   As was discussed earlier, it is perilous to interpret the behavior of someone not previously known to the officers. For example, the fact that a woman who has been raped appears "as though nothing happened to her" does not necessarily suggest she did not experience a trauma. It may simply mean she is in shock or denial and may need days or weeks before she can truly acknowledge what happened.

Pressure.   Victims are under enough pressure without more being placed on them by officers: "Look, the sooner you pull yourself together, the sooner you can tell us something about this guy so we can find him." This simply prolongs the amount of time it will take for the victim to think clearly.

Agitation.   Victims are usually in a state of heightened agitation when officers arrive. A common response by officers is this: "OK, calm down! We can't do anything until you calm down!" No one throughout the history of traumatic events has ever calmed down because someone ordered them to. In fact, such directives usually fuel, rather than extinguish, agitation. A better approach is to allow victims their agitation, encourage them to talk it out, and patiently wait until it subsides naturally.

Displacement.   Victims who are very upset often displace their frustration onto officers: "If you guys got out of your cars once in a while and patrolled the streets, this would never have happened to me!" This is a classic situation in which professional officers must transcend the trauma—that is, realize the victim is very upset, not thinking clearly, and lashing out at whoever is within striking range. Instead of defending their patrol policies, officers do better to ignore the content of the statement and respond to its source: "You have good reason to be upset about what happened to you. We can't change that, but what can we do now that we are here to help?"

Temptations.   In the midst of the high emotions and confusion often present when officers arrive at the scene, they may be tempted to do and say things that may not be helpful and, in fact, could make matters worse. Officers should use great caution in

- *Touching and hugging victims.* Although this is well-intentioned behavior on the part of officers, it is usually to be avoided unless victims throw themselves into the arms of officers. Often the last thing the victim needs, especially if the assailant was the same sex as the comforting officer, is to be touched or hugged by a stranger, even when it is an officer.
- *Making promises.* Officers should avoid making promises that are unlikely to be kept. Examples are promising confidentiality when "confidential" information will be necessary to make the case; promising to take a personal interest in the case and always "be there" for the victim in the future; promising to find the perpetrators and put them away for a long time.
- *Making ill-advised statements.* Officers should avoid making statements such as "I know how you must feel," which is not likely to be the case. They should also not talk for the victim: "You feel that if you would have been a little more careful, this would never have happened to you." This may be more the officer's sentiment than the victim's. Officers should also not inject philosophical or religious sentiments into the situation: "Well, I'm a firm believer that these things happen for a reason," or "If you put your faith in God, He'll get you through this."
- *Using humor.* Officers should not attempt to lighten the situation with humor. When victims are in the depths of their traumatic reaction, they generally fail to see much humor in anything. Moreover, they are likely to perceive the officers' well-intentioned attempts at humor as proof they do not grasp the gravity of the situation.
- *Referral.* Officers are not counselors and should not be expected to be. Therefore, officers should have referral sources to offer victims. However, care should be exercised even in this area. Most victims would rather get help from their families and friends and may take offense at the suggestion they need to see "a shrink." Referrals should be made in the spirit of "Some people find it helpful to see somebody who is trained in this area and has helped people through similar situations. Let me leave you some referral sources to consider so you can make an informed decision." To do more than this and pressure the victims to seek professional counseling often is ill advised.

- *Forecasting.* Just as there is not only one appropriate immediate response to a trauma, there is no one predetermined set of reactions that may occur at a later date. For this reason, it is unwise for officers to tell victims how they are likely to feel after the initial reaction wears off because this could create a self-fulfilling prophecy. For example, to tell victims they may experience sleeping and eating problems, withdrawal, phobias, memory problems, fits of crying, depression or rage, delayed stress disorders, sexual dysfunctions, nightmares, flashbacks, aversion to people of the same sex as the assailant, panic attacks, substance abuse, and so on, may contribute to the victim developing these disorders. All mental health issues should be left to mental health professionals to whom officers may refer the victim.

- *Questions.* Victims typically have many questions as to what will happen next. They want to know if they will be further contacted by officers or investigators; if they should be examined by a physician or consult a mental health professional; if they will have to meet with a prosecutor; if they will have to testify in front of a grand jury or in court; if the media will become involved; if there could be repercussions for going forward with the prosecution; if they will have to identify or confront the assailant; if the assailant will be able to get out of jail on bond; if they can be sued if the assailant is found not guilty; if the case will actually go to trial and, if so, when; and so on. Although these are ordinary questions, officers should exercise caution in responding to them. Some questions will be easy to answer, others will be more difficult, and still others should be referred to the appropriate people. Officers should avoid the temptation to give assurances that have no basis in reality; for example, that the assailant will be convicted, spend a long time in jail, not return to threaten the victim, and so on. Officers can assure victims that law enforcement will do everything possible to make the process as safe and stress-free as possible without making specific guarantees.

Personal Reflections

1. If you were the victim of a violent crime, what could officers do to place you at ease? What would make you very uncomfortable?

2. What do you think is the biggest mistake an officer can make when responding to victims of crime?

3. Respond to an officer's statement: "My job when responding to victims of crime is to get a solid statement and get out of there. It's up to family, friends, and counselors to help victims deal with the psychological effects of a crime."

UNEXPECTED DEATH

The survivors of the sudden and unexpected death of a loved one are considered co-victims because they can be as traumatized as any other victim. Unfortunately, sudden death survivors have not received as much attention as other victims from the general public and law enforcement. Because law enforcement has typically provided little education and training regarding death notifications, it is understandable that officers have not always handled these situations well.

Because death notifications must be made at all hours of the day and night, the officers on duty at the time will ordinarily be assigned to this task. Therefore, all officers need at least a basic knowledge of the nature of death notifications. The *Homicide and Sudden Death Survivors Guidelines* (1985) issued by the New Jersey Division of Criminal Justice highlight this point:

> Assuring that the needs of survivors are identified and that every effort is made to meet these needs are indeed monumental tasks. The need for a compassionate and dignified notification procedure, as well as access to information regarding the death, have been consistently identified as basic requirements for alleviating the trauma which results from the sudden and unexpected death of a loved one. The specific needs of survivors are unique and varied, and while many of them may not fall within the traditional purview of law enforcement responsibility, prosecutors, police officers, medical examiners, and others have a moral obligation to provide proper assistance to survivors whenever possible. (p. 1)

To this end, this section addresses some of the basic issues involved in death notifications.

Survivors

It is likely that the greatest trauma anyone can experience is the unexpected loss of a relative or close friend. Added to the trauma of the death itself is the "unexpected" element—the decedents were very much alive the last time survivors saw or talked with them. The sudden removal of a loved one from a person's life often leaves a void that may never be filled.

Before the notification, survivors are typically going about their normal day. The last thing they are expecting is that they will receive possibly the worst news of their lives. When officers arrive during daylight hours, the family is usually surprised to see them but not alarmed, but when the doorbell rings at 12 A.M., 2 A.M., or 4 A.M., the family feels instant dread, if not terror. A typical response when opening the door and seeing officers is "Oh, oh. This isn't going to be good, is it?" and the officers must confirm the people's worst fears. The survivors will have a wide range of reactions for which officers must be prepared. The following are typical.

Acceptance.   Some survivors accept the reality of a death notification for what it is. For whatever reasons, they cope well with their emotional reactions, comfort each other, understand what officers are saying, ask appropriate questions, and thank them for their time and compassion. This is the ideal situation for officers. They leave these encounters feeling good about how they handled the situation and genuine sympathy for the survivors.

Shock.   Perhaps the most typical reaction survivors have to a death notification is shock, a psychological defense that shuts down their response systems until they can gradually deal with the trauma. They experience psychological numbing in which they become dissociated from what the officers are saying and appear nonchalant, even disinterested to anyone who does not understand shock. Officers should not interpret this reaction as the survivors not caring about the death or what the officers have to say. Officers should not assume they were heard and understood by the survivors because the only thing people in shock hear, if they hear anything, is typically a "loud rushing noise" in their ears. Officers should exercise patience and repeat the details of the situation many times so they sink in gradually and are understood.

Hysteria.   In hysteria, survivors scream, sob, convulse, faint, and may become delirious. The trauma pierces the defense system and goes directly to the heart of the survivor. Many of these people sob, "My heart has been torn out," attesting to the depth of the wound. When survivors react with hysteria, the officers' task becomes much more challenging. Not only do officers have to give and receive vital information, but they must also calm down the survivors so that they can focus on the issue at hand, cooperate with the officers, and be capable of helping others through the crisis.

Denial.   Some survivors use denial as a defense that, like shock, gives them time to digest the news and eventually come to terms with it. These people typically respond to officers: "No, you've got the wrong people. My son couldn't have been shot. He's at work and will be home for dinner. He doesn't have an enemy in the world, so get out of here and find the right family!" Officers can allow the survivors to run out their string of denials over a period of time, which often allows the survivors to become more open to the possibility that the officer is telling them something they should hear. In cases of impenetrable denial, officers may be placed in the position of having to show the decedent's personal effects to the survivors.

Aggression.   Survivors may react with aggression, which sometimes includes violence toward anyone present: family, friends, and even the officers. Aggression acts like a psychological defense in that it focuses energy and attention away from the trauma and toward other issues, albeit irrational ones. The aggression is generally based on blame, blaming the death on one's spouse, other family members, friends, or society. The challenge to officers is formidable because of the imminent threat to everyone present, including the officers. This is one reason that two officers should be assigned to death notifications whenever possible, and the reason that many medical examiners will not send their staff to make death notifications unless they are accompanied by officers.

The first task of officers is to defuse the aggression, which is best accomplished by allowing people to vent their rage in an environment controlled by the officers, who listen respectfully and do not argue with the people. This may help the survivors accept the reality that a loved one has died suddenly and that attacking each other or the officers will not help the family make the important decisions required within the next few hours. If survivors turn their anger inward and seriously talk about suicide, officers should do what they would do in any similar situation—make a mental health assessment and take appropriate action.

Behavior of Officers

In addition to understanding the survivors' reactions to death notifications, officers should monitor their own behavior.

Balanced.   Officers need to be aware of their psychological state when making death notifications. These assignments are difficult because they often affect officers personally as well as professionally, sometimes on a very deep level, especially if a child is the decedent. Officers need to strike a balance between being emotionally distraught on the one hand and emotionally detached on the other.

Officers who become so emotionally undone by the situation that their main task is to rein in their own sorrow will not be able to communicate clearly or meet the needs of the survivors. On the other hand, officers who adopt a "this is just another call" attitude will likely be resented by the survivors and add even more anguish to the situation. Officers who are balanced feel the natural emotions of compassion and grief appropriate to the situation, while still being able to complete their task in a professional and helpful manner.

Transcendent.   As much as possible, officers need to transcend the shock, hysteria, denial, and aggression they encounter when dealing with survivors. If they fail to do this, they will become entangled in these dynamics and be of help to no one. Without proper education and training, officers can be thrown off balance by the reactions of survivors and respond with various, often unhelpful feelings that are communicated in one way or another.

- They may react to shock with confusion: "How can someone who has just been told their three-year-old drowned act like they just invited us in for tea?"
- They can react to hysteria with panic: "Oh, man, what do we do now that the whole place is in chaos?"

- They can react to denial with deep frustration: "What is it going to take to get these people to realize their kid is dead?"
- They may respond to aggression with their own aggression: "Look, we're sorry for your loss and all that, but if you're just going to attack us and each other, we're outta here."

Officers can rise above their confusion, panic, frustration, and aggression and accept survivor reactions for what they are: human, reflexive responses to a severe trauma that short-circuits rational thinking and behavior. These reactions do not define who these people are or their attitudes toward the trauma or the officers. Officers may develop some empathy for the survivors' plight if they reflect on how they have responded when faced with major stressors, even those far short of trauma, in their own lives. Officers may well have to admit they were not at their best and later felt bad about how they reacted.

Aware of consequences. Officers can be aware that their behavior may have lifelong consequences for the survivors. Few people forget where they were and what transpired when they were informed of a loved one's unexpected death. Therefore, the attitudes and behavior of the notifying officers create a lasting flashbulb memory for the survivors.

In this regard, notifying officers can have two basic attitudes. One attitude is this: "I really resent having to do this. It's not what I signed up for, and I'm not good at it. Let me say my piece and get out of here because I'm backed up three felony calls and six reports." These officers believe no one will be aware of their attitude because their overt behavior hides it. But this is unlikely because attitudes have a way of seeping into behavior, regardless of what officers think. The second attitude is this: "I'm really sorry to have to tell you this terrible news. This isn't easy for any of us, but I want you to know that I'm here to assist in any way and will remain as long as you need me." Clearly, the two attitudes generate very different behaviors. Both the attitudes and the accompanying behaviors will be with the survivors for the rest of their lives, increasing or decreasing their anguish and respect for law enforcement.

Competent. Officers need to feel competent and confident when making death notifications, so they can do a good job and be perceived by survivors as knowledgeable, trustworthy, and compassionate. The more officers can learn about death notifications by reading, attending workshops, and accompanying veteran officers on these assignments, the more competent and confident they will become. Unfortunately, death notification is rarely taught in training academies, so officers are left on their own to do the best they can, which is unfair to both the officers and the survivors.

When officers do not feel competent and confident, it is because they have been given no other choice but to "wing it," often struggling through the process, saying the wrong things, offering meaningless platitudes, becoming stymied by survivors' reactions, attempting to get in and out of the situation as soon as possible, and feeling foolish and frustrated after they leave.

Officer competence in death notifications means

- Making sure they are notifying the right people
- Learning enough about the nature of the death so they can give survivors a reasonable account
- Introducing themselves to the survivors and finding places where everyone can sit comfortably and see and hear each other easily
- Communicating the notification in a short, clear, and direct manner, and offering information only when certain of its validity
- Expressing genuine compassion to the survivors
- Answering questions in an honest yet diplomatic way
- Asking survivors if there is anything they can do to help
- Advising survivors as to what to expect with regard to further law enforcement involvement, if there is to be any
- Offering survivors referral sources to help them through the grief process
- Giving officers' names and phone numbers to the survivors in case they have follow-up questions

When officers do a competent job, and the survivor's reaction is accepting, the whole process may not take more than 15 minutes. However, the less competent the officers and the more agitated the survivors, the more prolonged and draining the notification will be for all concerned.

Practical Issues

While no two death notifications are the same, officers can consider some practical issues as they approach the prospect of doing them.

- Death notifications should never be made by phone. If survivors live outside the agency's jurisdiction, it can request officers in the survivor's jurisdiction to make the notification in person.
- Officers should make every attempt to locate the primary survivors and not settle for notifying other relatives, including the children or adolescents of the primary survivors.
- Two officers and, ideally, a member of the medical examiner's staff, should make the notification. It is generally asking too much of one officer to make the notification; on the other hand, bringing more than three people to the scene is likely to be cumbersome and distracting.
- When two officers respond, they should decide in advance who will be the primary notifier and who will monitor the reactions of the survivors to best respond to their needs. Officers should avoid talking in tandem, interrupting each other, and going off on different tangents, which will only confuse and distract the survivors.

- While there is no formula officers can use for death notifications, they should have a clear idea of what they are going to say before they arrive at the scene, for example: "We're sorry to have to tell you that your son Timmy drowned in a neighbor's pool earlier today. Officers and paramedics worked very long and hard to revive him, but were unsuccessful. We know this is terrible news, and we are here to offer any assistance we can." Notice that the son is referred to by name and not by terms such as *the victim* or *the deceased*.

- Officers should keep the discussion of the specific causes of death to a minimum. In some cases, the causes are self-explanatory, for example, in the case of a child drowning. However, if an adult drowns largely because he was highly intoxicated, this is not information loved ones need to know at this time.

- It is generally better for officers not to bring the personal effects (jewelry, wallet, clothes) to the notification, but to have them available if denial is impenetrable by other means.

- The situation can be particularly challenging if the decedent was a gang member killed by a rival gang or by police while committing a crime, especially when officers were placed in harm's way. In these cases, officers can separate the survivors from the deceased and realize the survivors may be good, law-abiding citizens who were deeply upset by the decedent's lifestyle. In any case, there is no place for judgmental attitudes in death notifications.

- Officers should not leave a survivor alone after a notification, but should make arrangements for survivors to be left in the company of others.

Of all the responses to violence discussed in this chapter, perhaps the most psychologically difficult for the officers are death notifications. These calls are unique in that the officers themselves bring the trauma to the people rather than responding to a situation in which a trauma is already present and a strong possibility exists that unlawful behavior has occurred.

In the latter cases, officers are on familiar ground because acts of violence fall directly within the purview of law enforcement, whereas death notifications present challenges with which officers are likely to feel less comfortable. Therefore, in order to respond in a truly professional manner, as physicians and clergy do, officers need specialized education and training because even though death notifications occur infrequently, they are critical events for both officers and survivors.

Personal Reflections

1. If you were making a death notification, what would be the most difficult part, and how would you handle it?

2. What do you think is the greatest positive action officers can take at a death notification?

3. What do you think would be the greatest mistake officers could make at a death notification?

*S*ummary

One of the main reasons that officers enter law enforcement is to help people. They can do this in two basic ways: by enforcing the law and by helping people when they are unable to help themselves. Examples of the latter have been discussed in this chapter: helping children and adults who have been victims or co-victims of particularly heinous crimes and unexpected deaths.

In the recent past, law enforcement has insidiously moved away from the helping role and concentrated more on its enforcement role. This is as understandable as it is unfortunate. Aside from finding lost children and responding to medical aid calls, there is no greater service officers can render outside of their enforcement role than to respond to the acute and critical needs of victims and co-victims of trauma. Yet, training academies typically either spend no time on this topic or dedicate only a few hours to it. Therefore, no one, least of all the officers themselves, can expect that officers will generally handle these calls effectively; that is, in ways that help them get good information on the perpetrator and, as important, have a therapeutic response to the victims and co-victims.

For this reason, it is important that training academies and continuing education workshops dedicate far more time than they do to educating and training officers to make an important difference when they respond to traumatic incidents, so that they become part of the solution rather than part of the problem.

*R*eferences

Bangham, L. (1986). Domestic violence: Too late to mediate. *The Police Chief, 53* (6), 52–54.

Crime and Violence Prevention Center, California Attorney General's Office (1997). *Domestic violence handbook: A survivor's guide* (rev. ed.) [Brochure]. Sacramento, CA: Author.

Davis, R.C., & Medina-Ariza, J.M. (2001). *Results from an elder abuse prevention experiment in New York City.* (NCJ 188675). Washington, DC: U.S. Department of Justice.

Dobash, R.E., & Dobash, R.P. (2000). Evaluating criminal justice interventions for domestic violence. *Crime and Delinquency, 46* (2), 252–270.

Garner, J., & Clemmer, E. (1986). *Danger to police in domestic disturbance: A new look.* Washington, DC: National Institute of Justice.

Gosselin, D.K. (2000). *Heavy hands: An introduction to the crimes of domestic violence.* Upper Saddle River, NJ: Prentice Hall.

Healey, K.M., & Smith, C. (1998). *Batterer programs: What criminal justice agencies need to know.* (NCJ 171683). Washington, DC: Office of Justice Programs, National Institute of Justice.

Hunter, S.M., Cewe, B.B., & Mills, J.L. (1997). *Police response to crimes of sexual assault: A training curriculum* (2nd ed.). Meriden, CT: Police Officers Standards and Training Council.

Karmen, A. (1996). *Crime victims: An introduction to victimology* (3rd ed.). Belmont, CA: Wadsworth.

Klaus, P.A. (2000). *Crimes against persons age 65 or older, 1992–1997.* (NCJ 176352). Washington, DC: National Institute of Justice.

Maxwell, C.D., Garner, J.H., & Fagan, J.A. (2001). *The effects of arrest on intimate partner violence: New evidence from the spouse assault replication program.* (NCJ 188199). Washington, DC: National Institute of Justice.

New Jersey Division of Criminal Justice (1985). *Homicide and sudden death survivors: Homicide and sudden death survivors' guidelines.* Retrieved June 14, 2002, from the World Wide Web: http://www.state.nj.us./lsp/dcj/agguide/homicide.htm.

Office for Victims of Crime, Office of Justice Programs (2001a). *First response to victims of crime.* (NCJ189631). Washington DC: U.S. Department of Justice.

Office for Victims of Crime, Office of Justice Programs (1997, 2001b). *Law enforcement response to child abuse.* (NCJ162425). Washington DC: U.S. Department of Justice.

Sadusky, J. (2001). Working effectively with the police: A guide for battered women's advocates. *Violence Against Women Online Resources.* Retrieved May 31, 2001, from the World Wide Web: http://www.vaw.umn.edu/BWJP/ policeV.htm.

Sherman, L.W., & Berk, R.A. (1984). *Minneapolis domestic violence experiment. A police foundation report.* Washington, DC: The Police Foundation.

Thurman v. City of Torrington (1984). 595 F.Supp. 1521 (D. Conn.).

11

Understanding Psychological Disorders

Dealing with psychologically disturbed people has become a standard part of law enforcement. As Arrigo (2000) states:

> Knowledge and attitudes by police officers toward the mentally ill have traditionally been those of ignorance and misunderstanding. Further, police officers have tended to have somewhat cynical attitudes toward the same population (Nunnally, 1961). This is not surprising, considering the tremendous amount of stress experienced by police officers every day. The failure of police academies and training programs to adequately address issues related to mental health has conceivably fostered the ignorance toward this specific population. (p. 69)

Typically, officers bring to the job all the misconceptions about psychological disorders they learned growing up, along with the pejorative labels often used to describe mentally ill people. This leaves them unprepared to deal with these people and their families in crisis situations. Therefore, it is important that officers develop some basic understanding of psychological disorders so they can respond professionally and helpfully to situations involving the mentally ill.

Officers are not expected to be diagnosticians or counselors on the same level as mental health professionals. However, professional officers should possess sufficient knowledge to deescalate difficult situations, transport a person to a mental health facility as expeditiously as possible, and write a report that reflects an informed understanding of the relevant issues. The report is particularly important because involuntary commitments initiated by officers are increasingly coming under legal scrutiny during which officers are required to explain the basis for their decision and how the person met the criteria for a mental health commitment.

Officers are often reluctant to become involved in mentally disturbed person calls for three reasons. The first reason is that officers typically receive little or no training in this area, with even the most progressive training academies dedicating only a few hours to the topic. When inadequately trained officers arrive at the scene of a "disturbed person" call, they are likely to overreact or underreact, the results of which can be troublesome if not tragic. The second reason is that some calls dealing with psychologically disturbed people involve them physically attacking officers, which can create a high-risk situation for all concerned. Wrightsman, Nietzel, and Fortune (1998) summarize this issue:

> The police are often asked to maintain public order and defuse volatile situations involving persons who are mentally ill, intoxicated, angry, or motivated by politically extreme views. Because of the instability of the participants in such disputes, they pose great risks to the police as well as to bystanders. (p. 140)

The third reason for officers' reluctance to become involved with the mentally ill is the "I'm not a social worker" syndrome, the implication being: "I'm not a social worker—we should leave the nutcases to them." Interestingly, these officers do not apply this type of thinking to any other part of their work. They do not say: "I'm not a professional race car driver, so I'm not going to get involved in pursuits," or "I'm not a doctor, so I'm not going to administer CPR." The fact is that dealing with psychologically disturbed people *is* a legitimate and important part of law enforcement. Officers have the choice of learning to deal effectively with these situations, just as they have learned to deal with domestic violence, or choose to remain uninformed, thus placing themselves and others in serious physical and legal jeopardy.

While volumes have been written on psychological disorders, this chapter will focus on some of the disorders that officers most commonly encounter. The following issues will be addressed: personality disorders, substance abuse disorders, mood disorders, suicide, schizophrenia, dementia, and Tourette Disorder. The chapter will conclude with a discussion of report writing. Because specific psychological disorders do not lend themselves to Personal Reflections, a set of Personal Reflections at the end of the chapter will address psychological disorders in general.

PERSONALITY DISORDERS

People with personality disorders have a dysfunction that is deeply rooted in their personality. They may manifest this disorder in childhood, but symptoms definitely will appear by adolescence or early adulthood. These disorders are manifested primarily in relationships with others and center on using, abusing, ignoring, or avoiding people. People with personality disorders possess little or no insight into their disorder, blaming others for whatever problems arise from it. They also experience little or no distress about their problematic behavior or its effects, and are more distressing than distressed.

Because people with personality disorders experience little subjective distress, they are unlikely to seek treatment. For the most part, the only time they enter a counselor's office is when they are pressured to make the appointment by family, employers, or the courts. Therefore, their prognosis for seeking and benefiting from treatment is generally poor. If they hurt other people, they typically feel little or no guilt, due to their lack of empathy for others. The only time they are likely to feel bad about causing problems is when they must pay some price for it.

There are ten personality disorders, but only the three that officers are more likely to encounter will be discussed here. It is important to note that psychological disorders are not all-or-nothing phenomena; the degree of impairment can be mild, moderate, or severe.

Borderline Personality

The term *borderline* refers to the idea that this disorder lies on the border between more serious disorders. People with a borderline personality possess the following traits.

Characteristics. People with borderline personalities typically are unstable and unpredictable; confused as to who they are and what they want; ambivalent about getting close to people; fearful of abandonment; bored with life, causing a feeling of emptiness; and destructive toward both themselves and others.

Behaviors. The above characteristics generate corresponding behaviors. The instability and unpredictability are manifested in impulsive behaviors, such as quitting a good job that supports a family in order to write a novel. Their identity confusion can be seen in excursions to "find themselves," which may include experimenting with drugs, embarking on spiritual journeys, traveling to distant places, and becoming involved in risky sexual relationships. Their ambivalence about getting close to people is demonstrated in behaviors such as being seductive toward people, suddenly rejecting them, and then begging them to return. Their fear of abandonment is seen, for example, in their choosing to remain in destructive relationships rather than be alone. Their boredom causes them to add spice to their lives by indulging in high-risk behaviors: abusing alcohol and drugs, gambling, running up bills, driving recklessly, entering into improbable relationships, and picking up strangers. Their self-destructive behavior can be seen in self-mutilation, bloodletting, binge eating, suicide attempts, and suicide. Their destructive behavior also can be antisocial, as seen in violence toward family, friends, coworkers, and in shoplifting, forging checks and prescriptions, sexually assaulting people, and getting in altercations with officers.

Antisocial Personality

It is likely that officers will encounter this psychological disorder more than all the others combined. The term *antisocial personality* replaces the older terms *psychopath* and *sociopath*, and the original one, which may have been the most descriptive—*moral insanity*.

Characteristics.   People with antisocial personalities are deficient in conscience development, which allows them to violate the written and unwritten laws of society and experience little or no remorse, guilt, or shame. They feel invulnerable and immortal. They are unable to experience normal feelings of love, empathy, guilt, and fear. Their feelings of entitlement lead them simply to take whatever they want from people and society without paying the price for it.

Behaviors.   People with antisocial personalities are impulsive, acting out aggressive and sexual feelings without considering the destructive consequences for their victims or even themselves. Their feelings of invulnerability allow them to act with impunity and to participate in high-risk behaviors without the slightest bit of trepidation: bank robberies, embezzlement, investment schemes, identity theft, rape, or murder.

These individuals are highly manipulative and exploitive, using clever combinations of flattery, pretense, seduction, lying, and intimidation to get what they want, from conning their teachers into giving them undeserved good grades, to seducing people into having sexual relations, to scamming insurance companies. They are irresponsible and uncommitted, unable to remain in relationships or jobs, or to meet their family, financial, employment, or legal obligations. They often leave a trail of broken hearts, lost jobs, and unpaid debts.

These people are unable to learn from experience. They can spend ten years in prison for armed robbery and commit another robbery one week after being released. Punishment, including loss of relationships, jobs, or reputation, has little or no effect with respect to modifying their behavior.

Because of their often attractive personalities, these individuals can act intelligent, cute, charming, fascinating, exciting, articulate, sympathetic, vulnerable, heroic, or religious. They are like accomplished musicians who know exactly what note to strike at exactly the right time. They can fool nice, intelligent, sophisticated, experienced people, including law enforcement officers, judges, and juries. The only people they have difficulty deceiving are other people with antisocial personalities, who know all the subterfuges and rationalizations because they are also experts in them.

It would be a serious mistake to think that these traits reside only in hoodlums and gangsters. People at all levels of intelligence, education, society, fame, and success can be antisocial personalities, including physicians, attorneys, stockbrokers, teachers, politicians, clergy, and law enforcement officers.

Schizoid Personality

The terms *schizoid personality* and *schizophrenia* are not synonymous, the latter referring to a more advanced and debilitating state of personality disintegration, which will be discussed later in this chapter. People with schizoid personalities possess the following traits.

Characteristics. Schizoid personalities are socially isolated, are content to be alone, and become agitated when others intrude into their lives. They do not need people or miss people and prefer to be left alone. They are found at every level of intelligence, industriousness, and creativity.

Their needs and emotions are muted. They have weak or nonexistent needs for excitement, novelty, adventure, success, sex, power, or prestige. Nor do they have normal feelings of affection, compassion, joy, or sorrow. This is reflected in their demeanor: bland facial expressions, little sign of emotion, flat voice, distant eyes, and indifference to the praise, criticism, kindness, or the pain of others.

Behaviors. Because people with schizoid personalities live in their own private world, devoid of normal interactions and stimuli, they can behave in odd and eccentric ways. Those who are quite impaired may focus all their emotions onto animals, collecting dozens of cats, for example. They may live like hermits without much shelter or convenience: no electricity, running water, radio, television, or automobiles. They may live the life of a survivalist or transient, living off the land and keeping away from people. Those less impaired may choose occupations in which they can work more or less alone: landscaper, artist, craftsman, librarian, inventor, handyman, cowboy, writer, researcher, bookkeeper, house painter, and so on.

The vast majority of people with schizoid personalities are quite harmless and keep to themselves. However, those who are very impaired can spend their time in isolation fantasizing about aggressive and sexual behaviors that they may occasionally act out, such as child molestation, rape, arson, and terrorism.

Officers who acquire at least a basic understanding of personality disorders are in a position to make at least a tentative assessment of the stability of these individuals, their truthfulness, their potential for violence, and the likelihood of their being cooperative. Obviously, people with personality disorders do not all act the same, but they do have certain tendencies of which officers should be aware.

SUBSTANCE ABUSE DISORDERS

Undoubtedly, one of the greatest challenges facing law enforcement today is substance abuse. It causes serious crime; destroys individuals, families, and communities; and poses a serious threat to the safety of officers. Criminals who are "drug sick" (experiencing withdrawal) or "high on drugs" are more likely than other offenders to attack officers.

Framework of Substance Abuse

Although there are volumes written about substance abuse, this section will focus only on information that is directly helpful to officers. The framework for this section is contained in Table 11.1 and the explanation that follows.

TABLE 11.1   *Psychoactive Substances*

SUBSTANCE	Death	Suicide	Psychosis	Withdrawal	Violence	Needles/HIV
Alcohol	Yes	Yes	Yes	Yes	Yes!	No
Barbiturates	Yes	Yes	No	Yes	No	No
Benzodiazepines	Yes	Yes	No	Yes	No	No
Inhalants	Yes!	No	Yes	No	No	No
Cocaine	Yes!	Yes	Yes	Yes	Yes!	Yes
Amphetamines	Yes	Yes	Yes	Yes!	Yes!	Yes
Opiates	Yes	Yes	Yes	Yes!	Yes!	Yes
Hallucinogens	Yes	Yes	Yes!	No	Yes!	No
Phencyclidine (PCP)	Yes	Yes	Yes!	No	Yes!	Yes
Cannabis	No	No	Yes	No	No	No

A *psychoactive substance* alters perceptions, thoughts, feelings, and behavior. These substances may be legal (prescribed), legal but illegally obtained (stolen or obtained by a forged prescription), or illegal.

The meanings of the columns in Table 11.1 follow. The *death* column indicates which substances can result in death due to toxic reaction, overdose (accidental or purposeful), respiratory and/or cardiovascular failure, or dangerous behavior, such as attempting to jump off buildings or walk on water.

The *suicide* column indicates which substances have been related to committing suicide. The *psychosis* column indicates substances that can cause psychosis, that is, a gross break with reality. The symptoms of psychosis follow:

- *Delirium:* an extreme state of confusion, inability to concentrate, memory loss
- *Disorientation:* marked confusion related to time (does not know the correct time, day, year), to person (does not know who he or she or others are), to place (does not know where he or she is)
- *Delusions:* beliefs that have no basis in reality; for example, believing that the officer is an agent of the devil
- *Hallucinations:* perceptions that have no basis in reality; for example, hearing God say: "Kill the officer who is an agent of the devil"

The *withdrawal* column indicates what substances, when suddenly discontinued, are likely to cause withdrawal (or abstinence) syndrome, dysfunctions of the central and autonomous nervous systems that, when untreated, can be fatal.

The *violence* column indicates substances related to violent behavior toward others, including officers. The *needles/HIV* column indicates that the substance can be injected intravenously and, therefore, these people may have needles in their possession and/or be HIV infected. *Exclamation marks* indicate those behaviors that have an especially high-risk factor.

Description of Substances

The following are brief descriptions of the substances listed in Table 11.1.

Alcohol. Withdrawal symptoms after prolonged use can cause delirium tremens: delirium, tremors, delusions of persecution, disorientation, and hallucinations (seeing animals and feeling spiders). These symptoms are part of an alcohol psychosis. Serious medical problems can arise, both during heavy drinking and withdrawal. The two immediate causes of death are cardiac arrhythmia and respiratory depression.

Alcohol has been implicated in explosive disorder in which violence occurs quickly and unpredictably. "Happy drunks" can turn into violent, powerful people in a nanosecond. Additionally, it is estimated that over 30 percent of suicides are alcohol related.

Barbiturates.   Barbiturates come in pill form and are highly addictive tranquilizers. They are prescribed to alleviate anxiety, pain, insomnia, and for the treatment of high blood pressure and epilepsy. They include drugs such as Amytal, Nembutal, Luminal, Seconal, and Tuinal, all of which induce euphoria.

Barbiturates cause a large number of overdose deaths and create a high potential for violent behavior. When barbiturates are combined with alcohol, a common event, the effects are four times more powerful than the effects of either drug by itself. This combination can cause heart and respiration rates to drop to fatal levels. Withdrawal can often be quite dangerous, even more than from heroin, consisting of delirium, convulsions, and death.

Benzodiazepines.   These anti-anxiety drugs come in pill form and initially cause euphoria but eventually lead to depression and loss of coordination. They also can act as analgesics to reduce pain. These drugs include Xanax, Valium, Halcion, Librium, and Qualudes. High doses can result in depression, disorientation, and delusions, as well as suicidal impulses.

Combining these drugs with alcohol multiplies each drug's sedative effects, potentially leading to respiratory and cardiac failure resulting in death. Withdrawal symptoms are often more dangerous than those from heroin and typically include delirium and convulsions that can be fatal.

Inhalants.   Inhalants are sold legally and include gasoline, glue, paint, paint thinner, hair spray, fingernail polish removers, lacquer thinners, kerosene, lighter fluid, and aerosols. These substances cause euphoria.

"Sudden sniffing death" can occur from the use of inhalants due to respiratory failure and cardiac arrest, as well as suffocation from the plastic bag containing the inhalant after the individual lapses into unconsciousness. Some substances, such as hair spray, cause fatalities by coating the lungs, which prevents the exchange of oxygen and carbon dioxide. Sometimes inhalants cause delusions leading users to believe they can fly or walk through glass doors, behaviors that often result in death.

Cocaine.   Cocaine is a stimulant that initially causes a rush of pleasurable feelings but eventually results in a "crash" (severe depression). Cocaine can come in fluid form, which is injected intravenously. It also can be a powder ("snow") that is snorted; it can be heated with ether and smoked ("freebasing"); or it can come in a pill ("crack", "a rock") and be swallowed.

Cocaine, even in moderate doses, causes rapid and dangerous increases in blood pressure and heart rate, as well as constriction of blood vessels, which can cause heart attacks, respiratory arrest, and convulsions, all of which can be fatal.

In high doses cocaine psychosis can occur, which includes severe depression and paranoia, usually delusions of persecution, as well as visual and auditory hallucinations. Typically, cocaine is used concurrently with other drugs to soften the "crash" that inevitably occurs. One combination is to mix cocaine with heroin ("speedball"), which is particularly lethal.

Withdrawal is typically severe and includes profound depression, paranoia, tactile hallucinations (feeling "cocaine bugs" on the skin), homicidal and suicidal thoughts and behavior. Cocaine, along with amphetamines, accounts for 40 percent of all substance-related cases that are seen in emergency rooms, and 50 percent of substance-related sudden death.

Amphetamines (stimulants).   Amphetamines are stimulants often prescribed to raise people's mood and energy level, to control weight, or to combat depression and fatigue. Amphetamines come in pill form: Benzedrine, Dexedrine, and Methedrine, which also can be homemade with toxic substances such as drain cleaner and lantern fluid. Recently, Ritalin, prescribed for children with attention deficit hyperactivity disorder, is being hijacked by juveniles, broken down, and snorted to obtain an immediate high. Amphetamines can also be smoked or snorted in a relatively pure form called "ice" or "crystal meth." "Speed freaks" inject Methedrine intravenously to experience an immediate, intense rush.

Amphetamines cause increased heart rate, blood pressure, and breathing rate, as well as chest constriction and irregular heartbeat, all of which can contribute to death. They also can cause amphetamine psychosis, which includes delirium, paranoid delusions (often of being stalked), and visual and tactile hallucinations (seeing nonexistent sores on their body or feeling snakes crawling over them).

After continual high doses ("speed runs"), the crash toward deep depression begins. In high doses, suicide and violent behavior may occur, especially when the drug is smoked or injected intravenously, and often occur as a reaction to delusions of persecution and terrifying hallucinations.

Opiates (narcotics). Opiates are analgesics (painkillers) that also produce euphoria. They blunt physical and psychological pain, as well as having a calming effect. Opiates include opium, morphine, and codeine. They are prescribed under names such as Percodan, Demerol, and Darvon.

Opiates can be smoked, snorted, or injected intravenously. Heroin is the most widely used of the opiates, usually injected beneath the skin ("skin popping") or intravenously ("mainlining"). Withdrawal symptoms for opiates, while very uncomfortable, are generally not life threatening. However, when opiates are combined with alcohol, cocaine, and/or marijuana, the potential for a lethal overdose is high.

Hallucinogens. Hallucinogens, also called psychedelics, are taken orally and produce powerful perceptual distortions. Hallucinogens include lysergic acid diethylamide (LSD), psilocybin, mescaline, and peyote. LSD, for example, produces hallucinations in all five senses, which can be beautiful or terrifying ("a bad trip"). It also produces delusions of grandeur and persecution. The hallucinations and delusions can cause people to attempt to fly from the tops of buildings, run through glass doors, or walk into the ocean to be "one with the universe." Terrifying delusions and hallucinations also can trigger suicidal and violent behavior. An overdose of hallucinogens does not appear to be life threatening, nor do withdrawal symptoms occur after discontinuation.

Phencyclidine (PCP). Phencyclidine (PCP) has depressant, stimulant, hallucinogenic, and analgesic properties. It is manufactured as a powder and can be snorted, smoked, or injected intravenously. Large doses can cause coma, convulsions, and death due to respiratory depression, as well as lead to suicide. Even in moderate doses, it often causes feelings of invulnerability, which can result in high-risk behaviors, such as walking in front of moving traffic. It also can cause paranoid delusions, auditory hallucinations, and violent behavior.

Cannabis. Cannabis is a substance that causes euphoria, perceptual distortion, and sometimes paranoia. Two kinds of cannabis are marijuana and hashish. Very high levels of cannabis can cause psychotic reactions in the forms of visual hallucinations, disorientation, and delusions of persecution. It also can significantly elevate blood pressure. However, cannabis is not known to be lethal at high doses or to cause withdrawal symptoms. Hashish is more potent than marijuana but has similar effects.

Cautions for Officers

Because officers may have frequent contact with people who are under the influence of alcohol and/or other drugs, knowledge of the various specific substances should be combined with the following general cautions:

Approach.   Officers should approach *all* intoxicated (on alcohol and/or other drugs) people as potentially dangerous, regardless of their age, gender, physical condition, or original disposition (happy, cooperative). For example, a "good trip" sponsored by LSD may abruptly turn into a "bad trip," causing the intoxicated person to attack officers violently without the least bit of warning. This fact, however, does not mean that officers should be overbearing, only very vigilant.

Emergencies.   Withdrawal symptoms, including cardiovascular and respiratory symptoms, suicide attempts, and psychosis, *always* represent emergencies and require immediate medical/psychiatric intervention because they could well be life threatening. Withdrawal symptoms should never be used as punishment or as a lever to extract information or confessions from people. It is likely that a high proportion of in-custody deaths that occur within 72 hours after arrest are related to untreated withdrawal symptoms, and this includes suicide.

Welfare of the person.   Once officers detain an intoxicated person, they are responsible for that person's welfare. Officers should not allow a situation to develop in which intoxicated people can dart into traffic, harm themselves or bystanders, or escape in a vehicle, including the officer's vehicle. Officers also should never leave an intoxicated person unsupervised in a police vehicle, interview room, or holding cell. Cardiovascular and respiratory reactions to withdrawal can be instantaneous and life threatening. An intoxicated person can look fine one minute and be dead the next, or be peaceful one minute and suicidal or homicidal the next.

Use of chemical agents.   Two points should be considered before using nonlethal chemical agents, for example, oleoresin capsicum (OC) aerosol spray, on intoxicated people. First, these agents are often ineffective with intoxicated and psychologically disturbed people and simply give them more time and opportunity to advance on the officer. Second, their use could exacerbate the cardiovascular and/or respiratory problems the person is already experiencing as a result of the intoxication or a preexisting condition. If this occurs, it could present a life-threatening situation.

Swift action.   Finally, it is helpful to realize that the longer the conversation lasts between officers and a highly intoxicated person, the more time there is for things to go wrong. Highly intoxicated people are not amenable to logical argument, counseling techniques, or even threat. Officers must give clear directions, repeat them once or twice, and, in the absence of compliance, take appropriate, professional action.

MOOD DISORDERS

Although there are several kinds of mood disorders, officers are more likely to encounter major depressive disorder and bipolar disorder. As is true with all psychological disorders, they can result in mild, moderate, or severe impairment.

Major Depressive Disorder

Major depressive disorder, also called unipolar disorder, has three categories of symptoms that are active when the person is not taking the appropriate medications.

Cognitive symptoms. Depressed individuals often have the following cognitions (perceptions, thoughts, beliefs): They believe they are worthless, stupid, evil, helpless, better off dead, and that people do not care about them, have abandoned them, and hate them. As a result they view life as meaningless, painful, cruel, unjust, and not worth the effort.

Affective symptoms. Depressed people have feelings of sadness, despair, helplessness, hopelessness, abandonment, loneliness, fear, anger, guilt, emptiness, and confusion.

Somatic symptoms. Depressed people experience insomnia (lack of sleep), hypersomnia (too much sleep), significant weight gain or loss, agitation or psychomotor retardation (slow thinking, speaking, acting), decreased energy, fatigue, crying, and anhedonia (inability to experience pleasure).

Officer response.   In most instances, officers become involved with depressed people when they talk about or threaten suicide. (See the section on suicide on page 300.)

Bipolar Disorder

Bipolar disorder, which used to be called "manic depression," refers to the fact that there are two "poles" to this disorder; depression lies at one pole and mania at the other. Some people with bipolar disorder may cycle, that is, go from one pole to the next, while others may experience only depressive or manic symptoms. Because depression was just discussed, the focus in this section will be on manic states, which have the following symptoms when the person is not taking the appropriate medications.

Cognitive symptoms. People in manic states believe they possess extraordinary beauty, creativity, brilliance, power, and abilities. They often believe they have insights and inventions that can change the world. They may contact the media or high-ranking government officials to offer their solutions to world hunger, nuclear proliferation, global warming. Their cognitions can include hallucinations ("God is asking me to help him") and/or delusions of grandeur ("I am a financial genius"). As a result of these cognitions, they make life-altering decisions, for example, sell all their possessions and invest the money in one of their dubious inventions.

Affective symptoms. They feel optimistic, exhilarated, ecstatic, enthusiastic, euphoric, powerful, and invulnerable. However, their positive moods often shift abruptly, and they can become highly irritable, angry, or enraged for no observable reason.

Somatic symptoms. They are hyperactive—talking, gesticulating, and pacing rapidly and endlessly. They have very rapid speech (pressured speech) and their ideas flit from one topic to another, even within the same sentence (flight of ideas). This can reach the point at which they become incoherent. They require little or no sleep and are continually in action: making phone calls at all hours, walking and driving aimlessly, beginning major projects only to discontinue them within minutes or hours, spending countless hours at a computer, and so on. Their energy and strength seem endless. They often use alcohol and/or drugs to slow down their thinking and behavior, which only compounds the problem.

Officer response.   People in manic states come to the attention of officers in the following ways: shoplifting, reckless driving, sexual acting out, barroom brawls, forging checks and prescriptions, harassing people (including government officials), disturbing the peace, committing vandalism, robbing banks, making threats, appearing naked in public, committing rape or murder. They may attempt suicide when cycling from mania into depression.

Officers need to exercise extreme caution with these individuals. They can become very violent and extremely strong very quickly. All the precautions covered in the section on dealing with intoxicated and depressed people also apply to people in manic states, including the use of nonlethal chemical agents.

SUICIDE

It is important for officers to know something about the nature of suicidal thoughts and behaviors, as they relate not only to depression but also to other psychological states.

Basic Facts

Statistics (Anderson, 2001) for 1999 indicate that over 29,000 people committed suicide in the United States, and there were approximately 725,000 suicide attempts. Suicide was the eleventh-ranking cause of death overall (homicide ranked fourteenth) and was the third-ranking cause of death for individuals between the ages of 25 and 34. The elderly made up 12.7 percent of the 1999 population but committed 18.8 percent of the suicides. It is also estimated that 5 million Americans have attempted to kill themselves.

Depressive disorders are involved in approximately 50 percent of suicides. On the other hand, a person need not be the least bit depressed to commit suicide. While any strong, negative feeling can trigger suicide or a suicide attempt, the most lethal combination seems to be hopelessness, rage, and guilt. Drugs also are often related to suicide. The combination of depression and alcohol is present in 57 percent to 86 percent of all suicides based on psychological autopsy studies (Murphy, Wetzel, Robins, & McEvoy, 1992). Suicide and suicide attempts often follow "exit events"; that is, a major loss in an individual's life such as death of a close relative or friend, separation or divorce, or loss of reputation, financial status, personal possessions, mental or physical health, or a job.

Myths Regarding Suicide

Officers should be aware of a number of myths that surround the issue of suicide.

- *Myth:* The more people talk about suicide, the less likely they are to commit it.

  Fact: Approximately 70 percent of people communicate suicidal intentions before committing suicide.

- *Myth:* People who unsuccessfully attempt suicide do not really want to kill themselves, or they would have done it.

  Fact: As strange as it sounds, many people do not know how to commit suicide. They do not know how many pills constitute a lethal dose, what caliber bullet will penetrate their skull, what kind of noose to tie in a rope. Suicide attempts can simply be a cry for help but, at the same time, they can also provide experience that will lead to a future successful attempt.

- *Myth:* People who have been depressed but suddenly become peaceful and even happy are no longer candidates for suicide.

  Fact: Suicidal individuals may suddenly appear calm and happy because they have decided to commit suicide in the near future, an act they believe will end their anguish.

- *Myth:* Happy, successful people do not commit suicide.

  Fact: It is important to understand a clinical entity called "smiling depression," which means that people can successfully put on a happy, ebullient façade but be very depressed in the recesses of their psyches.

- *Myth:* People who have never been depressed a day in their lives are not candidates for suicide.

  Fact: While it is true that 50 percent of suicides involve depressed people, it is also true that 50 percent of suicides do not. People commit suicide for many reasons: revenge, shame, boredom, stress overload, to escape pain, and as a result of hallucinations and delusions.

Officer Response

As is true for responding to any crisis call, there is no recipe that officers can follow when responding to threats of suicide. However, officers can keep the following points in mind.

Safety.   Officers must be concerned about their own safety. Increasingly, "suicide by cop," a situation in which distraught people force officers to shoot them rather than directly commit suicide, has become a valid concern for officers. The days are gone when all the officer has to worry about is the welfare of the person threatening suicide. There is a saying in law enforcement: "Suicidal can mean homicidal."

Quick intervention.   The sooner the suicidal person can be taken into custody, the better. Crisis intervention techniques have their place, but long, drawn-out, unproductive conversations with suicidal people only give them more time to get up the nerve to kill themselves and to conjure up more reasons to do so ("Nobody understands what I'm going through, not even these officers").

Rapport.   If the situation is such that the suicidal person cannot be taken into custody immediately (he has a gun aimed at his head), efforts should be made to draw out the person, establish rapport, and stall for time while waiting for assistance. Officers can keep the conversation going from a safe area, with prompts such as: "Tell me what's going on." "Why do you think this is a good decision?" "When did all this start?" "Would you like us to call anyone?" "OK, now I understand everything, except for the part about the situation at work." As the person addresses these prompts, officers may gain information that will offer possible solutions to the problem.

Improper statements.   Officers should avoid making statements that denigrate the person ("How could you be so stupid as to want to kill yourself?"), induce guilt ("How can you do this to your kids?"), minimize the situation ("I think you just want some attention"), challenge the person ("I think if you were really intent on killing yourself, you would have done it by now"), argue with the person ("I don't believe that your parents don't love you"), or diagnose the person ("You're talking crazy right now"). When people are seriously considering suicide, they do not need to be made to feel any more stupid, selfish, guilty, or crazy than they already do.

Options for help.   Many people intent on suicide see only two options: kill themselves or continue to live in a state of unbearable pain. Officers can attempt to pry these people loose from their no-win situation and offer a third option—to get the kind of help that will start them in a more viable direction. Officers should never take the word of suicidal people that they will "be all right now" and leave the scene. Officers should either transport the person to a mental health facility or see to it that family or friends take over responsibility for getting the person help. As soon as possible, officers should attempt to ascertain if the person is under a doctor's care and make the appropriate calls if such is the case, so that perhaps the doctor can converse with the person or offer advice to officers.

SCHIZOPHRENIA

Schizophrenia, which means "split brain" in Greek, ranks with the mood disorders as a very serious psychological disturbance. Over two million people in the United States suffer from schizophrenia, a number sufficiently large that officers will have relatively frequent contact with them, especially in urban areas.

There are five subtypes of schizophrenia, but paranoid schizophrenia is the most common, and the one officers are most likely to encounter. Schizophrenia, as is true with all psychological disorders, runs across every level of intelligence, education, and social class. The stereotype of the person dressed in rags talking to God on street corners represents only a small minority of chronic paranoid schizophrenics. Most are middle-class people of all races and educational and socioeconomic levels.

People suffering from paranoid schizophrenia typically exhibit the following symptoms when they are not taking the appropriate medications.

Symptoms

Cognitive.   Schizophrenic people often experience hallucinations, the most common being auditory. Two kinds of auditory hallucinations are command and accusatory. Command hallucinations order individuals to take some action, often to damage themselves or others. For example, a person may hear God command, in a very clear and authoritative voice, that if she sacrifices herself (or someone else), she will earn eternal happiness. Accusatory hallucinations consist of voices accusing the individual of horrible acts, for example, child molestation or murder.

Another common hallucination is visual, in which the individual sees deities, people, or objects that are not present in reality. For example, combining visual and auditory hallucinations, a person may see and hear a deceased parent. Typically, people with schizophrenia will talk back to their hallucinations, holding lengthy conversations and arguments.

Delusions are also a common symptom of schizophrenia. The most common delusions that people with schizophrenia experience follow.

- *Delusions of persecution:* the belief that people are plotting against them, spying on them, poisoning them, trying to get them fired, arrested, or killed.
- *Delusions of reference:* the belief that people are making secret reference to them. For example, a newscaster may report that "war is imminent" in some part of the world, but the schizophrenic believes that the newscaster is sending him a personal message that it is his responsibility to stop the war.
- *Delusions of thought insertion:* the belief that other people are injecting thoughts into their brain to control them or drive them crazy.
- *Delusions of thought withdrawal:* the belief that people are stealing their thoughts and using them for their own purposes.
- *Delusions of nihilism:* the belief that they are nothing, that they do not exist, or that they do not have a brain.
- *Delusions of thought broadcasting:* the belief that their thoughts are being broadcast to the world so that everyone knows what they are thinking.

With the exception of delusions of persecution, the remainder of these delusions tend to be unique to schizophrenia.

Affective symptoms.   People with paranoid schizophrenia tend to have relatively normal emotional reactions, except when they are delusional and/or hallucinating. However, chronic schizophrenics tend to have "flat affect," that is, to be emotionally unresponsive, detached, distant, and disinterested.

Somatic symptoms.   Again, between their delusions and hallucinations, people with paranoid schizophrenia appear relatively normal. However, as the disorder progresses, especially without medication or other types of treatment, they tend to regress and become chronic. When this occurs, they may manifest peculiar speech, mannerisms, and habits.

Their peculiar speech may consist of clang associations—putting words together because of the way they sound, not because of their meaning ("So you're a cop cop who goes clop clop"); neologisms—creating words that do not exist ("The tractile has become untracted"), and word salad—mixing words together that are unrelated ("My head is obnoxiously a petrified fence").

The peculiar mannerisms may consist of strange facial expressions, contorted posturing, and gesticulating that is unrelated to reality. Odd habits may consist of collecting objects (pieces of string, broken pencils, old newspapers) to which they often become very attached, sitting in a particular spot on the same sidewalk every day, or carrying a hat they never wear.

Officer Response

Officers responding to calls that involve schizophrenic people can be mindful of the following points.

Potential for violence. Paranoid schizophrenics can have a potential for violence. This is due to their command hallucinations ("The woman talking to you is Satan disguised as a police officer—you must kill her before she takes over the world") and delusions of persecution, believing that the officer is a hired killer. People experiencing these phenomena can become very violent, very abruptly, and possess the strength of five people.

Officers should remain hypervigilant without appearing as if they are about to pounce on the person. If officers have information from the reporting person that an individual is acting in a potentially violent manner, as many officers as possible should respond to the scene. However, their presence should be as unintimidating as possible, close enough to be of immediate assistance to the primary officer if necessary, but not so close as to surround the person or invade his or her space.

Need to build trust.   Officers can understand that a paradox exists with people who are paranoid schizophrenics. At the same time that they are clearly *out* of touch with reality, they are also clearly *in* touch with reality. They are often acutely sensitive to signs of disrespect, ridicule, trickery, and criticism and may react accordingly.

The main goals of officers' response are to deescalate the situation and get the person to a mental health facility. The best way to keep the person calm is to attempt to establish rapport. Even though people may be out of contact with reality and not grasp a good deal of what is being said, they can often *sense* the safety or danger in a situation. A calm voice that connotes gentleness, interest, concern, confidence, and helpfulness can have a soothing effect. The theme of the transaction can be this: Why don't you tell me what's going on, so I can understand it?

The purpose of these interactions is to help people ventilate, reduce anxiety, and begin to trust the officers. While ventilating, the people may provide clues to help officers decide what steps will help resolve the situation. Whenever possible, officers should try to ascertain whether the person is under a doctor's care and, if so, have a call placed to the doctor to get professional input and demonstrate that officers are doing everything possible to resolve the situation in a professional manner.

Actions to avoid.   When dealing with schizophrenics, officers should avoid the following measures:

- Invading the person's space by getting too close to or behind the person; making continual, direct eye contact; touching the person, even in what is meant to be a reassuring way.
- Getting tough with the person, using "shock therapy" to "snap him out of it." This could very well be perceived by the person as an attack and be responded to accordingly.
- Arguing with the person, employing logic to rebut the person's hallucinations and/or delusions, which only serves to entrench them and fracture rapport.
- Making what are meant to be good-natured, humorous comments to reduce tension. People experiencing a schizophrenic break with reality do not possess a sense of humor and typically perceive humorous comments as disrespectful or threatening.
- Pretending to believe that the person's delusions and/or hallucinations are true experiences ("Yes, the CIA *is* after you, but I can rescue you from them"). This serves only to increase the person's agitation because he believes *no one* can protect him from the CIA, which the officer has just confirmed is after him.

DEMENTIA

Dementia is basically caused by brain disease, injury, and stroke. Alzheimer's disease is the most common dementia. It is a progressive, irreversible neurological disease that destroys nerve cells. Its cause is unknown, and currently there is no cure. Its diagnosis comes about after a process of elimination of other brain disorders for which the causes are known. A definitive diagnosis cannot be made until an autopsy is performed because the anatomical abnormalities associated with Alzheimer's disease can be detected only with a high-power microscope.

Alzheimer's disease is the seventh-leading cause of death in adults over 65 (National Center for Health Statistics, 2001), and affects approximately four million people in the United States, a number that will increase as people continue to live longer, unless a cure is found. One in ten people over age 65 and nearly half of those over 85 have Alzheimer's disease. However, it is not necessarily an elderly person's disease; though rare, people in their thirties and forties have been diagnosed with the disease. People with Alzheimer's disease live an average of eight to ten years after diagnosis, although some have lived for twenty years or more (Alzheimer's Association, 2002).

The following symptoms of Alzheimer's disease can be mild, moderate, or severe, depending upon how advanced the disease is.

Symptoms of Alzheimer's Disease

Cognitive symptoms. The cognitive symptoms that accompany the disease are

- *Disorientation.* This occurs in time, person, and place—loss of sense of time, inability to recognize one's spouse or one's home.
- *Memory loss.* Recent memories are lost (what the person did five minutes ago), but distant ones are often retained (the names of schoolmates from a half century ago).
- *Delusions.* These are mostly delusions of persecution, the belief that someone, even a loved one, is stealing from or plotting against him or her.
- *Hallucinations.* Though rare, hallucinations can occur in all five senses; the most common are auditory, with Alzheimer's patients hearing voices talking to them or to others about them.

Affective symptoms. Emotions include anxiety, apathy, irritability, frustration, agitation, depression, anger, and deficits in feelings such as affection, warmth, compassion, excitement, joy, enthusiasm, hope, and peace.

Somatic symptoms. The following behaviors are typical in individuals with Alzheimer's disease:

- *Wandering.* These individuals may wander about the house or escape from caregivers and roam around the neighborhood, quickly becoming lost and often reacting with panic.
- *Communication problems.* Alzheimer's patients often have difficulty expressing their thoughts to others and understanding the communications of those around them, causing frustration on everyone's part.
- *Combative behavior.* Because of memory loss, disorientation, and delusions, these individuals can become very frustrated and frightened, causing them to lash out at the people trying to help them.
- *Loss of coordination.* In the late stages, motor activity can become impaired—walking, talking, sitting, eating, climbing, swallowing, grasping, and holding, as well as loss of bladder and bowel control.
- *Loss of inhibition.* This includes saying and doing aggressive and sexual things that the individuals would never say or do if they were well.

Officer Response

People with Alzheimer's disease come to the attention of officers in a number of ways. Many patients, especially in the early and middle stages of the disease, remain licensed drivers and continue to drive. Because of the symptoms already mentioned, they are likely to drive erratically, going through stop signs, driving on the wrong side of the road, striking cars and driving off because they were unaware or forgot that they were involved in a collision.

Officers who encounter these individuals often suspect that they are impaired by alcohol and/or other drugs because they may have an unsteady gait, talk to themselves, act strangely, and may be combative when approached by officers. Officers also may perceive them simply as being old.

People with Alzheimer's disease are often caught shoplifting because they picked up an item to purchase but forgot to stop by the cashier before exiting the store. Their genuinely confused reaction when contacted by officers is usually an indication that they are unaware of what they did. Often storeowners are sympathetic to the situation and are satisfied with simply receiving payment or having the merchandise returned.

Because of their lack of inhibitions, people with Alzheimer's disease may behave in aggressive or sexual ways in public. They may remove their clothes in public or assault people verbally, physically, or sexually. When confronted by officers, they may become verbally or physically combative because they are confused and frightened. Because such individuals are often older, fragile, and lack stamina, their assaults do not ordinarily pose a real threat to officers. However, if these individuals have access to deadly weapons (it is unbelievable how many caretakers have guns in the house), they can be as dangerous as any other impaired person with a lethal weapon.

Finally, people with Alzheimer's disease may report crimes to law enforcement agencies, which raises two cautions. The first is that the "crime" may be a product of the person's delusions: "My wife is trying to poison me and steal all my savings. . . ." These are common complaints of people in the middle and advanced stages of the disease. The second caution is that people with Alzheimer's disease *can be* real victims of crime, especially of elder abuse, because they can generate great frustration in caretakers. Therefore, investigating officers must keep one eye open for a delusional crime and the other for a real one.

It is important to note that people in the early, and even in the middle stages, of the disease can look physically healthy because their minds deteriorate long before their bodies do. Therefore, people's behavior should claim more attention than their physical appearance.

When contacting middle-aged or older people who are acting strangely, a few minutes of conversation will allow officers to rule out alcohol, drugs, or other factors and consider the possibility of Alzheimer's disease being the cause of the behavior. Often a simple way to ascertain whether a person has Alzheimer's disease, or some other dementia, is to ask such simple questions as these: "Where do you live? How old are you? What's your phone number, social security number? How did you get here? What is today's date, and what day of the week is it? Do you know where you are right now? Where are you going? Do you know who I am?" The main message officers should send is this: I am here to get you to a safe place. This can be communicated through a calm voice, a friendly expression, and a relaxed stance.

When interviewing an Alzheimer's patient, officers should remove the person from distractions: crowds, noise, and cars. The more the individual has only the officer to attend to, the more likely the person can focus on the officer. Communication should be kept very simple. Officers should speak in short sentences and ask questions that can be answered "yes" or "no." They should give positive directions ("Stand over here") in contrast to negative ones ("Don't stand there; you're blocking traffic").

Finally, officers can be aware of the Alzheimer's Association Safe Return Program. Among other services, this program provides a national registry of memory-impaired people, including their photographs and other identifying information, as well as emergency contact information, which can be faxed to law enforcement agencies. It has a 24-hour, toll-free crisis hot line (1-800-272-3900) that officers can call in their attempts to identify a disoriented, lost individual. People with Alzheimer's disease who are members of the association can carry an identification card, as well as wear a bracelet or necklace identifying them as members. Part of an agency's community service program can include educating citizens to this resource.

TOURETTE DISORDER

Officers may occasionally encounter a person with Tourette Disorder, which is manifested by vocal, motor, and complex tics that are sudden, involuntary acts. People who see a person with Tourette Disorder, especially one who is moderately or severely impaired, often become quite anxious, believing that the person is "crazy" and even dangerous. Officers who have not previously encountered people with Tourette Disorder may take them into custody for disturbing the peace or as being mentally ill. This could have serious public relations and legal ramifications, especially if medical, mental health, and civil rights advocates become involved in the situation. Therefore, it is important for officers who encounter people with Tourette Disorder to have a basic understanding of the disorder and take appropriate action.

The behaviors exhibited by those with Tourette Disorder that will create anxiety in people follow:

- *Vocal tics.* These consist of grunting, yelping, sniffing, tongue clicking, snorting, barking, and whistling, and making statements "out of the blue": "Oh, boy," "Shut up," "You're stupid." However, the vocal tic that will cause people the most distress is coprolalia, which is cursing, uttering obscenities, and making racial slurs. Although less than 15 percent of people with Tourette Disorder experience coprolalia, this symptom attracts the most attention in stores, restaurants, libraries, and churches. It also can cause serious altercations in which the person with Tourette Disorder is attacked when these epithets are aimed at people who take them as a challenge to fight.

- *Motor tics.* These include rapid eye blinking, facial twitches, shoulder shrugging, squatting, head jerking, grimacing, arm jerking, jaw snapping, tooth clicking. More impaired individuals may exhibit jumping, hopping, twirling, clapping, throwing objects, touching people, retracing their steps, striking out, writhing movements, rolling eyes upward, kissing, or hitting or biting themselves. Sometimes they may exhibit copropraxia, as in making obscene gestures or touching their genitals. They may also experience echolalia (repeating what others say) and echopraxia (imitating what others do).

As can be imagined, this is one of the more challenging calls officers receive because there are many things to consider. Are people with Tourette Disorder mentally ill? Most of these individuals are not mentally ill; in fact, they can be quite normal, have high intelligence, and graduate from college. Therefore, officers must be very careful before taking these people into custody on the basis of a mental health commitment.

Have they broken the law? Certainly, people with Tourette Disorder can break the law. However, in most cases, their "unlawful behavior" is the result of their tics and, thus, not likely to be viewed as the result of a specific intent to create disorder or harm people.

In most cases, when officers calm the person with Tourette Disorder and explain the situation to the complainants, the matter can be resolved. If the event has attracted spectators, it is often helpful for officers to offer a ride to the person with Tourette Disorder so as to remove him or her from the scene.

WRITING A REPORT

If a psychologically disturbed person commits a crime, officers write a standard crime report and let the prosecutors deal with the mental health issues. But if officers contact a psychologically disturbed person who has not committed a crime, they should write a different kind of report.

In today's litigious society, it is necessary to write a thorough report, *whether or not* the person is taken into custody for a mental health commitment. If the person does not meet the criteria for a mental health commitment (an imminent danger to self, others, or gravely disabled) and is released, and subsequently attempts or commits suicide or harms another person minutes, hours or even days later, the officer may be asked: "Why didn't you take him to the hospital? He was obviously distraught." For this reason, it is important to write a report immediately after the contact, detailing the situation, including reasons for not taking the person into custody.

When officers transport the person to a mental health facility, as part of a voluntary or involuntary civil commitment, they should also write a thorough report to document the circumstances. People who have agreed to a voluntary commitment have been known to change their mind, insisting they were forced to go to the hospital against their will. Those who were involuntarily committed can later insist they were perfectly sane, and officers took them into custody only because they yielded to the pressures of family or friends or because the officers were angry with them.

Details of the Report

For these reasons, a professional, thorough report is necessary. When preparing the report, the following points can be considered:

- Be specific, explicit, and descriptive. People reading the report should have a clear picture of what the officer saw, heard, said, and did. Special attention should be given to describing the person's appearance, demeanor, and statements. Generally, the more quotes from the disturbed person and from people at the scene, the more effective the report.
- Assume the case is going to court and that a judge and jury will be scrutinizing every word with a critical eye.
- Enumerate the reasons for taking the person into custody. For example, "The subject was taken into custody for the following reasons. One . . . , two . . . ," and so on.
- Refrain from using technical terms and diagnostic labels. For example, instead of writing: "She had delusions of persecution," write: "She said we were enemy agents."
- Obtain as much information as possible about the individual from family, friends, roommates: "Her mother said she had been diagnosed last year with bipolar disorder but refused to take her medications."
- Refrain from offering opinions: "I think her suicide attempt was just an effort to get her boyfriend back." Just state the facts.

Sample Report

The following report is meant to demonstrate some of the points previously discussed.

At 1400 hours I was dispatched to 1 Main Street where it was reported that a woman had locked herself in the bathroom and was possibly ingesting an overdose of Dexedrine, a stimulant. Officer Smith and I arrived at the scene at 1406 hours and were met by the subject's roommate, Helen Jones. Jones said that she and her roommate, Nancy Thomas, had quarreled and Thomas became very upset. She said that Thomas locked herself in the bathroom and yelled, "If you don't want me, then I'll give myself to God." Jones said she then heard the medicine cabinet being opened and water running into a glass. Jones told us that Thomas had been under psychiatric care and on medication, but had discontinued taking it when they became roommates two months ago. Jones said that Thomas apparently had attempted suicide "about a year ago" but was found when her father arrived home unexpectedly. As a result, she remained in a psychiatric unit for three days.

Officer Smith and I spoke to Thomas through the bathroom door, identified ourselves as police officers, and invited her to come out and talk with us. She opened the door and walked to a living room sofa, where she sat down. Jones counted the sleeping pills and said that none was missing. Thomas appeared very pale. She was wearing a bathrobe that hung open in front, revealing part of her naked body, but she did not seem to be aware of this or concerned about it.

Her hair was disheveled, and her hands were trembling a great deal, so much so that she held them between her knees to control them. She had a blank expression on her face and stared at the floor. When I asked her if she had taken any pills, she replied in a flat voice: "No, because I knew you were on the way, and I'd just have to go through the stomach pumping scene again, and I couldn't bear it."

I then asked Thomas if she could tell us what was upsetting her, and she replied, "I could, but I won't." Jones said, "Nancy, why don't you talk about it—I'll leave the room if it would help." Thomas replied, "No one can help but you and God, and I've lost all faith in you." From that point on, Thomas refused to talk. She sat, statue-like, staring at the floor as if no one else was in the room.

I asked her three separate times: "Do you feel all right now, or do you think you need to get out of here and get some help?" Each time she made no reply. Finally, I said, "I'm going to ask you that question one more time, and if you can't assure us that you are all right, I am going to consider your silence as a request for us to take you to the crisis center for some help." She did not reply, so we took her into custody at 1420 hours for the following reasons:

1. The apparent fact that she locked herself in the bathroom, opened the medicine cabinet, took a bottle of sleeping pills out, filled a glass with water, and said, "I'll give myself to God," indicated to me that she was contemplating suicide.

2. She apparently had made a serious suicide attempt approximately a year ago, which indicates to me that she was capable of repeating the act.

3. Her statement that she did not take the pills because she knew she would be rescued indicated to me that she could take the pills, or use some other self-destructive method, when she felt that she would not be rescued.

4. Her upset did not diminish in intensity during the fifteen minutes we were with her, leading me to believe that she was still capable of attempting a self-destructive act.

5. She has no one in the area that can take care of her, except her roommate, toward whom she is very antagonistic.

6. The fact that she may have had a chance to prevent herself from being taken into custody but declined to use it indicated to me that she was asking to be taken to the crisis unit.

For these reasons, I believe that I had probable cause to take her into custody pursuant to the Mental Health Code. She was transported by (names of officers) to the (name of) crisis center and admitted at (time of day).

As can be seen, simply completing the commitment form that the agency or mental health facility requires is not nearly sufficient to cover all the issues involved should the situation come under legal scrutiny.

Personal Reflections

1. What is your attitude toward psychologically disturbed people? Do you view them as having an illness like diabetes that was acquired largely through no fault of their own, or as people who developed a lot of their problems through poor decisions or moral weakness?
2. Why do you think that while law enforcement has become more enlightened and sensitive about gender and racial issues, it is still not unusual to hear officers refer to mentally ill people as "wackos," "crazies," "nutcases," and "retards"?
3. Do you think that how people refer to psychologically disturbed individuals affects how these people treat them?
4. In addition to being aware of officer safety, which is the most important thing officers should keep in mind when responding to "mentally ill person" calls?
5. Respond to this officer statement: "I didn't sign up to be a social worker, and I don't want to be a social worker. When we get a 'mentally disturbed person' call, we should only be required to secure the area and then let a team of experts take over."
6. Respond to this statement: "What's the use of taking mentally disturbed people to the crisis center? They'll be back on the streets before the officers are."

*S*ummary

Responding to calls that involve psychologically disturbed people can be challenging. Ironically, often law enforcement officers with little or no training in mental health issues are the first responders to critical situations, while fully trained mental health professionals do not become involved until the crisis is over and the person is brought to the hospital.

Some cities and agencies are attempting to mitigate this situation by having trained officers and mental health personnel respond as a team to crisis situations. This approach brings more expertise to the scene and relieves individual officers of having to shoulder the psychological and legal burden by themselves. As Klein (2002) notes:

> In some instances, having protocols, agreements, mutual aid assistance, or the assistance of a psychiatrist available still may not resolve a situation peacefully. However, having an extensive training and interactive working arrangement will

give the first-arriving officer more tools for achieving a peaceful resolution to a mental health crisis situation and can help law enforcement and mental health officials bring about a positive change in law enforcement response to individuals with mental illness. (p.14)

Because it may be some time before this situation becomes a standard practice in most jurisdictions, officers can learn as much as possible on their own or by taking workshops to help them become competent and confident when they encounter psychologically disturbed people.

References

Alzheimer's Association (2002). *Statistics: About Alzheimer's disease.* New York: Alzheimer's Disease and Related Disorders Association.

American Psychiatric Association (1994). *Desk reference to the diagnostic criteria from DSM IV.* Washington, DC: American Psychiatric Association.

Anderson, R.N. (2001, October 12). Deaths: Leading causes for 1999. National vital statistics reports, 71 (11). Hyattsville, MD: National Center for Health Statistics.

Arrigo, B.A. (2000). *Introduction to forensic psychology: Issues and controversies in crime and justice.* San Diego, CA: Academic Press.

Jordan, L. (2002). Law enforcement and the elderly. *FBI Law Enforcement Bulletin, 71* (5), 20–23.

Kendall, P.C., & Hammen, C. (1995). *Abnormal psychology.* Palo Alto, CA: Houghton Mifflin.

Klein, M. (2002). Law enforcement's response to people with mental illness. *The FBI Law Enforcement Bulletin, 71* (2), 11–14.

Murphy, G.E., Wetzel, R.D., Robins, E., & McEvoy, L. (1992). Multiple risk factors predict suicide in alcoholism. *Archives of General Psychiatry, 49,* 459–463.

Nevid, J.S., & Greene, B. (2001). *Essentials of abnormal psychology in a changing world.* Upper Saddle River, NJ: Prentice Hall.

Nunnally, J.C. (1961). *Popular conceptions of mental heath.* New York: Holt, Rinehart & Winston.

Sales, B.D., & Shuman, D.W. (Eds.). (1996). *Law, mental health, and mental disorder.* Pacific Grove, CA: Brooks/Cole.

Teplin, L.A. (July 2000). Police discretion and mentally ill persons. *National Institute of Justice Journal, 244,* 9–15.

Tourette Syndrome Association. (2002). *What is T.S.?* Bayside, NY: Tourette Syndrome Association. Retrieved November 10, 2002, from the World Wide Web: http://www.tsa-usa.org/what_is/Faqs.html.

Wrightsman, L.S., Nietzel, M.T., & Fortune, W.H. (1998). *Psychology and the legal system* (4th ed.). Pacific Grove, CA: Brooks/Cole.

Epilogue

Law enforcement has come a long way, even over the past quarter century, and this is to be acknowledged and celebrated. Yet, it still seems to have some distance to cover before functioning as effectively and ethically as it could and should. No simple prescriptions can be followed to bring this about, but five areas need to improve significantly.

First, society needs to support law enforcement better, both financially and socially. Most law enforcement agencies, especially state and municipal ones, operate on a shoestring budget. Salaries are generally poor and in some cases disgraceful, and the equipment that officers rely on to save the lives of others and themselves is often lacking or in a state of chronic disrepair. Today, some police departments are holding pancake breakfasts to raise money for necessary equipment, while others are getting corporations to buy police vehicles for their agencies in exchange for placing the corporations' advertising logos on the vehicles.

With respect to social support, society, including the media, is much more interested in law enforcement's failures than in its successes. If an officer makes a mistake or acts inappropriately, half the letters in the local newspaper's letters to the editor section will excoriate the officer, the agency, and law enforcement in general. When an officer engages in some heroic or compassionate act, appreciation for the officer's care and courage is rarely expressed by the public. There is a saying that communities get the level of law enforcement they want and deserve. Although one should not take that sentiment too far, it seems to hold a certain degree of truth.

Second, society and law enforcement must decide what kinds of officers they want. As long as a law enforcement agency believes that only white males can become effective officers, it will exclude candidates who may be more competent than those whom they are accepting. On the other hand, as long as race, gender, and/or political clout are weighted more heavily than the ability to perform the essential functions of the job, some competent candidates may be excluded.

In both cases, the ranks of the agency will be weakened, and no one can be legitimately surprised when problems arise.

Third, the selection process must be significantly improved. Four gates exist along the path to a career in law enforcement: selection, background investigation, training, and probation. Agencies rarely have equally secure gates at each of the four junctures. Some have solid selection procedures but slipshod background investigations; some have excellent training but probationary periods that no one but the least competent candidate can fail.

It is imperative that all four gates be strong, screening out candidates that fail to show great promise and screening in only those that do. Secure gates demand a high price in time, effort, and money, but the cost of not having them is significantly higher.

Fourth, law enforcement has made great strides in reaching out to the mental health professions for assistance, but reaching out on more levels is needed. Agency leaders seem to feel more comfortable doing this than do rank-and-file officers. Historically, some tension has existed between the law enforcement and mental health communities. Some law enforcement officers perceive mental health professionals as naïve and softhearted, while some mental health professions perceive officers as unsophisticated and heavy-handed. However, when both groups sit down in a professional atmosphere to discuss their perceptions and resultant tensions, understanding and better working relations typically result.

The mental health professions can offer law enforcement four important things. They can help agencies improve the validity and reliability of their selection procedures and background investigations; they can share the newest theories and research to help officers in their investigations; they can offer workshops on how to keep psychologically fit in a stressful job; and they can provide counseling to officers who are having a tough time, a service that may save an officer's health, career, or job.

Finally, law enforcement agencies have made some advances in ethics education and training, but not nearly enough. Many training academies provide no instruction in ethics or only a few hours, generally consisting of horror stories regarding what happened to officers who acted unethically or illegally. Because the people in the audience believe they could never be that stupid, the classes are entertaining but seldom helpful. It is not rare that even colleges with a criminal justice major do not offer a course in ethics.

So, while a great deal more can be done to make ethics an important part of academy education, it is perhaps even more important to offer continuing education workshops frequently throughout the careers of executives, managers, and officers. The undertow that can sweep officers into unethical behavior becomes stronger after a few years on the job, when they may get worn down by the temptations and pressures to act unethically.

However, it should be kept in mind that classroom teaching is only one kind of education. An even more influential form is role modeling by senior officers, managers, and executives. When these officers are scrupulously ethical, the message is clear: Do what I say *and* do what I do. But, when these officers accept free meals, discounts on merchandise, and free tickets to entertainment, their message drowns out those of even the best ethical curriculum: As officers, we are entitled to privileges that few other people in society enjoy. When this message is sent, agencies cannot feign surprise when ethical violations occur.

It can be said that law enforcement ranks with medicine and ministry as a means of helping people in ways that are challenging, awesome, and meaningful. All three occupations produce memories that will be among the most beautiful, humorous, frightening, and tragic that any human can ever have. But law enforcement is the *only* occupation whose mission is to stop people from hurting themselves and others and to bring to justice those who harm others. And that is what makes law enforcement the best occupation in the world for those who are called to it and who have the competencies and values to do it well.

Index